Lost Histories

HARVARD EAST ASIAN MONOGRAPHS 418

Lost Histories

Recovering the Lives of Japan's Colonial Peoples

Kirsten L. Ziomek

Published by the Harvard University Asia Center
Distributed by Harvard University Press
Cambridge (Massachusetts) and London 2019

The Harvard University Asia Center publishes a monograph series and, in coordination with the Fairbank Center for Chinese Studies, the Korea Institute, the Reischauer Institute of Japanese Studies, and other facilities and institutes, administers research projects designed to further scholarly understanding of China, Japan, Vietnam, Korea, and other Asian countries. The Center also sponsors projects addressing multidisciplinary and regional issues in Asia.

The Harvard University Asia Center gratefully acknowledges the support of the Association for Asian Studies First Book Subvention Fund.

Library of Congress Cataloging-in-Publication Data
Names: Ziomek, Kirsten L., author.
Title: Lost histories : recovering the lives of Japan's colonial peoples / Kirsten L. Ziomek.
Other titles: Harvard East Asian monographs ; 418.
Description: Cambridge, Massachusetts : Published by the Harvard University
    Asia Center, 2019. | Series: Harvard East Asian monographs ; 418 | Based on the
    author's thesis, issued under the title: Subaltern speak : imperial multiplicities in
    Japan's empire and post-war colonialisms (Ph.D.—University of California,
    Santa Barbara, 2011). | Includes bibliographical references and index.
Identifiers: LCCN 2018034043| ISBN 9780674237278 (hardcover : alk. paper) |
    ISBN 9780674237285 (pbk. : alk. paper)
Subjects: LCSH: Japan—Colonies—Asia. | Japan—Foreign relations—1868–1912. |
    Japan—Foreign relations—1912–1945. | Ainu—Ethnic identity. | Ryukyuans—
    Ethnic identity. | Micronesians—Ethnic identity. | Taiwan aborigines—
    Ethnic identity.
Classification: LCC JV241 .Z56 2019 | DDC 909/.0971952—dc23
LC record available at https://lccn.loc.gov/2018034043

Index by the author

∞ Printed on acid-free paper
Last figure below indicates year of this printing
28 27 26 25 24 23 22 21 20 19

For Craig, Lachlan, and Poppy

Contents

PART III. PERFORMING AND LIVING RACIAL-ALITIES

Maps and Figures

Acknowledgments

When I began this project ten years ago, I imagined I would spend most of my time in archives and libraries, scouring historical records trying to locate traces of the people I was writing about. While I have spent a good amount of time with written documents, it was the people I have met along the way who pushed my research into directions unanticipated and unimagined. I came to realize the significance of material objects, visual imagery, and oral testimony in helping reconstruct individual histories, especially of those who lived under colonial rule. To complete this book, I relied on the kindness of strangers, the generosity of the relatives of the people whom I write about in this book, and the assistance of scholars, colleagues, and friends.

This project began in graduate school at the University of California, Santa Barbara, under the mentorship and guidance of my wonderful adviser, Sabine Frühstück, without whom this project would have never gotten off the ground. I am grateful for her continued guidance and support, and I hope to be one-tenth of the scholar she is one day. The members of my dissertation committee, Luke Roberts, Paul Spickard, and Ann-Elise Lewallen, provided me with years of support and insightful feedback, continually challenging me to improve my thinking and approach to researching and writing histories of colonialism. Also at UCSB, Richard Backus, Cathy Chiu, and Sugawara Hiroko helped my research tremendously. I thank Sato Ari and Jo Yoshiko at the Inter-University Center for Japanese Studies in Yokohama. From my Fulbright dissertation research year at the Graduate School, Inter-faculty Initiative in Information Studies at the University of Tokyo, I thank my adviser, Yoshimi Shun'ya, and Soeno Tsutomu and Yamashita Daisuke for their assistance with the Tsuboi Shōgorō archives. I also thank the wonderful staff at the Jōhō Gakkan library.

I am grateful for being able to meet the relatives (and correspond with others) of some of the individuals I write about in this book, who shared their personal memories, photographs, and stories of their relatives who experienced Japanese colonial rule. Their contributions not only enabled richer and fuller stories to be written but remind us that this book is not about abstract ethnoracial groups but real people who led complex lives.

I thank Pedro "Sonny" Ada, Clara Ada, and Governor Joseph Ada of Guam. I am indebted to Mitsuishi Ayumi for her assistance with the photographs and records at the Nara University Library and Museum and Kitamura Miyako for her permission to view the personal correspondence of Kitamura Nobuaki. A special thank you goes to Chikamori Kiyomi and Deriha Kōji, whose assistance, generosity, and knowledge were indispensable to the book. I am grateful to have been able to have met and spoken with Kaizawa Seiko and was aided by Yamagishi Toshinori. Thank you to Chen Xing Sheng for his time and assistance, and to Li Wei Wei and Benson Chang, who made my stay in Fuxing so hospitable. Also in Taiwan, Lung-Chih Chang and Maleveleve Lin provided invaluable assistance for my research. Yupao Lee has been a great friend and supporter of my research in many ways. I also thank May-yi Shaw, Shiow-jyu Lu, Jing-ru Huang, Chia-yu Hu, the staff at Academica Sinica's Institute of Taiwan History (especially Yi-ling Lee), the staff of the library at the Museum of National Taiwan History, Yang Nanjun, Mr. Wei at SMC Publishing, and Teresa Huang at the Chinese Taipei Film Archive.

In London, thank you to Bill Tonkin, Beverly Cook at the Museum of London, Anne Wheeldon and Jane Kimber at the Hammersmith and Fulham City Archives, Sarah Walpole at the Royal Anthropological Institute, and Kiri Ross-Jones at the Archives at the Royal Botanic Gardens, Kew. Thanks to Jean Gosebrink at the St. Louis Public Library, Miranda Rectenwald at the Washington University at St. Louis Library, Galina Pluzhnikova and staff at the Russian Museum of Ethnography in

St. Petersburg, Jim Zobel at MacArthur Memorial Museum, Morioka Kenji at the Historical Museum of the Saru River, Murai Ichirō at Mitsukoshi, Matsunaga Masazumi at Osaka Human Rights Museum, Nomoto Masahiro at the Ainu Museum in Shiraoi, and Kinjō Kaoru of the Kansai Okinawa Bunko. Thank you to Stephan and Christian at Swirbul Library at Adelphi.

Because there are so many images in this book, the process of securing permissions was formidable. I extend a special thank you to Michiko Ito and Vicky Doll at the University of Kansas, whose assistance in securing permissions was invaluable. For kind assistance at the Nomura Archives, I thank Ishikawa Atsuko. Huang Wei-kang of the Tamkang University Maritime Museum went above and beyond to help me secure permissions. Thanks to Yan Guoming, Yan Guochan, Yuasa Hiroshi and the Moritani Company, Sunazawa Yoeko and Kosaka Yousuke, Kaizawa Toru, Hirooka Emi at the Biratori town office, Nibutani Ainu Culture Museum, Wei-Chin Lin and Annie Liu at the Shung Ye Museum of Formosan Aborigines, Inaba Kayoko at the University of Tokyo General Research Museum, Uehara Masami, the Itoman City Office, the Lake Chapala Society, Phil Peters, and Harley Hettick.

A special thank you to Paul Barclay, whose help and advice began when I was in graduate school and continue to this day. His scholarship on Taiwan, Taiwan's Indigenous Peoples, and empire in general has changed the field and helped pave the way for my work and that of other scholars. Without his help, and that of Matsuoka Tadasu and Ishikawa Takeshi, setting up the groundwork to start researching Taiwan's Indigenous Peoples would have been impossible. My research has benefited from the trailblazers in the Japan field who normalized Hokkaido and Okinawa as legitimate areas of colonial study; some of these forerunners are listed below. My work has benefited from the advice and feedback of colleagues including Ben Uchiyama, Greg Dvorak, Higuchi Wakako, Maki Mita, Iitaka Shingo, Yamaguchi Yoji, Kobayashi Izumi, Gregory Smits, David Howell, Katsukata Inafuku Keiko, Isa Shin'ichi, Jordan Sand, Richard Siddle, Ishii Hidekazu, Ishihara Makoto, Miyagi Kan, Itō Rumiko, Nishihira Renta, Shiode Hiroyuki, Donald Shuster, Aletha Chu, Miki Masafumi, Michele Mason, Christopher Frey, David Ambaras, Aaron W. Moore, Uemura Hideaki, Satō Yūji, Tomita Yūko, Kō Ikujō, Yoshihara Hideaki, Kawakami Satoru, Akino Shigeki, Nagano Tamaki,

Ono Kunio, Uchida Junko, Alfred Majewicz, Okada Kazuo, Suyun Lee, Hasegawa Yuuki, and Francis Hezel. Special shout out to our research support group in Tokyo from 2008 to 2009: Ben Uchiyama, Nick Kapur, Chinghsin Wu, Kari Shepherdson-Scott, and Kendall Heitzman.

Sections of chapter 1 originally were published in "The 1903 Human Pavilion: Colonial Realities and Subaltern Subjectivities in Twentieth Century Japan," *Journal of Asian Studies,* vol. 73, no. 2 (May 2014): 493–516. It is reprinted with the permission of Cambridge University Press. The first half of chapter 5 originally appeared in "The Possibility of Liminal Colonial Subjecthood: An Examination of the Tours to the Metropolis Program and the Search for Subaltern Histories in the Japanese Empire," *Critical Asian Studies,* 47:1 (March 2015): 123–50. I am grateful to Jeff Wasserstrom and Tom Fenton and the anonymous readers at both journals for their detailed feedback on the articles, which influenced for the better how I approached and revised the book.

My research over the years has been funded by a Fulbright IIE Doctoral Dissertation Research Fellowship; UC Pacific Rim Research Program Dissertation Fellowship and mini-grants; Title IV Department of Education Foreign Languages and Areas Studies (FLAS) grants, the University of California, Santa Barbara, Department of History; the Japan Foundation; the Kosciuszko Foundation; the Joseph E. and Gina Laun Jannotta Foundation; Hamilton College; and generous support of the History Department, provost, and the dean of the College of Arts and Sciences at Adelphi University.

Last, I am grateful to Bob Graham and the two readers at the Harvard University Asia Center for their invaluable comments and feedback, which have strengthened the manuscript. I thank Li Yang for his assistance with Chinese documents, Scott Walker for his expertise in helping create the maps in the book, and Julie Hagen for her keen eye in going over my manuscript. I am grateful to my parents, Lawrence and Virginia, and my sister, Nicole. Most of all I thank my husband, Craig, who has been with me from the beginning of this journey and whose feedback and advice over the years have been unwavering and invaluable. Without his support, this book would not have been possible.

Note to the Reader

All Japanese words have been transliterated according to the modified Hepburn system, except for places names like Tokyo, Osaka, and Hokkaido. Chinese words are written in Hanyu-Pinyin. In certain cases, for some information regarding Taiwan, I have provided the Chinese characters. In the case of Austronesian (Aboriginal) names, when the indigenous spelling of personal names or locations is known, I have used those spellings. When I have been unable to locate the indigenous spelling, I have used the romanized spelling of the Japanese *katakana* used for places or names. I have transliterated Ainu spellings according to Chiri Takanaka and Yokoyama Takao's *Ainu go eiri jiten*. All Japanese translations are my own. Chinese translations are my adaptions of translations provided by Li Yang.

Abbreviations

Organizations and Newspapers

ABSKSK	Ainu Bunka Shinkō Kenkyū Suishin Kikō
AS	*Asahi shinbun* (after 1945)
HKK	Hokkaido Kyōikushi Kenkyūjo
HSH	Hokkaido Shinbunsha Henshū
HT	*Hokkai taimuzu*
ILN	*Illustrated London News*
KNNS	*Karafuto nichi nichi shinbun*
KS	*Kobe shinbun*
KZW	Kirsten Ziomek website (www.kziomek.com), which holds additional images and documents
MY	*Mainichi* (Yokohama)
OA	*Osaka asahi*
OC	*Osaka chōhō*
OCC	Office of Court Counsel
OM	*Osaka mainichi*
OS	*Otaru shinbun*
OSWCC	*Otautau Standard and Wallace County Chronicle*
PSECC	Political Status Education Coordinating Commission
RS	*Ryūkyū shinpō*
SLPD	*St. Louis Post-Dispatch*
SLR	*St. Louis Republic*
TA	*Tokyo asahi*

TKHZRZ	Tokyo kangyō hakurankai zasshi rinji zōkan
TNNS	*Taiwan nichi nichi shinpō*
TNNSB	*Tokyo nichi nichi shinbun*
TSK	Taiwan sōtokufu keimukyoku
TSMKH	Taiwan sōtokufu minseibu keisatsu honsho
WLO	*West London Observer*
YSK	Yūki Shōji Kenkyūkai
ZHAMH	Zaidan Hōjin Ainu Minzoku Hakubutsukan

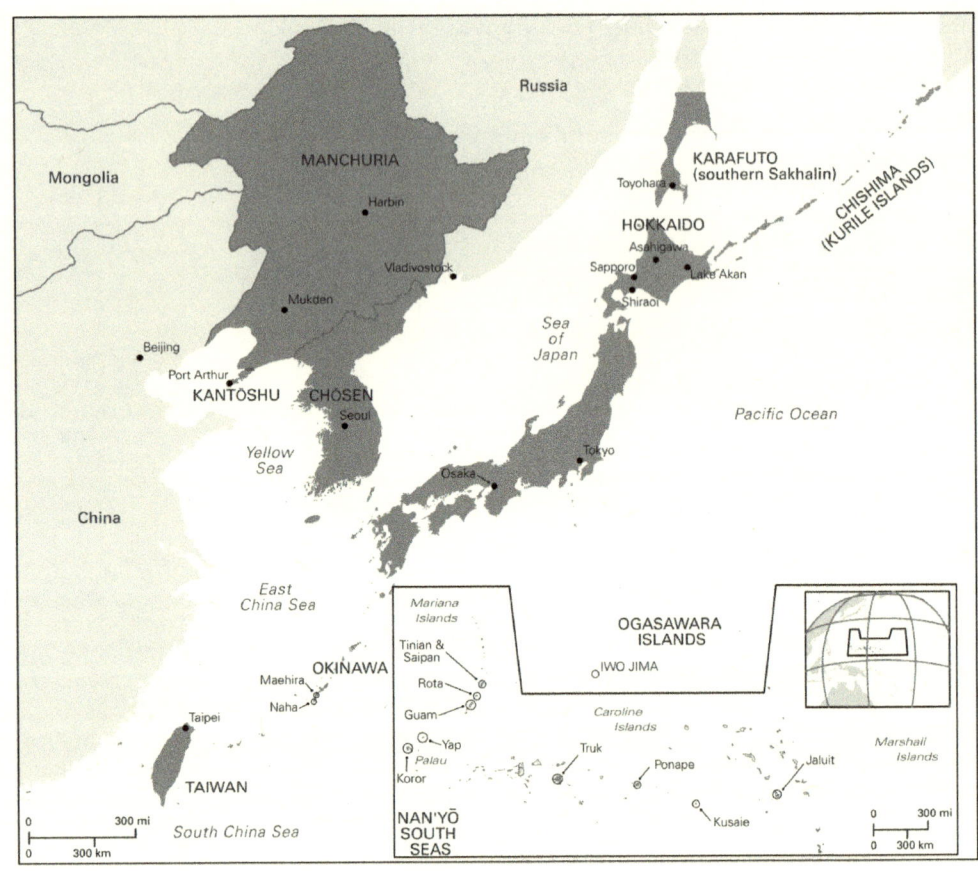

MAP I. Japanese empire circa 1935.

INTRODUCTION

> The task of the historian is to unearth both the conflicting force fields and the chains of individual choice; to rediscover the life that overflows categorical boundaries. The choices are of course unique. . . . No one story can represent all. But tracing one story in detail can remind us of the complexities and ironies concealed behind the grand labels of the moral narrative.
>
> —Tessa Morris-Suzuki, "Heroes, Collaborators and Survivors: Korean Kamikaze Pilots and the Ghosts of War in Japan and Korea" (2013)

Nakano Chūzō had wandered deep into the forests of Taiwan's mountains when he unwittingly entered what was known as the barbarian settlement of Dakekan, where a group of indigenous Atayal people lived. It was 1899, and Chūzō, a Japanese pharmacist, just eighteen years old, had traveled to Taiwan to collect medicinal plants. Atayal hunters seized Chūzō and brought their prize back to their chief, who was expected to chop off his head. As the story goes, Yayutz Bleyh, the chief's sixteen-year-old daughter, intervened on Chūzō's behalf and implored her father to spare the young man's life. Her father consented to her wishes, but Yayutz was forced to leave the mountains with Chūzō and move to the plains, owing to the shame she had brought on her father by making him appear weak in sparing the life of a foreigner. Yayutz was never to return to her home in the highlands.[1]

This romanticized narrative of the colonized woman, Yayutz, saving the colonizer, Chūzō, and thus consciously rejecting her native ways in favor of the colonizer's lifestyle, was widely circulated throughout Japan's empire. Too bad the events described—a clichéd story of redemption through service to empire—did not actually happen. According to what Yayutz's grandson told me in 2013, her heroic rescue of Chūzō never took place. He said Chūzō first encountered Yayutz under very different cir-

---

1. *TA*, April 30, 1912. Yayutz's name was rendered in katakana in many ways, including Yayutsu/Yajutsu and Yajitsu Beriya. I use the Atayal spelling found in Kang (2009).

cumstances: he was walking along the banks of the Daxi River collecting plants and he spotted her swimming, naked, in the river. This version of their meeting was never mentioned in the stories that circulated at the time. Her grandson's account is a hidden narrative, one that reconfigures the tale transmitted by government functionaries and the Japanese news media regarding Yayutz and her place in history. Furthermore, Yayutz did return to her home village after spending the early part of her life traveling back and forth between Taiwan and Japan. Although the conventionalized rescue narrative imagines Yayutz as someone who left her native ways behind, there is much evidence—oral, material, and written— to suggest otherwise. Perhaps most indicative of this is the fact that Yayutz has two gravestones—one in Japan and one in Taiwan. The liminal nature of her life offers a vivid manifestation of the complex effects of colonialism on the lives of Japan's imperial subjects, whose actual experiences diverged from the versions in nationalist and anticolonial narratives that cast them as, at best, bit players in a larger story. Accounts like the story of Yayutz delineate what Morris-Suzuki, quoted in the epigraph, calls "the complexities and ironies concealed behind the grand labels" of conquest, assimilation, progress, and dispossession by recovering the experiences of subjects whose lives were not contained by the rhetorical roles assigned to them in Japanese and postcolonial historiography.

The protagonists profiled in this book, such as Yayutz Bleyh, evoke a different shape of power and show us that imperial subjects could occupy vital positions in Japan's sprawling Asian empire (see map 1). They command our interest because they simultaneously participated in the work of empire building and pursued individual ambitions. Some defended or even celebrated local, kin-based, or tribal interests and identities, whereas others saw a new destiny and new possibilities for themselves as Japanese subjects. What this book explores, then, is not a model of empire resembling concentric circles, radiating out from an imperial core to a subaltern far periphery, but an expansive and variegated terrain of networked relationships in the Japanese empire that left more space for personal, local, and regional agency across the empire than hitherto imagined in one work.[2]

2. Scholarship on Japan's empire that has focused on local agency include Barclay, *Outcasts of Empire*; Brooks, "Peopling the Japanese Empire"; Henry, *Assimilating Seoul*; Howell, *Geographies of Identity*; Matsuda, "Becoming Japanese"; and Morris-Suzuki, "He-

Main Arguments

In this book I challenge conventional narratives of Japan's colonial history by taking the usual sites of dominance and oppression and reverse engineering them to focus on colonial subjects from four groups in the empire: the indigenous people of Taiwan (today comprising sixteen ethnicities), Micronesians, the Ainu of Hokkaido, and Okinawans. All four groups were geographically far from the Japanese metropole, the center of the empire—in the case of the Micronesians, at its farthest end. Although the Ainu and Okinawans eventually gained the full rights afforded to Japanese nationals because their status placed them somewhere between national and colonial subjects, their experiences often resembled those of other colonial subjects more than those of their Japanese compatriots. Although these groups had varying experiences under Japanese rule, government officials, anthropologists, and others tended to compare them, often through hyperracialization. This entailed exaggerating and even inventing racial markers to further distinguish these groups from the Japanese. All four groups fit the least easily into the concept of *dōbun dōshu* (common culture, common race), which was based on the understanding of a shared Sinitic culture that united Japanese, Koreans, and Han Taiwanese.

This book illustrates the breadth of the Japanese colonial project by showing that different racial and social hierarchies operated throughout the empire, and the modes of colonial rule differed according to those hierarchies and local geographies. Prior to their incorporation into the empire, the islands of Micronesia had been under European rule, Taiwan had been under Chinese rule, Okinawa (the former Ryūkyū Kingdom) was under the influence of both China and Japan, and the Ainu in Hokkaido had been under varying and inconsistent Japanese influence. With diverse histories preceding Japanese rule, it is no wonder that the experiences of Japan's colonial subjects reflected local power structures and led to different understandings of empire. With such a far-reaching empire, I tell different individuals' stories to convey a sense of the diversity

---

roes, Collaborators." My work is distinct in that it provides in-depth windows into local agency throughout the empire and follows individuals as they traverse the empire, showing commonalities and disparities of the colonial experience beyond one colony's borders.

of the empire and the commonalities of the colonial experience. Their stories serve as a starting point, opening the possibility of understanding the empire from a variety of perspectives reconstructed from materials within and beyond the colonial archive. They also reveal two main arguments about the empire: Japan depended on its colonial subjects to enact its rule, and ethnoracial differences among colonial subjects were used to the advantage of both colonial administrators and colonial subjects.

DEPENDENCY ON COLONIAL SUBJECTS TO RULE

The sheer diversity and expanse of Japan's empire meant that colonial officials were forced to adapt to established hierarchies of power that differed according to locale. Governing was easier when the Japanese could graft their imperial projects onto the remnants of previous colonial rulers. In areas where administrative apparatuses were lacking, colonial officials relied on individual power brokers and people of influence.

The limits of colonial control were perhaps most visible in the highlands of Taiwan and the islands of Micronesia, where the Japanese were more flexible in their modalities of governing and relied on colonial subjects to facilitate their rule while keeping traditional power structures in place. In the cases of the Ainu and the Okinawans, the leaders and power brokers who were influential in their local communities before Hokkaido and Okinawa were incorporated into the empire were the same elites after incorporation who were instrumental in shaping local policies and economies in these areas. As other scholars have shown, the commencement of Japanese rule did not eviscerate local power networks, and at times those networks and their elites were forceful actors in shaping local destinies.[3]

The various people profiled in this book are similar in that they were not nameless, nor were they randomly chosen from within their communities to work with Japanese officials. Over time, these once-powerful men

3. See, for example, Barclay, *Outcasts of Empire*, and Matsuoka, "Gendai Taiwan," on the indigenous Taiwanese; Matsumura, *Limits of Okinawa*, on Okinawan elites; and Siddle, *Race, Resistance*, and Howell, "Making 'Useful Citizens,'" on Ainu leaders in Hokkaido. Howell describes the Ainu–Japanese relationship prior to 1868 as one of "mutual dependence and constructive misunderstanding" (*Geographies of Identity*, 112).

and women were transformed into anonymous ethnotypes; once known and written about, they became nameless people whose histories were lost.[4] In reconstructing their histories, things will inevitably be lost and misportrayed in rewriting their narratives. Nonetheless, the composite images that reemerge show us that who they were mattered in their time. They had influence in their communities, which is why the Japanese authorities interacted with them in the first place.

These individuals were the intermediaries, the translators, and the men and women of influence on which the empire was run, although they cooperated to differing degrees in maintaining imperial rule. Japan's reliance on such intermediaries to facilitate colonial rule was downplayed in the Japanese mass media, for example, but other evidence indicates that the Japanese would have been lost without the behind-the-scenes help of certain colonial subjects. In other cases, Japan's blatant interference with local leadership structures in the colonies can be seen when comparing colonial documents with oral histories and interviews conducted after the colonial period. Although Japanese authorities appointed their own proxies in the colonies, indigenous sources reveal that local leaders were still acknowledged, despite the Japanese government's attempts to circumvent local sources of power. Sometimes the Japanese even relied on leaders whom they had previously targeted and attacked as rebels, converting them into allies who could help justify the regime. These accounts indicate that it is a mistake to understand the relationships as a one-way process in which the Japanese always controlled their subjects.

ETHNORACIAL DIFFERENCE AS ADVANTAGE

Recent studies of Japan's empire have relied on a periodization of colonial rule in which the experiences of colonial subjects shifted from an initial period of assimilation (*dōka*) to imperialization (*kōminka*), starting in the 1930s.[5] This view suggests that as time went on, the goal for colonial subjects was increasingly to eradicate the differences separating them from

4. Barclay, "Playing the Race Card," demonstrates how it is possible to name the people who have become racial ethnotypes on postcards.

5. Ching, *Becoming "Japanese,"* and Chou, "Kominka Movement."

the Japanese. Although "becoming Japanese" was a familiar talking point, I argue that understanding colonial subjects' experiences solely through the lens of assimilation does not take into account the more complicated and codependent relationship between those usually delineated as "colonized" and "colonizer." Although some colonial subjects did in fact identify as Japanese, they often did so as a strategy to obtain rights or the same treatment other Japanese nationals received. By claiming they were also "children of the emperor" or "Japanese," they hoped to evoke an emotional connection to their compatriots while advocating for equal opportunities. Furthermore, colonial authorities who worked closely with Micronesians and the indigenous Taiwanese, for example, at times found it in their best interest to emphasize the ethnoracial distinctions that set them apart from the Japanese.

In contrast, the Japanese did not identify "traditional" Koreans or Han Taiwanese as ideal intermediaries, as they did the Ainu, Micronesians, and indigenous Taiwanese. At the start of colonial rule in Korea and areas of Han Taiwan, the Japanese had to rely on traditional groups, such as the Confucian elite.[6] But over time in Taiwan, the Japanese chose to work with the children of the Confucian elite, who were educated in Japanese schools and had less of a connection to past ruling systems.[7] In Korea, "traditional-ness" was not evoked as a positive quality but was seen as evidence of low culture or a lack of modernity.[8]

I also challenge the notion that the Japanese used ethnoracial difference primarily to denigrate or highlight the savagery of the people they were ruling to clarify their own position of power, as some have emphasized.[9] Instead, the emphasis on ethnoracial differences had more to do with the precariousness of Japanese rule. The Japanese had to adjust their strategies—just like their ideological justifications—for colonial rule constantly as real-world conditions proved not to be static and simply reactionary to Japanese action but involved complicated and autonomous structures of power the Japanese had to try to slip into when supplanting

6. Tsurumi, *Japanese Colonial Education*, 160; Uchida, *Brokers of Empire*, 124.
7. Phillips, *Between Assimilation*, 22–23.
8. Henry, "Sanitizing Empire," 668.
9. See Tierney, *Tropics of Savagery*; Atkins, "Colonial Modernity"; Matsuda, *Teikoku no shisen*.

these power structures was not possible. In some cases, maintaining local power structures was beneficial, necessitating more involvement from those putatively under Japan's rule. From the perspective of colonial authorities, it was often better to show a model colonial subject who was ethnoracially distinct and cooperating with administrative rule than a subject who was Japanized. In Taiwan, for example, potent images of indigenous leaders now tamed were used to garner support from local populations; they were not deployed merely to underscore the dichotomy between the so-called civilized Japanese and barbaric indigenous peoples. Instead of trying to Japanize or assimilate Bunun rebel leaders, the Japanese encouraged certain leaders to serve as traditional representatives of the past to maintain peace and stability in their local communities. Japanese rule was more tenuous than was often conceded and the divergent strategies of colonial rule that were used included policies that were different to assimilation policies.

In fact, I argue that emphasizing ethnoracial differences was a strategy used by both colonial authorities and colonial subjects. For colonial subjects, stressing their ethnoracial differences could be a means of protest; examples of this can be found across the empire. Koreans emphasized their ethnoracial differences from the Japanese when protesting Japanese rule.[10] Ainu leaders in the postwar period stressed their ethnoracial differences to bolster the importance of preserving their own culture and to gain recognition from the government.

While I certainly discuss several people who spoke of the value of "becoming Japanese," I also illustrate how the process of becoming Japanese simultaneously entailed the loss of indigenous ethnoracial identities—something that is less often a focus. This book widens the discussion on colonial ideology and assimilation policies by minimizing the importance of such rhetoric in Japan's empire.[11] Instead, I discuss situations in which the Japanese and their colonial subjects saw value in emphasizing ethnoracial differences.

10. Henry, "Assimilation's Racializing Sensibilities," 16; Ruoff, *Imperial Japan*, 127.
11. Henry, *Assimilating Seoul*; Caprio, *Japanese Assimilation*; Ching, *Becoming "Japanese."*

Methodologies of Re-Creating the Colonial Archive

When I embarked on this project ten years ago, it was in the context of reading histories of Japan's empire that focused on government figures and everyday Japanese settlers. But there were these unknown entities who were hinted at, referred to, yet not really discussed—the colonized people. What did they think, and how did they operate? Although they were portrayed as subaltern, as faceless and undifferentiated people, mere representations of ethnoracial types, I wondered, could their histories be told?

Through my research I discovered that to write the histories of colonized people we must rely on unconventional means and sources beyond the colonial archive. These include oral histories, visual imagery, and material objects. By incorporating ethnography along with documentary evidence and visual images, I have been able to reconstruct histories of individuals whose traces in government documents may be incomplete and one-sided. In some cases I use visual evidence and imagery in the way Roland Barthes describes: seeing a specific photograph by looking beyond its "referent (from what it represents)" to "perceive the photographic signifier [a sign's image as distinct from its meaning]." "It requires," according to Barthes, "a secondary action of knowledge or of reflection."[12] The various connotations of a particular image, as well as the interpretations it can lead to when analyzed in conjunction with other images, provide an alternative mode of interrogating the colonial experience. This original manuscript had more than 150 images. Fortunately, I was able to publish more than eighty images in this book (please visit my website to view the rest of the images).[13]

Allowing personal belongings, photos, and oral histories to lead the reconstruction of colonial narratives offers more of a chance to witness the multidimensionality of the colonial experience than we can get by relying solely on documents written by colonial officials. Yet I do not disavow the colonial archive, as some contend we should.[14] Colonial documents often reveal the deprecatory attitudes officials directed toward

---

12. Barthes, *Camera Lucida*, 5.
13. See www.kziomek.com (referred to as KZW in subsequent chapters).
14. Smith, *Decolonizing Methodologies*, and Lorde, "Master's Tools."

certain peoples under Japanese rule, but they can also illustrate the complexities of the colonial relationship, based on what details were recorded and how. By drawing from a range of sources, the fuller narrative that emerges does not become more straightforward, however. Rather, it raises more questions than answers about our ability to capture even one moment in all of its complexity, let alone the fullness of a person's life. Acknowledging and gravitating toward these ambiguities enables us to reconsider the breadth of individual colonial experiences. Thus, I have used colonial documents as well as written, visual, oral, and material sources beyond the colonial archive to gain access to information about people who have been misrepresented, ignored, or forgotten. As Ann Stoler and Frederick Cooper have pointed out, because the task of writing such a colonial history "is unwieldy and not easily carried out . . . [w]e need to create . . . a new archive of our own."[15]

In my work I have drawn inspiration from the methodological techniques of some scholars of colonial history outside of the Japanese empire, including Pekka Hämäläinen (the Comanche empire), Saloni Mathur (India), and Clare Anderson (the Indian Ocean world), who all use a range of sources, written and visual, to excavate the voices of those who have not been heard.[16] In Hämäläinen's groundbreaking work, *The Comanche Empire*, he "prioritized accounts that recount, even in a mutated form [the] Comanche voice—while keeping in mind that the voice is recorded through a cultural colander." Hämäläinen also cross-checked multilingual "documents against one another to create more stereoscopic and arguably more accurate portrayals of Comanche intentions and objectives."[17] This awareness of what he calls a "cultural colander" is important and, like Hämäläinen, I have tried to

---

15. Stoler and Cooper (eds.), *Tensions of Empire*, 16.

16. In Saloni Mathur's *India by Design*, she reads visual representations of empire critically against written texts and oral testimony. Her analysis of how the travel of poor Indians recruited to the London exhibition became a problem for the British and Indian elite alike offers a counterpoint to previous work that defined travel at this time as a mostly bourgeois experience. Clare Anderson, in *Subaltern Lives*, makes use of an array of sources, combing through the colonial archives and plucking names out of obscurity—from penal records and the like—to follow the trail of people across the vast territories of the Indian Ocean.

17. Hämäläinen, *Comanche Empire*, 13.

address the difficulties of re-creating histories of Japan's colonial subjects by cross-checking sources in Japanese, Chinese, and English. By following the path of pioneering works that pushed the methodological envelope in their examination of colonial relationships, I hope to inspire a reexamination of whose stories can be told from times of empire and how to tell them.

Overview of the Book

Throughout the chapters I emphasize the movement of colonial subjects throughout Japan's empire. The book is divided into three parts, with a detailed overview introducing each part. Part I focuses on the people involved in the human displays that were popular in the early twentieth century at expositions held in the Japanese metropolis, in Osaka and Tokyo, and at international expositions like those held in St. Louis in 1904 and London in 1910. By looking at the participants' varied motivations, experiences, and recollections, we see that they were multifaceted individuals, not one-dimensional ethnic models. The displays thereby defied their characterization as representing Japan's imperial power over its colonized peoples. In addition, the public's reactions to the displays reveal that contrary to expectation, both colonial subjects and the Japanese questioned the boundaries determining who was a colonial subject.

Part II focuses on the tours to the metropolis (*naichi kankō*) program, a colonial policy that sought to bring the indigenous people of Taiwan and Micronesia to Japan and show them the wonders of Japanese civilization. The tours serve as a jumping-off point from which I explore the complexities of the colonial relationship, rather than assessing the efficacy of the tour program as intended by Japanese authorities.

Part III examines the outerlands of the empire, addressing the Ainu tourist villages of Hokkaido, the leaders who initiated the tourist industry that developed in Shiraoi in the early twentieth century, and the entrepreneurial Ainu who built the tourist village at Lake Akan in the postwar period. Some of the Ainu leaders involved in the operation of these villages fought for Japan during the Asia-Pacific War, and their wartime experiences in different parts of the empire, including Okinawa, reinforced their sense of identity as members of an indigenous group distinct from the Japanese. Their experiences away from Hokkaido—in Manchuria, Okinawa, and Micronesia—inspired them to use the platform of Ainu tourism not only to preserve and reteach Ainu culture to their people and others but to advocate for Ainu rights.

This book focuses on individuals, to see what their lives can tell us about colonialism. The processes of revelation do not simply result in uplifting stories of power and agency. Often it is by revealing the actions and motivations of colonial subjects that we can shift the narratives of colonialism. In some cases in this study, while the oppressive nature of Japan's colonial policies is maintained, the narrative is enriched by focusing on how colonial subjects acted within that oppression, revealing the limits of power on both sides. At other times, the contestations in colonial subjects' local communities are more important to understanding certain aspects of colonial life. In all, the result is a more nuanced analysis of how colonial subjects moved and lived within Japan's imperial spaces.

Colonial relationships in imperial Japan were fluid, and this dynamism was often revealed when the Japanese and the indigenous populations they ruled encountered each other outside of their familiar realms. My work intersects with those scholars who reveal this dynamism, as well as recent work focusing on Japanese travel across the empire.[18] Building on those works, I show how the travel of certain people to other locations in the empire had the ability to transform their standing and place in the empire. Not only were colonial subjects traveling throughout the empire and beyond, they were involved in creating tourist sites. By discussing their movement, I do not mean to entirely rewrite the narrative of travel within the empire but to challenge presumptions about the use and place of colonial bodies within Japan's imperial project.

18. Sand, "Imperial Tokyo as a Contact Zone"; Brooks, writing about Koreans in Manchuria, argues that both the Taiwanese and the Koreans "fell into grayer, often impermanent categories when displaced to other realms of empire" ("Peopling the Japanese Empire," 26). Matsuda, on the other hand, argues that Yaeyama migrants to Taiwan did not fulfill the traditional role as colonizers from *naichi* because they left the rural margins and went to the modern center of Taipei ("Becoming Japanese" and "Moving Out"). For Japanese travel, see McDonald, *Placing Empire*, 52, and Ruoff, *Imperial Japan*, 82.

Japanese Imperial Expansion, 1868–1945

Before we follow various individuals in different locations and as they journey across the empire, I offer a quick overview of Japan's imperial expansion to set the scene for the following chapters. As the empire transformed, so did the language that defined it.

Japan's empire building in the mid-nineteenth century began when it initiated processes to incorporate Hokkaido and Okinawa in 1868 and 1872, respectively, adopting a primarily defensive posture against Western imperialism. Areas like Hokkaido and Okinawa were in some ways seen as equivalent to newly acquired colonial acquisitions, like Taiwan and Korea. During the Meiji period, the islands of Honshu, Kyushu, and Shikoku were viewed as part of Japan's interior territory (*naichi*), and territories outside of that, including at times Okinawa and Hokkaido as well as other colonial territories, as external territory, or *gaichi*.[19] Understandings of *gaichi* fluctuated over time, as did the labels for imperial spaces and the people within those spaces.[20] Both Taiwan (1895) and Korea (1910) were eventually incorporated as colonies, but the imperial Diet debated whether they should instead be administered as prefectures, like Okinawa, illustrating that how territories were added to the empire was not self-evident; instead, expansion was a highly contingent process based on economic and political concerns.[21]

Japan's victory in the Russo-Japanese War in 1905 and the resulting Treaty of Portsmouth led to the colonization of Korea and Japan's acquisition of the South Manchurian Railroad and the Kwantung Leased Territory on the Liaotung Peninsula. This initiated emigration to the area and justified the presence of Japan's Kwantung Army to defend Japanese interests in Manchuria. Furthermore, Karafuto, on southern Sakhalin Island, was recognized as a Japanese colony; in 1907 it was redesignated a

---

19. Chen, "Attempt to Integrate," 240–41.

20. The terms' referents changed depending on who was speaking. Ainu, Okinawans, Taiwanese, and Micronesians often referred to Japanese as *naichijin* (people from the interior lands), as a way to signal Japanese "apartness" from themselves. So while Hokkaido would at times be seen as *naichi*, the Ainu still viewed the Japanese (and not themselves) as *naichijin*. See Oguma, *"Nihonjin" no kyōkai*, for more discussion.

21. Chen, "Attempt to Integrate," 248–51; Yamamuro, "Evolving Meiji State," 15–16.

prefecture (despite its majority-Japanese settler population, it was still considered *gaichi*).

As Britain's ally during World War I, Japan occupied German colonial territories in the Pacific and placed them under Japanese naval administration. After Germany's defeat, Japan governed the Micronesian islands (Nan'yō guntō) according to a Class C mandate from the League of Nations (see map 1 for all islands under Japanese jurisdiction). This position confirmed Japan's rising status as an imperial power, in the company of Western powers that governed with similar mandates over territories elsewhere in the world that had been deemed incapable of governing themselves. In 1931 the Manchurian Incident, in which the Japanese Kwantung Army blew up its own railroad tracks and blamed it on the Chinese, was used to justify Japan's invasion of Manchukuo, which the Japanese then proclaimed a sovereign state (but effectively ruled as a puppet state).[22]

During World War II, after attacks launched elsewhere in conjunction with the 1941 attack on Pearl Harbor against the United States, Japan occupied several former colonies of Western powers under the pretense of liberating them. In 1942 the administration of Taiwan, Korea, and Karafuto was shifted to the Japanese Ministry of Home Affairs, and responsibility for Micronesia and the Kwantung Leased Territory was turned over to the Ministry of Greater East Asia Affairs (Daitōashō).[23] Burma and the Philippines were given nominal independence and concluded treaties of alliance with Japan, but not much was done to facilitate their independence.[24] In March 1945, the Diet's lower house accepted a petition abolishing use of the term *gaichi*, or outer territories, to refer to possessions outside of metropolitan Japan.[25] All of the empire was now *naichi*. The Japanese empire's remarkable evolution underscores how Japan, like other imperial powers, constantly changed the rhetoric of empire as its physical integration of outside territories continued, thus seeking to mask the violence that imperialism perpetuated.

22. Duara, "New Imperialism," 6.

23. Chen, "Attempt to Integrate," 243.

24. Other areas, like Indonesia and Malaya, were designated "imperial territories" in May 1943 and were ruled by Japanese military governments. Gotō, "Cooperation, Submission," 277.

25. Fujitani, *Race for Empire*, 66.

Bringing Subalternity to Crisis, or the Unwriting of Subaltern Histories

I contend that it is possible to write colonial histories in which the colonial subject is paramount. In her well-known essay "Can the Subaltern Speak?," published in 1988, Gayatri Spivak stated four times that the subaltern cannot speak.[26] Spivak wrote this essay in the context of her critique of the Subaltern Studies group, founded in India, whose purpose was to write new histories of protest and insurgency from the point of view of those who protested, without relying on elite sources. She rewrote her essay in 1999 in response to critics who claimed she did not recognize that the subaltern does have a voice and that she was not allowing resistance to speak.[27] In subsequent interviews she clarified that she meant subalterns can talk but cannot be heard.[28] Although Spivak has explained that her passionate lament that the subaltern cannot speak was intended to voice a sense of rhetorical anguish, she has maintained her original argument.[29]

This book builds on Spivak's theorization of the subaltern and shifts the focus from writing subaltern histories to unwriting them. Instead of trying to preserve imperial Japan's most marginalized colonial subjects as perpetual subalterns, I believe it is possible to unwrite their subalternity through what Spivak calls "bringing subalternity to crisis."[30] I argue for understanding subalternity as a malleable status that varies with gradations of mobility and proximity to institutions and structures that write events and people into the conventional historical record.

Prominent voices in colonial studies, following Antonio Gramsci, have used the term *subaltern* to refer to groups in society that are subject to the hegemony of the ruling class or "colonizer." Spivak disagrees with

26. Spivak, "Can the Subaltern Speak?," 287, 295, 308.

27. Landry and MacLean, "Subaltern Talk," 287.

28. Landry and MacLean, "Subaltern Talk," 292; Spivak, "Extempore Response," 143–46.

29. Landry and MacLean, "Subaltern Talk," 289; Sharpe and Spivak, "A Conversation."

30. Spivak, "In Response," 229.

the wide application of the term.[31] "[One is] not 'subaltern,' she writes, "simply by being postcolonial or a member of an ethnic minority."[32] To Spivak, a subaltern is "a person without lines of social mobility."[33] Therefore, once subalterns are able to access paths of mobility, she says, or "when a line of communication is established between a member of subaltern groups and the circuits of citizenship or institutionality, the subaltern has been inserted into the long road to hegemony."[34] When this happens, their subalternity is brought to crisis. Arguing against the Subaltern Studies group, which trained its focus on subalterns engaged in protest, Spivak believed such acts of militancy meant the protesters were no longer subaltern. She explained:

> You have the foreign elite and indigenous elite. Below that you will have the vectors of upward, downward, sideward, backward mobility. But then there is a space for all practical purposes outside those lines. Now if I understand the work of the Subalternists right, every moment of insurgency they have fastened onto has been a moment when subalternity has been brought to a point of crisis: the cultural constructions that are allowed to exist within subalternity, removed as it is from other lines of mobility, are changed into militancy. In other words, every moment that is noticed as a case of subalternity is undermined. We are never looking at the *pure subaltern* [emphasis added]. There is, then, something of a not-speakingness in the very notion of subalternity.[35]

In Spivak's conception of bringing subalternity to crisis, an act of militancy (as well as access to lines of mobility) eradicates subaltern status.

Bringing subalternity to crisis is desirable, Spivak writes: "Unless we want to be romantic purists or primitivists about 'preserving subalternity'—a contradiction in terms—this is absolutely to be desired."[36]

31. Landry and MacLean, "Subaltern Talk," 291; The Subaltern Studies group expanded it as the "name for the general attribute of subordination in South Asian society whether this is expressed in terms of class, caste, age, gender and office or in any other way." Ashcroft, Griffiths, Tiffin (eds.), *Post-Colonial Studies*, 215–16.
32. Spivak, "Can the Subaltern Speak? Revised," 65.
33. Spivak, *Critique of Postcolonial*, 28.
34. Spivak, "Can the Subaltern Speak? Revised," 65.
35. Landry and MacLean, "Subaltern Talk," 288–89.
36. Spivak, "Can the Subaltern Speak? Revised," 65.

Spivak flipped the criticism that she was preserving subalternity by asserting that true subalterns were unknowable, accusing her critics of the same thing: claiming that when discussing certain subalterns' access to mobility, they still insisted on ascribing to them subaltern status.

If subalternity is essentially unknowable, what of the people who are slightly outside or above the state of subalternity?[37] I argue that those on the peripheries of empire experienced different degrees of proximity to subalternity because they had different levels of access to power. Donna Landry and Gerald MacLean interviewed Spivak in 1993 and asked her about the subaltern functioning "as an ever-receding horizon of possibility."[38] Taking this formulation as a point of departure, it seems possible to conceptualize different gradations of proximity to subalternity. At one extreme is the place where true subalternity lies in obscurity, according to Spivak. At the opposite end of the spectrum are subalterns whose access to or disruption of lines of mobility has removed their subalternity. Then there are all those who fall somewhere in between. The people I discuss in this book are not true subalterns according to Spivak's definition, because such a condition would place them beyond the realm of historical reconstruction. The fact that I can tell their stories reveals that their subalternity has been brought to crisis. They have escaped from the muting that envelops absolute subalternity.

Whether someone is relegated to the obscurity of subalternity has more to do with the inscription of events and personalities in the historical record and the subsequent writing of history than with their actual efficacy as historical actors. If dominant narratives of history place certain people in footnotes, or describe what happened to them instead of what they did themselves, their subalternity is reinscribed—a condition that replicates itself as historians build on previous scholarship.[39] Although Marxist critiques of colonialism remind us that it was often the indigenous people of empires who suffered the brute violence of the imperial state in its drive for primitive accumulation, in these critiques indigenous people are rewritten as dead labor or as bodies meant for extermination.

37. In explaining Spivak, Morris also writes, "true subalternity remains in shadow." "Introduction," 7.

38. Landry and MacLean, "Subaltern Talk," 292–93. They asked her if she had a formula for "tracing the ever-receding horizons of subalternity," to which she responded no.

39. Trouillot, *Silencing the Past.*

The lived experiences of colonial subjects detailed in this book challenge the undervaluation of the mobility of colonial bodies and urge a move away from the rigid framework of empire that reimagines imperial power as unilateral and absolute.[40]

Finally, any discussion of Spivak and her conceptualization of the subaltern must mention one of her original and ongoing critiques: that the writing of subaltern histories has the potential to reinscribe imperialist power structures. She criticizes scholars like Foucault, whom she labels a "first world intellectual masquerading as the absent nonrepresenter who lets the oppressed speak for themselves."[41] Taking this criticism to heart, I nevertheless contend that it is possible to hear colonial subjects speak, even as I acknowledge that as a historian, I select and present their stories to form a historical narrative. While the dynamics of power in an empire give greater weight to perspectives that lend themselves to certain genres of narration and preservation, they do not destroy the voice of the colonized completely. At the same time, although it is possible to hear subalterns speak, their utterances, like the utterances of those whose voices have accreted greater historical weight, are imperfect, and the two sides are often in dialogue with each other. We must not reify their voices to the extent that suggests it is possible to extract one singular and true voice of the radically marginalized, or, for that matter, that those who relegated them to the shadows were a monolith. There is no "repressed" version of events waiting to be uncovered that could completely supplant conventional historical versions of events.

I recover the histories of radically marginalized people, or strip them of their subalternity, not as proof that the truly oppressed can speak, but as a demonstration that subalternity is not a permanent condition. If we cannot get to pure subalternity of the past—in any representable way— we can at least get to the conditions and circumstances of those who have emerged from its shadows.

40. For Driscoll, "one of the tactics of biopolitics [was] to 'direct population flows,'" which involved the movement of colonial bodies for labor and exploitative purposes, to fuel the empire from the periphery (*Absolute Erotic*, 15).

41. Spivak, "Can the Subaltern Speak?", 292.

A Note on Ethnoracial Terminology

Throughout the text I use the term *ethnoracial*, which I have adopted from Paul Spickard's work on world ethnic systems and Tessa Morris-Suzuki's work on migration in the prewar Japanese empire.[42] I use this term to circumvent a dichotomized understanding of race and ethnicity. As Spickard remarks, "To distinguish between 'race' and 'ethnicity' is to give in to the pseudoscientific racists by adopting their terminology. It is to conjure up visions of large, physical, immutable races, and smaller, cultural subgroups that are ethnic."[43] Works by scholars of Japan's empire have illustrated that the discourse from the late nineteenth to the twentieth century was so varied that the different peoples of the empire were classified according to both ethnic and racial differences.[44]

During times of Japanese empire, the hyperracialization of ethnoracial subjects also prevailed. Paul Barclay has written about the importance of taking race seriously in discussions about Japanese empire. He writes that despite the fact that race has been debunked as "a form of pseudoscientific false consciousness," it was still "subjectively experienced by racializers and the racialized in the event of its historical emergence."[45] Okinawans, indigenous Taiwanese, and Micronesians were often described by the Japanese as "black" or "dark" (*kuroi*) in terms of their physical appearance. Along with the Ainu, they were compared to African Americans, at that time referred to as Negros (*niguro* or *neguro*) and black people (*kokujin*), by various groups of Japanese educators, officials, and Christians in framing the colonial subjects' sociopolitical status (with its racial implications) vis-à-vis the Japanese. The specter of Booker T. Washington was often upheld as proof that assimilation and edification were possible for the "lower" and "primitive" races of Japan's empire.[46]

As noted, indigenous peoples also understood their relationship to the Japanese in ethnoracial terms. This was not a matter of merely adopting

42.   Spickard, "Race and Nation"; Morris-Suzuki, "Migrants, Subjects."
43.   Spickard, "Race and Nation," 12.
44.   Frühstück, *Colonizing Sex*, 19–20; Weiner (ed.), *Japan's Minorities*; Doak, "What is a Nation."
45.   Barclay, "Playing the Race Card," 39.
46.   Inoue and Uchimura, *Seibanki*.

the language of the colonizer but was rooted in longer historical relationships with the Japanese, especially among the Ainu and Okinawans. The terms Japan's colonial subjects used to refer to the Japanese include *wajin, Yamatojin, Yamatochū, naichijin,* and *shamo,* and all are ethnoracially based. Some mobilized these terms to maintain their distance from the Japanese and assert their own subjectivity. Others determined to pass as Japanese and, through Japanization, sought to eradicate ethnoracial differences. By paying attention to the language colonial subjects used, one can see how they reinforced distinctions between themselves and the Japanese.

PART I

Boundaries of Late Meiji Colonial Subjecthood

Part I Introduction

Chapters 1 through 4 look at Japanese empire from the perspective of colonial subjects featured in the human displays at expositions held in Japan and abroad. The experiences of the various individuals who were on display, as well as the diverse reactions to these displays expressed by Japanese and colonial subjects, demonstrate an uncertain and fluctuating notion of colonial subjecthood during the late Meiji period.

Chapter 1 explores the first human display in Japan, the Human Pavilion at the Fifth Domestic Industrial Exposition, held in Osaka in 1903. The pavilion included imperial (or national) subjects—Ainu and Okinawans—and individuals from recently colonized Taiwan and from Korea, which was yet to be colonized. It also displayed people from such exotic locales as Java and India. The fact that Japanese imperial subjects were included in the pavilion with other, non-Japanese races indicates that imperial subjecthood was not a criterion in determining who should or should not be showcased.

How the inclusion of the Ainu and the Okinawans was understood and debated reveals the different ways each group saw their new status vis-à-vis the empire. Ainu Fushine Kōzō advanced a notion of imperial subjecthood in which one could be Ainu and also a loyal subject of the Japanese empire. Fushine urged that the Ainu be treated equitably, not because all races were equal (a rather modern notion) but because he viewed imperial subjecthood as predicated on military conscription and being included as "children of the emperor." Two Okinawan women,

Nakamura Kame and Uehara Ushi, were removed from the display amid a larger debate in which competing visions of imperial subjecthood and what it meant to be civilized were tied up with the charge that the pavilion's treatment of people as objects posed a humanitarian concern (*jindō mondai*). The Human Pavilion became a nexus between colonial and imperial subjects that, rather than reifying distinctions between the two, called into question the coherence of civilizational taxonomies in Japan and the world.

In chapters 2 and 3, I examine the Ainu who were involved in the human displays that Japan presented abroad at the 1904 Louisiana Purchase Exposition and the 1910 Japan-British Exhibition in London, as well as the Taiwanese Aborigines involved in the 1910 exposition. The international settings recalibrated the place of colonial subjects because in some cases Japanese participants were also on display, right next to their colonial subjects. The experiences and reactions of participants in the human displays show that some questioned their characterization as colonial subjects who were primitive and uncivilized; the Japanese were even occasionally seen as being less civilized than their colonial counterparts. In the case of the Taiwanese Aborigines, by following accounts of the participants after they returned to Taiwan we see how their experiences in London emboldened them to critique Japan's backwardness in comparison with the Western powers.

Chapter 4 focuses on the 1912 and 1913 expositions in Tokyo and Osaka, respectively. In contrast to the 1903 Human Pavilion, which was designed as an anthropological showcase, the display in Tokyo was meant to serve as an imperial nexus point, where Japanese visitors and the colonial subjects on display could meet and learn about the various races of the empire. Touting its diversity, this was the first time the empire was explicitly linked to a human display, and it represented a snapshot of the empire that was both contested and incomplete. Advertised as exhibiting all the ethnoracial groups of the empire, the 1912 human display did not feature Korean subjects—although Korea was a colony by this time—owing to reservations on the part of the colonial government, whereas it did feature Ainu from Hokkaido and Karafuto (technically not colonies at the time), as well as Nivkh and Uilta people from Karafuto. Taiwanese subjects of Han ethnicity, the majority population in Taiwan, were almost absent, with the indigenous people of Taiwan being the main representatives of

Taiwanese culture in the exhibit. These sorts of peculiarities indicate that a territory's official nomenclature—"colony" or "prefecture"—was not important; what qualified certain colonial subjects for inclusion in the display were their perceived ethnoracial differences from the Japanese, rather than whether their territory was called a colony.

Planners of the 1913 exposition in Osaka followed a similar pattern in terms of the composition of the human display, but the tenor and feelings surrounding the exhibit were dramatically different. This was the last time such a display of various colonial subjects was attempted in Japan, and unlike other empires where colonial expositions were a way of life, in the Japanese metropolis human displays came to be seen as an inappropriate way to visualize the empire.

CHAPTER I

Colonial Reality and
Subaltern Subjectivity

The people in the crowd elbowed one another as they tried to get a better position, craning their necks to see the man who had become the overnight sensation of the Human Pavilion (Jinruikan), the first anthropological display at an exposition in Japan that featured living humans. The undisputed star of the pavilion, according to reporters who had visited the exhibit in its opening days, was an Ainu man named Fushine Kōzō.[1] He was on display in a two-story wooden building outside of the main exposition grounds, in the entertainment section of the Fifth Domestic Industrial Exposition in Osaka. The 1903 exposition was larger than any of the four that preceded it, in terms of space, number of exhibitors, and the number of visitors it attracted (an estimated 4,351,000).[2] For many in the crowd, this was the first time they had seen an Ainu person in the flesh.

The Human Pavilion was located alongside the exposition's zoo and what was called the Mystery Building (Fushigikan), which featured Carmencella, a US actress whose performance was enhanced by an electric light show. Although some have dismissed the importance of the Human Pavilion, saying it was not actually part of the exposition owing to its location in the entertainment district, in fact references to the building were included in exposition documents and even in the exposition

1. *OM*, March 6 and 9, 1903; *OA*, March 8 and 24, 1903, April 8, 1903.
2. Yoshimi, *Hakurankai no seijigaku*, 127; see KZW for a map of the exposition.

FIG. 1.1. The people in the Human Pavilion. Credit: *Ehagaki ni miru Okinawa Meiji Taishō Shōwa*. Naha: Ryūkyū shinpōsha, 1993, 194. Courtesy of Ryūkyū shinpōsha.

song.[3] After paying the ten sen fee to enter the Human Pavilion, Japanese spectators could see people from such exotic locales as Africa, Java, India, the Ottoman Empire, and the Malay Peninsula.

The Human Pavilion included people who had become Japanese subjects: Okinawans, Ainu, Taiwanese of Han ethnicity, and Taiwanese Aborigines (fig. 1.1). The exhibit's organizer, anthropologist Tsuboi Shōgorō, announced that his goal was to showcase the various races of the world.[4] Many observers pointed out that no Japanese individuals or Westerners were included.[5] The pavilion featured only peoples deemed barbaric and primitive, and thus the Japanese and Westerners were exempt.

3. Stanza 89 of "The Fifth Domestic Industrial Exposition Song, a guide to the premises" reads: "the Human Pavilion shows throughout the manners and customs of the Ainu, Taiwanese, Ryūkyūans, Koreans, Indians, Javanese that are gathered" (*Daigokai naikoku kangyō hakurankai jōnai annai shōka*, 45).

4. The genesis of the pavilion has been attributed to Osaka businessman Nishida Masatoshi, who enlisted Tsuboi Shōgorō as the official organizer.

5. *Nihon*, May 4, 1903; *RS*, April 7, 1903.

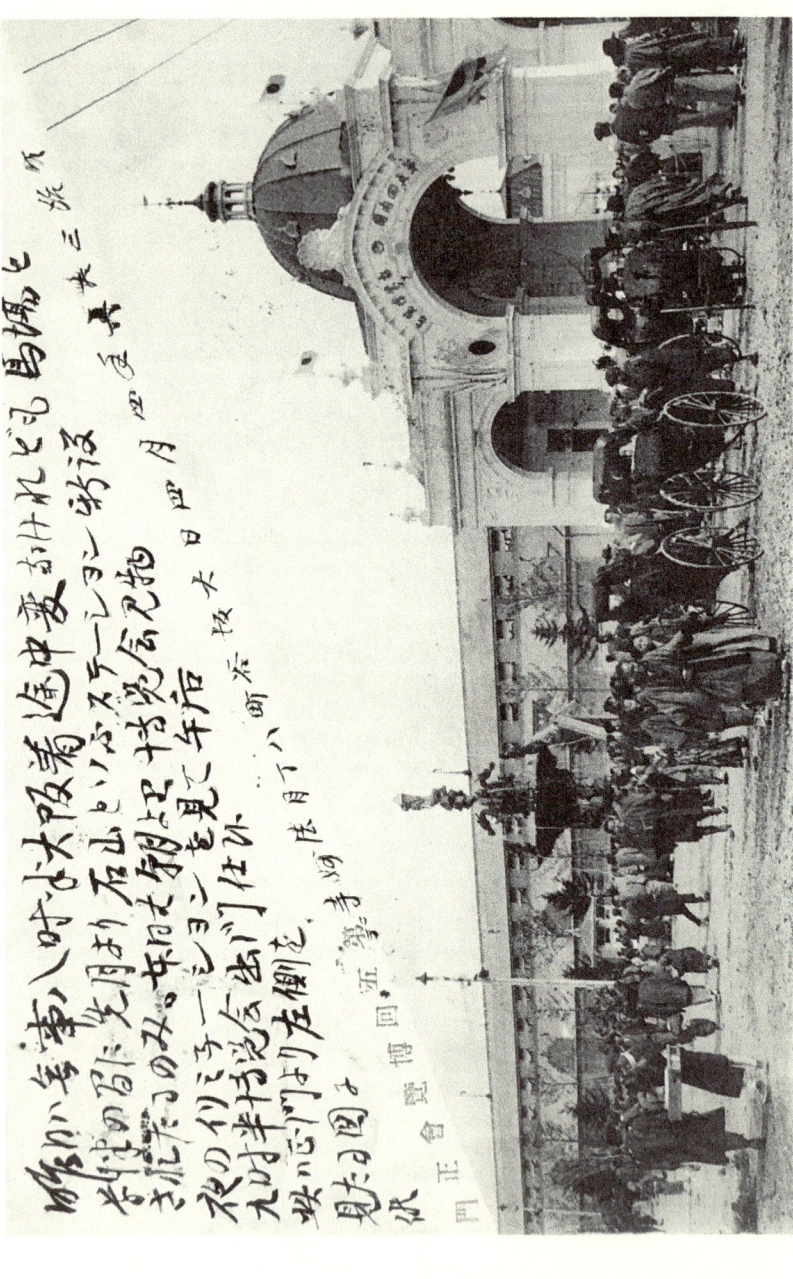

FIG. 1.2. Postcard featuring the entrance of the 1903 Fifth Domestic Industrial Exposition. Courtesy of Collection NOMURA Co., Ltd., Japan.

This first human display in Japan has been described by Yoshimi Shun'ya as born out of the tradition among Western imperial powers of displaying colonized peoples at expositions in the mid-nineteenth century.[6] Arnaud Nanta argues that the Human Pavilion brought Japan closer to being on par with the other imperial powers, and Matsuda Kyōko has characterized it as an illustration of Japanese orientalism at work: through Japan's display of its primitive "other," the image of the Japanese as civilized was reinforced.[7] Scholarship focusing on the protests that erupted over the display of Okinawans, Koreans, and Chinese has situated the travesty of the pavilion in the protesters' jockeying for position on the scale of civilization—that is, in their claims that being associated with other primitive peoples was demeaning and their inclusion in the pavilion was a threat to their country's national prestige.[8]

As "big-ticket spectacles," expositions and world fairs are often viewed as barometers for a nation's current progress and prestige (fig. 1.2). Although, as Susan Fernsebner reminded readers in her article "Expo 2010: A Historical Perspective," which reflected on the 1910 Nanyang Exposition from the perspective of 2010, expositions can offer a more complex story—in China's case, articulating "a vision of the future rather than guaranteeing the capacity of the state to achieve it."[9]

In a similar vein, a more complex story unfolds with regard to the 1903 Human Pavilion. Views of the pavilion did not line up neatly according to two dichotomized groups, with the Japanese supporting the display of primitive people and those whose people were on display protesting against it. Rather, some Ainu did not view their participation in the pavilion as a humanitarian problem, whereas some Japanese did. This chapter offers new perspectives on understanding the pavilion as a symbol of Japanese imperialism by introducing the diverse protests of the Japanese people. In addition, through the words and recollections of some of those who were dis-

6. Yoshimi, *Hakurankai no seijigaku*, 212–13.

7. Nanta, "Colonial Expositions," 248–58; Matsuda, *Teikoku no shisen.*

8. For Okinawan protests, see Christy, "Making of Imperial" and Ōta, *Okinawa no minshū.* For Chinese protests, see Claypool, "Sites of Visual"; Gen, *Nihon ryūgaku*; Hur, "Staging Modern"; Kitaoka, "Daigokai naikoku"; Sakamoto, "Chūgoku minzokushugi"; and Sugano, "Osaka hakurankai (1903)." For Korean protests, see Kwon, "Study on 'Korean Displays'" and "Analysis of Korean Intellectual Responses."

9. Fernsebner, "Expo 2010," 675.

played, rather than seeing a black-and-white image of oppression we get a more complicated picture of their experience. This chapter adds further layers to the story by situating the Human Pavilion within the larger history of expositions, in which the Japanese have been objects of curiosity at Western expositions, a fact not lost on some who protested the pavilion.

The Intersection of Nation and Empire Building: Hokkaido and Okinawa

Out of all the exoticized people on exhibit in the Human Pavilion, Fushine became the star because he was an Ainu who spoke fluent Japanese, the language of the metropolis. He possessed exceptional oratory skills, which he put to political use. On March 13, 1903, Fushine gave a public speech that began with a bold request:

> Ladies and Gentleman, I am an Ainu called Fushine Yasutarō.[10] The reason why I am here in Osaka this time is to appeal to you for a helping hand in fulfilling my hopes. Being Ainu, I can say that we feel that we are Japanese. At this very moment we Ainu can now appear for the conscription examination and loyally serve his Majesty the Emperor. It is sad that we cannot become decent soldiers because we Ainu do not have education. It has been my goal for many years to strive however I can to enhance Ainu education.[11]

Rather than denying his Ainu ethnicity to assert his position as a loyal Japanese subject, Fushine spoke as a representative of the Ainu people. In this, he was in line with other prewar Ainu whom David Howell has characterized as asserting "the possibility of a distinct Ainu ethnicity compatible with imperial subjecthood."[12] I build on Howell's argument by showing how Fushine's actions at the Human Pavilion exemplified this

---

10. Fushine's Ainu name was Chanraro, and his nickname was Hotene. He changed his name to Fushine Yasutarō in November 1898, and then to Fushine Kōzō in May 1916. Hokkaido Kyōiku Kenkyūjo (ed.), *Hokkaido kyōikushi*, 813. Fushine Kōzō is the name most often used to refer to him.

11. *OC*, March 13, 1903.

12. Howell, "Making 'Useful Citizens,'" 21.

compatibility: he spoke as a proud Ainu, and he stressed the importance of military service to the emperor, education, and, as I discuss later in the chapter, solving humanitarian problems (*jindō mondai*).[13] Fushine appealed to the Japanese based on their commonality as imperial subjects, all children of the emperor.

Fushine articulated a notion of imperial subjecthood in which he, an Ainu, could also be a loyal subject. In contrast, Okinawans protested against the inclusion of Okinawan subjects in the display, arguing that there were no ethnic distinctions between them and the Japanese. How had the Japanese state melded nation and empire so successfully that by 1903 the Okinawan people proclaimed themselves to be Japanese? As Alan Christy has asserted, while cultural-assimilation projects were carried out in all the colonies, "the fact that in Okinawa alone did the targets of the project widely come to identify themselves as 'Japanese' has no doubt contributed greatly to the propensity to ignore the possibility of ethnic contradiction in Okinawa."[14] In contrast, why did the Ainu, as exemplified by Fushine's thoughts and actions, view their inclusion in the empire so differently? Furthermore, how did Japanese reactions to the two groups differ when they confronted imperial subjects displayed next to individuals from foreign nations?

To answer these questions, I turn to the debates that arose over the controversial Human Pavilion. On the surface, the arguments seemed to be concerned about notions of civilization and barbarity: whether displaying people violated notions of what it meant to be human and whether Japan was aping the West by displaying its colonial "others." But on a more discrete level, issues of imperial subjecthood and colonial subjecthood were also being fleshed out and debated. Some Japanese argued that compatriots (*dōhō*) like the Okinawans and the Ainu should not be treated in the same manner as people from foreign nations. Others saw the inclusion of the Taiwanese in the empire as being the same as that of the Ainu and Okinawans, calling them "new Japanese" (*shin Nihonjin*) and not colonial subjects.

13. Howell mentions Fushine's participation in the pavilion but focuses on Nukishio Kizō and Iboshi Hokuto as illustrating a distinctly Ainu yet fully Japanese identity ("Making 'Useful Citizens,'" 15).

14. Christy, "Making of Imperial," 610.

AINU FUSHINE KŌZŌ

In character and appearance, Fushine Kōzō stood out among the Ainu in the exhibit. For one thing, he had chosen to appear in the Human Pavilion as a way to raise money for native schools (*dojin gakkō*) for Ainu children. One reporter remarked favorably on his resemblance to someone from the metropolis (*naichijin*) and provided evidence of Fushine's loyalty as an imperial subject, for he had "contributed money to the land army during the 1894–95 Sino-Japanese War and frequently gave money to charity."[15]

Although he appeared to be Japanese in his patriotic actions, Fushine's presence was nonetheless Ainu, as distinguished by the attention reporters paid to his speech given in Japanese and his non-Japanese facial features that looked more like those of Caucasians. (In reference to one of the other, older Ainu in the Human Pavilion, a reporter said he "bore a striking resemblance to Tolstoy."[16]) Fushine blurred the expectations the audience had about what place the Ainu should have in the empire. At the same time, the principle behind the Human Pavilion—the idea of humans displaying other humans—was called into question. As the exhibitors and their motivations came under scrutiny, debate broke out in the public arena over who should be in the pavilion, if anyone. This debate was embodied in the person of Fushine Kōzō, a man who was both Christian and modern, who usually dressed in Western clothing, such as a frock coat and trilby hat, and carried a gold pocket watch worth more than 100 yen, but donned traditional Ainu clothing for the display. In this way, Fushine represented the complexity of the lives of those caught between the boundaries of colonial subjecthood.

In his speech, Fushine asked his audience for donations to construct an Ainu school in Fushiko.[17] At the time Ainu children were segregated and could not attend school with Japanese children, in accordance with legislation that was not abolished until 1937. Although article 9 of the 1899 Protection Act stipulated that funds for establishing schools for the Ainu

15. *MY*, April 23, 1903.
16. *Miyako*, April 29, 1903.
17. *OM*, March 6, 1903; *OA*, April 8, 1903.

were to be provided by the national treasury, in reality money was neither immediately nor systematically provided.[18]

As Fushine explained, he had worked for many years to advance educational opportunities for Ainu children. He had met the Christian
missionaries John Batchelor and Charles Nettleship in the late nineteenth
century and was greatly impressed by their dedication to helping the Ainu
people. Fushine had been a wild youth growing up, with a penchant for
gambling and drinking. The message of the Protestant missionaries who
came to Hokkaido and were involved in the temperance movement appealed to him. He converted to Christianity. By adhering to the missionaries' encouragement of temperance, Fushine was able to heed his
mother's dying wish for him to stay away from sake. She had reminded
him about the evils of drinking and how Ainu who exchanged goods for
sake with Japanese traders often ended up dependent on the traders for
alcohol and lost their livelihood as a consequence. When Christian missionaries opened the Hakodate Training School in the late 1890s, Fushine
paid the fees to send two Ainu children to the school and provided for
their travel expenses and new clothes.[19] He also schooled children in his
own house, and hired a Buddhist monk, Yamagata Ryōon, to teach them
at a time when there were no schools yet built in his village.[20] In 1899 he
began to raise money for a school in Fushiko that was established in 1901.
Missionaries helped him find a teacher for the first class, which included
twenty-five Ainu children.[21]

Because of the difficulty of maintaining the school, Fushine asked
the local government officials for funding, which they denied. When they
told him about the Osaka exposition and suggested it as a venue where
he could raise money for the school's operation, Fushine embraced the
opportunity.[22] Before he began appearing in the Human Pavilion in April,
he toured the country to raise funds, visiting Hakodate, Sapporo, and

18. Siddle, *Race, Resistance*, 72. Fushine advocated for segregated schooling for the
Ainu, as the Ainu were teased by Japanese children, which made learning difficult
(*OM*, March 6, 1903). In areas with smaller Ainu populations, Ainu attended Japanese
schools but were taught separately. Ogawa, "Ainu gakkō" and "Hokkaido kyūdojin."
19. Yoshida, *Higashi Hokkaido*, 19–20.
20. Hisaki, "Yamagata Ryōon," 8.
21. Hokkaido Kyōiku Kenkyūjo (ed.), *Hokkaido kyōikushi*, 813.
22. *OM*, March 6, 1903.

Otaru in northern Japan and Tokyo, Kobe, Kyoto, Nagoya, and Mae-
bashi in central Japan.[23] His decision to go to Osaka to raise public awareness of the Ainu reflects his dedication to improving the lives of the
Ainu members of his community. Fushine was no stranger to the metropolis; he had first traveled to Tokyo in 1898, visiting the Ministry of
Internal Affairs, where he met with politicians Gamō Sen (1856–1908) and
Saigō Tsugumichi (1843–1902) about education and the development of
agriculture for the Ainu people.[24]

Few Ainu would have had the funds to travel to the metropolis, but
Fushine was one of the Ainu elite and one of the richest men in his village; over his lifetime he employed forty to fifty Japanese and Ainu
workers in his six fisheries.[25] Born in 1874, he was descended from the
family lineage of Sansōtona, son of the Ainu chief Shatsunai and his
wife, Perupune.[26] Fushine's father owned more than 100 horses, which
he raised on a large tract of land.[27] His father had interactions with
Japanese traders and often told Fushine and his siblings how important
it was to get an education.[28] Thus Fushine had grown up in an envi-
ronment conducive to learning Japanese. Still, it was his conversion to
Christianity and his interactions with missionaries, most notably John
Batchelor, that enabled him to actively support education for the
Ainu.[29]

Although Fushine was from a well-to-do background and was reported by some newspapers to be the chief of the Tokachi region—and
even designated by others in quite hyperbolic fashion to be the chief of
all the Ainu in Hokkaido—he was not a chief.[30] He was certainly a man

23. Hokkaido Kyōiku Kenkyūjo (ed.), *Hokkaido kyōikushi*, 813; Yoshida, *Higashi Hokkaido*, 21.

24. *OS*, February 26, 1898; Hokkaido Kyōiku Kenkyūjo (ed.), *Hokkaido kyōikushi*, 813; Murakami, *Ainu jinbutsuden*, 55.

25. Arai, *Ainu jinbutsuden*, 28; Fushine employed more than thirty Japanese work-ers on his farm (Hokkaido Shinbunsha Henshū [ed.], *Hokkaido daihyakka jiten*, 349).

26. Hokkaido Shinbunsha Henshū (ed.), *Hokkaido daihyakka jiten*, 349.

27. Umeki, *Ainu dendōsha*, 110.

28. Yoshida, *Higashi Hokkaido*, 18.

29. Fushine learned Japanese when he was seven years old. Yoshida (19–21). Nishi-hara, *Watashitachi no rekishi*, speculated that John Batchelor influenced Fushine to go to Osaka considering their close relationship (38–40).

30. *OM*, March 6, 1903; *OC*, April 5, 1903.

of influence in his region, and in his later years he became a leader of the larger Ainu community in general, yet he was humble about his status as someone who was uneducated. Fushine could speak Japanese fluently and was a fine orator, but he keenly felt his lack of schooling. He did not hide from his audiences the fact that he could not read and could write only a little.[31]

In a speech given on April 5 in the Human Pavilion, Fushine further delineated the disadvantages the Ainu faced because of their lack of education. First, he explained that the Ainu as a people had never had a written language; they tied knots in ropes to secure contracts with one another and looked to the changing seasons—when the snow melted in the mountains, or when the first green leaves appeared in spring—to know when a specific task needed to be carried out. But with the recent influx of Japanese coming to Hokkaido who relied on money to arrange contracts, Fushine said, the Ainu were prone to mistakes when doing business on Japanese terms. Second, Fushine touched again on the fact that although the Ainu were eligible for military conscription, many could not be hired for jobs because they could not read. He emphasized that although he himself was uneducated, he was the one teaching more than eighty Ainu children. His actions portrayed the dire situation of the Ainu, for he, an uneducated man, had taken on the task of educating the children. In his closing remarks, he described how his everyday life was affected by not having an education. He relayed how, when he first came to Osaka, he had mistaken an udon (noodle) shop for the police station. He tried to convey to the Japanese audience how simple things they might take for granted—such as reading signs—were an everyday struggle for him and other uneducated Ainu. He ended his appeal by affirming that the Ainu people, although a race distinct from the Japanese, were united with the Japanese under the bonds of subjecthood: "The Ainu people, 16,000 in number, are a pitiful race [*jinrui*]; ladies and gentlemen, if you embrace the concept that we are all subjects of the empire [*teikoku no shinmin*], raise your hand if you would like exert your efforts in helping Ainu education."[32]

31. Takakura, "Ryokushō ni kataru," 92.
32. *OC*, April 5, 1903.

Fushine demonstrated with his speech that he did not believe he had to deny being Ainu to bolster his stance as an imperial subject. In his closing lines, he urged the audience not to miss out on seeing the only authentic house displayed in the pavilion, which was a chance for them to see a representation of the Ainu way of life. The house had been purchased from its occupant, an Ainu named Itakupaku from Horobetsu village, Iburi province, and moved to Osaka, where it was displayed in the Human Pavilion along with a traditional storage house and an *inaw netopa*, a large piece of wood to which *inaw* (whittled pieces of willow, lilac, and other wood shavings, seen as offerings to gods) were tied.[33] While Fushine urged the audience to give money for Ainu education, he also believed in educating the Japanese about the Ainu's distinctly non-Japanese culture.

Besides giving speeches to raise money for schools, Fushine, with his wife, Fumi (Ainu name Arushito), and twelve-year-old nephew Keiichi (Ainu name Ukantokuaino), raised money by selling Ainu handicrafts at a booth sponsored by a wealthy Osaka resident.[34] Fushine informed his audiences about the Ainu's current situation by handing out pamphlets titled *An Account on the Protection of the Ainu*.[35] A reporter described him in the following way: "[Fushine,] as a believer in Christianity, is a man of exemplary conduct, and as he sells goods in this exposition, at the same time he solicits contributions from public-spirited persons. He has a subscription list open to support the expansion of education for the natives, and it shows many donors who have made contributions of fifty sen or one yen."[36] By the end of the exposition, Fushine had raised an estimated 80,000 to 100,000 yen for running the school.[37] The next year, the school Fushine had established was promoted to the status of a public school and renamed No. 2 Fushiko Elementary School.[38]

---

33. *Miyako*, April 29, 1903; *OC*, March 14, 1903. *Miyako* reports that Horobetsu was in Ishikari province; other reports place Horobetsu in Iburi province. *OC*, March 14, 1903.

34. *OM*, March 6, 1903.

35. *OC*, March 14, 1903; *MY*, April 23, 1903.

36. *OC*, March 14, 1903.

37. Estimate of 80,000 yen: *OA*, July 12, 1903; 100,000 yen: *OM*, July 12, 1903.

38. Hokkaido Kyōiku Kenkyūjo (ed.), *Hokkaido kyōikushi*, 813; Umeki, *Ainu dendōsha*, 113.

OKINAWANS NAKAMURA KAME AND
UEHARA USHI

While Fushine's efforts were directed toward educating visitors about
the reality of Ainu life in Hokkaido, for the two Okinawan women in the
Human Pavilion, Nakamura Kame and Uehara Ushi, representing the
reality of their life was not as important as meeting the expectations of
visitors and, to a certain extent, providing entertainment. Robert Bogdan has criticized the exhibitions of non-Western peoples generally, saying they were intended to show those on display as "exotic, but exotic is
an understatement for what [occurred]. Showmen elaborately embellished
the exotic and wrapped it with a profusion of creative tales and twists,
finally packaging it all within a pseudo-anthropological framework."[39]
This could be seen with the Okinawan women's display, with a surprising twist: the women were presented to Japanese visitors as aristocratic
members of the Shuri royal family, when in reality they were prostitutes
from the Tsuji red-light district in Okinawa.[40]

Two contrasting narratives emerged relating to how the Okinawan
women were treated in the Human Pavilion and their attitudes toward
their time there. Importantly, the dominant narrative of the tragedy behind
the display of these Okinawan women is the one Okinawan histories
refer to when describing the long history of Japanese discrimination against
Okinawans.[41] Intriguingly, some evidence points to an alternative story
that has not been considered in depth.[42] I argue that the second narrative is
not considered because it opens up the possibility that the women might
have been complicit in their display, suggesting that instead of being a
black-and-white case of Japanese oppression, there were some gray areas.
Although I do not have enough evidence to prioritize one version over the
other, it is important to consider how the narratives diverge and what their
implications are.

The story about Nakamura and Uehara published in the Okinawan
newspaper *Ryūkyū shinpō* claimed that they were tricked into going to

39. Bogdan, *Freak Show*, 178.
40. *RS*, April 7, 1903.
41. Christy, "Making of Imperial"; Uechi, "'Jinruikan' jiken"; Ōta, *Okinawa no minshū*.
42. Matsuda, *Teikoku no shisen*, 208, n. 10 mentions this article.

Osaka to work in the human display, having been told that they would work in a shop selling Okinawan goods. They were promised 1 yen a day and an advance payment of 200 yen, plus adequate food and shelter.[43] But once they arrived in Osaka, they were taken to the Human Pavilion. An Okinawan resident living in Osaka at the time, Mr. Gachō, sent a letter to the *Ryūkyū shinpō* claiming that he saw the Okinawan women in the Human Pavilion moving at the command of a man holding a whip, who pointed at them "no differently than how one would point at a monkey or animal." He wrote that the guide commanded the women, whom he referred to as "broads" (*koitsu*), to move their arms and legs. According to another report, the women were prohibited from leaving the pavilion. Mr. Gachō further asserted, "We cannot but be troubled to understand the reasons for *restrictively confining man*—who is the spiritual head of all beings—and turning him into a spectacle."[44]

In contrast to the characterization of the Okinawan women as captives, a second narrative suggested that at least one of the women was complicit in their display. In response to the reports printed in *Ryūkyū shinpō*, the *Osaka asahi* investigated the matter and concluded that there had been no ill treatment of the women:

> We reported in the margin of the previous issue the fact that an Okinawan newspaper has now also written about some Okinawans, and recorded that the Human Pavilion was maltreating them. But when we just now personally looked into the real facts and internal situation of the pavilion, we found that they were providing about two chickens a day to the so-called barbarians and giving an allowance above and beyond regular meals, and that therefore there was no reason to suppose that they were being hard-hearted only to the Ryūkyūans. But the head of the pavilion was greatly concerned about there being such criticism, and he talked to the two Ryūkyū women, Nakamura Kame (twenty years old) and Uehara Ushi (twenty-three years old), saying he would leave it up to them [to decide] on what they should do.[45]

43. *RS*, April 27, 1903.
44. *RS*, April 7, 27, April 7, 1903; emphasis added.
45. *OA*, May 8, 1903.

According to *Osaka asahi*, Nakamura Kame wanted to return to Okinawa, but Uehara Ushi wanted to remain in Osaka. Nakamura wanted to return to Okinawa because of homesickness, and Uehara wanted to stay in Osaka because of lovesickness:

> Since Nakamura Kame is a farmer's daughter and has parents and siblings, naturally she has missed her home and felt a desire to go back. But Uehara Ushi has a lover in a relationship dating from the time when she worked as a waitress in Okinawa, who is currently at the Okinawan booth. She stated her decision that she would act together with her lover and he is going to stay until the exposition closes.[46]

A week after the report in *Osaka asahi*, *Ryūkyū shinpō* reported the arrival of the ship *Satsuma* at the Okinawan port of Naha, with both women on board. It was reported that although they had been promised 400 yen, each received just 126 yen, leaving 148 yen unaccounted for.[47] Whether Uehara had had a disagreement with her boyfriend or changed her mind, or the organizers had forced her to leave to quell the protests, can only be speculated. The discovery in 2010 of a second photograph of the Human Pavilion confirms the presence of an Okinawan man who could have been Uehara's lover. On the back of the photograph it is recorded that there was an Okinawan man, although official reports do not count him in the tally of participants.[48] Therefore the second narrative is possible—that one of the women regarded the experience of being on display in Osaka as an opportunity, or at least a better alternative to the red-light district. Only one newspaper reported that there was a man with a whip in the pavilion, commanding the women to move, just as only one newspaper reported that one of the women wanted to remain in Osaka. Today only the story of the man with the whip has endured, and the story about Uehara wanting to stay is never considered.

To substantiate the reports in *Ryūkyū shinpō* regarding the man with a whip, I surveyed a variety of newspapers from the metropolis for any reports on the Okinawan women (fig. 1.3, top row right). The few reports

46.   *OA*, May 8, 1903.
47.   *RS*, May 19, 21, 1903.
48.   *Okinawa taimuzu*, September 5, 2010.

that did describe the women described scenes of boredom, and on certain occasions when reporters visited, the women's absence, suggesting they were sometimes in places other than their Okinawan house. An account published in the *Miyako* described their lack of interest in showing their wares: "Next came the Ryūkyū booth, where ceramic tobacco pipes, fans, and lacquerware were lined up on the floor, but the proprietress was in the middle of a noon nap, lying in a corner with her clothing pulled over her head."[49] Another account published in *Osaka asahi* described the shop, with its various products from Ryūkyū: "These Ryūkyūans are such shiftless types that they never bothered to show up in the shop, so it seems none of the goods are sold. I peeked in, wondering how they were doing, and saw the two together lying on their stomachs and shelling peanuts."[50] Their reported listless behavior stands in sharp contrast to Fushine's ardor, which was fueled by his efforts to raise money for the Ainu schools, his ability to communicate with the audience, and his position as a well-to-do Ainu with Japanese supporters. The Okinawan women, on the other hand, revealed the tedium of being on display with no purpose other than exhibiting their "Okinawaness." These reports, which depict the women as sleeping or absent, also contrast with the indelible image of a man with a whip ordering them to move. Of all the numerous articles written about the Human Pavilion at the time, the only paper that mentions him is *Ryūkyū shinpō*. This does not mean the man with the whip did not exist, but it does cast doubt on his dominant presence.[51]

While most accounts described only the general scene of the Okinawan section of the pavilion, one from the *Osaka chōhō* gave readers a more personal description of the women. The reporter apparently found them attractive, writing: "Their hair was done up in the usual coiled bun fastened by silver hairpins, but unlike the Korean girls, they had a simple and somewhat refined manner about them." He described Uehara as dark-skinned and Nakamura as fairer and very attractive. The reporter even claimed sensationally, "Miss Kame sometimes makes eyes at men she

49. *Miyako*, April 26, 1903.
50. *OA*, April 17, 1903.
51. In Chinen Seishin's 1976 play *Jinruikan* (Human Pavilion), written and performed in *uchinā yamato-guchi* (a mixture of Okinawan and Japanese), the man with the whip is one of the main characters. It fuses the pavilion with Okinawan experiences of the Asia-Pacific War.

thinks are handsome."[52] Both women could speak Japanese well enough to talk to reporters without a translator. Kame demonstrated to one reporter that she could write her name, and both were said to be elementary school graduates.[53]

Once Okinawans living in Osaka learned that Okinawan women were on display in the Human Pavilion, word quickly traveled back to Okinawa and a protest was mounted. Beginning in April, Ōta Chōfu, one of the founders of the *Ryūkyū shinpō*, which printed the majority of the protest articles, led the outcry. In the late nineteenth century, right after the Ryūkyū Kingdom was abolished and incorporated into the Japanese empire, Ōta had been part of a group of Okinawan students selected to go to the metropolis to study at the government's expense.[54] By the turn of the century, Ōta was a well-known advocate for Okinawan assimilation, believing that becoming Japanese meant modernizing and that once Okinawans were modernized they would receive equal treatment from the Japanese government. At this time, a number of discrepancies existed in how Okinawa was administered in comparison with other prefectures, something Ōta fought with his encouragement of assimilation.[55] In 1900 he gave a speech, subsequently referred to as "Kushameron" (On sneezing), in which he argued that Okinawans must assimilate to the point that they even sneezed the same as the Japanese.[56]

It is important to note that before Ōta urged Okinawans to assimilate, he had tried to encourage Okinawan rule by Okinawans. After the Ryūkyū Kingdom was abolished, the former king, Shō Tai, was forced to move to Tokyo. The first governor of Okinawa and all subsequent ones were appointed from Tokyo (similar to the governors of Japan's other prefectures), a practice that continued until 1945.[57] Ōta had been one of the founding members of the Kōdōkai, a group that advocated Okinawan leadership of Okinawa. The Kōdōkai hoped to install Shō Tai as the

52. *OC*, March 14, 1903.

53. *OA*, May 8, 1903.

54. Ōta studied in the metropolis in 1882. Smits, "Jahana Noboru," 102.

55. Mizuno, "Meiji Policies"; Okinawa was a prefecture but was "treated like a foreign colony," Smits, "Jahana Noboru," 101–2.

56. "Sneeze" in Japanese is *kushami*. In the Ryūkyūan language, it is pronounced *kushame*. Uechi, "'Jinruikan' jiken," 22.

57. Smits, "Jahana Noboru," 102.

governor of Okinawa and proposed that a hereditary governorship be maintained through the relatives of the former king. According to historian George Kerr, it was hoped that "if the king was granted the nominal title and honors of governorship, the most stubborn anti-Japanese elements in Okinawa would unite with the liberal advocates of modernization."[58] The Kōdōkai was short-lived, though, as the government in Tokyo soon abolished it, seeing it as a threat to the legitimacy of the newly appointed governor from the capital. Thus Ōta's support of assimilation can be seen as something he came to gradually, after he and others failed to preserve some aspects of the traditional Okinawan leadership structure after the islands' incorporation into the Japanese empire.

Before the controversy over the Human Pavilion erupted, Ōta had already expressed his concern over the presence of Okinawan dancers at the Osaka exposition. He believed the traditional dancing was counterproductive to Okinawan attempts to assimilate—that cultural performances, such as the Okinawan "hand dance" (*teodori*), planted the idea in the heads of the Japanese (*yamato*) that Okinawan culture was inherently different, overshadowing his people's commonalities with the rest of the nation. Such differences become exaggerated, he said, and then become grounds to justify discrimination against Okinawans.[59]

When reading about Ōta's conviction that anything that highlighted Okinawan difference inevitably led to discrimination, one can understand more fully his critique of the Human Pavilion. In an article protesting the pavilion, Ōta wrote that Okinawans had already become Japanese, and although there were certainly small regional differences between Okinawans and the Japanese, these kinds of regional variances could be found in all the prefectures, and none was so large as to mark the Okinawans as dramatically different from the Japanese.[60] The display of Okinawans not only identified them as being distinct from the Japanese by displaying them alongside people of other nationalities, it portrayed them in a primitive manner by having them live in a grass-covered hut alongside outdated implements, such as ancient Korean (Goguryeo) ce-

58. Kerr, *Okinawa*, 425.
59. *RS*, February 25, 1903.
60. *RS*, April 11, 1903.

ramic tobacco pipes. For Ōta, this primitive and inaccurate depiction of Okinawans implied that they were no more modern than the Ainu and the Taiwanese Aborigines (whom he viewed as uncivilized), next to whom they were displayed.[61] Furthermore, the pavilion's presentation of Okinawan culture, in which "two prostitutes from the Tsuji district of Naha" were displayed as royalty, insulted the legacy of the former kingdom and made a mockery of everything Ōta was trying to promote, namely, that Okinawans were modern and advanced.[62]

Ōta's unhappiness with the association of Okinawans with other primitive people was similar to the discontent expressed earlier by Chinese protesters. One Chinese writer had asserted that it was intolerable to be displayed side by side with races that were known to be inferior, such as "the Indians and Ryūkyūans who came from dying countries and were now under the control of the British and Japanese, and the Koreans, who relied upon the protection of Russia and Japan, and the Javanese, the Ainu, and the barbarians from Taiwan who are among the lowest races in the world, and are no different than deer and pigs."[63] The inclusion of the Chinese among such a motley crew of colonial subjects in the Human Pavilion, including a Turk from the Ottoman Empire (referred to as the "sick man of Europe" at the time), suggested the vulnerability of Chinese political sovereignty. Protests from Chinese students studying in Japan and from the Chinese embassy convinced the Japanese foreign ministry to pull the Chinese people from the exhibit before it officially opened. Despite this resolution, shortly afterward word reached a group of Chinese students in Tokyo that there was a Chinese woman displayed in the Human Pavilion, and they sent a delegation to investigate the conditions inside. There they found a Taiwanese girl dressed in traditional Chinese clothing with bound feet, serving tea to visitors. The students negotiated for her removal and transfer "to a decent tea house in Osaka, thereby putting the issue to rest."[64] According to Hur, one of the student protesters, Zhou Hongye, believed that since "Taiwan officially belonged to Japan as its colony . . . further problematization of

61. *RS*, April 7, 1903.
62. *RS*, April 10, 1903.
63. Sakamoto, "Chūgoku minzokushugi," 78.
64. Hur, "Staging Modern," 78.

this issue could lead to an international conflict."[65] The important point here is that the Chinese students' intervention did not extend to the Taiwanese Aborigines on display in the pavilion. They intervened in the case of the Taiwanese girl in Chinese clothing and only because her presence in the pavilion misrepresented China. The Taiwanese Aborigines were of no concern because they represented Japan's colony.

In contrast to the Chinese, the Koreans who protested, like the Okinawans, used their affinity to the Japanese, in having the "same race and same language" (*dōshu dōbun*), as the rationale for protesting. Korea was increasingly losing its independence under the growing influence of Japan at this time, and protesters turned to the notion of a pan-Asian identity for the reason Koreans should not be in the pavilion (fig. 1.3, bottom row, middle), writing in the *Osaka mainichi*:

> Ryūkyū, Hokkaido, and Taiwan are within Japan's territory. However, we are concerned about whether there was consent between the two governments regarding the display of the Chosŏn [Korean] women. According to what we have seen and heard, the women were enticed by a Japanese person to the exposition. Will you correspond with that person to resolve this problem? Is this not against the good neighbor policy? We believe people of good intentions and heart understand each other. They say the three Far Eastern countries share the same ethnicity and cultural fidelity (*dōshu dōbun*). . . . We are distressed as people of the same ethnicity and fidelity.[66]

While the Korean protesters attempted to transcend national boundaries by promoting a pan-Asian identity, *Osaka mainichi* illustrated the blurring of national identities when it reported an encounter in which a Western woman asked a Korean woman in the Human Pavilion if she was Korean. She replied: "No, I am not Korean, I have become Japanese."[67] In this case, being Japanese was not something that was imposed from the top down by a colonial power but was asserted willfully by a Korean woman who was not yet a Japanese subject. (That occurred seven

65. Hur, "Staging Modern," 78.
66. *OM*, March 19, 1903.
67. *OM*, March 15, 1903.

years later.) The Korean protests, like those of the Chinese, were successful and resulted in the Korean women's withdrawal from the pavilion.

Ōta reasoned that if the Chinese and Koreans, as people from foreign countries, were upset about their inclusion in the pavilion, the Okinawans, who were compatriots, should feel the insult twice over. Other letter writers joined in his anger and denounced the Japanese public as enemies for remaining silent and therefore complicit in the operation of the pavilion. One of the last articles on the topic in the *Ryūkyū shinpō* presented a particularly harsh depiction of the pavilion, likening it to a zoo in which young Okinawan "girls" (*shōjo*) (who were previously referred to as women or prostitutes) had been kept among black slaves (*dorei*) in huts.[68]

Ōta's optimistic belief in 1903—that if Okinawans were the same as Japanese there would be no basis for discrimination—eventually weakened as Okinawa continued to be treated as a second-rate prefecture.[69] In 1915 Ōta was obviously dismayed, writing that "to put it simply, although Okinawa prefecture is part of the empire's internal lands [*naichi*] the Okinawan residents are natives of a colony [*shokuminchi no dojin*]."[70]

An Okinawan activist and founder of the Kansai Okinawa Bunko (Culture Center), Kinjō Kaoru, told me that in Okinawa it is said that one of the women from the Human Pavilion built a large house with the money she had earned after she returned to Okinawa.[71] While I was in Okinawa I talked with several people who had heard this story (including a government official and the director of a documentary about the pavilion), but they could not identify anyone who could elaborate. If the story is true, and if one of the women had wanted to stay on in Osaka, what would this say about their treatment and the meaning behind their return to Okinawa? Is it possible that in the contestation over female bodies and who has the right to display or violate them, the women's subjectivity was erased and their mistreatment overemphasized to strengthen the claim of injustice and facilitate their removal—thus serving the

68. *RS*, April 7, 27, July 23, 1903.

69. Christy writes, "As if to confirm their worst fears, news of a plan to rescind the prefectural status of Okinawa and place it under the jurisdiction of the Taiwanese governor-generalship was leaked in 1908, causing panic among Okinawan intellectuals and elites" ("Making of Imperial," 621).

70. Ishida, *Okinawajin no genronjin*, 188.

71. Personal communication, November 2008.

interests of the Okinawan elites who worried that their presence tarnished Okinawa's image? The story of Nakamura and Uehara illustrates that the power politics involved were not dictated by Japanese-Okinawan relationships alone; the Okinawan male elite also played a key role in affecting the fate of the Okinawan women.

During my research, while looking through numerous bound volumes of *Ryūkyū shinpō* I stumbled on a short article published on October 27, 1912. It reported the suicide of a prostitute named Nakamura Kame (age twenty-eight), the daughter of a farmer. According to the article, she began to work as a prostitute in the Tsuji red-light district in 1903. She was described as a quiet girl who had lately turned despondent; she had killed herself by jumping into the sea. I believe this is the same Nakamura from the Human Pavilion (who was from a farming family) who had wanted to return to Okinawa because she missed her father and her siblings. The age matches, for in 1903 the Okinawan woman in the Human Pavilion was reported to be twenty, and in 1912, nine years later, the woman who jumped into the sea was reported to be twenty-eight. These lingering, unsubstantiated stories, one a rumor about a woman building a house on her return, and the other a newspaper clipping about a suicide, are whispers of the women's subjectivity that prevent us from completely transforming them into subaltern objects of discrimination.

Reaction to Taiwan, Japan's First Official Colony, and Colonial Subjects

It is remarkable that for a display so often labeled as an expression of Japanese imperialism, that attention paid to Japan's first display of subjects from an official colony (Taiwan) was overshadowed by the concern that Japanese subjects (Ainu and Okinawans) were on display next to individuals from foreign countries. If the breadth of the empire was on display in the Human Pavilion, it had less to do with what many historians call Japan's first colony, Taiwan, and more to do with how the people from Hokkaido and Okinawa were implicated in the entanglement of imperialism and nationalism. The few reports published on the Taiwanese Aborigines in the pavilion did not single them out as Japan's first colonial subjects. Absent from descriptions are the terms "colonial subjects" and "colony." Compared with the rhetoric at similar British and French expositions, it is surprising that although the Human Pavilion elicited a wide array of opinions on who should be displayed and whether the human display was an abomination, there was a noticeable absence of colonial rhetoric applauding the civilizing of Taiwanese colonial subjects or the necessity of the imperial project in Taiwan.

The few depictions of the Taiwanese Aborigines were far from favorable; most reports depicted them as unruly, prone to squabbling among themselves, frequently smoking opium, and needing to be bribed with alcohol to perform. One reporter, for example, said he learned from the staff working at the Human Pavilion that although a man in the exhibit named Ji Yinglai had submitted to the rule of the governor general early on and was largely obedient and docile at the exposition, his Atayal wife, Gyajin, was a different matter:

> But [Gyajin] had only recently come from the mountains and had not lost her savage temperament, so that she easily took offense and frequently caused problems. Fortunately, they said this woman enjoys sake; therefore if you want to have her play a tune on the barbarian flute, assign her two or three pints of Masamune and she will play you a tune on request.[72]

Many accounts of the Taiwanese Aborigines dramatized their perceived savagery; for example, a *Miyako* reporter remarked, "At first sight you'd be scared to look at them, the man with a head of tangled hair looking like a demon, and the woman with red hair parted and bound at the nape of her neck, and a tattoo in the shape of a rod drawn vertically between her eyes, in a dark indigo."[73] Conversely, others remarked that they were not as savage as expected. A reporter for the *Osaka chōhō* commented Ji Yinglai "is not at all a savage [*seiban*], he seems to have been picked from the so-called semi-civilized savages [*jukuban*]." His final assessment flew in the face of conventional imperialist attitudes when he concluded, "In any case all men are brothers, including barbarians."[74] One report

72. *OC*, March 13, 1903.
73. *Miyako*, April 29, 1903.
74. *OC*, March 14, 1903.

did fall into the common trope of suggesting the civilizing effects of being in the metropolis: "It is said [that Gyajin] was black when they first came here but now she has turned quite white in color," and "her dress was no longer of the native type either."[75]

Some observers noticed that the Taiwanese Aborigines' savage nature was partly contrived. Their house was described as a "pitiful lonely dwelling" that had thick bamboo posts, a thatched roof, and walls constructed from strips of *shuro* palm bark. On a shelf were three human skulls (only one of which was real), which caused the "fainthearted girls [to] hurry past with their faces muffled in their sleeves" (fig. 1.3, bottom row, right). Many of the reporters from different newspapers stressed that two of the skulls were fake, demonstrating an attempt to distinguish performance from reality, although those lines were often blurred.[76]

In addition to reports that depicted the Taiwanese Aborigines as savage or questioned the contrived nature of their barbarity, there were articles that lampooned the Japanese and their fear of the native Taiwanese. A satirical work (*gesaku*) written about the Human Pavilion in a exaggerated tone poked fun at the commotion over the purported savagery of the Aborigines. The *gesaku* writer described an imagined scenario in which the Indians provoked a riot in the Human Pavilion by playing their drums and chanting, causing the others in the Human Pavilion to join in and chaos to ensue. He described how the Aborigines were provoked by the commotion, which also led Gyajin to start a fight with her husband:

> Well, when matters reached that stage, how could the usual unmanageable savages stay silent at the sidelines, especially the wild goblin woman with the tattoo in the middle of her forehead?
>
> "All right, say it again!" she roared. "Go on, spit it out! You may not know it from the way I look now, but you're looking at a woman who had her first baby bath in hell in the pool of blood while glaring at the mountain of skulls over on one side. You're the husband! Act like a husband and bring me twenty or thirty heads strung up on spears of bamboo grass." As she berated him, she rampaged, stabbing the air with a pair of iron tongs. Such

75. *Miyako*, April 29, 1903.
76. *MY*, April 26, 1903; *Miyako*, April 29, 1903.

a thing would never happen. It would never happen, but suppose for a min-
ute it did happen, that would be a terrible thing to occur.

From the tone, it is clear that the writer of the piece was making fun
of Japanese characterizations of the Aborigines as fierce savages, with
Gyajin demanding thirty heads. No one was safe from the satirical wit
of the *gesaku* writer, not even Fushine, who was caricatured at the end of
the piece as the one to end the riot by assembling everyone in the pavilion and converting them to Christianity. The writer continued, "Not
only that, but this meeting motivated the formation of a wonderful
league of peace for all the races of mankind lasting generations under
the leadership of the Ainu."[77] The Human Pavilion was thus satirized
from all sides, from the purported savagery of the Taiwanese Aborigines
to the praise of Fushine as the hero of the display.

In the small number of published responses to the display of the Taiwanese Aborigines, I could not find one that spoke favorably of Japan's
civilizing mission. If the Taiwanese Aborigines were mentioned at all, it
was in the context of an opinion that they should not be displayed.

Debating Human Rights and
Who Belongs to the Nation

Although there were countless illustrations in the newspapers of the various ethnoracial groups in the Human Pavilion (fig. 1.3), the coverage on
the lives of the people on display, as well as the pieces that satirized Japanese depictions of who was savage and who was civilized, showed that
the people on exhibit mattered to the Japanese audiences, beyond their
role as ethnotypes. The Human Pavilion led more often than not to people
questioning its purpose and the intended representations of the people on
display.

The various Japanese voices in the debate on the legitimacy of the
Human Pavilion reveal that Japanese perspectives were just as multifari-

77. *OM*, April 10, 1903.

FIG. 1.3. Montage of the people of the Human Pavilion. Credit: L to R, top to bottom: row 1: *HT*, April 15, 1903; *OC*, March 17, 1903; *OM*, March 14, 1903; row 2: *Miyako*, May 26, 1903; *Miyako*, May 21, 1903; row 3: *OA*, March 9, 1903; row 4: *OM*, April 22, 1903; *Miyako*, May 19, 1903; *MY*, April 26, 1903.

ous as those of the colonial subjects. The controversy over the Human Pavilion sparked an interesting debate among several Japanese newspaper writers about whether Japan could be called a civilized country when the countrymen of Japan condoned turning its subjects into a sideshow. Some Japanese writers sympathized with the Okinawans in particular, seeing them as compatriots (*dōhō*) and therefore as deserving better treatment.[78] Shortly after the Korean protests erupted, a writer from *Osaka chōhō* reported that Osaka's Mayor Tsuruhara went to see the Human Pavilion for himself. Tsuruhara declared that at the pavilion "humans were being treated like animals" and that the "Japanese were insulting their compatriots."[79]

In a consecutive two-day front-page special in the *Miyako* in May, a column titled "Human Spectacles" proclaimed its support for the Okinawans and Ainu:

> This cruel exhibit is criticized by people of countries other than the Japanese. And what is worse, Japanese subjects go calmly along and never give it a second thought. I have heard that as countrymen of an advanced nation of East Asia, the Japanese are a civilized race [*bunmei jinshu*], second to none of the peoples of Western Europe. Even when the two races of the Ryūkyūans and Ainu, who are our compatriots, are treated with contempt, can we still go calmly along and put up with insults heaped on our countrymen?
>
> I do not know if the Japanese people at last have become a civilized race or not. However, as Japanese people, if we say we are a civilized race, as a so-called civilized race we are offering as materials for spectacles the uncivilized races. More so than the uncivilized races, in the end we have become the inferior ones.[80]

In this excerpt, it is notable that the Japanese writer used the insulting behavior toward compatriots—Okinawans and Ainu—as the basis for questioning the civilized nature of Japan. The writer accepted that there were different degrees of civilization among races. He was not critical of the treatment of the Okinawans and the Ainu because he considered

78.   *OA*, April 27, 1903.
79.   *OC*, April 1, 1903.
80.   *Miyako*, May 20, 1903.

them as civilized as the Japanese; rather, he believed that countrymen, regardless of how civilized they were, should be treated with decency. He did not believe that the level of civilization of a certain race depended on immutable characteristics inherent to specific races, as strands of social Darwinism suggested. Instead, it was such uncouth actions as putting humans on display that affected a nation's standard of civilization. The writer's critique of the pavilion was more of a rallying cry in the spirit of national pride.

Moving beyond whether Japan's national prestige was tarnished by the display, another report questioned the boundaries between empire and nation. Lines between imperial and colonial subjects were blurred in the Human Pavilion, and as one reporter remarked, "It has revealed one kind of humanitarian problem directed toward the Ainu, Ryūkyū, and Taiwanese."[81] This type of critique, in which treatment of the Taiwanese was considered alongside that of the Ainu and Okinawans, is noteworthy for illustrating that divisions between colonial subjects (those from Taiwan) and imperial subjects had not yet crystallized. In fact, none of the reports referred to the Taiwanese as colonial subjects, and in one report they were even called "new Japanese" (*shin Nihonjin*).[82]

Incorporating Taiwan into the empire was often talked about in the same language used for the inclusion of Hokkaido and Okinawa. In lieu of calling it a colony (*shokuminchi*), Taiwan was described as having become a part of Japanese territory (*hanto ni hairimashita*), a phrase also used to describe Hokkaido's and Okinawa's inclusion.[83]

The sympathy directed toward Human Pavilion participants varied. A reporter from *Osaka chōhō* expressed sympathy only for the Okinawan women, saying, "I don't think one can feel very good about having compatriots from the same homeland put up for exhibit as human specimens."[84] With regard to the Ainu, some were confused by the contradiction be-

81. *OM*, March 21, 1903.

82. *OC*, March 14, 1903.

83. Tsuboi, "Meiji irai teikoku." The term *hanto* (版図) was commonly used in the Meiji period to refer to a country's territory. Fraleigh, "Transplanting the Flower," 179, discusses the use of *hanto* instead of *shokuminchi* (colony) during Japan's early colonial period with regard to Nitobe Inazō's writing.

84. *OC*, March 14, 1903.

tween how the Ainu acted (with grace, and therefore like the Japanese) and the differences that marked them as Ainu—their clothing, tattoos, and speech. Some compared the Ainu to the Taiwanese Aborigines because both had tattoos and customs that the Japanese viewed as distasteful. One reporter likened his impression of the Ainu section to the one he had when he visited the Taiwanese Aborigines: "Next to the storage bin stood a fence made of staves out of which the *inaw netopa*, or votive poles, projected with three bear skulls displayed on the tips. The bear ritual of the Ainu leaves us with a strange feeling little different from that of the head-hunting ritual of the Taiwan savages."[85]

Other reporters commented that Fushine and his wife seemed more like the people of the metropolis (*naichijin*) than natives (*dojin*).[86] Another reporter praised Fushine's wife, stating that "the way [she] makes the beads fly on the abacus, you can tell that some of the inhabitants of the big cities of Japan are several degrees inferior to her in mastery."[87] Her tattoo was a source of debate, one reporter remarked: "Although she is called a beauty among the Ainu, I must say that the tattoo on her lips makes her an odd kind of beauty indeed."[88] Another commented, "It was amusing the way the young woman who was his wife, also with a dark tattoo on her upper lip, conveyed an image of metropolitan grace as she offered pictures of the exposition for sale."[89] Fumi's tattoo contradicted the refined manner in which she moved, which the reporter viewed as a distinctly metropolitan. Their nephew Keiichi was described as having "set his heart on enlisting in the army and serving as a soldier, although he was a native."[90] Rather than confirming their primitive nature, the Ainu people in the pavilion made spectators realize their similarity to them.

Furthermore, in the *Nihon*, a writer identified as Professor Takebe articulated a notion of imperial subjecthood premised on seeing all Japanese subjects as children of the emperor—the basis from which Fushine had made his appeal. Takebe proclaimed:

85. *Miyako*, April 29, 1903.
86. *OA*, May 8, 1903.
87. *OC*, March 14, 1903.
88. *OC*, March 13, 1903.
89. *Miyako*, April 29, 1903.
90. *OC*, March 13, 1903.

I cannot but feel overawed to think that such barbarities are being staged right next to the exposition which is favored daily by visits from His Majesty and members of the imperial family and are being practiced on people who are equally His Majesty's children or else belong to allied and friendly nations.

He further attacked the Human Pavilion from a universal humanist standpoint, saying that displaying people in any type of human spectacle was tasteless:

According to the map of the distribution of human races made by Professor Tsuboi and displayed in the pavilion, Western people also should be displayed along with the Ainu and raw savages, the Indians and the Turks. If we ask why this has not happened, is it due to the fact that Western people are civilized people? Is it that if they are Westerners we respect them, and if they are Indians or Turks, it doesn't matter if we display them? Regarding the matter of all human spectacles, whether it is the people who are displayed or the people who display them or the people who see them, they all together vulgarize the human character.[91]

Takebe protested against the Human Pavilion by arguing that the Japanese were engaging in a practice that had been inflicted on them at previous expositions overseas. He referred to a previous British exposition that had a "Japanese village in which our countrymen were put on show," and to the 1900 Paris Exposition and its "Around the World" panorama, which had featured fifteen Japanese geisha.[92] He wrote that although the Japanese envoys stationed in France had brought this display to the attention of France's Ministry of Agriculture and Commerce, the ministry, "whose concern with financial profit was unparalleled, was completely insensitive to the issue of human character [*jinkaku mondai*] and humanitarian concerns [*jindō mondai*], and proceeded to inflict on the honor of our nation a great disgrace by such behavior." He criticized the

91. *Nihon*, May 4, 1903.

92. A Japanese village in London in 1885 outraged Japanese residents of the city because people of a low socioeconomic class represented Japan (Scholtz, "'Almond-Eyed Artisans'"). Their letter campaign to prevent the opening of the village failed. On the Paris Exposition, see Berg, "Sada Yacco," 369–71.

Human Pavilion in Osaka as aping Western practices: "Sure enough, the people appearing in earlier exhibits that ignored human character are now the exhibitors who blithely view these entertainments."[93]

When the *Osaka chōhō* reported on the Korean protests, it also referred to the Paris Exposition, where it said two or three Japanese people were displayed.[94] Both references to the Paris Exposition were intended to remind readers that not too long ago, the Japanese had been protesting against the same thing the Koreans, Chinese, and Okinawans were protesting now, with the same rationale. In *Osaka mainichi*'s letters to the editor, participants in the "loud debate" (*yamashi giron*) over the Human Pavilion and the Chinese and Korean women brought up a London exposition held in 1902 in Earl's Court in which women from Europe, Japan, China, India, Egypt, Persia, and other countries were gathered in a panorama.

> In front of each room there was a sign on which was written "talking with the women is allowed" which the writer likened to being similar to a zoo with signs that read "do not give food to the animals without reason." In 1902 it had been argued that "although the displays show manners and customs, because the Japanese were placed together with barbarians it was distasteful."[95]

The letter writer highlighted the irony of an argument that had been employed by the Japanese in 1902 falling on deaf Japanese ears one year later.

Although some saw displaying humans as distasteful, and even hypocritical, others thought the issue was more complex when taking into account the position of the displayed people. A famous writer of the time, Kamitsukasa Shōken (1874–1947), remarked:

> There was a sideshow at the Osaka exposition called the Human Pavilion where living human beings from the Ryūkyū Islands, Taiwan, and the Malay Peninsula were collected and displayed. It aroused much controversy as a humanitarian issue, but on the other hand, some people like to will-

93. *Nihon*, May 4, 1903.
94. *OC*, April 1, 1903.
95. *OM*, March 23, 1903.

ingly let themselves be displayed before a crowd as *tableaux vivants* or cinematic advertisements. Humanitarian issues are maddeningly elastic.[96]

Kamitsukasa compared the pavilion with another entertainment popular in Meiji Japan, *tableaux vivants*, or living pictures (*katsujinga*). In these performances, actors posed before an elaborate backdrop—of the countryside, for example, or a Renaissance scene. Kamitsukasa thought that since the people in the pavilion let themselves be displayed, its characterization as a humanitarian problem was not straightforward.

More important, Fushine Kōzō, himself on display in the pavilion, did not view it as a humanitarian problem. He believed that the Human Pavilion was a respectable venue for himself and other Ainu. Nevertheless, it was reported that one afternoon when Fushine was walking across the exposition grounds, he encountered a group of Ainu selling seal meat and singing Ainu songs to attract the attention of customers. A crowd had gathered around them, and Fushine, perhaps assuming the crowd was there more to gawk at the Ainu than to buy their wares, was angered. He urged the Ainu to work inside the Human Pavilion with him.[97] Bearing in mind Ōta's unhappiness with the Okinawan prostitutes representing Okinawa, it seems that Fushine could have been worried that what he viewed as embarrassing behavior would reflect poorly on the Ainu image he wanted to promote.

In the 1930s, Fushine spoke about his time in the Human Pavilion with Japanese educator Yoshida Iwao, who had dedicated his life to teaching the Ainu. Fushine recalled that his primary purpose had been to educate the Japanese audience about the Ainu, and he recalled some of his own impressions. He said, "In the Human Pavilion, I personally undertook the task of explaining such customs as the Ainu bear festival that could serve as scholarly reference under the leadership of the late Dr. Tsuboi. I even saw how *seiban* [savages] and Indians turned blood red while fighting. It was also the time of stupidity when I had the money in my sleeve stolen by a pickpocket."[98]

96. *Yomiuri*, August 4, 1903.
97. *HT*, April 15, 1903; *OS*, April 14, 1903.
98. Yoshida, *Higashi Hokkaido*, 21.

Fushine remembered his time in Osaka not for the controversy over the pavilion but for a different humanitarian problem that arose at the same time. It involved a group of Ainu who were performing in the Dōtonbori entertainment district of Osaka, near the exposition grounds. Fushine described their situation as a violation of their human rights:

> Just at this time, eight Pichari Ainu from the Hidaka area were made to perform *shinotocha* [tones gliding into song], *upopo* [songs], and *yaishama* [popular love songs] under the manipulation of some Japanese, in a small playhouse in the Osaka Dōtonbori district. Learning of this, I could not hold back my indignation at a situation where persons who, as subjects of Japan, are equally children of the emperor, and yet see their human rights [*jinken*] ignored. With the backing of the *Osaka mainichi* and *Osaka asahi* newspapers and the help of Kanda Kahei I was prepared to bring the matter up in court, but due to the philanthropy from people in religion and education, we were able to return the eight to their homes safely and thereby proclaimed the solution of a humanitarian problem.[99]

For Fushine, Ainu performing or exhibiting themselves was not the issue (he was doing this himself), but the conditions under which such a performance was carried out were crucial. Although his account did not detail what it was about the Dōtonbori Ainu group that constituted a humanitarian problem, other sources shed light on their circumstances. The Ainu group from Shiraoi, led by chief Nomura Shpanram, talked with a theater critic about their working conditions. They said that having to constantly dance in circles and sing on stage was intolerable and hot and more labor than the work they did at home in their villages.[100] According to the critic, the show was not successful because it was conducted in the Ainu language, and no one in the audience could understand what was going on. Although all the Ainu performers could speak Japanese, the manager did not want them to perform in Japanese. The extent of their ill treatment was confirmed in an account written by Wacław Sieroszewski, a companion to the Polish cultural anthropologist

99.   Yoshida, *Higashi Hokkaido*, 21.
100.   Heishi, "Ainu shibai," 52–54.

Bronisław Piłsudski, who studied the Ainu and had encountered the group from Shiraoi in Hakodate in 1903. Nomura told Piłsudski that a Japanese visitor had tempted him with a promise "of a huge income" if he, his wife, and his neighbors went to Osaka and imitated an Ainu village and demonstrated the bear festival. "They kept 'demonstrating' it for three months; the Japanese entrepreneur cheated them, did not pay a single sen, got bankrupt and escaped." Even after hearing about their plight, for Piłsudski everything was still a transaction with the Ainu, as he gave them food and money in exchange for Nomura's pledge of assistance with his research.[101]

The fact that their plight reached Fushine's ears while he was in the Human Pavilion and he worked to set them free illustrates the complexity of determining what constituted a humanitarian problem. While an Okinawan writer wrote that he could not understand how in an enlightened age the organizers were not ashamed of infringing on human rights [jinken no jūrin], Fushine did not see the pavilion in the same way.[102]

Although Fushine had many Japanese friends, he was not blind to the injustice inflicted on the Ainu, and he condemned those Japanese policies and people who treated the Ainu unfairly.[103] For example, a reporter from Osaka asahi relayed how, in one of Fushine's speeches in the pavilion, he had criticized the Japanese who cheated the Ainu. Fushine pointed to the storehouse in the Ainu exhibit and explained:

> This is the Ainu people's storehouse. If you put something in it, it will be safe no matter how many years you kept it there. However, recently bad men came [to Hokkaido] from the metropolis, and have been teaching bad things, and so robberies have begun to happen. The people from the metropolis are really not honest people. They do not try to protect the poor Ainu but cheat them instead.

---

101. Sieroszewski, "Among Hairy People," 667–68. In Sieroszewski's account, there is no mention of Fushine's help. Nomura said that to leave Osaka "they sold whatever they possessed; their clothes, kettles, pots, silver jewelry. . . . The money was sufficient just for a ticket to Hakodate." For pictures of Nomura and Piłsudski see Majewicz (ed.), The Collected Works, 647–48.

102. RS, April 7, 1903.

103. Fushine, "Ainu seikatsu," 52–72.

The reporter remarked, "Fushine is most eloquent in expressing his indignation and seems quite capable of speaking with logical clarity."[104] Although he was trying to raise money for Ainu education, his view of his place in the empire was colored by good and bad experiences, and he felt no need to hold his tongue in critiquing the Japanese who exploited the Ainu.

The debates about the Human Pavilion opened up a space for members of the empire to articulate what it meant to be an imperial subject. Although Fushine did not enter these debates the same way as those who sent letters of protest, the story of why he had come to Osaka and the speeches he gave were printed in the same newspapers. His words added to the cacophony of voices debating imperial subjecthood. Fushine, as well as the Okinawans and ordinary Japanese people, understood the boundaries of imperial subjecthood differently. Ōta's shame about the Okinawans' primitive grass hut and Fushine's pride in the Ainu house offer a telling point of comparison for how colonial subjects articulated their place as imperial subjects differently in a nascent empire. Some Japanese disagreed with Tsuboi's racial division of imperial subjects (although they supported civilizational differences) and saw themselves as allies of their compatriots, belying a characterization of the Human Pavilion as an indefatigable symbol of Japanese imperialism. Rather than perpetuating the myth of an established and coherent imperial taxonomy—created and supported by the Japanese—the Human Pavilion in Osaka highlights the complicated nature of imperialism and the numerous people involved in the formation of imperial mentalities.

The 1907 Tokyo Industrial Exposition and the Failure of the Human Display

Unlike Britain, France, and the United States, where expositions featuring colonial subjects were a consistent feature of modern imperial life, in Japan, the controversies that ensued over the 1903 Human Pavilion in Osaka led to big changes by 1907, at the Industrial Exposition held in Tokyo. Although a building called the Human Pavilion was established at the

104. *OA*, April 17, 1903.

exposition, it functioned differently than its predecessor. Unlike the first pavilion, this exhibit, again under the direction of Tsuboi Shōgorō, had no living humans on display—only anthropological and ethnological goods.[105] The sole living human displays at the 1907 exposition were two Ainu men in the Ainu Building and two Koreans, a man and a woman, in a venue called the Crystal Palace. These displays could be called failures in the sense that they were not popular with visitors, and in the case of the Ainu, the two participants became fed up with being swindled by their Japanese manager and returned home before the end of the exposition. Protests from Koreans living in Japan criticized the practice of displaying Koreans at expositions, this time in the Crystal Palace.

When the Ainu Building opened, it received scant attention in the press. A reporter wrote that although "its name suggests that it would be grand, in reality it is nothing more than a small shop" where Ainu handicrafts were for sale. A tea shop was established next to it, and when the reporter visited, it was recommended that he try an Ainu sweet for five sen. When he entered the shop, he wrote, he could not find any Ainu. He also reported that he found no customers there.[106]

The two Ainu men who worked in the Ainu Building had come from Harutori, in Kushiro, Hokkaido. Twenty-one-year-old Yūki Shōtarō had entered into a contract with a Japanese entrepreneur from Tokyo, Tamura Kō, in the spring 1906. Ainu elder Gen Tarō accompanied Yūki. In 1903, the year of the first Human Pavilion, Gen had been a member of a twelve-person Ainu group called the Ezo Theatrical Company (Ezo engekidan), led by two Japanese promoters. The promoters had paid the five Ainu members from Akkeshi and seven from Harutori twenty yen each in advance. They were supposed to tour all over Japan, but while the group was performing in Niigata, some of its members fell sick and one died. The group did not have enough money for the journey home by ship, but the people of Niigata took pity on them and gave them the money for their passage.[107]

Four years later, when an opportunity to make money in the metropolis presented itself, Gen, undeterred by the failed venture of 1903, agreed to

---

105. *Engei no tomo*, 21.
106. *Yomiuri*, April 1, 1907.
107. Nakamura, *Nagakubo Shūjirō*, 208–9.

participate, along with Yūki. Researchers have linked their participation in the Tokyo exposition to the influence of another Ainu, Pete Gorō, and his success after returning from the 1904 Louisiana Purchase Exposition in the United States (see chapter 2). Gorō had earned more than 800 yen, some of which he used to build a new house for his parents. His success would certainly have influenced Yūki, who had attended the same Ainu school in Yachigashira as Gorō and was just eight years younger.[108]

The men had been promised 1,000 yen to be paid out over two periods, but shortly after they arrived in Tokyo they ran into problems. Gen wrote to Nagakubo Shūjirō, a Japanese missionary who lived in Harutori, asking his wife to send them clothing and implements for performing the Ainu bear festival. This would seem to indicate that once they had started appearing at the exposition, they found their simple presence in the Ainu Building was not been enough to attract the business Tamura had anticipated. The request Gen sent via Nagakubo to his wife suggests an attempt to make their show more entertaining.

It is important to note that throughout the exposition there was no media coverage of the Ainu Building. A report in early March said there would be several stores at the exposition where three or four Hokkaido Ainu would sell handicrafts and demonstrate weaving and the making of other goods, but it is not clear if Gen and Yūki were a part of those activities, or if theirs was a different enterprise.[109] The lack of media coverage is evidence that the Ainu Building did not attract many visitors, supporting the theory that either the manager or the Ainu were trying to think of ways to make themselves more marketable. Gen's wife refused to send the sacred clothing and tools to the metropolis. Instead, she told Nagakubo to relay to her husband that because of seasonal work she was busy, and that she was concerned about her health and wanted Gen to return home as soon as possible. In the beginning of May 1907, Yūki and Gen sent telegrams to Nagakubo referencing a falling out with Tamura and requesting thirty yen to return home. Nagakubo wired them the money and they returned home by the second week of May, before the exposition ended. Although it is not clear exactly what caused the Ainu

---

108. This information about Yūki comes from his son, Yūki Shōji, a famous activist for Ainu rights. Yūki Shōji Kenkyūkai (ed.), *Yūki Shōtarō kenkyū*, 691.

109. "Tokyo kangyō hakurankai ekai," 20.

men to break with their manager, it is evident that they suffered an economic loss and did not receive the money they had been promised. After their return, both Yūki and Gen, as prominent members of their community, helped the Ainu community with land reform and worked with younger Ainu.[110]

Although their venture was ultimately a failure, the story of how they came to go to Tokyo illustrated two facts. First, there was a precedent for Ainu performing in the metropolis, and the fact that some found it to be financially advantageous encouraged others to follow suit. Second, the Ainu who ventured to the metropolis were usually well connected to the Japanese living in Hokkaidō and other well-to-do Ainu. Just as such connections had facilitated their contract with their manager, Tamura, they also helped in achieving their safe return home.

The protests over the presence of the two Koreans in the exposition's Crystal Palace were mostly carried out by Korean students studying in Japan. The Crystal Palace was a space that housed different attractions, including a cave of horrors. The Koreans, a twenty-four-year-old man named Park Yang hang (in Japanese, Boku Ryōkō) and a twenty-year-old woman named Jeong Myeong seon (in Japanese, Tei Meikō), were employed at the Crystal Palace as barkers; they wore signs over their traditional Korean clothing and worked to entice customers into the building.[111] When Kin Chinsho, a Korean who lived in the Hongō area of Tokyo, and six other Koreans learned of their presence, they loudly denounced the Crystal Palace for turning Koreans into spectacles. They also claimed that displaying Korean people in this manner was an insult to Korea. The building operator scorned this accusation, saying there was no harm done because they were being paid a salary and had agreed to work there. Kin voiced his anger with numerous government authorities, including the Ministry of Internal Affairs, and on June 15 he met with the manager of the Crystal Palace to demand that the Koreans be released.[112] Prior to that, a first-year student at Tokyo Industrial High School, Kin Shōshaku, had met with the manager of the Crystal Palace on May 25 and demanded

110.   Nakamura, *Nagakubo Shūjirō*, 211–13.
111.   According to *Fuzoku gahō*, she is called Tei Meikō, but *TA* calls her Tei Meisen. *Fuzoku gahō* 369 (1907): 28.
112.   *TA*, June 16, 1907.

their release.[113] Despite these protests, one report claimed that the Korean woman did not actually want to return to Korea.[114] As Kwon demonstrates, Japanese newspaper coverage emphasized that the Koreans came of their own free will, whereas reports in the Korean papers emphasized how they were misled about their role at the exposition and, upon discovering the true nature of their jobs, were disgraced.[115] In a scenario reminiscent of the removal of the Okinawan women from the 1903 exposition, it is possible that as much as their presence upset their fellow compatriots, the participants themselves wanted to be there. In both situations, understanding how the displayed Okinawans or Koreans felt about their involvement is less apparent than how Okinawan and Korean elites rallied around the displays as violating their inclusion in the empire (in the case of the Okinawans) or their national honor (for the Koreans). Eventually, owing to the protests, the Koreans were removed from the Crystal Pavilion.

During the uproar over the Koreans in the Crystal Palace, the Okinawan *Ryūkyū shinpō* published a report on the exposition in Tokyo that was cause for concern, warning of what it called "a second Human Pavilion." According to an April report, women from Okinawa had been recruited to dance in Ueno Park during the day and, after nightfall, to work as prostitutes. The girls were promised thirty yen a month, and the reporter said they had been sweet-talked into going to Tokyo—where, they were told, they would sightsee, eat delicious foods, and wear beautiful clothing. Instead, the writer of the report contended, "They are devoured by the money owners, and [Ueno Park] has become a second Human Pavilion, [with] terrible eyes looking at people that have been turned into laughingstocks."[116]

The title of the article, "Tokyo Exposition, Again the Display of Prostitutes," and the reference to a second Human Pavilion make it clear that the 1903 controversy had not been forgotten. But the furor over the 1907 Tokyo exposition was not driven by the exposition's Human Pavilion, which, despite the name, did not have any people in it. The controversy concerned the hiring of Okinawan dancers, which had also been

113. *Miyako*, May 26, 1907.
114. *Yomiuri*, June 17, 1907.
115. Kwon, "Analysis of Korean Intellectual Responses," 25.
116. *RS*, April 20, 1907.

a source of contention in 1903. The situation in 1907 was different from 1903, when Ōta expressed his concern that the Okinawan hand dance, or *teodori*, emphasized Okinawan culture as distinct from Japanese culture. In 1907 the focus was on the dancers themselves, who were also prostitutes. According to the reporter, the fault lay with the women who chose to ruin their lives for a salary of thirty yen a month, thus bringing shame on themselves. The report referenced the 1903 Human Pavilion controversy and claimed it was clear that the 1903 attempt to bring beautiful Okinawan women to Osaka from Tsuji had failed. Four years later, according to the writer, they succeeded in bringing only ugly Okinawan women who were not worthy of being sold in the red-light district in Tokyo. Nevertheless, the women attracted many customers at two or three times their usual rate from among the likes of sailors. He remarked that their popularity could compete with that of the Kabuki actor Ennosuke. The writer was outraged that the police did not intervene because the women's daily performance of the *teodori* justified their presence.[117]

The protests from Koreans and Okinawans during the 1907 exposition illustrate that the memory of the Human Pavilion in Osaka was still raw. Although the 1907 Tokyo exposition is rarely talked about in conjunction with its predecessor, it is important to look at them side by side. Then, instead of assuming that the 1903 Human Pavilion set the precedent of displaying colonial subjects to propagandize the imperial might of Japan, we can see a different unfolding of events. For whatever reason, Tsuboi did not have people on display in his second Human Pavilion, although he kept the exhibit name, perhaps in defiance of his critics.

Finally, the story of Gen and Yūki illustrates that factors within the Ainu community—namely, Gorō's success at the 1904 exposition in St. Louis—influenced other Ainu to embark for the metropolis. Their decision to leave the Tokyo exposition early presents them as masters of their own fate and not mere pawns of a Japanese entrepreneur. Indeed, the Human Pavilion in Tokyo was not a remarkable event. In Tsuboi's archive at the University of Tokyo, there are only a few postcards from the exposition in general to connect him to the second Human Pavilion. Often, silence speaks louder than words. Filling the vacuum left in the absence of living human displays, an exhibit featuring life-size dolls from

117. *RS*, April 2, 1907.

all over the world was presented for visitors to the exposition. The public would have to be content with that depiction of humanity for now.

Conclusion

What does the return of the Human Pavilion four years later, but without people of different ethnoracial groups in it, say about Japanese reactions to the first human display? First, the controversies regarding the first Human Pavilion were enough to dissuade Tsuboi from creating a similar enterprise in 1907. Second, the echoes of the first Human Pavilion's legacy show that reactions against human displays were not quelled.

What has endured, besides the notoriety of these events, are stories of the people who participated in the 1903 and 1907 expositions. While many of the participants have been lost to history, it is possible to locate some of them in documents and through their descendants. Some Ainu participants, like Gen, Yūki, and Fushine, became powerful leaders in their communities and advocated not only for the Ainu people's welfare, education, and equal inclusion in the empire but also articulated what it meant to be Ainu. Fushine's inclusion in the Human Pavilion was just one moment in his long career as an advocate for Ainu causes. His respected position as one of the leading Ainu voices of the early and mid-twentieth century is illustrated by the numerous articles and photographs that continued to feature him until his death in 1938.

CHAPTER 2

Meeting the Man on the Other Side

Soon after the opening of the Louisiana Purchase Exposition in St. Louis, Missouri, in 1904, a newspaper headline screamed: "Ainu Baby Turning White!" The sensationalist report explained how a very much doted-on two-year-old in the fair's Ainu exhibit, Kiko, was kissed so often by visitors that she was now kissing the dolly that she had been given, adopting a custom the Ainu had not previously known. She was also demanding kisses from her mother and would give them in return. Furthermore, the reporter claimed, her once-tan complexion was now getting whiter each day.[1] Apparently the transformative power of US culture was such that it could change Kiko's customs and even her appearance. Her story took a further twist when, ninety years later, a documentary by the Japan Broadcasting Corporation (NHK) revealed that Kiko could have been characterized more accurately as having turned Japanese, as it turned out that she was actually Japanese, not Ainu. NHK reporters had tracked down Kiko's eldest son, who was unaware that an Ainu couple had adopted and raised his mother and that she had traveled to St. Louis for the exposition. When Kiko was older, she left her Ainu home in Biratori and moved to Hokkaido's capital city, Sapporo, where she married a Japanese man and never revealed her Ainu past (fig. 2.1).[2]

1. *SLR*, April 26, 1904; April 24, 1904.
2. Nihon Hōsō Kyōkai, "Taiheiyō wo watashita Ainu" (3rd evening), June 12, 1996, mentioned in Refsing, *Early European Writing*, 1:77.

FIG. 2.1. Two-year-old Kiko photographed by Charles Carpenter. © The Field Museum, Chicago, Il, ID no. CSA13221.

At the time Kiko was born, it was not uncommon for Ainu families to adopt Japanese babies. The Meiji government in the 1870s had enticed Japanese settlers to go to Hokkaido by giving them free plots of land, but often the reality of colonial life proved too much, and some children had been abandoned—with only the Ainu to take them in.[3] Other children were offered up for adoption to the Ainu directly by Japanese settler families who could no longer care for them. The adoption process could vary. One Ainu informant described it as a mutually beneficial arrangement

3.   Mason, "Manly Narratives," 20–22.

in which no money was exchanged. Others described the Ainu "as often childless" who "habitually adopt Japanese children"; it could be a calculated endeavor where the price of the child was debated.[4]

The Ainu adoptions of Japanese children illustrate how ethnoracial categories linked to colonial status—colonized Ainu and colonizing Japanese—could be unstable. Furthermore, as the display of Kiko as an Ainu shows, ethnoracial status could be performed, misportrayed, and even faked—a common occurrence at such expositions.[5] In reality, as we will see, the different experiences of the various people on display defy the dichotomy of colonizer/viewer and colonized/viewed usually underscored in exposition studies. In St. Louis, for example, the Ainu were displayed among the exposition's "anthropological villages," whereas the Japanese exhibit, called Fair Japan, in which more than 300 Japanese people participated, was with those from other "civilized countries." Despite Japan's status as a rising imperial power, many fairgoers viewed the Japanese in Fair Japan with the same curiosity as they did Japan's colonial subjects in the villages.[6]

The title of this chapter, "Meeting the Man on the Other Side," alludes to how American and European visitors described meeting native people in the human displays at the Louisiana Purchase Exposition in 1904 and the Japan-British Exhibition in London in 1910. Visitors used the phrase to describe encounters with those on the other side of the exhibit fence, connoting the notion of a divided space in which the viewer was distinct from those who were viewed. I want to flip the phrase by contextualizing those on the other side as complex individuals with differing experiences and flesh out "the other side" to make it a concrete place instead of an abstract notion from the perspective of the viewer. By looking *from* the other side *at* exposition visitors, the one-dimensional notion of colonial subjects as objects collapses to make way for a glimpse of them as people involved in a dynamic cultural interaction. With regard to the Louisiana Purchase Exposition, Ainu participant Pete Gorō, for example, had actively

4.   Conversation with Ainu informant in Asahikawa, December 2010; "A Chat with Dr. Munro," 454.

5.   Durbach, *Spectacle of Deformity*, 147–53. British and Irish performers were painted to look like Africans (148).

6.   See KZW for postcards of Fair Japan as well as exhibits featuring Japanese from earlier expositions.

lobbied to go to St. Louis; when it was time to return to Japan, he wanted to remain in the United States. Gorō's personal photo albums illustrate that his time in St. Louis involved sightseeing and developing friendships with Americans. The photographs and the souvenirs he brought back to Japan reveal that for him the exposition was a place of intercultural exchange, belying a view of expositions purely as displays of imperial power.

The 1904 Louisiana Purchase Exposition

When anthropologist Frederick Starr, the US organizer of the native villages at the Louisiana Purchase Exposition, went to Hokkaido to recruit Ainu participants, he enlisted the help of John Batchelor, a British missionary who would spend over sixty years in Hokkaido. Batchelor's work had resulted in many Christian converts among the Ainu, and he strove for improvements in their social welfare and education. He was known for his criticism of the Japanese government as the cause of the Ainu's downtrodden state.

As the Japanese government pushed to Japanize the Ainu in the early twentieth century, Batchelor recorded the customs of the Ainu in one of the first efforts to preserve their language and culture. Batchelor was even involved in the creation of schools for the Ainu where they learned to read and write in their language. Through this missionary and educational work, Batchelor had developed a network of contacts throughout Hokkaido, which Starr made use of.

All nine of the Ainu participants who went to St. Louis had a direct relationship with Batchelor. Kutoroge and his wife, Shutratek, Kiko's parents, had connections to the Ainu chief Penri of Biratori, a close friend of Batchelor's. Batchelor had stayed with Penri in 1879 when he first arrived to Hokkaido and had learned the Ainu language from him.[7] Because of this relationship, Kutoroge, Penri's nephew, felt obligated to go to the United States when Batchelor urged him to. Starr described the scene: "Mr. Batchelor called [Kutoroge] back. He told him that we wished

---

7. See http://www2s.biglobe.ne.jp/~matu-emk/bachel.html (last accessed September 27, 2015).

him, with his wife and child, to go with us to the United States; that he would be gone nine months; that he should go. A look of blank helplessness came over his face, but he replied that he would have to go, of course, if *he* said so."[8]

Starr wanted an "old man" to balance out his collection of Ainu, and he asked Kutoroge's father to go to St. Louis as well, but he refused. Kutoroge persuaded Hiramura Sangyea to fill the place of an "old graybeard." Sangyea brought with him his wife, Santukno, and their five-year-old daughter, Kin.[9]

The other Ainu participants worked for Batchelor at his house in Sapporo, including Ozara Fukotaro, known as Yazo, and his wife, Shirake. According to Starr, they were ideal candidates: because they were "already familiar with white people and their customs," he explained, "we felt that they would be a good influence in keeping others satisfied."[10] Yazo had worked for Batchelor for ten years, since the age of fourteen. He owned a small farm with horses, and Starr described him as industrious and progressive.[11] The final participant from Batchelor's household was Pete Gorō, who came from a family linked to early Meiji assimilation projects (fig. 2.2).[12]

Gorō's grandfather had been selected by the Japanese to attend school in Tokyo in the 1870s. At that time the government had forced the Ainu to adopt surnames; some surnames were assigned, but Gorō's grandfather chose his own. Pete comes from the Ainu name Pet-un-kuru, meaning "a man who passed over the river"; it referred to Gorō's great-grandfather, who had crossed a river and lit a signal fire that saved the lives of many in his village when a rival Ainu group had attacked them.[13] Thus Gorō's

8.   Starr, *Ainu Group*, 56.

9.   Starr, *Ainu Group*, 66.

10.   Starr, *Ainu Group*, 16.

11.   Starr, *Ainu Group*, 16.

12.   Some English literature, including John Batchelor's writings, have used the spelling of Bete instead of Pete. Pronunciation is *pe-tei*, like "tei" in table. His granddaughter Chikamori Kiyomi and Ainu language specialists use Pete. In the Ainu language, there is no distinction between the B and P sound, but why Batchelor chose to use B is unclear. Written communication with Deriha Kōji, February 1, 2018.

13.   Hilger, *Together with the Ainu*, 23, 110. This likely refers to the agricultural school in Tokyo whose goal was to train Ainu as farmers, which ended in failure.

FIG. 2.2. John Batchelor and Pete Gorō pictured in 1914. Courtesy of Chikamori Kiyomi, photo by Deriha Kōji.

grandfather chose a surname that celebrated his Ainu lineage, even as the Ainu were being forced to conform to Japanese customs.

Years later, Gorō's granddaughter Chikamori Kiyomi said that everyone except her grandfather had agreed to go to St. Louis because Batchelor, who had looked after them, had asked them to go. In contrast, Gorō wanted to go to the United States so much that he approached Starr. According to Chikamori, Gorō had mastered writing in English, so he was seen as useful in communicating with the Americans.[14] Starr had originally thought Gorō was too Westernized because he wore European clothing and was clean shaven. "All this is highly commendable," Starr remarked, "but it is no qualification for figuring in an Ainu group at the

14.   Chikamori, "Ainu bunka," 68.

Exposition." In the end, though, Starr decided that because Gorō was "lively and happy and anxious to go," his influence would cheer the group.[15]

Another Ainu connected with Batchelor who expressed a strong desire to go to America was Sangyea's son Tuperek. When the young man heard about his father's upcoming journey, he also approached Starr. Tuperek had lived with Batchelor before he was selected to attend the Hakodate Training School (run by the Church Mission Society), where students were taught in the Ainu language.[16] The night before the Ainu group's departure, Tuperek and Sangyea called on Starr together.[17] "[Tuperek] begged to be taken to the Exposition; as they sat upon the floor before us, they wept as they pleaded," Starr recalled. Tuperek was clean shaven and wore Japanese clothes; Starr recounted that Tuperek "knew that [his appearance] was against him, but he [said he] still had an Ainu costume and his beard would soon grow!"[18] In the end Starr refused Tuperek's request. For Tuperek, going to America was a once-in-a-lifetime opportunity—for adventure or perhaps monetary gain—but Starr had his group selected and he was not to be swayed by emotional appeals.

Each Ainu traveling to the exposition was given a contract, the signing of which was witnessed by a police officer. Starr agreed to pay each couple one month's salary in advance, fare for their return voyage home, money for food, and a salary of thirty-five yen per month per person.[19] In return, they agreed to remain with the exposition until December 1904 and "erect a house, and live, dress, and act in a way true to Ainu life." They would be allowed to sell anything they made and keep the profits, but they were instructed not to reveal this to other native groups, who reportedly were forbidden from keeping the profits from the items they sold.[20] Deriha Kōji conducted research at the Field Museum in Chicago, and he

15. Starr, *Ainu Group*, 77.

16. Frey, "Ainu Schools," 212. Fushine Kōzō of the 1903 Human Pavilion was so impressed by the school, he funded two Ainu boys to attend. Yoshida, *Higashi Hokkaido*, 20.

17. *HT*, March 29, 1904.

18. Starr, *Ainu Group*, 93–94.

19. Fowler and Parezo, *Anthropology Goes to the Fair*, 84. For comparison, two Ainu were hired for a job in the Saru River region in 1893, at seven yen for one month. Miyatake, "Hakurankai no kioku," 71.

20. Fowler and Parezo, *Anthropology Goes to the Fair*, 84.

found records that showed Gorō, Sangyea, Kutoroge, and Yazo all sold items they had owned or had made to the museum, and each received compensation. Kutoroge earned the most of the four, with $42.70.[21]

Both Starr and the Ainu understood the performative aspect of their display. Gorō vowed to change his Westernized look and grow out his beard, and while in reality Yazo, Shirake, and Gorō lived with Batchelor in a Western-style house, in St. Louis they would live and be displayed in a traditional Ainu house.

LIFE AT THE EXPOSITION

The Louisiana Purchase Exposition was held from April to December 1904. Newspapers told of fairgoers' favorable view of the Ainu group (fig. 2.3).[22] Some visitors, at first disappointed that they were not dirty and savage, were fascinated by their gentle demeanor and polite manners.[23] "The little baby [Kiko] was a particular object of admiration[,] and if yesterday's record is duplicated every day the baby Ainu will have enough property to start a junk shop by the time the World's Fair has ended."[24] Another report said, "Visitors gave them small coins and other gifts so often that most of their time seemed to be spent in bowing and gesturing their elaborate thanks."[25]

In contrast, the Ainu were often affronted by the visitors' actions. People looked into the windows of their house, something they deplored because they held the east window of a house to be a sacred window to the gods.[26] Sangyea understood it was natural for visitors to be curious, but he was upset by their rude behavior, as he relayed through their translator, Inagaki Yochitarō:

21. Deriha, "Furederikku Sutā," 99–101, 106–7.
22. Previous scholarship (Vanstone, "Ainu Group") has misidentified the Ainu participants due to the inaccurate cataloging of photographs taken by Charles Carpenter at the Field Museum. For detailed information see Deriha, "Shashin ni nokosareta," 42–48; Deriha, "Sento Ruisu bankoku hakurankai," 26–32; and Miyatake, "Hakurankai no kioku," 91.
23. Hanson, *Official History*, 393; "Racial Exhibit," 414; "Native Dwellings," 218.
24. *SLR*, April 8, 1904.
25. Fowler and Parezo, *Anthropology Goes to the Fair*, 213.
26. Munro, *Ainu Creed*, 57–59.

We do not mind the people coming in at the doors, but we do object to them coming to the windows and peering in. We consider that very impolite. In our country it would never be thought of, but here more than half of the people that visit us come to the windows and look in and grin and chatter. I cannot understand how they could be so impolite. The doors are made for people to enter the house, and those within the house to go out. The windows are for those in the house to look out, but not to go out. People who are not within the house have no right at the windows. Why have they? Only robbers go to the windows of houses. . . . I am from the village of Piratori, and such a thing as looking in the windows at the people in the house was never heard of. I never heard of such a thing until we got settled in our own house.[27]

Sangyea did not object to being looked at by visitors, he said, but he cared about the way they were observed. He continued, "We did not mind in the least that the people gathered around and watched us at our work in constructing the house, for we know that our house is strange to visitors." When asked how he felt about being looked at all the time, Sangyea's comments revealed the duality of being on display: he was aware that he and the other Ainu were of interest to the onlookers, and at the same time, the onlookers were a curiosity to the Ainu. He remarked,

No, we don't object to be looked at. Of course, some of the people talk and laugh when they look at us as if we were freaks in the museum, but that can be expected. You are also strange to us. Your houses are odd, and you dress funny, and your talk sounds odd, and you are as much of a curiosity to us as we are to you. We like it here very much, but we are afraid of the hot weather.[28]

According to reports, "Their interpreter [Inagaki] spent much of his time guarding the building and corralling insistent visitors who expected an exception to be made for them."[29] Contrary to official exposition photos, which always depicted the Ainu alone, fig. 2.4 shows visitors in the Ainu house.

27. *SLR*, May 29, 1904.
28. *SLR*, May 29, 1904.
29. Fowler and Parezo, *Anthropology Goes to the Fair*, 272.

FIG. 2.3. On top ledge: Kin, Gorō holding Kiko; standing from left: Kutoroge, Shutratek, Yazo, Shirake, Santukno, and Sangyea. Photographed by Jessie Tarbox Beals. Courtesy of Missouri History Museum, St. Louis.

FIG. 2.4. Kiko gazes at the camera as her mother, Shutratek, weaves in the foreground; in the background, visitors watch from inside the house. Courtesy of Schlesinger Library, Radcliffe Institute, Harvard University.

The *St. Louis Post-Dispatch* reported on how the visitors' rubbernecking affected the Ainu. According to the article, one day fifteen people pushed into the Ainu's house without asking permission. The Ainu asked the official on duty to get them out of the house. As they were leaving, the reporter wrote, one of the female spectators exclaimed, "Well, I'd like to know what they are here for," and the official responded, "It may be that they are here to teach Americans gentle manners." It was also reported that crowding at the windows darkened the inside of the house, making it difficult for the Ainu to do things inside, and they had become sullen and no longer smiled and bowed. The Native Americans in the neighboring display had solved this problem by "posting a sign which reads: 'Admission, 10 cents,'" the newspaper noted, adding, "As for him and his, they will get along without privacy as long as it pays."[30]

30. *SLPD*, May 22, 1904.

INTERCULTURAL EXCHANGES

By the end of the exposition, the Ainu had earned a good income from their salaries and the sale of their handicrafts, and some had developed friendships with visitors and the other people living in the neighboring villages. The Ainu's interpreter-caretaker, Inagaki, wrote an article for a Japanese Christian newspaper that detailed the Ainu's interactions with their next-door neighbors the Patagonians, as well as with the Cocopa and Pueblo Indians. Inagaki wrote that contrary to the expectation that bringing many primitive groups together would lead to fighting and make them regard each other as enemies, "they associate with each other with warm feelings and sympathy and love; it is extremely beautiful." The Ainu often exchanged meat and seeds with other native participants, and they visited each other's houses. Although they could not communicate directly, they relied on translators and gesturing.[31] Sangyea explained: "Oh yes, the others visit us. We cannot understand them, of course, and now and then only it is possible to understand what they mean, but we go by their grunts and their smiles and motions."[32] In one account, a third US translator was called in to help facilitate communication between the Ainu and Tehuelche translators because they "failed to get together on their English."[33]

GORŌ'S PHOTO ALBUMS

Nothing serves as greater evidence of the varied relationships the Ainu forged at the exposition than Gorō's two photo albums, which are now in his granddaughter Chikamori's possession. The albums include about fifty photographs that were either taken at the exposition or given to Gorō by friends while he was in St. Louis. Miyatake Kimio, a cultural anthropologist, was the first to catalog the photos in these albums.[34] While Miyatake discusses and publishes three of Gorō's photographs in her 2010 book, my work is the first to publish three album pages in their entirety and consider the pages' composition.[35] I identify some of the Americans

31. Inagaki, "Genshi jinshu"; *SLR*, May 8, 1904.
32. *SLR*, May 29, 1904.
33. *SLR*, April 16, 1904.
34. Miyatake, "Aija ni okeru hakurankai," 35–36.
35. Miyatake, *Umi wo watatta*, 91–93.

FIG. 2.5. Photograph of a Patagonian man with smaller photographs of another Patagonian and American man. Courtesy of Chikamori Kiyomi, photo by Deriha Kōji.

in his albums. In Gorō's albums, there are two pages that exclusively have photographs of American friends (including fig. 2.12). Seven pages have a mixture of photographs of American friends, the Ainu while in St. Louis, and other participants of the exposition, like the Patagonians (fig 2.5). These photographs substantiate reports that the Ainu developed a relationship with the Patagonians. It was reported that the young Ainu men picked up some English, and a seven-year-old Patagonian girl, Giga, "acquired considerable Japanese from Kiko the Ainu girl, with whom she played, as the camps of the two adjoined."[36]

There are three formal exposition photographs that feature the Japanese participants (including the Ainu) or possibly some Japanese visitors who visited the exposition. However, the majority of the pages have a montage-like composition, intermixing candid shots showing Yazo,

36.   Carlson, "Giant Patagonians," 22; Miyatake, "Aija ni okeru," 35; *SLR*, December 3, 1904.

Shirake, Gorō, and Inagaki while they were sightseeing in St. Louis next to photos of American friends Gorō had met (fig. 2.6).

Gorō's albums contrast with narratives in which foreign participants in the exhibits were mere objects in the spectacle. The albums indicate that the participants were looking back and that Gorō wanted photos of his American friends and the other participants to remember them. They show that the Ainu participants had many experiences beyond the reconstructed Ainu house official exposition photos typically placed them in. In a further blurring of the official exposition visual record and Gorō's personal visual records, there is a copy of an official portrait of the Ainu group taken by Jessie Tarbox Beals in one of Gorō's albums. The photograph in this album is from a series taken by Beals that are held by the Missouri History Museum (fig. 2.3). The folded creases of Gorō's copy show that after receiving the photo, he folded it up to bring it back to Japan (fig. 2.7).

The meaning of Beal's photograph changes in Gorō's album. In the museum, the photograph reflects a cold and detached view of the Ainu. Creased and weathered, and pasted in Gorō's album, the photo becomes just one memento of his experiences abroad, juxtaposed with photos from different periods of his life. The photo was placed on an album page along with photos taken from different times of Gorō's life and candid shots of the Ainu while in the display village.

Some pictures show Gorō with the Krieckhaus family, who befriended him. One notable photo shows one of the Krieckhaus sisters dressed in Ainu clothing (fig. 2.8).[37] This photo is unique; there is no evidence that the Ainu sold the privilege of dressing up in Ainu clothing. It shows that a friendship must have existed between the sisters and Gorō. Another photo shows Gorō with Mathilda Krieckhaus in Western clothes outside the Ainu house (fig. 2.9), and there are pictures that show the Krieckhaus sisters (fig. 2.10) and the Ainu at the Krieckhaus home (fig. 2.11). According to Chikamori, the Krieckhaus sisters taught Gorō how to sew, a skill he later taught the Ainu women of his town, including his granddaughter.[38]

The albums document Gorō's many encounters with American friends. He wrote their names, sometimes with the caption "friends while in America," underneath the photos. One American family he identified

37. Miyatake, "Aija ni okeru," 44.
38. Chikamori, "Ainu bunka," 69.

FIG. 2.6. A page from Pete Gorō's photo album, featuring photographs of American friends he met while in St. Louis. Includes a photograph of him, Yazo, Shirake, and their translator Inagaki, sightseeing. Courtesy of Chikamori Kiyomi, photo by Deriha Kōji.

FIG. 2.7. Gorō's creased copy of an official exposition portrait taken by Jessie Tarbox Beals. Courtesy of Chikamori Kiyomi, photo by Deriha Kōji.

FIG. 2.8. Gorō and one of the Krieckhaus sisters dressed in traditional Ainu clothing. Courtesy of Chikamori Kiyomi, photo by Deriha Kōji.

FIG. 2.9. Gorō with Mathilda, who is identified in English and Japanese. Courtesy of Chikamori Kiyomi, photo by Deriha Kōji.

FIG. 2.10. The Krieckhaus sisters. Courtesy of Chikamori Kiyomi, photo by Deriha Kōji.

FIG. 2.11. Taken at the Krieckhaus home. Courtesy of Chikamori Kiyomi, photo by Deriha Kōji.

in his album was the Proetz family, including a sixteen-year-old boy named Arthur, who worked at the exposition and was related to the Krieckhaus family (fig. 2.12).[39]

In his memoir, Arthur Proetz described the wacky Krieckhaus family as a "circus."[40] He recalls that

> as the fair was being assembled the town began filling with foreigners from everywhere, and the aunts, *toujours gaies*, kept turning up with some exotic specimens. One afternoon [Aunt] Tut brought home a baroucheful of Hairy Ainus, the Japanese aborigines with long beards or tattooed lips, and names like Bete [*sic*], Shirokke [*sic*], and Kiko.

Proetz remarked, "They spent their lives in huts without chimneys and smelled like smoked hams."[41] In addition to bringing the Ainu home for tea, Tut brought other foreign visitors, including a Japanese man Proetz referred to as the "diminutive oriental Kohan Akita, who owned a Buddhist temple on the Pike."[42] From his comments it is clear that Proetz viewed Kohan Akita in the same light as the Ainu—all were exotic foreigners.

By the end of the exposition, Gorō was not looking forward to going back to Japan. He wrote to Starr, requesting that he ask Batchelor for permission for him to stay longer. Unfortunately, Batchelor's letter agreeing to the proposition did not reach Starr in time, and Gorō had to return with the rest of the group.[43] Gorō later described his feelings about the exposition and his experience.

> I had really wanted to go the exposition and I kept asking until I was finally allowed to go. The exposition was fairly difficult, however there are also precious memories. At that time there were three American women [Krieckhaus family] who had an interest in the Ainu and they visited us

39. Proetz, *I Remember*, 14–15. At the exposition, Proetz was on display at the Berlitz exhibit learning French.

40. Proetz, *I Remember*, 167. Thanks to Miranda Rectenwald at Washington University at St. Louis, Special Collections, for her assistance with the Proetz papers.

41. Proetz, *I Remember*, 160.

42. Proetz, *I Remember*, 160.

43. Vanstone, "Ainu Group," 89.

FIG. 2.12. Individual members of the Proetz family, identified, including young Arthur (upper left corner). Middle caption reads: "Friends while in America." Courtesy of Chikamori Kiyomi, photo by Deriha Kōji.

often. . . . After the exposition I had wanted to stay one or two years longer in America and asked for Batchelor's permission, but while his answer
was in the middle of being delivered the group had to return. Mr. Inagaki
would not give me permission.[44] I was extremely disappointed, but I returned home. Batchelor had come to meet us at the station and when he
saw me he said, 'Why did you come back? It would have been alright if
you had wanted to study a little longer over there.' I was again sorely
disappointed.[45]

Gorō's remarks about wanting to stay longer in the United States, along
with his photographs and the captions he wrote in his albums, reverse
the conventional narrative that the colonial subjects were there simply to
be looked at; Gorō himself was also eagerly looking.[46]

THE EXPOSITION AS LABORATORY AND THE
CROSS-ETHNICKING OF OBJECTS

Expositions were also sites where scientific studies were carried out with
native participants. In St. Louis, Casper Mayer made fifty-five life casts
depicting the various races at the exposition, including casts of Gorō,
Yazo, and Shirake.[47] Hearing tests were conducted on participants, including the Ainu.[48] Casts were also made of the Ainu's feet, as an orthopedic
doctor wanted to study the natural shapes of feet of people who did not
wear shoes. Another doctor measured the Ainu participants' heads as part
of a long-term study of Japanese craniums.[49] Frederick Starr gave anthropology lectures, including one on the Ainu, and used native participants as live models.[50] A two-day athletic meet involving participants
from the native villages, called Anthropology Days, was held to test
whether white men were superior athletes.

44. Refsing, *Early European*, 5:144.
45. Reprinted in Miyatake, "Hakurankai no kioku," 78–79.
46. Corbey, "Ethnographic Showcases," 349–50.
47. Chikamori, "Ainu bunka," 70; Miyatake, "Shikago Fui–rudo," 49; Preston,
Dinosaurs in the Attic, 189–91.
48. Bruner, *Hearing of Primitive*, 44–45.
49. Fowler and Parezo, *Anthropology Goes to the Fair*, 317.
50. *SLPD*, August 30, 1904, September 1, 1904.

The Ainu's time at the exposition involved interactions with others beyond the typical fairgoers. In addition to visiting the Krieckhaus home, several times they attended services held at an Episcopal church.[51] They interacted with other native people and participated in the economy of the exposition as both sellers and buyers. It was common for participants to buy each other's handicrafts as souvenirs; for example, a Nootka participant named Dr. Atlieu used the money he earned from the exhibit to purchase souvenirs from the Ainu, Moros, and Maoris. In Chikamori's possession is a bracelet Gorō bought from a Native American participant. The beaded pattern on the bracelet includes the fleur-de-lis, a symbol of St. Louis, which appeared on many commemorative items sold at the fair.[52]

Interestingly, two objects currently at the Russian Museum of Ethnography in St. Petersburg came from the Ainu who had been in the exposition. Russian ethnologist Viktor N. Vasilyev bought the items from Ainu who had gone to St. Louis when he visited their village in 1912 (fig. 2.13) during a trip to Sakhalin and Hokkaido.[53] Vasilyev had secured assistance from John Batchelor and others during his travels to help him in his effort to collect Ainu goods. At Biratori, the hometown of the Ainu who had gone to St. Louis, the "Ainu themselves kept bringing in ethnographic objects from morning till night." Within five days he bought more than 800 articles from them, and it was said that he only stopped collecting more objects when he ran out of money.[54]

Among the items Vasilyev purchased from the Ainu is a small beaded bag displaying a design similar to the one on Gorō's Native American bracelet, with what looks like a fleur-de-lis pattern in one corner (fig. 2.14). He also acquired a necklace, called a *rekutōnpe* in Ainu, that has a medal sewn onto the cloth that reads on one side, "You Have Got to Show Me, I'm from Missouri. World's Fair St. Louis 1904."[55]

51. Everett, "Mysterious Little Japanese," 394.

52. Miyatake, *Umi wo watatta*, 173–74.

53. *KNNS*, August 25 1912; August 29, 1912; *OS*, May 6, 1912, *Omskaiᾱ*, 78–79.

54. See http://www.ethnomuseum.ru/collections-relics-culture-ainu-japanese-chinese-koreans-mongols?language=en (accessed August 2, 2018).

55. On the opposite side, emblazoned over the design of a male rooster, or cock, are the words "Presented for Having the Largest" (*Ainu no bi*, 106–7). This medal illustrates the Victorians' penchant for raunchy jokes (Mike Truax, 1904 World Fair Society, personal communication, May 11, 2010).

FIG. 2.13. Photograph of 1904 St. Louis participant Shutratek that Vasilyev took during his visit to Nibutani in 1912. Courtesy of the collections of the Russian Museum of Ethnography, St. Petersburg, Russia.

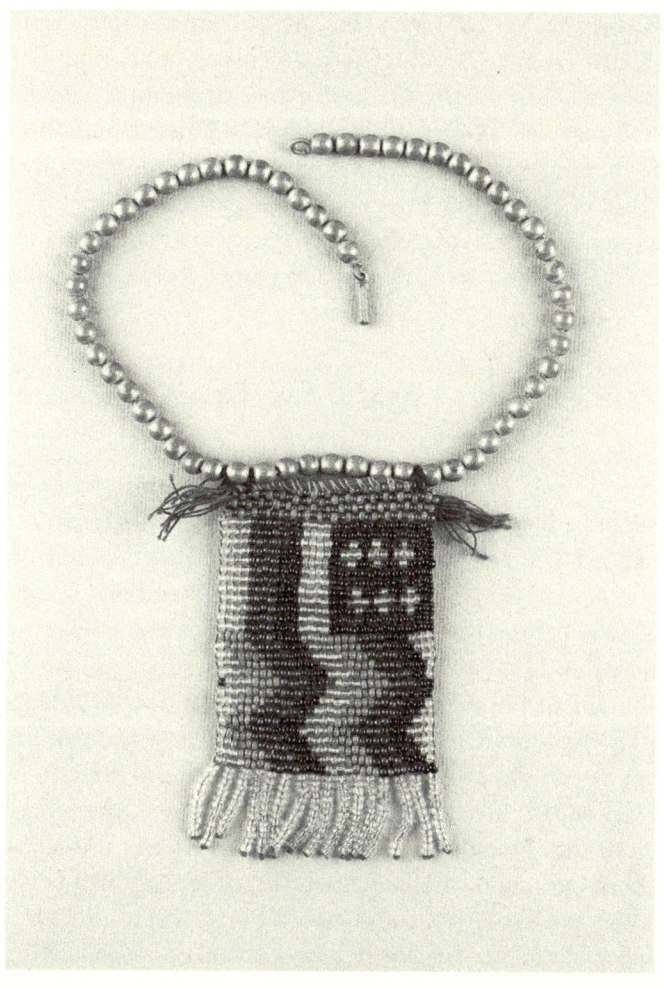

FIG. 2.14. Vasilyev's beaded bracelet that he purchased in 1912 from the Ainu in Biratori who went to the Louisiana Purchase Exposition in 1904. Courtesy of the collections of the Russian Museum of Ethnography, St. Petersburg, Russia.

Vasilyev had wished to buy Ainu items for a Russian ethnography museum and ended up buying a foreign (apparently Native American) handicraft and a souvenir medal from the Louisiana Purchase Exposition that had been refashioned into a traditional-style Ainu necklace. These American- and Native American–made objects, originally acquired in the United States, were transformed into economic capital for the Ainu when they sold them to Vasilyev, who then used them to depict Ainu culture. Through this "cross-ethnicking" (a term coined by Jennifer Robertson) objects that were originally made in America became Ainu.[56] The exchange and movement of these objects as they crossed cultures facilitated their refashioning and cross-ethnicking, transforming them into objects of hybrid signification. The objects, like the participants' personal experiences, demonstrate that categories of ethnicity are malleable and that the Ainu played an active part in refashioning and hybridizing their culture.

The 1910 Japan-British Exhibition in London

In the cold winter of December 2010, Ainu Kaizawa Seiko, then age seventy-eight, smiled at me warmly as she softly touched a white and blue porcelain bowl. "What they did was heroic," she said decisively.[57] She was referring to her father's and grandparents' journey to London more than a hundred years before. Kaizawa's father, Zensuke, was only ten years old when he went to London with his parents, older sister, and six other Ainu from Nibutani and Monbetsu, Hokkaido. The purpose of their trip was to bring an Ainu house to London for the 1910 Japan-British Exhibition, where they would show visitors their everyday life and customs. The bowl she held was one of three her family brought back with them (fig. 2.15). Of all the goods they brought back, including leather bags, leather boots, formal clothing, pots, and various household goods, only two bowls remain in Kaizawa's possession to commemorate her family's sojourn abroad. Most of the objects they bought or were given are now gone.[58]

Oral testimony passed down by relatives of the participants reveal aspects of their experiences not found in the official records of the exposition, or even in the accounts of those who took part in it. For example, one

56. Robertson, *Takarazuka*, 96–97.

57. Interview conducted in December 2010 in Nibutani, Hokkaido. Follow-up written correspondence with Kaizawa's contact, Mr. Yamagishi, who visited Kaizawa several times in 2014 to confirm details of the 2010 interview.

58. Hamada, "Nibutani no ekashi," (1991) 166. Hamada Hiroshi, the grandson of Kaizawa Shirabeno, described a fire that burned down a storage house that had held his grandfather's notebook, among other things.

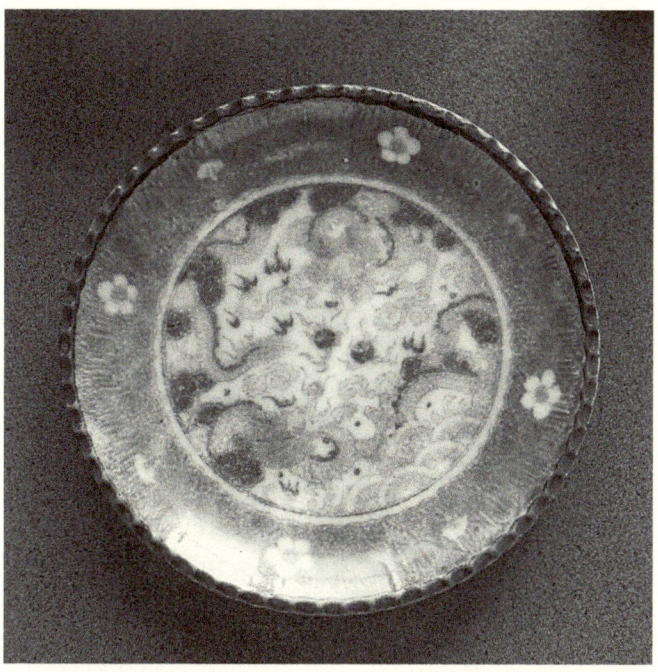

FIG. 2.15. The bowl pictured is one of the last remaining objects that Kaizawa Seiko has from the items that her family brought back from the 1910 Japan-British Exhibition in London. Courtesy of Kaizawa Seiko, photo by Yamagishi Toshinori.

story tells of an Ainu participant who bought a pair of chopsticks while in London and then carried them in his pocket wherever he went. After he returned to Hokkaido, if he was at someone else's house to eat he always used those chopsticks, which he still brought with him everywhere.[59] If not for objects like Kaizawa's bowl and the stories that are still remembered and retold, the Ainu's experience in London would be lost, just like the objects that were once treasured as mementos of their time abroad.

JAPAN'S INTERNATIONAL STANDING IN 1910

The year of the Japan-British Exhibition, 1910, was a pivotal moment for Japan as an emerging colonial power. Japan's victory over Russia in the Russo-Japanese War in 1905 had been a shock felt around the world.

59. Hamada, "Nibutani no ekashi" (1991), 172.

Reactions in the West to Japan's victory ranged from deep concern to racist and belittling disparagement. After 1905, the influx of Japanese settlers to Manchuria and Japan's increased presence in Korea raised eyebrows among the Western powers, including the British.[60] Japan had been allied with Britain since 1902, when they formed the first alliance between a non-Western and a Western nation. Although Japan had initially hoped to further raise its international profile by hosting an international exposition, it saw its participation as a sponsor of the Japan-British Exhibition in London as a way to reassure Britain, which was growing wary of Japan's growing empire, and showcase its standing as a modern, civilized empire.[61]

In reality, the allies were anything but equals in organizing the exposition. The British government did not play any official role; instead, entrepreneur and businessman Imre Kiralfy (known for producing theatrical spectacles and expositions) coordinated all British involvement, working with the Japanese government. This unequal partnership did not sit well with the Japanese.[62] Kiralfy insisted on including native villages in the amusement section of the exposition, for without them, he warned the Japanese, the event would not generate enough interest or money. Despite their initial reluctance, the Japanese agreed that, at Kiralfy's urging, in addition to an Ainu village and a Formosa hamlet housing Taiwanese Aborigines there would also be a Japanese village, called Uji village, that would showcase traditional Japanese life and crafts. The Japanese did not originally conceive of using Ainu and Formosa villages to showcase its empire; the fact that the British planner forced them to include a Japanese village alongside the native villages of their colonial subjects demonstrates the complexities involved in mounting an exhibit of the Japanese empire in an international context. Rather than presenting an image of a modern nation, Japanese critics lamented that the Uji village portrayed an unrealistic and overly feudal representation of Japan. Visual montages in British newspapers, such as a drawing titled "Characters and Curiosity at the 'Jap-Anglo' Japanese, Ainus, and Formosans at Shepherd's Bush,"

---

60. Hotta-Lister, *Japan-British Exhibition*, 117–18.

61. Hotta-Lister, *Japan-British Exhibition*, 115.

62. See KZW for postcards showing how the British depicted the Japanese at the exposition, as feminized and "learning from the British," as well as images from Uji village.

LEAVES FROM AN ARTIST'S SKETCH-BOOK: THE ANGLO JAPANESE EXHIBITION, AS SEEN BY FRANK REYNOL

FIG. 2.16. The montage of Ainu, Japanese, and Taiwanese Aborigines at the exposition. Credit: *ILN*, July 9, 1910.

placed all three groups together as objects of curiosity, blurring Japan's colonial hierarchy (fig. 2.16).[63]

The portrayal of Japan's empire in an international context like the Japan-British Exhibition was complicated by Japan's position as a non-Western nation. The British conflated the Taiwanese Aborigines and the Japanese, and the fact that the Ainu were discussed as a potential "lost white race" threatened Japanese claims of superiority over them, in Western eyes. Furthermore, the experiences of those in the villages and their wide array of interactions with fairgoers and others while in London demonstrate that they were not just "objects on display" representing Japan's empire but were individual people whose experiences at

63. *ILN*, July 9, 1910.

the exposition shaped their view of their own place in the empire well after their time in London.[64]

RECRUITMENT

The Kaizawa family was recruited to go to London because of the affluence and stature of the head of the family, Kaizawa Shirabeno.[65] Shirabeno was the largest landowner in the Ainu village of Nibutani when he was approached by officials to go to London. When Shirabeno was a young man, he had been forced to work at a fishery in Atsukeshi, owing to a system of compulsory labor (*basho ukeoisei*) imposed on the Ainu during the Tokugawa period. Japanese officials had visited Ainu villages, selecting who they wanted to work at the fisheries and separating family members. After a year of compulsory labor, Shirabeno received a lacquer cup (*tōki*) as compensation.[66] As prominent Ainu leader Kayano Shigeru later recounted, "Even today, lacquerware obtained as payment for labor or in trade exchanges with the Japanese can be found in Ainu homes. It is rarely known who received these and how, but the lacquer wine cup on a stand that Kaizawa Shirapeno [*sic*] had treasured until his death around 1940 is known to have been his payment for a year's labor in Atsukeshi in his youth."[67]

After one year, when Shirabeno left Atsukeshi to return to Nibutani, he took a horse with him. Most of the villagers ridiculed him about the utility of a horse, since no one owned one in their village. Kaizawa Seiko's brother Hamada Hiroshi remarked that their grandfather had had foresight when he brought the horse. From the end of the Meiji period to the beginning of the Showa period, Shirabeno became the best horse breeder in the Saru River region.[68]

---

64. Zwick, *Inuit Entertainers*, 2.
65. Hamada, "Nibutani no ekashi" (1983), 334–42.
66. Hamada, "Nibutani no ekashi" (1991), 163.
67. Kayano, *Our Land*, 36. Kayano later acquired this wine cup, which is now on display at the Nibutani Museum of Ainu Cultural Resources. Kayano documents the forced labor of his grandfather, who deliberately cut off his own finger in an attempt to make himself ineligible from work (26–36).
68. Hamada, "Nibutani no ekashi" (1991), 164.

Shirabeno amassed a large farm and hired many workers, who lived in outbuildings on his land. He hired around ten daily laborers and had many business transactions with various people. He recorded these transactions in a notebook, writing in kana (Japanese characters), recalled Hamada, who had once seen the book. Because the first school in Nibutani was not built until the late 1880s, his grandfather had never attended. Hamada identifies his grandfather's period of forced labor at the fishery as when he learned to speak Japanese and write. In his grandfather's circle of acquaintances, whoever knew katakana taught the others.[69]

Kaizawa Seiko remembered Shirabeno's wife, her grandmother, Anretoku, to be a strict and beautiful woman. She was an exemplar of Ainu womanhood, as she was proficient in sewing, including making Ainu rugs and kimonos, and she knew the proper preparations for ritual ceremonies. Because she was the wife of the village chief, she played a central role in the village.[70] Shirabeno and Anretoku did not have any children, so they adopted a girl, Kokin, and a boy, whom they named Zensuke, from an Ainu couple from Penakori.[71]

When Shirabeno was around forty and already a wealthy man, officials in England contacted the head of the registry department in Biratori with a request for an Ainu family to work at the London exposition. The head of the office approached Shirabeno, saying, "Shirabeno-san, because I think you are the most suitable, please go to England." The manager of the Ainu group in London, Yoshida Hideatsu, told reporters that Shirabeno and his family were selected because their behavior was proper, they worked hard at their family business, and they were classic Ainu types (*tenkeiteki* Ainu).[72] Shirabeno told a reporter for *Tokyo asahi* what the registry head had said to him: "You are someone who takes care of the village, this is a lucky break for you, and everyone will look after you, won't you please do me the favor of going this time?" Shirabeno said he was thrilled to go. He showed the reporter a letter written by the registry head that was to be shown to people during his journey whenever he needed assistance.[73] According to a report in the *Kobe shinbun* the Ainu group

69. Hamada, "Nibutani no ekashi" (1991), 166.
70. Written correspondence, Yamagishi, February 27, 2014.
71. Hamada, "Nibutani no ekashi," (1991), 167, 167–68; Tamura, *Ainugo onsei*, viii.
72. *TA*, February 13, 1910.
73. *TA*, February 13, 1910.

went to London because of John Batchelor, who had also helped Frederick Starr recruit Ainu for the Louisiana Purchase Exposition.[74] There is no other evidence to substantiate this claim.[75]

From the beginning, Shirabeno was eager to go to London, and his family accompanied him.[76] From Nibutani, twenty-four-year-old Kaizawa Kenji, his twenty-eight-year-old wife, Utarashino, and their two-year-old son, Chūji, also went to London. Hiramura Kanekatoku, age sixty-two from Biratori, and Monbetsu Shinotsukaten and his wife, Nukatsutoke, both fifty-five and from Monbetsu, rounded out the group. The Ainu took with them housing materials, from pillars to support the roofs of their Ainu houses (*chise*) to everyday tools and utensils.[77]

The Ainu group spent a few days in Tokyo before their departure for London. A reporter visited their hotel on February 14 and encountered Shirabeno, Zensuke, and Kanekatoku, who were going out to buy provisions for their journey. The reporter offered to be their guide for their shopping trip in the city's Ginza district. He described Shirabeno as a fairly agreeable man with a long beard and hair who was wearing a brown trilby hat and a black two-layer overcoat and carrying a carved wooden cane. Shirabeno's speech was clear, and the reporter said that if he did not have a beard, one would not think he was Ainu. Zensuke was wearing traditional *hakama* pants, a large black hat, black lace-up shoes, and an overcoat with gold buttons. According to the reporter, Zensuke was no different from any other elementary school student from the metropolis. The reporter described Kanekatoku as wearing "barbarian clothes" from Hokkaido: a *chikarakarpe* (an Ainu embroidered kimono). With his white hair and beard, the reporter thought he looked like an Ainu gentleman in a typical bear festival photograph.[78]

74. *KS*, February 18, 1910.

75. In Batchelor's records, he only wrote about the Ainu who went to St. Louis in 1904. There is circumstantial evidence that suggests that he was connected to Ainu participation at three expositions. Nishihara, *Watashitachi no rekishi*, 28–39.

76. According to Hamada, Kokin was eighteen at the time of the trip; see also *KS*, February 18, 1910. According to Tamura, Kokin was born in 1897, which would have made her thirteen (xii).

77. *Miyako*, February 9, 1910; *OS*, February, 16, 1910.

78. *TNNSB*, February 15, 1910.

During their shopping trip, Zensuke bought a book for third-year students. For readers who doubted that an Ainu boy could read and write, a newspaper printed Zensuke's handwriting showing his name and age. This visual proof of his aptitude as novelty shows the prejudice the Ainu faced. A ten-year-old boy from the metropolis who could write his name would be of little consequence, but the fact that Zensuke was Ainu and could write was something that warranted evidence.[79] The article listed the prices of all the items they bought to show that these Ainu were wealthy. The reporter made a point of indicating that Shirabeno's wealth was the result of his own success and described him as wealthy man who owned fifty to sixty horses and fields used for cultivation.

Shirabeno explained how he and his family were approached about participating in the exposition. "It was through the official's discretion that we were selected and how we came to go to England. I think that it is truly an honor. Up until now I have been to Sapporo, Otaru, and Muroran. This is the first time I have been to Tokyo."[80] Another report said that Shirabeno was surprised and pleased by the Tokyo scenery.[81] He talked about going abroad: "I had many worries about going to the Japan-British Exhibition, but they said they are going to take good care of us so I became reassured. Among those in the village, some were jealous and others were threatened." He explained how he had become wealthy by buying an agricultural machine.[82] These reports revealed Shirabeno to be a savvy, self-made man who was looking forward to his upcoming journey.

Although the Tokyo reporters were sympathetic toward the Ainu, some Japanese were not as considerate. Because the Ainu women were tattooed on both hands and around the mouth, wherever they went they heard jeers of "Ainu, Ainu" and unkind remarks about their tattoos. Yoshida, their manager, vigorously defended them, pointing to the Ainu women's chastity and the great skill involved in the intricate embroidery work on their *chikarakarpe*. Yoshida asserted, "If you see this . . . you

79. See KZW.
80. *TNNSB*, February 15, 1910.
81. *OS*, February 14, 1910.
82. *TA*, February 13, 1910.

[will] know that one must not sell short the intelligence of the Ainu."[83] Later, their scheduled performance of the Ainu bear ceremony, which was supposed to be filmed, was canceled owing to the weather. Their stop in Tokyo reveals that even before their departure for England, interest in the Ainu in the metropolis was evident in the consistent newspaper coverage.[84]

LIFE AT THE EXPOSITION

On April 15, 1910, the *Kagamaru* arrived at the Albert Docks in London, and the disembarking Ainu and Taiwanese Aborigines drew much attention. A Japanese newspaper reported that Englishwomen forgot their train departure times and gathered around the Ainu.[85]

In the Ainu village on the exhibition grounds, there were three houses. One served as living quarters for six people, another housed three, and in the third lived the eldest of the group, Hiramura Kanekatoku, known during the exhibition as the "Bear Killer." He was popular owing to his appearance, which many likened to Santa Claus, and other fanciful characters, such as Father Time.[86] Kaizawa Kenji remarked that because Kanekatoku looked like Tolstoy, he was held in high esteem.[87] It was reported that he had a kimono embroidered with a family crest of three oak trees in gold thread that had been presented to his relatives by the Matsumae domain when it presided over Hokkaido (during the seventeenth to mid-nineteenth centuries).[88] He was also one of the few transmitters of Ainu oral stories and epic poetry known as *yukar*.[89] Although Kanekatoku's knowledge of *yukar* was not widely recognized at the time, scholars who went to the exposition to conduct research on the Ainu realized what a rare treasure he was.

---

83. *TNNSB*, February 15, 1910.
84. *OS*, February 18, 1910; *TA*, February 16, 1910.
85. *TNNS*, May 26, 1910; see KZW.
86. *OSWCC*, August 16, 1910; *TNNSB*, February 18, 1911; see KZW.
87. *TNNSB*, February 18, 1910.
88. *Daily News*, March 25, 1910.
89. Nihon Koten Bungaku Daijiten Henshū Iinkai (ed.), *Nihon koten bungaku daijiten*, 6:101.

Kanekatoku received innumerable visitors. Among them was Alan Ostler, a reporter who visited him with a Japanese translator. We have only two in-depth descriptions of the Ainu village at the exposition; Ostler's account is one of them:

> [Kanekatoku's] venerable countenance was expressive of woe. He had been trying to light a fire, and had nearly succeeded in burning down the roof that sheltered him.
>
> "Not that that would be a great loss," he murmured sorrowfully, "for it doesn't shelter me any too well." He hugged himself and shivered. "Hokkaido is cold," he added. "But this place—ugh! I thought I should freeze hard last night like a piece of dried fish." . . .
>
> I told him that to see him[,] people came a day's journey, that he had been mentioned in all the newspapers, that ladies thought him simply sweet, and children believed him to be Santa Claus. And as the interpreter made the best of these compliments, a happier expression flitted across the old face, and a hairy hand stroked the venerable beard complacently.
>
> "And did the English know of the Ainu before we came here?" he asked.
>
> I said "Yes," and to prove it showed him a copy of the second part of "Old and New Japan," wherein are photographs of the hairy people in their native land.
>
> The old man was delighted. . . .
>
> "They stand up," he said, running the tip of his forefinger round the outlines of the figure of an Ainu fisherman in one of the illustrations. He spent a long time poring delightedly over the book, asking what the letter press meant, and turning page after page with absorbed interest.
>
> "It is for you to keep," explained the interpreter when, with a sigh, the old man prepared to hand the volume back to me. He was astonished.
>
> "But—but such a book as this," he said. "It is too great a gift. Surely it is priceless." And he obviously disbelieved me when I said that the book cost about one-fourth of a yen.
>
> After that he asked me many questions about the country in which he now finds himself. What was it like outside the Exposition? Were there people in the north of England like those in the north of Japan? . . . "This is the most wonderful book in the world," he announced decidedly. "When I look at its pictures I am back again in my own home."[90]

90. *OSWCC*, August 16, 1910.

This rare account is valuable because it provides us with a snapshot of the interactions Kanekatoku had with his visitors. The sad and whimsical portrait that emerges evokes his longing for Hokkaido.

The other firsthand account we have of the Ainu village in London was written by Uchigasaki Sakusaburo.[91] Uchigasaki was not like the majority of Japanese residents in London, who saw the Ainu and Japanese villages in the exposition as a disgrace to Japan's national character. Uchigasaki "felt proud to be Japanese and he felt pity for those unperceptive Japanese who were unhappy with the exposition." His feelings were reflected in how he treated the Japanese artisans and workers at the fair and the Ainu, with whom he visited and chatted. Uchigasaki described the atmosphere of the Ainu village:

In the first hut, an old man of fifty or sixty, sitting with one knee raised, was bowing politely to the visitors who peeped into the hut. The second hut, which contained a family of six[,] was very popular with the crowds. I went into the third one, which received many visitors. As one of the Ainus pushed himself out of the crowds, I asked him if he spoke Japanese. He indeed spoke excellent Japanese. He appeared to be a bright middle-age man[,] with a thick black beard. When I began to ask many questions about the Ainu, we were surrounded by a crowd of about fifty or sixty people. A kind old woman said sympathetically that it could not be pleasant to be surrounded by such a big crowd and worried what it would be like on a hot summer day.[92]

Uchigasaki helped Kaizawa Kenji and his son, Chūji, move through the large crowds so they could get to a space clear of people where Chūji could play. He then described them in detail:

This man was called Kaizawa Kenji and he had come with his wife and their three or four year old son. The visitors were very friendly towards them and began to give some coins to the boy. According to Kaizawa, he was the first Ainu to join the Japanese army. He was very pleased to be able to explain his customs and traditions to many visitors through my interpretation. I promised that I would see him again and expressed my hope that

91. Uchigasaki, *Eikoku yori*; "Ainu mura no daihanjō," 47–48.
92. Uchigasaki, *Eikoku yori*, 245–46.

I would see a growth in the Ainu population in Japan. I had seen the Ainus before when I was very small, but it was the first time I had ever spoken to them. Kaizawa and the old man left me with a very good impression of them and I think that it would be our duty to preserve and keep the Ainu race in Japan. I would like to draw to the attention of our nationals that it is important to give an adequate education to the Ainus so as to give them the same opportunities as the Japanese.[93]

Uchigasaki's sympathetic feelings for the Ainu and his call to promote educational opportunities for them put him in a small but vocal minority of progressive Japanese who advocated on behalf of the Ainu people. Compared with the rude treatment the Ainu experienced in Tokyo before they departed for London, Japanese like Uchigasaki illustrated the diversity of Japanese opinion about the Ainu. Still, for every person sympathetic to the Ainu's situation, there were others who made fun of them. One British visitor sent a postcard that featured Kanekatoku's image to a Miss Dawkins, writing, "This is a gentleman we saw in the Aino home. How would you like him for a young man. A. L."[94]

Besides the tone of such written messages on postcards, the cards' pictures themselves reveal information about the experiences of the Ainu in London. The images on two postcards depicting the Ainu village, for example, appear at first glance to be identical, but there are some crucial differences. Comparing a black-and-white card with a hand-colored version of the same photograph, it is clear that the light just under the eaves of the building and the amusement ride visible beyond the fence have been airbrushed out of the colored image. Two attendants who appear in the background in the black-and-white photo have been erased in the color version. These changes serve the same purpose—to make the Ainu village look more authentic by erasing any indications that it was a constructed set. Thousands of copies of the color postcard were sold, while the black-and-white version was not mass produced; the indicators that marked the Ainu village as contrived were caught just in time.[95]

93. English translation in Hotta-Lister, *Japan-British Exhibition*, 143–44. She did not translate all of Uchigasaki's writings. Original text in Uchigasaki, *Eikoku yori*, 244–48.

94. Author's collection, KZW.

95. See KZW.

The erasure of the things that disrupted the picture's representation of authenticity reminds us that the authenticity of the Ainu exhibit was constantly under construction, not only by the participants but also by others like the postcard makers. Just as tourists who go to Egypt today take strategic photos of the pyramids that crop out the modern buildings in the background, the alteration of the postcard image sought to eradicate anything that called the scene's authenticity into question.

In another example of the contrast between perception and reality, information in the exhibition's guidebook, which described the Ainu almost romantically "as a dying race comparable to Native Americans," differed greatly from the information in less conventional sources from the same time.[96] For example, police reports in the local newspapers in the Hammersmith and Fulham city archives in London tell the following story regarding the Ainu. In mid-October Shirabeno, Anretoku, and Zensuke appeared at a courthouse in west London for the trial of a man accused of robbery in the Ainu village on October 8. With a Japanese official translating for them, each Ainu witness took the oath in English. According to the *West London Observer*:

> The principal witness was the wife who stated that on the previous Saturday her husband was dancing on the platform in the village, and she was lying down, ill in the cottage. Presently she heard the sound of the chink of money, and she looked up and saw the prisoner in the act of putting money into his left hand coat pocket. He then crawled out of the cottage and afterwards her husband came back and found that his wallet had been stolen from a bamboo basket. She saw the prisoner that day amongst other men at the Police Station, and she picked him out. She knew him well, as he used to work at the Ainu village. Evidence was also given by the Ainu boy, by the name Zensky [*sic*], who said he saw the prisoner come out of the cottage. He had previously been playing with him.[97]

The defendant, William Bustin, a thirty-four-year-old laborer who had worked as an attendant at the Ainu village, was accused of stealing "a leather wallet, containing two pounds, two schillings and six pence

96. *Japan British Exhibition, 1910 Official Guide*, 89.
97. *WLO*, October 21, 1910.

and a receipt for 300 yen, the property of Shirabeno, a farmer." A week later the verdict was announced: "The defendant (Bustin) denied the charge and it was stated that he had hitherto borne an excellent character. The magistrate did not think that any jury would convict, and he discharged the accused."[98] Numerous thefts occurred at the exposition, some leading to sentences of hard labor.[99] The fact that the magistrate did not think any jury would believe the word of the Ainu family over a British man speaks to the reality of the Ainu's situation. Still, the matter had been taken to court; the Ainu had not been denied the right to attempt to gain justice. Looking at the postcards again, the erasure of the two attendants in the compound strikes a chord with the story of the robbery by William Bustin, who had also worked as an attendant in the Ainu village. Just like the postcards, events like the robbery, although not recorded in the official histories, reveal the nonperformative aspects of exposition life. The police reports push back against a characterization of the Ainu as solely representative figures (exemplars of a dying race). They remind us they were actually real people with diverse experiences.

The experience of living in the Ainu exhibit was not limited to meeting curious visitors. Real life went on for the Ainu participants, and on August 31, 1910, Kaizawa Kenji's wife, Utarashino, gave birth to a baby boy.[100] Headlines proclaimed: "First Ainu Baby Born in Europe!"[101] A christening ceremony for the new baby was held shortly afterward.[102] According to the local Fulham birth registry, the baby was named Hidehiro (also referred to as Eihaku in some documents).[103] The characters of his name (英博) literally mean "England" and "exposition," and Hamada explained that "he was named in commemoration of their going to

98. *WLO*, October 28, 1910.

99. *WLO*, July 8, 1910. Fushine of the 1903 Human Pavilion also had his wallet stolen. The robberies indicate that the large amount of money they received made them targets for thieves.

100. Birth certificate for Kaizawa Hidehiro, 31 August 1910, Fulham Registration District, Birth in the Sub-district of North Hammersmith in the County of London, General Register Office.

101. On September 2, 1910, *WLO* mistakenly reported the baby to be a girl.

102. *WLO*, September 16, 1910.

103. Birth certificate for Kaizawa Hidehiro.

England."[104] Baby Hidehiro survived the return journey back to Japan but later died at the age of twenty-three years.[105]

EXPOSITION AS LABORATORY

In London, as in St. Louis, the exposition site became a research laboratory for scientists and anthropologists. Most notably, Polish scholar Bronisław Piłsudski, who had lived in Karafuto for more than twenty years and conducted research in Hokkaido, worked closely with the Ainu in London. Piłsudski was fluent in the Ainu language and had recorded many of their oral stories that had been passed down through the generations. This was not his first encounter with Ainu who participated in such human displays; as detailed in chapter 1, he had met the stranded Dōtonbori Ainu in Sapporo in 1903 and given them money to complete their journey to Shiraoi. He wrote about his fortuitous chance to meet the Ainu in London in 1910, proclaiming, "I received permission from the Exposition authorities to talk freely with the natives as much as I chose. Notwithstanding the necessary inconvenience and drawbacks of conversation under such circumstances as accompany a public exposition, I was able to note down a great many valuable data, especially as concerns folklore; I wrote out more than fifty tales."[106]

Piłsudski thought his interactions with the Ainu in London lifted their spirits: "They were extremely pleased to find themselves treated, not as curiosities or beasts in a show, but as men; my talks with them raised the level of their dignity as members of the same human family, and they felt deeply grateful."[107] Piłsudski stayed in London throughout the exposition and became "their assiduous friend." With their help, he was able to review and complete 300 Ainu texts he had at hand, as well as his Ainu dictionary of 8,000 words, including 1,000 words that had not previously been recorded.[108]

104.   Hamada, "Nibutani no ekashi" (1991), 172.
105.   *KS*, December 15, 1910. In the papers of Dr. Munro held at the Royal Anthropological Institute in London, Hidehiro's death is confirmed, as are that of all the children of Kenji and Utarashino from tuberculosis in 1935, including Chūji. ("Relationships of Kaizawa Kusuashte, set 53," Dr. Neil Gordon Munro papers, MS 249/2/9, Royal Anthropological Institute).
106.   Piłsudski and Rozwadowski, *Materials*, xiv–xv.
107.   Piłsudski and Rozwadowski, *Materials*, xiv–xv.
108.   Rousselot, "Phonétique," 8.

French linguist L'Abbé Rousselot, a friend of Piłsudski's and a professor of phonetics at the Collége de France, came to the exposition in mid-August to undertake a linguistic study of the Ainu language.[109] For eight days, during the Ainu's free time, he and the Ainu participants worked in a large room Rousselot called "a wonderful laboratory," in a hotel near the exposition grounds.[110] He also took a portable recorder with him to the Ainu village and made recordings there.

Rousselot found the Ainu to be gentle, confident, and eager to please. "Once, I met resistance," he recalled. "Mr. Pilsudski asked for a young girl's love song (usually when an Ainu woman composed her own song of love for her fiancé). At our insistence she [Kokin] resisted, first with tears and then finally saying that she could not sing in front of men of her country. They went out, and she sang with grace."[111] Recording the language of the Ainu involved using a device that had special palates attached to two drums: one for the mouth, the other for the nose. Kanekatoku, Shirabeno, and Kokin used the recording machine skillfully. Rousselot had each person repeat the same word or sentence numerous times, which gave him some interesting variants he could use for controls.[112] Besides Piłsudski and Rousselot, the Ainu manager Yoshida recounted other kinds of visitors, including an artist who came to draw them, photographers, and a designer who studied the architecture of the Ainu houses.[113]

SIGHTSEEING IN LONDON

The Ainu often went sightseeing around London or were invited to Londoners' homes.[114] In his memoirs, British journalist Philip Gibbs wrote how he once rode around London atop a double-decker bus with one of the Ainu.[115] Yoshida recalled how "once, the group dressed in their

109.   Piłsudski and Rozwadowski, *Materials*, xv; *KS*, December 15, 1910; Rousselot, "Phonétique," 8.
110.   Rousselot, "Phonétique," 10.
111.   Rousselot, "Phonétique," 10.
112.   Rousselot, "Phonétique," 11; see KZW.
113.   The Ainu manager Yoshida mentioned two scholars, one from Poland and one from Paris. *KS*, December 15, 1910.
114.   Hamada, "Nibutani no ekashi" (1991), 169–70.
115.   Gibbs, *England Speaks*, 176; Gibbs, *Crowded Company*, 81. The *Sydney Morning Herald*, February 4, 1950, also mentions Gibbs's meeting with the Ainu.

distinctive Ainu clothing strolled in the large city that sparkled like a galaxy."[116] Shirabeno, Anretoku, and Zensuke went on a tour around London by motorcar, which was explained to the family as something that was like a wagon that runs without oxen. "The little boy laughed with glee as it shot forward along Holland Park Avenue. They looked at the mansions along Bayswater Road with admiration and when Shirabeno asked what kind of people lived in them he was told that they were the homes of rich people." They also went to Ellington Park and visited Buckingham Palace.[117]

From these accounts it is clear that the Ainu were often outside the exposition grounds. Zensuke went to a nearby British school where he played with the children. He made many good friends and learned to speak English very well. His parents encouraged him to play with the children who came to the exposition. Through these interactions, it was observed that Zensuke was very bright and had the capability to do well in school, which led to an offer to have him stay in London for his education and train to be a doctor.[118] Although he wanted to stay, his parents refused. Years later, during the height of a tuberculosis epidemic that ravaged his village in the 1930s, Zensuke would wonder whether he might have better helped his community if he had indeed stayed in London and then returned to Hokkaido.[119]

Before the Ainu left London, they sent a message to Piłsudski. Their letter was published in the newspaper after their departure, under the title "Ainus' Farewell: How London Impressed the Curious People":

> We had heard long ago of the great English country and its beautiful capital, London, but we never have thought before that we might see it some day. It happened so that we have passed more than six months in London, and though we are gladdened by the prospect of seeing again our country and those who are our nearest, yet we are sorry that we have to leave. We have seen so many things not known before to us, and were astonished to

116. *KS*, December 15, 1910.
117. *Grey River Argus*, October 14, 1910. Translated into Japanese in *TA*, September 28, 1910.
118. Kaizawa Seiko interview, December 2010, and written correspondence, Yamagishi, March 8, 2014.
119. Hamada, "Nibutani no ekashi" (1991), 170.

see waters gushing out of the earth, vanishing and coming again to our houses. (A reference to the water supply.) We have seen light coming out of the earth when a button was pressed down, and the light running up a mountain before our eyes. We admired the length of the town, which has no beginning and no end. We admired the cars running of themselves, the innumerable throng of people, high houses where people are living one above the others; marvelous animals we have never seen before (a reminiscence of the zoo). We were delighted by the tall figures of men and women.

But most of all we were astonished and captivated by the kindness of the people of England, and still more by the kind and tender heart of the English women. For this we feel more grateful than for anything we admired, and when we return to our country we shall tell our people of this rich country, of the Women of the Good Heart, that the tale might be transmitted to our children and grand-children.[120]

While their letter spoke of their positive memories, they had faced hardships: being robbed, enduring the cold, facing crowds of people, and the tedium of exposition life. Once they arrived back in Japan after their year in London, a reporter asked them how they would describe their experience in England. One of the Ainu replied, "There were interesting times, but we also faced some trouble." They talked about performing the Ainu dance every day. When they were asked what the most interesting thing was, one member of the group said it was leaving the port in Singapore and seeing the huge expanse of ocean before them, as the waves made the 8,600-ton ship shake like leaves on a tree.[121]

Another report told how Kenji and Utarashino, who had their baby in London and named him "English Exposition," had sent home 3,500 yen in savings.[122] A lot of the Ainu's money came from British fairgoers, who gave money to the children and showered the baby with attention. The Ainu's monetary success at the Japan-British Exhibition was apparent. On arriving back in Tokyo, the group visited the Mitsukoshi department store where, Kanekatoku reported with pride, each person spent forty to fifty yen on "mountain like piles" of Japanese souvenirs and goods.[123]

120. *Daily News*, November 2, 1910. Reprinted in Japanese: *OS*, December 21, 1910.
121. *TA*, December 16, 1910.
122. *TNNSB*, December 18, 1910.
123. *TNNSB*, February 18, 1910.

The Ainu were impressed by London, particularly the large parks, the fully equipped transport system, and the magnificent homes. At the time of their departure, the Ainu had warmly shaken hands with the British people seeing them off and the British women had kissed the Ainu women good-bye, causing Kokin to be very embarrassed.[124] They were given presents, including watches, and they wore brand-new Western clothes, as they had traded their *attush* clothing for frock coats.[125]

According to his grandchildren, when Shirabeno returned to Nibutani, he regaled the villagers with his tales of London. He talked about being with the Taiwanese Aborigines and about his experience riding the subway for the first time, remarking, "I thought it was a house, and I entered, and was there for a little, and then the house began to move, and house began to run; I was surprised." Zensuke's impressions of London were recorded when he returned:

> Everyone treated me very well, they invited me to come out and play and took me out to dinner at different places. I also received a ton of interesting things. When we went sightseeing around London, Kenji and I wore Western clothes and wore shoes. Everything was really interesting, but the most interesting was when we saw the Thames from London Bridge. I also saw an airplane flying.[126]

Years later, Hamada recalled how his father, Zensuke, talked about how he had played with British boys and been invited to people's houses.

One poignant memory for Zensuke was stopping at the ports of England's colonies on their return. They sailed into Bombay, Calcutta, Singapore, and Hong Kong. While the ships were docked for a night or two, Zensuke would gaze at the harbors. Locals would paddle out to the ship in little boats, and he remembered passengers on the ship throwing coins into the water and the people in the boats jumping into the sea to get the money.

124. *TNNSB*, February 18, 1910.
125. *KS*, December 15, 1910.
126. *TNNSB*, February 18, 1910.

AFTER THEIR RETURN

Hamada said he did not know how much money his grandfather had received from his time abroad, but each day at the exposition visitors to the Ainu exhibit had put money in a rucksack, which filled to the brim with coins and bills. This money supplemented the salary they were paid of one yen a day until their return to Japan. During their absence the Kaizawa family had left the running of the farm to their hired laborers, and Hamada speculated that to take a break from farming for a year they must have received a very good income from the exhibition. From the time Shirabeno returned from England until the beginning of the Showa period (1926), he enjoyed prosperity, although there were also difficulties. There was a time when his family had more than 100 horses, and there was one year when the winter's snowfall was so heavy that about sixty horses died. Nevertheless, Shirabeno always remained in good spirits.[127]

In a film featuring the Ainu bear ceremony made by Scottish doctor and anthropologist Neil Gordon Munro in the 1930s, Shirabeno and Anretoku are shown greeting Munro.[128] Shirabeno collaborated on the project with Munro, who lived in Nibutani and studied the Ainu culture for twelve years, until his death in 1942. Shirabeno and Anretoku's house served as the backdrop for the film, further illustrating the centrality of their role in Nibutani. Since Shirabeno had agreed to help Munro, other Ainu in the community followed suit, including many who had also participated in the international expositions.

Interestingly, if one looks at the photographs Munro took of Shirabeno and the other Ainu (including Pete Gorō, who is pictured in another, similar photograph held in the archives) who helped him with his research without knowing Shirabeno's and the others' history, it would be easy to see the photos simply as a Westerner's classification of Ainu anthropometry (fig. 2.17). The fact that Munro recorded the names of the people on the backs of their portraits shows that it mattered to him who they were. Nevertheless, in his book *Ainu Creed and Cult*, he treats his

127.   Hamada, "Nibutani no ekashi" (1991), 172.

128.   Uchida, "A Witness to History: Photographic Introduction to Items from the Collection," http://www.rekihaku.ac.jp/english/outline/publication/rekihaku/141/witness .html (accessed August 2, 2018). Kayano recalled being at the bear ceremony that Munro filmed at Shirabeno's house (*Iyomante no hanaya*).

informants as one-dimensional vessels of knowledge about Ainu culture and not as complex individuals—despite the fact that Shirabeno, for example, was a powerful leader and in 1931 had sold Munro the land on which he built his house.[129] We must read each source—whether visual, oral, or material—within the context of other sources, to ensure that our understanding of colonial subjects is not limited by one source's characterization.

Zensuke worked for Munro as his assistant in the 1930s. In Munro's notes and letters at the Royal Anthropological Institute in London, he mentions Zensuke's role in helping him interview Ainu *ekashi* (elders) for *Ainu Creed and Cult*. According to Zensuke's daughter Kaizawa Seiko, her father encouraged the people in Nibutani to try to live like people in the West. To improve his community's living conditions, he urged his children to become educated, and he became a member of the town council. Shirabeno worked to improve the lot of the villagers and also joined the town council. In particular, he worked to protect the Ainu farmland in Kasenshiki and suggested the construction of a levee to protect the land from the damage inflicted by heavy rains. He used his own money to help those in Nibutani.[130]

When Sister Inez Hilger, an anthropologist who studied indigenous people all over the world, visited Hokkaido in the 1960s, she asked people who the last great Ainu leaders in their area were. Kayano Shigeru told Hilger that he remembered "Shirampano [*sic*]" to be "a dignified leader in the Nibutani area."[131] Shirabeno died in 1943, while his grandson Hamada was serving in the army in Manchuria.[132] For the Kaizawa family, the family's journey across the ocean was something they continued to carry with them. In 1998 Hamada journeyed to London to walk where his grandfather and father had once walked.[133]

129. Ainu Bunka Shinkō Kenkyū Suishin Kikō (ed.), *Umi wo watatta*, 171.
130. Yamagishi, written correspondence, February 2014.
131. Hilger, *Together with the Ainu*, 104.
132. Hamada, "Nibutani no ekashi" (1991), 174.
133. *AS*, July 22, 1999.

FIG. 2.17. Munro's photographs of informants; they are named on the back of the photo. Second row center is Kaizawa Uesanashi who went to the 1912 Tokyo and 1913 Osaka expositions. Third row left is Kaizawa Shirabeno; third row center is Zensuke. Credit: 300_249-01-19.01. "Some Ainu portraits." N.G. Munro Collection, 1930s © RAI.

CHAPTER 3

The Paupers' Grave at Margravine Cemetery

Unlike the Ainu participants at the 1910 Japan-British Exhibition (discussed in the previous chapter), tracing the Taiwanese Aborigine participants and their experiences in London proved to be more elusive. They did leave tangible clues regarding their London experiences, but these clues—oral, visual, and material—have remained disparate traces until now. When viewed as a whole, these traces counter previous one-dimensional depictions of the indigenous Taiwanese participants' time in London as a way to view Japan's modern civilizing mission. In fact, the 1910 exposition, in which the Japanese were displayed in villages, just like the Ainu and indigenous Taiwanese, did more to complicate understandings of imperial hierarchies than to reinforce them.

The Story of the Taiwanese Aborigines

After their year in London at the Japan-British Exhibition, the Aborigines (of the Paiwan ethnic group) stopped in Japan before the final leg of their journey back to Taiwan. Reporters asked them what had been the saddest time at the exposition for them. They responded that it had been the death of a member of their group, Ruji Suruchan, who had died of a heart attack, they said.[1] Another Japanese newspaper report identified Ruji as a woman.[2]

Determined to find out more about this death, I scoured the archives in London and Japan, looking for any mention of it. I was finally able to locate a death certificate registered in the Fulham district of London that revealed the following details. On October 25, 1910, Ruji Suruchan, an eighteen-year-old male, died at the Hammersmith infirmary, located near the exposition grounds of the Japan-British Exhibition in Shepherd's Bush. His cause of death was listed as "gastric ulcer and perforation shock."[3] Ruji's death was kept under wraps and not reported in the major or local British newspapers. Besides two sentences in one Japanese newspaper, his death was not mentioned during the exposition, nor is the story known today. Hoping to find out more, I searched the burial records at the Fulham archives in London and almost missed the listing of his death because he was recorded as "Ruggi Swinehard."

Although the name was spelled differently, in the column of the register headed "who brought the deceased" the Japan-British Exhibition was named, and the age given matched that on the death certificate for Ruji Suruchan. According to the registry he had been buried in an unmarked, unconsecrated mass grave (paupers' grave) in the Margravine Cemetery in Hammersmith on October 27, 1910. The cemetery was right next door to the archives, so I decided to seek his gravesite with the help of a map given to me by the archivist. I came across the part of the cemetery where he was buried, but there was no gravestone or marker to identify the space as his final resting place or that of the countless others buried there with him (fig. 3.1).

When Ruji Suruchan's death was mentioned in the Japanese newspaper, he was mistakenly identified as a woman. Furthermore, the person who wrote his name in the burial registry in London transformed it by giving his foreign name an Anglo-Saxon version: Ruggi Swinehard.

1. *KS*, February 13, 1910.

2. *OM*, December 15, 1910.

3. Death certificate for Ruji Suruchan, October 25, 1910, Fulham Registration District, Birth in the Sub-district of North Hammersmith in the County of London, General Register Office, UK. See KZW for death certificate, image of Ruji Suruchan, and burial records.

FIG. 3.1. Site of unmarked paupers' grave where Ruji Suruchan was buried in London's Margravine Cemetry in 1910. Credit: Author.

His death, which occurred in a London hospital just four days before the Ainu and the Taiwanese Aborigines were to depart for Japan, was an anonymous affair, his burial took place without ceremony, and his final resting place was an unmarked grave thousands of miles from his Taiwanese home village. British officials distorted his name, and Japanese reporters changed his gender. His death mattered little to anyone except the other Taiwanese Aborigines in his group, who mourned him and said his death was the most distressing thing about the exposition.

The death of Ruji Suruchan, revealed by a subaltern's utterance but not found in the exposition histories, nor in the countless documents about the Japan-British Exhibition, demonstrates the human dimension of the subaltern experience. Nothing during the Paiwan participants' time in London caused them more grief than the death of one of their own. That their statement was verifiable—even if through distorted renderings—reminds us that subaltern histories are indeed traceable, and they can reveal histories that are not part of the official narrative.

In contrast to the individual narratives that emerged from the Ainu who went to London, stories about the individual Paiwan participants involved in the exposition's "Formosa Hamlet" were more elusive. Children of one of the participants, Chaibaibai, were interviewed by the Japanese channel Nihon Hōsō Kyōkai (NHK) for its 2009 documentary series *Japan Debut*.[4] They said that their father had never talked about his time in London, and they were shocked to see his image when the producers showed them a postcard from the exposition.[5] This documentary provoked controversy in Japan and Taiwan. First at issue was the filmmakers' labeling of the Formosa Hamlet as a "human zoo" (*ningen dobutsuen*). Second, Chaibaibai's daughter, on seeing the postcard of her father, was reported as commenting, "It's too sad, I can't talk about it." She later said the interview was edited to make it seem like she and her brother were ashamed of their father's role in the Formosa Hamlet, when in reality they were saddened only by seeing him in the photograph. The Paiwan translator said that the Japanese interviewers had never used the words "human zoo" when they asked their questions and criticized the translation as inaccurate.[6] Criticism also arose over the fact that Chaibaibai's son was so infirm that he was not coherent, and some said filming him had been exploitative.

The backlash against the NHK program was led by a conservative Japanese TV channel, Japan Cultural Channel Sakura, and supported by some Paiwan representatives, as well as some of the Taiwanese interviewed for the documentary, who said their positive statements about Japan had been edited out. The controversy led to two class-action lawsuits filed against NHK in 2009, with the involvement of the Paiwan (fig. 3.2) and more than 10,000 people.

Although these class-action suits were not successful, the controversy surrounding NHK's documentary illustrated the continuing struggle over how the indigenous people of Taiwan fit into the legacy of colonial rule. Some Taiwanese of Han ethnicity, whose views of the colonial period ranged from ambivalent to nostalgic, criticized NHK's negative portrayal of the Japanese colonization of Taiwan. In contrast, Paiwan representatives

4. I am using the spelling of Chaibaibai that was given in the documentary. The postcard that features him spells his name as Chaibai Pujajon.

5. "Shiri-zu Japan debū."

6. See http://mamoretaiwan.blog100.fc2.com/blog-entry-1792.html (accessed August 2, 2018).

パイワン族の名誉を汚したのか、その子孫である
人たちを傷つけたのか、全く理解できません。

FIG. 3.2. A still from the press conference regarding the class-action lawsuit against NHK, October 6, 2009. A Paiwan representative holds an image from the NHK documentary. She stated: "The honor of the Paiwan is damaged, and we can't understand why they hurt our descendants." © Japan Cultural Channel SAKURA.

pushed back against labeling the Formosa Hamlet as a human zoo, which they said rendered the Paiwan as people to be pitied.

Unlike the Ainu from Nibutani, whose descendants have shaped and informed their relatives' legacy by retelling their stories, less is known about how the Paiwan participants experienced their time in London. Why is there such a discrepancy? First, although stories were told by the Paiwan participants during and after their journey, as I will show, there are no accounts from their descendants. Second, the Formosa Hamlet simply generated less interest at the exposition in comparison to the Ainu village. The lack of interest in the Paiwan as individuals resulted from the fact that although the Ainu were romanticized and beautified and seen by many as relics of an idealized past, the Paiwan were depicted as violent savages who loved war and headhunting. We see this in the account of a British woman, Charlotte Salwey, who wrote after her visit to the exposition,

The mild Ainu, barbaric, still in many ways quiet, gentle, inert and contented to-day, brought with them a savour of Old Japan. The Ainu contrasted widely with the furious "head-hunters," who sojourned for the time being in the Formosa Sha [village] at Shepherd's Bush, for their warlike weapons were always ready to hand, decorated with trophies of human hair depending therefrom. The very manner in which these men prepared and consumed their food was a sufficient guarantee of their savage descent.[7]

The Paiwan people did engage in headhunting, as did the Atayal and Bunun. The practice was a tradition associated with the passage into manhood and linked to notions of bravery. But British writers did not attempt to explain this and instead transformed it and other customs into examples of savagery.

Given the relative lack of oral histories, postcards from the Japan-British Exhibition—their images and what was written on them—have become one of the most important tools for verifying the experiences of the Paiwan in London. An analysis of postcards featuring Formosa Hamlet participants reveals that their activities extended beyond simply being on display and in fact included learning English and communicating with fairgoers. The postcards illustrate their experiences at the exposition in a valuable, multidimensional way.

The Paiwan experience is substantiated by the writings of an Englishman named William Price, whose diary and private papers are found at the Kew Gardens Botanical Archives. In 1912 Price, a botanist, traveled throughout Taiwan and visited the Paiwan people who had gone to London for the exposition. His diary, which is discussed later in the chapter, provides a fascinating view of the Paiwan people. Price saw them as more sophisticated than the Japanese who ruled over them, owing to their facility with English and their courteous manners.

Throughout the exposition, the characterization of the Paiwan participants as savages coincided with an almost nonexistent photographic record of them in comparison with the Ainu.[8] One British postcard company, Valentine's, published a six-card series of color postcards depicting the Ainu village, as well as black-and-white cards depicting Chūji and Kokin, who were popular with fairgoers; the only image of the

7. Salwey, "Japanese Monographs no. XV," 351.
8. The Paiwan were pictured in Japanese newspapers during their journey to London and upon their return. There were no photographs in the British papers.

Tugie Kalowan, Chief.

Formosa Village. Japan. British Exhibition 1910.

Famous "head-hunter" of tribe. Has taken 37 heads. His signature in back of card. P.T.O.

FIG. 3.4. "Tugie Kalowan, Chief." Credit: Bill Tonkin

Baruharu—Chaco.

FIG. 3.3. "Baruharu-Chaco." Credit: Bill Tonkin

Formosa Hamlet printed by a major postcard company featured a hut in the village, without any Paiwan people.[9]

The contrast between the eight cards that featured the Ainu and the one black and white card showing the Formosa village symbolically illustrates people's emotional detachment from the Paiwan at the exposition. It seems that the first postcard company gambled that the Formosa Hamlet would not be popular and produced no cards of that exhibit and its participants; at the same time, it elected to produce several cards featuring Uji Village (the Japanese village) and the Ainu village.

Postcards of the people in the Formosa village were eventually produced but were printed by a private company or individual unrelated to the major British postcard manufacturers. The cards that feature Paiwan individuals from the Formosa Hamlet have no identifying language linked to a manufacturer or to the exposition (fig. 3.3). For one postcard collector, Bill Tonkin, it was only when he came across the card titled "Tugie Kalowan, Chief" with notes written on it by a fairgoer that he realized the card depicted a man from the Formosa Hamlet (fig. 3.4).[10] The fairgoer's notes identify the scene as "Formosa Village, Japan-British Exhibition" and describe the man pictured: "Famous 'head-hunter' of tribe. Has taken 37 heads. His signature on of back of card." In stark contrast to postcards of the Ainu exhibit, countless numbers of which were circulated and which can be easily found today, far fewer cards featuring the Paiwan were circulated, and they are hard to find. The scarcity of actual photographs of the Formosa Hamlet, absent those in the Japanese newspapers, make the postcards even more important. For twenty-three of the twenty-four Paiwan participants, cards were printed with their name and image (and one person's photograph was identified with two different names). There is also one postcard from the series that features twelve participants with the group's manager.

Among the Paiwan participants, three were women; two men were identified as chiefs (the only two Paiwan identified with any information beyond their name). Each of the chiefs is posed holding a knife, raised high, in his right hand (see fig. 3.4). This staged but menacing

9.   See KZW.

10.   For years, British collector Bill Tonkin sought out cards from the Formosa village, eventually collecting more than thirty. I have eight cards in my collection, some acquired from Tonkin and a few purchased at postcard fairs in London.

FIG. 3.5. Postcard captioned "Taiwan Savages." Digital image courtesy of East Asia Image Collection, Lafayette College Libraries, Easton, PA.

posture was a common motif in contemporaneous postcards featuring Taiwanese Aborigines, like fig. 3.5, which had several Tsou men brandishing daggers.

By studying the cards in Tonkin's collection and my own, I have been able to discern patterns in how they were circulated. The Paiwan earned some income by selling these postcards; according to one report, visitors coveted them.[11] The Paiwan would authenticate the postcards as souvenirs by writing their signatures on them, signing their names in Japanese katakana, Chinese characters (kanji), or English letters—sometimes in cursive, sometimes even written backward (fig. 3.6). This mix of signature styles serves as a telling snapshot of the Taiwanese Aborigines' position as colonial subjects living abroad. Unlike souvenir postcards of the Ainu, of which I have found only one signed in katakana, the Paiwan signed their cards in different ways, perhaps in an effort to practice their new language skills or accommodate purchasers of the cards.

A reporter who visited the Formosa Hamlet remarked how the Paiwan had been actively memorizing English, more so than the Ainu. They used

11. *TNNS*, September 9, 1910.

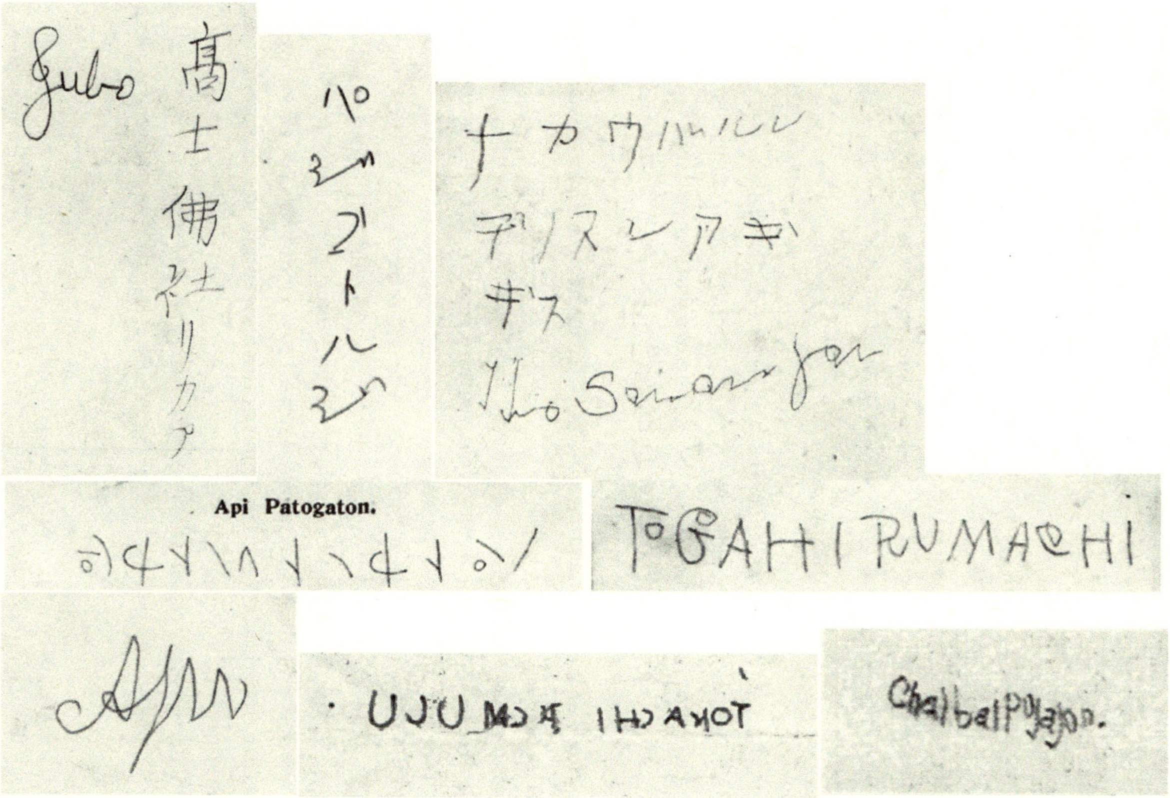

FIG. 3.6. Montage of Paiwan signatures from various postcards. Credit: Bill Tonkin and Kirsten Ziomek.

phrases like "thank you" and "good morning." The Paiwan said it was easier to memorize English than Japanese, and they were proud of their ability to speak English.[12] One postcard described a fairgoer's interactions with the Paiwan and confirmed reports about their ability to pick up English. On the back of a postcard labeled "Chaibai Pujajon," the visitor had written:

This is from the Exposition. We all shook hands with the man on the other side. They all seem to understand a little English and say how do you do, how are you, England very cold but nice people, goodbye and various other phrases. I'm just off to Fulham. Had a lovely time here. Oct 20th 1910.[13]

It is no coincidence that this postcard pictured Chaibaibai. On another postcard with his image on it he wrote his name in English, testifying to his skill with the language (fig. 3.6). A postcard with Chief Tugie Kalowan's picture on it described another fairgoer's interactions: "Formosan headhunter. This chief gave me his flute."[14]

The majority of the fair's Paiwan participants came from Kuskus village in Koshun (today known as Hengchun), southern Taiwan (see map 2). There are still residents in Kuskus who recall stories about those who went to London. In 2009, a seventy-two-year-old Kuskus resident named Valjluk Mavaliu told a Japanese reporter that as a boy he had heard others in the village speak of the people who went to London. It was said that the participants spoke English after they returned, and others in the village picked up some English from them. Valjluk sang part of an English song for the reporter from Channel Sakura. "How would I know this song, if it wasn't true?," he asked. He spoke of the Paiwan group's experience as a point of pride.[15]

The souvenir postcards also reveal that fairgoers mixed up whether the Paiwan were Japanese or Taiwanese Aborigines. The message written

12.   *TNNS*, September 9, 1910, January 8, 1911.
13.   Bill Tonkin collection.
14.   Bill Tonkin collection.
15.   He could identify six of the people who went to London. Interview on Channel Sakura TV program June 13, 2009.

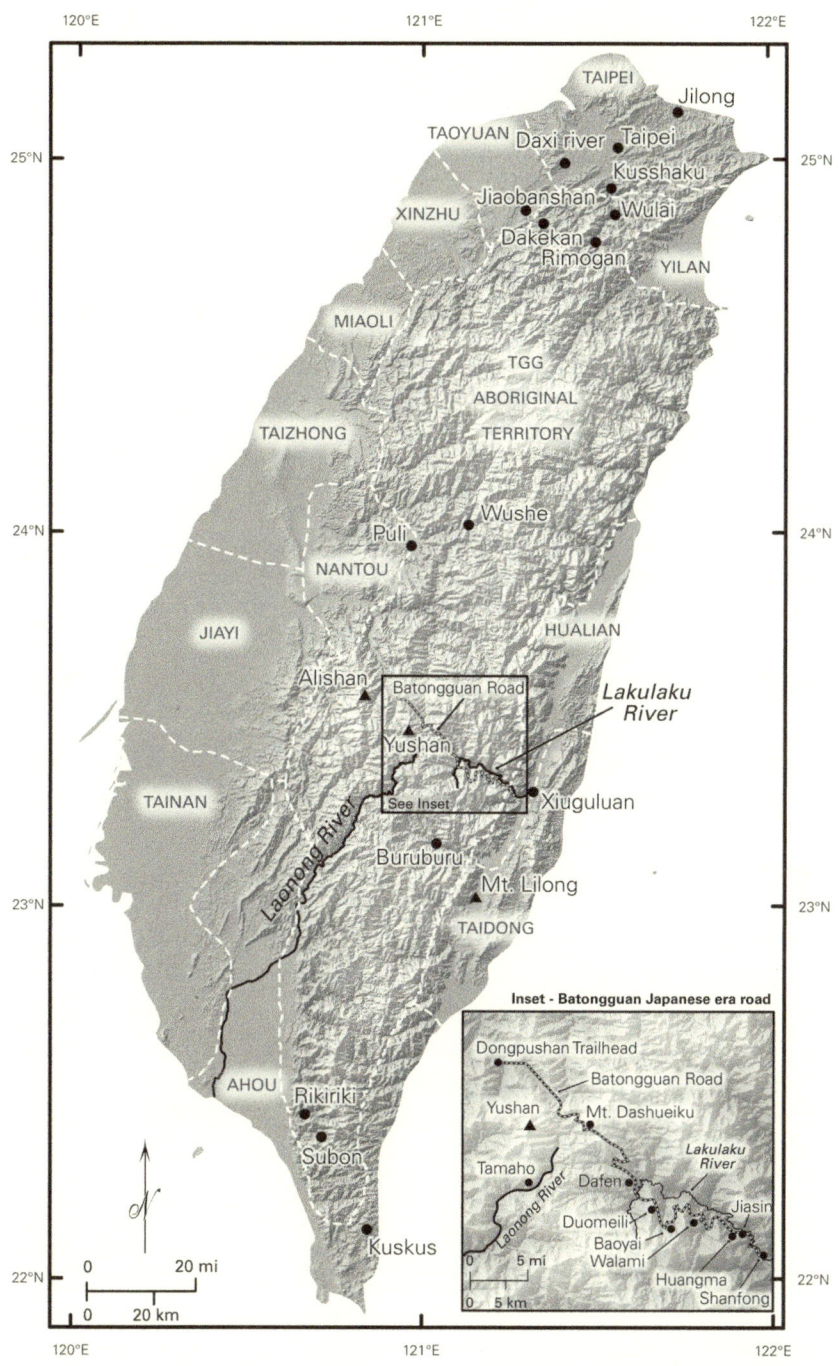

MAP 2. Taiwan circa 1930.

on a card bearing the image of Bachago Bagaban, one of the Paiwan, reads:

> Dear Gwyneth,
>   We went to the Jap Escibition [*sic*] last Saturday and spoke to the Japanese. This is a photo of one. Thank you for your postcard. I hope you are enjoying your holiday. Love from Olive Aug 25 1910.[16]

For British visitors, the line between the Taiwanese and Japanese at the exposition was blurred. In a letter to researcher George Ithell, Norah Gallagher, who as a young girl worked in the Irish village in the exposition, relayed her memory of making friends with the Paiwan chief.

> Near the village there was an Iron Jeliside [?] kiosk where I remember two kind ladies. There was also a Formosan village and I made friends with its chief, thus causing some apprehension. My father seems to have trusted these people but I remember that I was forbidden to go near the Japanese. . . .
>   Yours sincerely, Norah Gallagher 14 February 1986.[17]

Norah's interactions with the chief are substantiated by a postcard showing the Paiwan Togachi Rumuchi standing in front of a pillar that reads "Irish Village," indicating the proximity of the two villages. The meaning of Gallagher's sentence "My father seems to have trusted these people but I remember that I was forbidden to go near the Japanese" is ambiguous. Did she mean that her father trusted the Taiwanese, and not the Japanese, or was she referring to the Taiwanese Aborigines as Japanese? The conflation of the groups challenges the contention that the villages demonstrated how the Japanese were civilizing the savages, because at times the so-called savages were mistaken for Japanese.

In addition to interacting with British visitors, the Paiwan occasionally had Japanese visitors.[18] It was reported when Japanese fairgoers unexpectedly entered the village and asked if the Paiwan were from Tai-

16. Bill Tonkin collection.
17. Bill Tonkin collection; see KZW.
18. *TNNS*, September 9, 1910.

FIG. 3.7. Five "Sinicized" members of the Paiwan group that went to London. Credit: Endō Hiroya, *Taiwan banzoku shashinchō* (Taipei: Endō Hiroya, 1912), 54. Courtesy of the Archives of the Institute of Taiwan History, Academia Sinica.

pei, the Paiwan participants got very nostalgic and bowed politely, and there were even some who greeted them in Japanese.[19]

RECRUITMENT

It is not clear how the Paiwan individuals were selected to go to the exposition.[20] Those who participated were described as Sinicized, meaning their interactions with the Chinese during the Qing period had led them to take on Chinese manners (fig. 3.7). As we will see, the inclusion of Ainu, Formosa, and Japanese villages in the exposition was suggested by the British producer of the fair, not by the Japanese. Japan's colonial government officials were not thrilled about sending the Paiwan to London, fearing that any resulting unhappiness on the part of the Paiwan after their return could enflame anti-Japanese opposition on the island. A document

19. *TA*, July 6, 1910.
20. Yamaji, "Nichiei hakurankai," 10. For more on the Paiwan of Koshun and Kuskus in particular, see Barclay, *Outcasts of Empire*, 146–48.

sent by Japanese officials details an earnest appeal to exposition officials to ensure the protection of the Taiwanese Aborigines while abroad.[21] Like the Ainu, the terms of participation for the Paiwan were spelled out in a contract, and each person was to be paid one yen a day from the date of their departure to the date of their return. Participants and overseers were to be paid weekly in advance.[22] Yamaji Katsuhiko, a Japanese scholar, quantifies this awesome amount: "In 1900 a starting elementary school teacher's monthly salary was 10–13 yen and in 1918 a monthly salary was between 12 and 20 yen." According to government documents, among the Paiwan the least amount of money saved was 200 yen and the most was 500 yen.[23] Still, compared with the Ainu, they took home less money, and they also more than likely received less money from visitors.

LIFE IN THE FORMOSA HAMLET

The recognized leaders in the Paiwan group, identified as chiefs on the postcards and in Japanese newspapers, were Tugie Kalowan and Tibo Salongai.[24] According to the passenger list of the *Kagamaru*, which took them to London, two policemen, Itakura Jutarō and Ishikawa Tanozō, accompanied the group.[25] The presence of policemen with the Paiwan reflected how the Japanese colonial administration governed the indigenous Taiwanese compared with the Taiwanese of Han ethnicity. Police stations were set up in the indigenous areas of Taiwan, where they served as mediation points between indigenous communities and the colonial government. Although the presence of police officers with the Paiwan reinforced their image as ferocious people who posed a threat, in reality it reflected Japan's administrative relationship with the Aborigines.

21.   Yamaji, "Nichiei hakurankai," 10–11.

22.   Clause 7 and clause 12, "Formosa Hamlet Contract," accession no. 82.232/352, Museum of London.

23.   Yamaji, "Nichiei hakurankai," 11; Suzuki, *Taiwan no banzoku kenkyū*, 377.

24.   *TNNS*, September 9, 1910. I am using the spellings of participant names used on the postcards featuring each person; there are variable spellings of their names in Japanese katakana depending on the source.

25.   Copy of *Kagamaru* passenger list shown to me by Anne Wheeldon (personal copy) at the Hammersmith and Fulham Archives in April 2010. Ishikawa was in first-class steerage and Itakura in second-class. The Ainu manager, Yoshida Hideatsu, was in second class, while the Ainu and the Paiwan were in third class; see KZW.

Initially the Paiwan were unhappy in London and wanted to return to Taiwan. One of the first journalists to report on the Formosa Hamlet was Hasegawa Nyozekan of *Tokyo asahi*.[26] Hasegawa wrote in July that the exposition organizers had not fulfilled their contract and buildings and insulation were not completed, and the natives were suffering and wanted to return home. The Paiwan had arrived in London in late April, so when Hasegawa reported that they were unhappy, they had been in London for about two months. Hasegawa reported that the Japanese who accompanied the Paiwan remained close-lipped regarding whether they wanted to go or stay.

When a *Taiwan nichi nichi shinpō* reporter visited the Formosa Hamlet in September, four months into the exposition, he also formed the impression that the Paiwan wanted to go home. He speculated that they must not have known how far away England was. They had thought the journey would take a week, but it took two months and had been tedious. They also complained to their manager that for four months, since their arrival, they had been cooped up in small huts. They wanted to walk in the fields and mountains, but it was not allowed, and they were already getting tired of the exposition. The Paiwan thought the mountains of Taiwan were better than London, and they pressed the director for a quick return. On hearing this, the director called Taiwan and was told that if they returned halfway through the contract they would be cowards. He was told to assure them that if they stayed for the whole term, they would be able to bring back a lot of souvenirs from London. When the Paiwan learned they could not return, they became standoffish and quiet.[27] But the mood of the group improved when temperatures got warmer, and they began to feel revived.[28] When the reporter returned to their village three weeks later, at the end of the month, there was no longer any talk of going home.[29]

Life in the village finally settled into a routine, which was described as follows: the Paiwan participants awoke at 6:00 am and took a hot bath, then had an hour of recreation, after which they had breakfast at 8:00

26. Hasegawa was a well-known liberal social critic in the Taishō and Shōwa periods. Hotta-Lister, *Japan-British Exhibition*, 145.

27. *TNNS*, September 9, 1910.

28. *TA*, July 6, 1910.

29. *TNNS*, September 30, 1910.

am; at 12:30 they had lunch, and at 7:00 pm they had dinner; at 10:20 pm they went to sleep. They danced four times a day, reportedly for their health, and it was said that as a result they were as healthy as when they were home.[30] Instead of thinking of their health, exposition organizers probably saw entertaining audiences of fairgoers as the more important impetus for daily dancing. Their war dances were popular among the visitors, who described them as thrilling.[31] At the exposition the Paiwan were allowed to drink whiskey, which, their manager remarked, was doled out according to the circumstances, although they usually were given a lot to drink on Saturday and Sunday.[32] According to their contract, "Tobacco and liquor [were to] be given to the natives at the discretion of the overseers, the expense[s] of which devolve upon the second party."[33] This stood in contrast to the alcohol policy for the Ainu, who were forbidden to drink, owing to the belief that sake had been their downfall in the past.[34]

The Paiwan were presented as violent people even when they participated in special events held during the exposition. On a day set to celebrate Inari, the Japanese goddess of the rice harvest, every Japanese subject at the exposition participated (including those in the Japanese, Ainu, and Formosa villages), a total of 300 to 400 participants. The Taiwanese Aborigines had "spear throwing contests" and "a sham fight, demonstrating their methods of fighting and head hunting," performing alongside the Ainu, Japanese sumo wrestlers, and other Japanese entertainers.[35] Much of the reporting on the Paiwan focused on their so-called violent nature, which they may have played up to live up to their own reputation. "When the reporters from the newspapers tried to take the picture of the Taiwanese Aborigines they drew their swords. It was said if their food was late, they said the food tasted bad and they would take out their spears. The officials as a principle respect them and so would [concede to their demands], saying yes, yes." The Taiwanese Aborigines

30.   *TNNS*, September 9, 1910.

31.   *Japan British Exhibition: The Official Guide*, 88.

32.   *TNNS*, September 9, 1910.

33.   Clause 11 of "Formosa Hamlet Contract," accession no. 82.232/352, Museum of London.

34.   *OM*, February 18, 1910.

35.   *WLO*, August 19, 1910.

were reported to be carrying guns, spears, and knives. They were also said to have human hair from the scalps of those they killed hanging from their belts, and to have guns loaded with real bullets that they would not remove.[36] Inside their living quarters were guns, the bags used to carry heads when headhunting, spears, hatchets used for working in the mountains, and ceremonial wine cups.[37] The human hair can be seen in the images on the postcards (fig. 3.4), but the guns apparently were not theirs, as the Paiwan later said that they wished they owned the guns.

One of the British visitors to the Formosa Hamlet was journalist Alan Ostler, who had also visited the Ainu. He wrote:

> There I stayed a little while among savages, whose teeth are blackened with the perpetual chewing of the betel nut, who melt up the pennies and three penny bits given to them by visitors and convert them into copper bangles and silver earrings, whose chief complains that he does not think much of the garden allotted to him, because at home he has a far bigger one, with palings round it, and with 75 human heads on these palings.[38]

Those in the Formosa Hamlet received foreign visitors like Ostler, and they left the exposition grounds occasionally. They went on sightseeing trips around London, just as the Ainu did.[39] The *Daily News* reported, "Savage Formosans in their war paint, . . . made quite an unwonted stir" at London's Zoological Gardens in September. There, when the Formosans were met with photographers they

> exhibit[ed], in common with many English people, an antipathy to the camera, [and] the operators who sought to snapshot them unawares in the gardens had a lively time endeavouring to secure "cover" from which to operate. The whole of the gardens were visited, but the only place which seemed to arouse any exceptional interest was the monkey house, the Formosans especially shouting to the interpreter that here were animals such as they had at home.[40]

36. *TNNS*, May 26, 1910.
37. Yamaji, "Nichiei hakurankai," 11.
38. *OSWCC*, August 16, 1910.
39. *TNNS*, September 30, 1910.
40. *Daily News*, September 17, 1910.

When the British queen and king visited the Formosa village, the Japanese papers reported it, unlike the British papers.[41] According to the report, the visit was mutually uninspiring. The king and queen talked with the three Paiwan women, and for ten minutes they observed various items in the exhibit and took a photograph of the Paiwan group. One Japanese reporter was astounded that the queen and king had such little security, remarking that "even the policemen of Taiwan when they go to the native settlements bring with them numerous security guards, however with the King there were just two or three equerries that followed them." The Paiwan were equally surprised that the queen and king traveled so humbly by car and did not think the king had the appearance of royalty.[42]

One notable event in the Formosa village was the "birth of a baby to twenty-four-year-old Ruji Gadeku Rugayo, who had found out she was pregnant while at the exposition. The father of the baby was her betrothed, Chabibai Butsuapaberi [sic], who was also at the exposition and had been labeled a 'lady killer.'"[43] To avoid the potential scandal of having a child born out of wedlock at the exposition, it was reported that before the couple's departure for London, a marriage agreement had been arranged and wedding preparations had begun. In the meantime, because they were not married, they were not allowed live together. Reporters sensationalized the relationship with narratives like "Since they arrived in England they pursued this dangerous love in the dark and first light of the morning."[44] Rugayo gave birth in September to a boy, who was later named Hieihiro 日英博 (meaning "Japan-British Exhibition").[45] In remarkable contrast to the birth of the Ainu baby, which was seen as cause for celebration, photographs, and a christening, the only reports of the child born in the Formosan village were tacked on at the ends of articles

41. *ILN*, August 13, 1910; *The Times* (London), August 8, 1910.

42. *TNNS*, September 30, 1910.

43. These names link to the names on the postcards of participants. There is a postcard with a female pictured as Rugayo. The second name, Chabibai Butsuapaberi, is a mix of two participants: Chaibaibai Pujajon and Buchaburi Salangai. Other reports suggest the groom is Buchaburi Salangai.

44. *KS*, December 15, 1910.

45. *TNNS*, September 30, 1910.

in just two papers.[46] This lack of coverage was no accident; it reflected the general disinterest in the Paiwan on the part of the British press, which maintained its distance from the participants and sensationalized their savage nature.[47] The manager of the Formosa Hamlet, Ishikawa, confirmed that the Paiwan were not received as warmly as the Ainu were.[48]

Three weeks before Rugayo gave birth, a wedding ceremony was held in the village, purportedly to legitimize her romance with Buchaburi. Although the plans for the wedding had been publicized from the start of the exhibition, a reporter for *Taiwan nichi nichi shinpō* said the wedding plan arose out of necessity of the impending birth. The *Times* of London explained, "This interesting event is a sequel to a romance which commenced in Formosa. Commercial as well as sentimental considerations entered into the alliance, the heads of the two families arranging the matter by a gift from the man's father to the girl's father of a number of human heads that were trophies of war."[49] Interviewed in 2009, Kuskus resident Valjluk Mavaliu remembered hearing the stories about the wedding and recalled they had killed a pig to celebrate the occasion.[50]

THE RETURN OF THE HIGH-COLLAR BARBARIANS

"The Formosans had been accustomed to the horrible savage world, but like flowers they gazed at the streets of the large city."[51] This romantic description in a Kobe newspaper captured how their London experience was seen to have changed the Paiwan. When the Paiwan stopped in Japan on their return from London, they were portrayed in the media as cultural interlocutors who spoke with authority on life in London

46.   *WLO*, September 30, 1910; *Daily News*, November 2, 1910; *KS*, December 15, 1910, names them as Ruji Karurunga and Chanha Futsuapiri.

47.   *TNNS*, May 26, 1910.

48.   *KS*, December 15, 1910.

49.   *WLO*, September 2, 1910; *The Times*, September 5, 1910, claimed, "Sarongai-Busabirce, the bridegroom, is 24 years of age, and Rungayo Rugigasela, the bride, is 21, and they had been betrothed since infancy."

50.   Interview on Channel Sakura TV program, June 13, 2009.

51.   *KS*, December 15, 1910.

compared with the state of affairs in Japan. They arrived in Kobe on December 17, and according to one article, when a group of girls saw them on the street, they greeted them with shrieks of "Barbarians, barbarians!" as they pushed through the crowd to get closer. One of the so-called high-collar (*haikara*) barbarians reportedly chided the children, saying, "'Oy, do not be so noisy, I am a Japanese from Taiwan, in England they would not have their roads be so crowded.' As people cleared the way for them, they said, 'Kobe is like the countryside [*inaka*], isn't it!'"[52]

There are several things of note in this description of their return. First, the word *haikara* used to describe the Paiwan was a loaded term. As Jason Karlin has noted, the word—which refers to the high collars on Western shirts—was coined by journalist Ishikawa Yasujirō in 1898 to describe "the foppishness and novelty of the followers of Western styles."[53] It was first used to criticize Japanese officials who upheld the opinions of the West in a superficial manner, where presenting oneself as modern mattered more than actually being so.[54] In its later application, *haikara* came to refer to those who were sophisticated and advanced.[55] The Paiwan's chastisement of the children placed them as world travelers who knew what constituted a modern city, while the locals were like frogs in a well, unaware of the outside world.

In Japan the Paiwan also visited the office of Aboriginal Affairs in Osaka, where they were interviewed about their experiences in London. They were taken on a sightseeing tour around Osaka, and saw the bronze statue of Toyotomi Hideyoshi and Himeji Castle. When they saw the buildings of the rich people in Osaka, they said they looked like the houses of the lower classes in foreign countries. They compared things in Japan to those in England and claimed that everything was bigger in England.[56]

The Paiwan were said to have been more changed by what they saw and heard than were the Ainu. It was reported that "the beauty among the Taiwanese Aborigine women, Jyaran Tajiyakaru[,] eighteen years old, wanted to imitate the Western women and has been pressing the

---

52. *TNNS*, January 9, 1911.
53. Karlin, "Gender of Nationalism," 61.
54. The kanji for *haikara* include the characters for ash (*hai*) and shell (*kara*), suggesting the "empty superficiality with which it was associated."
55. Karlin, "Gender of Nationalism," 64.
56. *TNNS*, December 15, 1910; *TA*, February 13, 1911.

director to buy her shoes." They were said to have become embarrassed by their bare feet and heads, as they had not seen any Westerners without shoes and hats.[57] The Paiwan were impressed by the White City district, where the fair was located in Shepherd's Bush, and by the bathrooms with running water.[58] Even though they were impressed by the grandeur of London, there were some things they found fault with. They were angered by the unsuitable practice among English men and women of walking hand in hand and were concerned that few women carried their children on their backs (a practice common in Taiwan and Japan).[59] The transformative power of London was limited, as one reporter noted, for not all of their "barbarian" tendencies had disappeared. "As barbarians they still go to war, and the number one thing they wanted among the exhibited goods were the weapons. They remarked, 'If we had these guns, how well we could fight and we could also hunt.'"[60]

The group arrived back in Taiwan on January 7, 1911. There, Governor-General Sakuma Samata questioned them about their time in London.[61] The fact that Sakuma met with the London group was not unusual; he consistently engaged in audiences with those he viewed as advanced Taiwanese Aborigines. As discussed in a later chapter, although Sakuma pursued a vicious campaign to subjugate the Atayal people in northern Taiwan, he simultaneously pursued the colonial policy of tours to the metropolis, which was meant to "civilize the savage" by sending them to Japan's capital to witness modern society for themselves. Sakuma often met with returning tour participants to hear about their experiences in Japan. Japanese writer Nagai Kafū, whose father worked for the colonial government in Taiwan, described the group's visit to the Taiwanese Bureau in his diary. He wrote that the Paiwan asked the officials when such grand and large buildings like the ones they were overwhelmed by in London would be built in Taipei.[62] Tōsei Hideru relayed one of the participant's thoughts on Japan and England:

57. *TNNS*, September 9, 1910.
58. *TNNS*, September 9, 1910.
59. *TNNS*, September 9, 1910, January 9, 1911.
60. This statement shows that the guns they were exhibited with were not their own. *KS*, December 15, 1910.
61. *TA*, February 13, 1911.
62. Suzuki, *Taiwan no banzoku kenkyū*, 377–78.

I have heard often that Japan and England are brother countries. But because I have not heard which is the big brother and which is the little brother, I was happy this time to go to England and make sure for myself. I took notice of many things. The people in England have very robust frames and they are very tall, their actions are very energetic, and the structures of their houses are huge and grand. I was impressed by their machinery; no matter where I looked England seemed like the older brother and Japan very much like its younger brother.[63]

A few years later, in 1915, novelist Nakamura Kokyō met one of the participants identified as a chief, Tibo Salongai, who told Nakamura about his impressions of England. He remarked how astonished he had been to see the large houses and streets in London. He had wanted to telephone Taiwan and have his whole family move to London to live with him. Numerous things surprised him, including the fact that although there were no fields, there were plenty of oranges and vegetables. He wondered how English women could walk around, considering how small their waists were. He was impressed by the bright lights of the city and by the subway and being able to end up anywhere, and come up right in the middle of the street. He remarked that even the Japanese policemen who accompanied them were impressed by these things. Last, he said the most surprising thing was when they saw what looked like a large box flying in the sky above the exhibition grounds. Inside the box were two people who he had thought would surely die. He had seen his first airplane.[64]

WILLIAM PRICE'S VISIT

One year after their return to Taiwan, in 1912, the full extent of the Paiwan participants' ability to speak English was revealed during a visit to Taiwan by British botanist William Price. Initially Price traveled around Taiwan with his renowned colleague Henry John Elwes, but they parted ways halfway through their trip. According to Elwes, he had been dis-

63. *TA*, February 13, 1911.
64. Brief excerpts from Nakamura Kokyō's "Banchi kara," originally published in *Chūō kōron* in July 1916, are reprinted in Yamaguchi (ed.), *Kōza Taiwan*, 63–68. Nakamura mentioned by Obata, "The Display," 62.

suaded by Sakuma from visiting the "savage parts of the island" because the "aboriginal tribes were still at war with the Japanese." He left for Japan while Price continued his travels.[65]

During the Japan-British Exhibition, Price had only briefly visited the Formosa Hamlet; at the time, he said, it "rather bored [him] and [he] did not stay long."[66] Now, during his tour of Taiwan, a meeting was arranged with the Paiwan who had traveled to England. Japanese accounts of the event dramatized the meeting, which they said Price had sought out, as a reunion of old friends.[67] According to Price, the Japanese arranged the visit, and he wrote that the Paiwan were "very excited at the news that I was coming. The reason was apparently that [in England] they had 'been very well treated and had enjoyed themselves very much.' They consequently wished to show their gratitude to the British by showing me hospitality in return."[68]

Before I located Price's diary and papers at the Kew Gardens Botanical Archive in 2016, the information available from oral histories recorded in Kuskus, colonial records, and postcards from the exposition had indicated that the Paiwan learned English better than the Ainu did while they were in London. Valjluk recalled stories of Price's visit, indicating that it had been talked about for years. Surprisingly, Price's diary entry about the encounter inverts the standard narrative in Japanese colonial accounts, which celebrated the Paiwan's embrace of civilization and their vow to educate their children in England and eradicate their savage ways.

Price's diary and versions of a manuscript he eventually published in 1982 reveals that after traveling throughout Taiwan collecting plant specimens for several months, he was much heartened to be able to communicate with the Paiwan who had gone to London and had picked up English better than many of the Japanese he encountered in Taiwan. In Price's eyes, the so-called savages were not savage at all; in fact, he writes that he found their courteous manner to be superior to that of the Japanese, and he felt a clear affinity with them. His impressions of their meeting in June

65. Elwes, *Memoirs of Travel*, 229.
66. Price, *Plant Collecting in Formosa* (1982), 93.
67. Taiwan sōtokufu keimukyoku (ed.), *Riban shikō*, 2:291–92; *TNNS*, June 7, 1912; Suzuki, *Taiwan no banzoku kenkyū*, 377–78.
68. Price, *Plant Collecting in Formosa* (1982), 93.

stand in stark contrast to the attitude Price expressed at the beginning of his travels. Early on, he described the thrill that came over him as he encountered an Aboriginal camp that was littered with animal bones, bringing to mind "Robinson Crusoe entering a dark forest with remains of cannibal feasts lying around." He wrote that he explored "without apprehension" because the "savages of the southern part of Formosa were such jolly fellows," but at times, being away from the group caused others to worry he had "been head-hunted."[69] Throughout Price's writings he employs the word *savage* without reflection until he writes about his visit with the Paiwan who had gone to London. In his diary he acknowledges how prevalently the term *savage* is used, and after visiting a "savage school" in Kuskus, where a Japanese instructor and a "savage" teacher were teaching the Paiwan boys simple sentences in Japanese, Price writes that he walked around the village saying *watakushi banjin arimasu*—"I am a savage"— much to their delight.[70] (For the book he published in 1982 and the 1961 version of the manuscript based largely on these 1912 diary entries, he omitted this part.) In a telling contrast, on the first day of his visit with the Paiwan, he used *savage* without reflecting. But by later that day, when the Paiwan came to meet him for dinner he wrote: "long after dark the ~~savages~~ "ten" appeared."[71] Price's decision to cross out the word *savages* shows his reflection over its use. While he reflects on the appropriateness of the use of *savage* a day later in his diary, by June 2 he went back to using it to describe the Paiwan when they gathered to say goodbye.[72]

Price met with ten of the Paiwan who had gone to London and was amazed that they could speak English better than the Japanese he met in Taiwan. He found the Paiwan especially courteous in that they knew how to extend their hand to shake hands with him and in the gifts they offered to him. In his diary he remarks on how beautifully they were dressed and says that he found them attractive in appearance and—in particular, the elder headmen—energetic and intelligent.[73] He also met one of the Japanese police officers who had accompanied the group to London but found his English poor in comparison with the Paiwan and could

69.   Price, *Plant Collecting in Formosa* (1961), 44.
70.   Price, personal diary, June 1, 1912, 252.
71.   Price, personal diary, June 1, 1912, 254.
72.   Price, personal diary, June 2, 1912, 259.
73.   Price, personal diary, May 31, 1912, 251.

not communicate with him. This officer showed him the many things he had brought back from London, including a bicycle, which Price thought was quite useless in the mountains.[74]

Japanese newspapers had described their meeting as a party, with food, drink, song, and dance—including three different types of food: Japanese, Western, and Aborigine—and Price's diary corroborates that he contributed a can of tinned beef, along with some brandy, while the Paiwan bought some beer for him.[75] They also drank sake. Price recalled:

> A chair was brought and I was made to sit in it as the seat of honour. . . . Conversation then begun. Three of the men and one of the women could talk English quite fairly well, and understood a surprising amount of what I said. This in itself indicates what a superior type of people they are. The policemen on the other hand couldn't talk English at all, and even Kikuchi's English was inferior to the savages! It was a fantastic situation, the savages and I having an English conversation, while the Japanese sat dumb and awkward. I felt I must exercise all possible tact.[76]

Just as this passage indicates, Price was aware of the power dynamics of their meeting, in which the Paiwan were communicating better, leaving the Japanese out of the loop. These uneasy dynamics continued throughout their exchange. At dinner, Price was seated at the head of the table. On one side was Kikuchi, his research assistant, and on the other the local schoolmaster, then the two police officers, and then the "ten savages with their headman at the bottom of the table," Price wrote. "It was the weirdest dinner I ever sat down to. I could talk to everyone in a sort of way in pigeon [*sic*] English or pigeon [*sic*] Japanese, but the savages understood me best in English. The more they talked, the more I talked, and the more the poor Japanese became silent, so that I had to try a few remarks with the schoolmaster."[77]

Besides revealing how he got on better with the Paiwan than the Japanese, throughout his account Price describes the tension he felt as he

74. Price, personal diary, May 31, 1912, 251.
75. *TNNS*, June 7, 1912.
76. Price, *Plant Collecting in Formosa* (1982), 96.
77. Price, *Plant Collecting in Formosa* (1961), 130.

imagined that the Paiwan at any moment might provoke the Japanese by saying something inflammatory. At one point in the evening, the Paiwan tried to communicate something startling to Price in English. Price believed that they were trying to tell him that they "wished they were subjects of England!" Sensing the danger of such a statement in front of the Japanese, Price responded by jumping up and saying "as clearly and emphatically" as possible, 'No, you subjects of Japan—you part Japan empire"!"[78] He later reflected, "Perhaps they didn't understand a word, because they all cheered tremendously, but I think the Japanese did, or Kikuchi told them, as they looked pleased."[79]

Throughout his conversation with them, Price reflected, "I tumbled to something critically important, and that was, that 'Formosa people' meant the savages of Formosa; in other words Formosa in their eyes was *their* country, they were the rightful owners. I was most nervous, but so far all three nationalities continued to beam friendliness."[80] Price recalled that he tried to tell them he thought highly of them and their country as they continued to put down Taiwan and elevate England: "I carefully kept off the words 'savage' and 'ban-jin' and addressed them as Formosa peoples. I told them their country was not as bad as they seemed to think it was."[81] Price elaborated more in his diary on his conflicted feelings about addressing the Paiwan as savages. He wrote, "I suddenly found myself not knowing how to address them. I remembered having used the word Savages towards them previously, but they had not objected and evidently did not understand the adjectival form of the word, which was perhaps fortunate. Then I remembered that they had called themselves 'Formosa People,' so the question was solved."[82]

After a while the Paiwan told him he must be tired and that they should go. Price wrote in his diary how their awareness of how he was tired reflected their "European manners."[83] He later wrote,

78. Price, personal diary, June 1, 1912, 257.

79. Price, *Plant Collecting in Formosa* (1982), 96.

80. Price, *Plant Collecting in Formosa* (1982), 96; "their" is not emphasized in the published volume, but it is underscored in the 1961 draft at the Kew.

81. Price, *Plant Collecting in Formosa* (1961), 131.

82. Price, personal diary, June 1, 1912, 258.

83. Price, personal diary, June 1, 1912, 258.

This was without any doubt at all an example of their native culture and good manners, head-hunters or no, in fact they could have given us all lessons in courtesy and good manners. An article I read later describing the way in which Toke-tok the great chief in the 1870s entertained an English party at his house somewhere near here, bears out the truth of these people's possession of these extraordinary advanced natural social attributes.[84]

The day Price left Kuskus, he gave the only things he had, some needles, as gifts to the women and wrote, "I felt very sorry to leave my friends. We all shook hands, only English was spoken, and there were endless 'good byeees' and 'come back' and 'thank you,' and we marched off waving at them all standing a row."[85] During his visit Price posed for a picture with members of the Paiwan group (fig. 3.8), and unlike another photograph taken during his trip in which he is pictured with the Tsou people (fig. 3.9), in this image he is standing shoulder to shoulder with the Paiwan, smiling with his gaze averted. In contrast, in fig. 3.9 Price's position of authority is marked by the Tsou's position, standing behind him and the Japanese policemen, as well as by Price's and the police's confident posture as they sit with their arms crossed, gazing directly at the camera.

Price's visit with the Paiwan was recorded in the newspapers and government records. Those accounts mention that the Paiwan spoke to Price in English, but of course they do not convey that their English ability was superior to that of the Japanese. Ironically, while Price thought the Paiwan were trying to communicate to him that they would rather live in England than be ruled by Japan, Japanese accounts relayed a completely different version of events, as we can see in an article titled "The Barbarians' Japan-British Alliance," a reference to the 1902 alliance made between Japan and Britain.[86] Tibo Salongai reportedly told Price, "After we saw England, our thinking changed. We are still savages [*yaban*]; in order to escape this condition, we must obtain the power of education. Since our return, we make our children study, and someday we will have them study abroad in England; the day will come when our lifestyle is the same

84. Price, *Plant Collecting in Formosa* (1961) has "natural" handwritten above social attributes, 131; unlike Price, *Plant Collecting in Formosa* (1982), 97.

85. Price, *Plant Collecting in Formosa* (1961), 132.

86. *TNNS*, June 7, 1912.

Self = Paiwan Savages at Kusukusu - 1912

FIG. 3.8. William Price standing with Tibo Salongai (left) and other London participants. Credit: William Price Papers, *The Life of a Botanist*, PR1/2/2, folio 20a. Image reproduced with the permission of the Board of Trustees of the Royal Botanical Gardens, Kew.

Party climbing Mt Morrison 1912

FIG. 3.9. William Price with Japanese police officers and the Tsou. Credit: William Price Papers, *The Life of a Botanist*, PR1/2/2, folio 20a. Image reproduced with the permission of the Board of Trustees of the Royal Botanical Gardens, Kew.

as the people of the world."[87] While the Japanese stressed how being in England had transformed their point of view, Price emphasized their distinct identity as non-Japanese and how his interactions with them forced him to reconsider the appropriateness of referring to them as savages.

The Paiwan group's transformative experience in London was later linked to the success of one of the former participants, the Paiwan chief Tugie Kalowan who went to work for the colonial government (figs. 3.4 and 3.10). In a publication on the state of education for the Aboriginal people of Taiwan, Tugie was upheld as proof of the transformative power of becoming civilized through tourism.[88]

The article named two pioneers (*senkakusha*) who fought on the Japanese side to quell rebellions started by other Aborigines. Several tribes in Koshun had risen in rebellion in 1915, attacking local police stations and killing the officers and their families as well as construction workers. The rebels took the heads of the local mailmen, destroyed telegraph poles, and cut wires.[89] Members of Rikiriki village surrounded Subon village and attacked the colonial government office there (see map 2). One of those who fought against the rebels was identified as Subon village chief Tugie, whose participation in the 1910 exhibition was also noted. Tugie led the opposition attacks against the rebels and was credited with saving the people of Subon and five people from a nearby village.[90] His actions "distinguished him in the southern barbarian rebellion in 1915." In his obituary in 1926, his many achievements in helping the colonial government, his choice of the next chief to succeed him, and his selection to go to London for the Japan-British Exhibition were all mentioned.[91] In addition to Tugie, a photograph of one of the Paiwan women who went to London, Baru-haru Chaco (fig. 3.3), was featured in a 1915 article. It described that after she returned from London, her previously unadorned body was now covered in elaborate jewelry (fig. 3.11).[92]

---

87.   Fujisaki, *Taiwan no banzoku*, 668–69; Suzuki, *Takasagozoku*, 113. In Suzuki, *Taiwan no banzoku kenkyū*, the speech is different, 377.

88.   "Chief of Subon village." Tugie's name is spelled as Karoun Tsujiyui.

89.   Yamaguchi (ed.), *Kōza Taiwan*, 66–67.

90.   "Chief of Subon village."

91.   "Nanban no kyoseichi ni otsu," 336–37; Taiwan sōtokufu keimukyoku, *Takasagozoku no kyōiku*, 18.

92.   "Paiwan woman in full dress."

（蕃下排彎）女の裝正　搖動の族ンワイパ

The Woman in Full Dress.

The Chief of Subon Village.

目頭が社ンギ、ス搖動の族ンワイパ・

FIG. 3.10. "Chief of Subon village," *Taiwan shashinchō* 1, no. 7 (1915). Digital image courtesy of East Asia Image Collection, Lafayette College Libraries, Easton, PA.

FIG. 3.11. "Paiwan woman in full dress," *Taiwan shashinchō* 1, no. 5 (1915). Digital image courtesy of East Asia Image Collection, Lafayette College Libraries, Easton, PA.

The Paiwan group's time in England was not just an opportunity to reflect about their own level of civilization vis-à-vis Japan's and Japan's progress as a modern country. It was also, again, an occasion to question the legitimacy of human displays such as the Formosa, Ainu, and Japanese villages at the London exhibition. After the Paiwan group's return, "there was much criticism that showcasing [them] violated humanitarian principles."[93]

Save the Elephants and the Pigs! British and Japanese Responses to the Human Displays

In 1908, letters written to the editor of the *Times* in London had revealed a flood of protests against what many saw to be a display of cruelty: in the Indian village at the 1908 Franco-British Exhibition, elephants were sent careening down a slide into a pool of water as part of a theatrical performance. It was not the treatment of the numerous Indian dancers, craftsmen, or acrobats on display at the Indian village but the welfare of the elephants that inspired people to complain. One letter writer, Reverend J. G. Cornish remarked, "There is something degrading in seeing so dignified and intelligent an animal treated as a mere means of provoking thoughtless and heartless laughter, for that I suppose is the object."[94]

In 1910 great concern was shown for the welfare of a pig that was to be killed for the celebrations following the wedding held in the Formosa Hamlet. According to the *Times*, "a small black Berkshire pig, which had been received at the village the previous night, was carried into the centre of the village and killed. Mr. A. Pinson-Case, veterinary surgeon, and five inspectors attended on behalf of the Royal Society for the Prevention of Cruelty to Animals and certified that the animal had been humanely killed."[95] This type of concern over the treatment of animals, when less attention was paid to the welfare of the humans in the displays, reflected a general sentiment among the British public.

93. *TA*, February 13, 1911.
94. *The Times*, August 21, 1908, and letter to the editor on August 26, 1908.
95. *The Times*, September 5, 1910.

In contrast, Japanese politicians and Japanese residents of London proclaimed the Ainu Village, Formosa Hamlet, and the Uji Village to be humanitarian problems. Their adverse reaction to the villages—as well as the background on how these villages came to be at the exhibition—should caution us from jumping to the conclusion that the Japanese were intentionally trying to demonstrate their power by putting their colonial subjects on display.

By the end of the Japan-British Exhibition, the Japanese government's reaction and public opinion were mixed with regard to whether Japan had been fairly represented. Most historians have reached the consensus that the British reaction to the exposition was more favorable than the Japanese one.[96] Japanese criticism of the exposition focused on three main issues.[97] First, while the Japanese government had taken an active role in securing exhibits and funding, the British government had played no official role in producing and hosting the exposition. Second, interest in the exposition among the British was lackluster compared with the effort Britain had put into the Franco-British Exhibition of 1908.[98] Japan accused the British of instead concentrating on the exhibits they sent to the Brussels International Exposition, which was also held in 1910. The Japanese had not sent anything to Brussels in order to concentrate fully on the exposition in London.[99] Third, and most significant, the perceived failure of the exposition, in Japan's view, was attributed to Imre Kiralfy's insistence on having native villages in the amusement section of the fair. Coerced by Kiralfy, the Japanese had acceded to his demand, but by the end of the exposition, they were lamenting that modern Japan had been misrepresented as an old-fashioned feudal society, primarily through the Uji Village display. Japan's image as a nation of "quaint backwardness" had been reinforced by what it was pressured to put on exhibit: producers wanted only traditional Japanese artwork, for example, because any Western-style paintings by Japanese artists were considered simply pale imitations.[100]

The Japanese empire was officially on display in the exposition's Palace of the Orient, which featured exhibits on Japan's protectorate Korea,

96.   Hotta-Lister, "Japan Seeks," 133.
97.   Nish, "On the Commercial," 62–63.
98.   Tsuzuki, "Conditions in Japan," 10.
99.   Hotta-Lister, "Japan Seeks," 127; Cortazzi, "Overview," 20.
100. Cortazzi, "Overview," 23; Hotta-Lister, "Japan Seeks," 128–29.

Taiwan, the South Manchurian Railway, and the Kwangtung government.[101] Historians such as Peter O'Connor have speculated that the timing of the formal annexation of Korea, which occurred in August, midway through the exhibition, helped temper international reaction, because the exposition had "made more of Japan's right to belong to the order of imperialist nations."[102] While the Japanese ambassador Katō in London had reported unfavorable British reactions to the prospect of annexation in May, Britain's official reaction after the annexation was finalized was to stay out of it so as to avoid interfering with ongoing Japan–Britain talks regarding tariffs.[103] British public reaction to Korea's annexation was also muted.[104] In reality, though, the Palace of the Orient did not draw as much attention as the villages did.

Instead of thinking of the Ainu and Formosa villages as examples of Japan proudly showcasing its empire, documents reveal that the Japanese organizers had to be cajoled into having the village exhibits at all, and they had been especially reluctant to place a traditional Japanese village alongside the Ainu and Formosa villages.[105] The Japanese had a long history of protests against Japanese villages at European and North American expositions, and they were reluctant to send these village exhibits to London. But Kiralfy had organized numerous expositions, and he knew what the public expected—namely, amusements. He always tried to outdo the exposition of the previous year.[106] In his correspondence with Count Mutsu, who was in charge of the Japanese side of the exhibition, Kiralfy was dismayed by the resistance in Japan to the establishment of Japanese villages. In a series of letters written to Mutsu (now in the archives of the Foreign Ministry in Tokyo), Kiralfy's frustration with the Japanese reticence is palpable. To prove that Japanese villages were necessary, he listed the profits from the amusements and villages, including mention of the Senegalese, Ceylon, and Irish villages at the 1908 Franco-British

101. Hotta-Lister, "Japan Seeks," 123.

102. O'Connor, "Exhibition and the Media," 99.

103. Nish, "On the Commercial," 61.

104. O'Connor, "Exhibition and the Media," 97–99.

105. Yamaji, "Nichiei hakurankai," 10.

106. A pamphlet for the 1911 Coronation Exhibition reads: "Because you paid a visit last year it is a great error to imagine that this year it is the same. [. . .] The Great White City is this year more original, more entertaining, more instructive and more fascinating." Accession # 82.232/327, Museum of London.

Exhibition.[107] In another letter penned a week later, he listed various exhibits of old streets and villages at expositions since 1885, writing, "I will pick out just a few, to show what villages and old streets they had and I leave it to you to say whether these are legitimate expositions." He referenced old London streets at the 1885 London International Inventions Exhibition, Japanese villages at the 1893 World's Columbian Exhibition in Chicago, and the Japanese village (Fair Japan) at the 1904 Louisiana Purchase Exhibition. He closed the letter by writing, "Now can one imagine a Japan-British Exposition without Japan being presented in a characteristic and picturesque way?"[108]

In the end, Kiralfy got his way. The Fair Japan exhibit had craftsmen demonstrating their work, similar to the exhibition called Old Japan at Earl's Court in 1907. The Uji Village exhibit showed Japanese farmers going about their daily life in a farmlike setting. Japanese journalist Hasegawa Nyozekan called it unrealistic, saying he had never seen such things as the water wheel that was in the village. He remarked, "I was convinced that this kind of village of low grade status could not have existed even in the previous century in Japan or anywhere else and could only exist at the Japan-British Exhibition."[109]

Such criticism of the Japanese village was often coupled with criticism of the Ainu and Formosa villages. One article, titled "The Japanese Village in London," said the majority of Japanese correspondents in London "look[ed] askance at the Japanese side-shows at the exposition."[110] A different Japanese reporter remarked that Fair Japan, "with craftsman of different trades, and the farming village of Uji, are like the Ainu and Formosa villages where you pay sixpence to get in; are all the same—nothing more than spectacles." The reporter blamed the villages on the "the deep desires of a Jewish man, Kiralfy, the representative of the exposition, who has used these spectacles as crowd pleasers and as a means to make the exposition flourish and bustle." The Japan-British Exhibition was viewed by Japan as a failure because of these spectacles.[111] Although the journalist Hasegawa was highly critical of the Uji Village and how it represented

107. Kiralfy to Count Mutsu, August 12, 1909, Gaimusho archives, Tokyo.
108. Kiralfy to Count Mutsu, August 19, 1909, Gaimusho archives, Tokyo.
109. *TA*, July 6, 1910.
110. Hotta-Lister, *Japan-British Exhibition*, 132.
111. *TNNS*, September 30, 1910.

Japan, he viewed the displays of the Ainu and Paiwan, with visitors looking at them as if they were rare animals in a zoo, as a matter of humanitarian and moral concern.[112] For some other observers of the Uji Village, worries over national representation trumped issues of humanitarian concerns.

Kurahara Korehiro, a member of the Japanese Diet who stayed in London for four months during the exposition, expressed his disapproval of the villages in Diet proceedings on January 25, 1911. He believed that the exposition fostered anti-alliance and anti-tariff feelings. One of the reasons for this, he said, was because the "British had lost their respect for Japan because many Japanese participants in the exposition, including native peoples such as Ainus and Formosans as well as sumo wrestlers and some artisans, had been of low class or uncivilized origin, and this showed the very humble lifestyles of these peoples as if [they] were the norm in Japan."[113] Although Kurahara talked of the display of the Japanese along with the Ainu and Taiwanese Aborigines, his later comments distinguish how the Ainu in particular upset the British. He explained,

> Following this exposition there are many who see Japan as a midrange country, with many low-class people. If you ask why, it is because this exposition was an exposition for amusement. There were countless spectacles, but the four most popular attractions were sumo, the Taiwanese barbarians, Hokkaido Ainu, and the Taiwanese teahouse. However, with respect to the barbarian and Ainu problem, the English humanitarians have asked why do you take ten or twenty pence admission fee for people like the gentle Ainu at the exposition? Upperclass English women, crying, have made appeals to me about this injustice. We could not answer anything to this. Each time they see the Ainu, with kind tears flowing, they give the Ainu various things, as well as comfort. I saw how they wanted to make the Ainu happy and help enable them to return home.[114]

The Ainu were the objects of pity more often than the Paiwan or the Japanese participants in the Uji Village. Although the press never mentioned any British discomfort with the villages, Kurahara's account shows

112. *TA*, July 6, 1910.
. 113. Okurashō Insastsukyoku, *Shūgiin Gikai*, 34. Thank you to Hamazaki Kenichi for providing me this reference.
114. Okurashō Insastsukyoku, *Shūgiin Gikai*, 34.

there was some. One British woman who expressed sympathy for the Ainu was Charlotte Salwey, who remarked, "It is certainly with pleasure that we shall remember their presence in our great metropolis, for in their present state they bear few marks of their early barbarism. Their simplicity of life, their contentment with few surroundings, and their dignity under trying circumstances of being made objects of curiosity speak well in their favour."[115]

Kurahara's condemnation of all the villages was based on humanitarian concerns voiced earlier in 1903 and 1907: "In reality to use our country's compatriots as materials for spectacle and take an admission fee, I think this is a huge failure in humanity."[116] However, Fair Japan and the Uji Village were mainly discussed with respect to how they misrepresented Japan's national stature. One Japanese reporter remarked, "The Japanese village is a mere sketch of the life of the lowest class of peasants in the north east of Japan and is a sight which must fill Japanese gentlemen with nothing but displeasure and shame." He critiqued the disgraceful behavior of some artisans who had been employed by Kiralfy and who "were so low a class that they freely and shamelessly begged for money from the visitors." Despite his critique of the behavior of those in the Japanese villages, he viewed their display differently from that of the Ainu and Paiwan. "The exposition of the Ainu and Formosan natives together with their native huts and so forth to public gaze might also have been regarded as raising the question of personal rights."[117]

Japanese criticism of the villages in the Japan-British Exhibition were part of a consistent Japanese dismay over turning humans into spectacles for profit, an issue that first arose during the 1903 and 1907 domestic expositions. In assessing why the British showed a relative lack of concern for the peoples on display (with the possible exception of the Ainu, as just mentioned), some scholars, like Ayako Hotta-Lister, have concluded that the difference had to do with the Japanese viewing the Ainu and Taiwanese Aborigines as being the same race as them. The British, French, and Americans saw their colonized peoples as "belonging to entirely different races, or even as aliens" and thus had less sympathy for them. Hotta-Lister explains:

115.   Salwey, "Japanese Monographs no. XIV," 330.
116.   Okurashō Insastsukyoku, *Shūgiin Gikai*, 34.
117.   Hotta-Lister, *Japan-British Exhibition*, 133.

Japan was an inexperienced latecomer into the imperial club. . . . It seems to reveal that imperialism in the Western sense was still not yet fully developed or grasped by even the articulate and educated Japanese class. Instead of behaving in a similar way to the general public in Britain, . . . the Japanese (the colonizer) regarded the natives from Taiwan and the Ainu (the colonized) as though they were their fellow citizens.[118]

Hotta-Lister concludes, "It probably never occurred to them (the colonizer) that they (the colonized) were a different race from themselves, so they (the colonizer) utterly condemned such forms of exposition, dreading to think that it was exposing Japan's backwardness (not the backwardness of subject peoples) to the British public."[119] This idea that the Japanese had a racial affinity for those they ruled can be found in the work of scholars such as Mark Peattie and Ramon Myers.[120] Nevertheless, I do not believe that racial affinity was the reason the Japanese opposed the displays. By 1910 a public discourse was being shaped by Japanese anthropologists that delineated the Ainu and Taiwanese Aborigine as races separate from the *yamato* or *wajin* (Japanese). At this time mixed-race theories about the origins of the Japanese were popular, but there was still a distinctive understanding that the Ainu and the indigenous people of Taiwan were distinct from the Japanese race. Although the Japanese used words like *compatriots* (*dōhō*) to refer to the other subjects of the empire, that does not mean the Japanese saw the Ainu and Taiwanese Aborigines as racial equals. Concern among the Japanese for their compatriots' welfare did not negate their understanding that their colonial subjects were different from them racially and in their eyes culturally more primitive.

For example, the Ainu village caused concern prior to the group's departure for London. Educators and numerous religious people called the Ainu display "irreconcilable with humanity" (*jindō ni haihan*). Kozaki Hiromichi, a prominent Christian who was a president of Dōshisha University, spoke out about this humanitarian concern. He had seen the 1909 Alaska-Yukon-Pacific Exposition in Seattle, where Eskimos, Native Americans, and Africans had been displayed in what he called human

---

118. Hotta-Lister, *Japan-British Exhibition*, 192.
119. Hotta-Lister, *Japan-British Exhibition*, 192.
120. Peattie, "Introduction," 7.

pavilions (*jinruikan*). He said that although on the surface the reason for the Ainu's display in London was to demonstrate bear hunting, the bear festival, and various crafts, in reality they were on display as a race with curious features and customs. Kozaki said Japan needed to protect and help develop what he referred to as the inferior races. He called for an end to turning the handicapped and freaks into spectacles and said it was a national disgrace to display inferior races in the name of art or entertainment.[121] Kozaki's argument against the display of the Ainu evokes arguments directed against the first human display in Japan, in 1903, with his employment of phrases like "human pavilion" and "humanitarian concern." Despite using terms like *compatriots*, or *dōhō*, it was precisely because these races were inferior that Kozaki championed the idea of protecting them against exploitation.

Conclusion

The displaying of Japanese people at international expositions had caused concern at home that it reflected poorly on Japan's national status. As Kozaki Hiromichi argued in 1910—and Professor Takebe argued in 1903 (see chapter 1)—the human displays sullied Japan's name. In contrast, criticism of the Ainu Village, and to a lesser extent the Formosa Hamlet, at the Japan-British Exhibition in London focused on the argument that humans should not be turned into spectacles. The Japanese reaction to these displays within the international context should dissuade us from characterizing Japan as an imperial power eager to showcase its subjects. Not only were the Japanese themselves displayed in the same way as their subjects, the Ainu and Taiwanese Aborigines, but the international audience at the exposition also confused who was Japanese and who was not, calling into question the whole appearance of the Japanese imperial project. At the 1910 exposition in England, displaying Japan's empire in the international context reflected Japan's insecurity as an upcoming imperial power that did not entirely belong among the other Western and white nations.

121.   *TNNSB*, February 12, 1910.

CHAPTER 4

Welcome to the Empire

The 1912 Tokyo Colonial Exposition was the first time the various races were brought together expressly in the name of promoting Japan's diverse multicultural empire. But all was not as it seemed at the exposition. Some colonial subjects, like the Koreans, were conspicuously absent, whereas the Ainu from Hokkaido (a place whose colonial status was ambiguous) were prominently featured. Others, like the Taiwanese Aborigines (who were the minority population of colonial Taiwan) commanded much attention while the Han Taiwanese participants (the majority of Taiwan's population) were almost invisible. The stories behind the individuals who were featured (or not featured) at the exposition illustrate the tensions behind the commercialization of one of imperial Japan's largest anthropological showcases held at that time.

1912 Tokyo Colonial Exposition

The black-and-white image on the postcard in fig. 4.1 gives a somber view of the different people representing the various ethnoracial groups in Japan's new empire. Pictured along with exposition officials, the people from the Tokyo Colonial Exposition's human displays stand or sit stoically, gazing straight at the camera.

This image was reproduced many times, including on a flyer for the exhibition (fig. 4.2), but it takes on a new meaning when we consider a

人　土　の　土　領　新　各

FIG. 4.1. Caption: "The natives of each new territory." Tsuboi Shōgorō, organizer of the human displays, is in the back, fifth from the right. Credit: Author's collection.

story about the taking of the photograph, featured in an article written by organizer of the human displays, Tsuboi Shōgorō, for a children's magazine called *Shōgakusei* (Elementary student). Tsuboi explained for young readers the place of these colonial subjects in the empire: "All of them are the same as Japanese, and if we think of them as subjects of the Japanese empire, isn't it wonderful? However, their customs are clearly different. Their words, of course, are different, and from the top of their heads to the tip of their toes, they are different people."[1] In acknowledging the ethnoracial differences of the colonial subjects, Tsuboi reinforced their common bond with the Japanese people as subjects of the emperor. Then, with his story about taking the photograph, he emphasized the universal kinship shared by all the different people pictured, including the Japanese. At the exposition, he recalled, everyone had gathered to take the memorial photo. But just as the picture was about to be taken, the bench broke, and everyone on it crashed to the ground. Because of this, everyone laughed so hard their stomachs

1.   Tsuboi, "Nihon zenjinshu," 16.

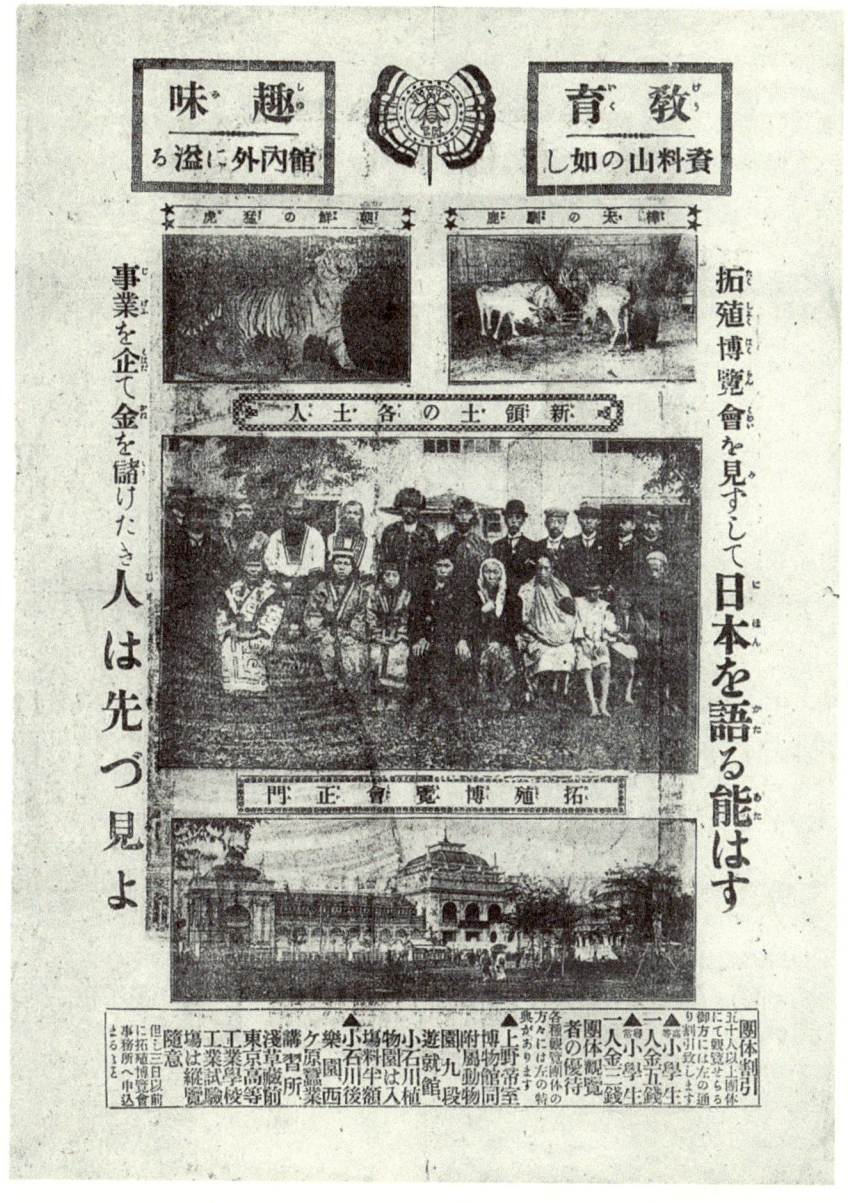

FIG. 4.2. 1912 exposition flyer. Courtesy of Collection NOMURA Co., Ltd., Japan.

hurt. Tsuboi explained how this simple story illustrated a much bigger idea. When faced with the same experience, people from all the different races had the same reaction. This was an important lesson he wanted the children to learn: they were all humans, just like the Japanese.[2]

Although written for a young audience, Tsuboi's words are significant; they explain the place of the different peoples in Japan's empire in a succinct way that even small children could understand. Tsuboi believed that all Japanese people, including children, should be educated about the different races in the empire. He encouraged taking a humanist view toward all, despite their differences. When the article was published, cultural expositions and imperialism were explicitly intertwined for the first time in Japan at the 1912 Tokyo Colonial Exposition; yet his unique vision of the empire does not square with how Japan's empire is often represented today.

Both the 1912 Tokyo Colonial Exposition and the 1913 Osaka Colonial Exposition included human displays of colonial groups. The 1912 exposition promoted a dynamic two-way exchange I call imperial knowledge production, in which metropolitan Japanese visitors interacted with colonial subjects in the human displays, and colonial participants were introduced to each other as well as to Japanese culture in Tokyo. The exposition site served as an important demonstration of the pedagogics of empire that sometimes blurred into the theatrics of empire, all predicated on understanding the Japanese empire as a multiracial empire.

The 1913 Osaka Colonial Exposition, in contrast, destroyed all illusions of performance when participants in the human displays openly voiced negative opinions about their experience. For the most part they complained of poor treatment, bad food, and the tedium of their daily life on display. Their complaints, combined with those of other critics of such exhibits, reveal how human displays continued to provoke debate about colonial roles, not only among the participants but also among the Japanese.

2.   Tsuboi, "Nihon zenjinshu," 14–17. See KZW for the picture in *Shōgakusei*.

EXPOSITION AS CLASSROOM:
EDUCATING A PRINCE AND THE
EMPIRE'S SMALLEST SUBJECTS

On a crisp fall morning in October, Crown Prince Hirohito, the eleven-year-old future Shōwa emperor, and his entourage came to Ueno Park in Tokyo to visit the exposition. As they toured the various pavilions, different professors, including the human display's organizer, Tsuboi Shōgorō, were on hand to answer the prince's questions. The prince greeted the people of various races, and they bowed in return. A nineteen-year-old Nivkh boy named Punyon from the colony of Karafuto (the southern island of Sakhalin) rode around on a reindeer for the prince.[3]

When the imperial entourage took a rest at the Taiwanese teahouse, Taiwanese Aborigine children ran out into the garden chasing each other, blithely unaware of the prince. He asked one of the professors about their lifestyle, including whether the Aborigines had seen Tokyo and what kind of souvenirs they were bringing back with them to Taiwan. He went to the Tokyo Anthropological Society's exhibit to see dolls of all the races found in Japan and throughout the world (fig. 4.3).[4] Tsuboi Shōgorō, Matsumura Akira, and Inoue Seisuke created these dolls. Their mass production (they were sold for one yen and fifty sen) represented the mass commercialization and dissemination of anthropological ideas to ordinary Japanese.[5] Just like the article in *Shōgakusei* magazine, the commercialization of the dolls represent how understandings of the different peoples living in Japan and other races of the world were conveyed to everyday people.

Before the prince left the exposition, he gave 100 yen to be divided among the different participants of the human displays; in turn, he received goods from the Taiwan colonial government and the Hokkaido government office, as well as handmade presents from the people in the displays.

3. *Jinruigakui zasshi* 29 (January 1913), photo on unnumbered page; see KZW. Punyon, or Okuda Momotaro, was later known as the "Nivkh who met the emperor" because of his participation in the exposition. Thirty-three years later, in 1945, Punyon, a soldier in the Japanese imperial army, was shot to death by Soviet troops. Tangiku, "Aru Nivufuhito," 132; http://www.sangiin.go.jp/japanese/joho1/kousei/syuisyo/173/syuh/s173079.htm (accessed August 1, 2018).

4. Nishino, "Meiji 37 nen no Tsuboi Shōgorō," http://umdb.um.u-tokyo.ac.jp/DKankoub/Publish_db/1997Archaeology/04/40500.html (accessed August 8, 2018).

5. Originally found at http://buyee.jp/item/yahoo/auction/h301795097 (accessed May 13, 2018) (listing no longer available).

FIG. 4.3. Tsuboi Shōgorō, Matsumura Akira, and Inoue Seisuke created dolls to represent the races of the world. Created from 1910–1913. Courtesy of the University of Tokyo General Research Museum.

Hirohito's introduction to the empire's colonial subjects, with professors from Tokyo Imperial University standing by to answer questions and gifts of toys handcrafted by people of the different races, was an experience truly tailored for a prince. Tsuboi, an anthropologist by training, typically lectured about the nature of empire and the growing consciousness of colonial populations in terms of the emerging field of anthropology. But in lieu of a formal lecture, on this day the young emperor-to-be was treated to a day of gentle instruction and an exchange of gifts. It had to be fun, after all.[6]

The living displays at the exposition were in fact marketed directly to Japanese children as a way for them to learn about the various races of the empire. Tsuboi had maintained the educational aspect of human displays in the anthropological sense since the first human display he organized in 1903. But with the 1912 exposition, he wrote articles for many children's magazines, encouraging children to attend the exposition

6.   *TA*, October 31, 1912; see KZW for a picture of young Hirohito.

primarily to meet their fellow subjects in the empire. In *Shōgakusei* Tsuboi introduced readers to the idea that Japan was becoming a leading country in the world. He explained the value of the exposition for young children in helping them

> measure the large development of Japan's future, and for the people of the metropolis to learn in detail the appearance of these new lands. It is necessary to study the characteristics of the inhabitants who live in these areas. In order to do this, we are able to see the real thing [at the exposition], not just pictures or words. The people of these lands have done us the favor of coming here, and everyone should come to the exposition to learn about their appearance and characteristics.[7]

Tsuboi believed that human displays should be interactive, and he reminded his readers to have respect for the participants:

> At this exposition, there are . . . Taiwanese (Han ethnicity), savages [*seiban*, referring to the Taiwanese Aborigines], as well as the Karafuto Ainu, Uilta and Nivkh—everyone has come. These people are different from goods and animals; they are the same as human beings and we cannot make them into spectacles. They are fortunate because houses are built for each group, and among them they do skilled arts. We are lucky to be able to see them.[8]

Testimonials written by children describe their experiences at the exposition. In *Yōnen sekai* (Young people's world), a young boy named Taro gave a firsthand account of his visit: "I went and saw the colonial exposition that opened. There were many goods from our land, which has grown large since the Meiji period including Hokkaido, Karafuto, Korea and Taiwan. Also I saw the natives of Karafuto and the savages of Taiwan. When I think how large Japan's territory has become, I couldn't be happier."[9]

7. Tsuboi, "Nihon zenjinshu,"16.
8. Tsuboi, "Nihon zenjinshu,"16.
9. Taro, "Takushoku hakurankai," 24.

TEACHING AND LEARNING FROM BARBARIANS

During the 1912 exposition, the prince and other Japanese children were not the only ones learning about the empire they lived in. Most visitors had never seen people of the different races on display. Tsuboi and linguist Kindaichi Kyōsuke produced a book titled *The Languages of the Various Races within Japan* (Nihon kokunai shojinshu no gengō), designed "for those spectators at the exposition who wished to exchange even just one word with a native." It included nineteen pages of basic vocabulary words in Japanese and five of the six languages spoken by the different people in the exhibition (Taiwanese was not included). There was a conversation section that included phrases like "What are you doing now?" and "What are you making?" Other sentences, such as "I came by again" and "I am giving this to you," pointed to the kinds of interactions organizers expected onlookers to have with display participants.[10]

The phrase "Once you have finished eating, come out and play again," indicated one of the problems encountered with living displays of people—what to do when they were not interacting with visitors and were staying inside their houses.[11] Sometimes participants chose to take a nap or eat inside their house, away from the constant gaze of visitors. According to one account, on a day when it was very cold and rainy, the Taiwanese Aborigines (in this case, the Atayal) had been shuddering in the cold wind all morning, and in the afternoon they were getting warm by a fire inside their house. When they did not come out to the front of their house, the spectators shouted in loud voices, "Come out! Come out!"[12]

Tsuboi and Kindaichi's book was meant to help bridge the limits that the exhibition's fences maintained between onlookers and participants, although the conversational template in the book in many ways reinforced the parameters of their encounters. But Kindaichi went beyond the typical interactions when he met Ainu Nabezawa Kopuanu, who had come

10.   Tsuboi and Kindaichi, *Nihon kokunai*, 21–26.
11.   Tsuboi and Kindaichi, *Nihon kokunai*, 25.
12.   *KNNS*, October 20, 1912.

FIG. 4.4. From left Uesanashi, Kishino, and Kopuanu. Credit: Author's collection.

to Tokyo from Biratori with Kaizawa Uesanashi and Kopuanu's grand-daughter Kishino (fig. 4.4).[13]

Kindaichi's encounters with Kopuanu had ramifications for his future linguistic research and his recordings of *yukar* (Ainu epic poetry). Kopuanu, who was from the village of Shiunkotsu, had traveled to Tokyo more than eight times to sell goods at expositions. She told Kindaichi that she was able to make a lot of money doing this.[14] On the opening day of the 1912 exposition, Kopuanu, who had tattoos on her arms and around her mouth, spoke with reporters in a subdued voice, in Japanese: "I just make things that don't make money," she said, and then reportedly laughed like she was crying.[15] When the prime minister visited the exposition and inquired after her family's health and asked if they found it cold, Kopuanu reportedly replied, "excellently in the language of the

---

13.　Uesanashi was a man of influence in his town and was well known for his wood carving. He was the only participant in the 1912 exposition who returned for the exposition in Osaka in 1913.

14.　Satō, "Zakkan tenjisareta Ainu," 19.

15.　*TA*, October 1, 1912.

metropolis, 'It's not cold and I don't want to return, I am used to it so there is nothing in particular that is awful.'"[16]

Kindaichi met with Kopuanu at the exposition every day to get her assistance in his study of the Ainu language. He asked her question after question, recorded Ainu epics (jōjishi), and received help translating yukar. At the time, Kindaichi was a poor struggling scholar, and he seized on his fortuitous opportunity to work with Kopuanu in Tokyo. At night he gathered the Ainu from Hokkaido and Karafuto, and he would ask them to clarify the meaning of certain parts of the yukar. He said these sessions were joyful experiences and the participants were happy to explain the parts he did not understand.[17]

Kopuanu told Kindaichi about Nabesawa Wakarupa, a blind transmitter of yukar, who later became an integral source for much of Kindaichi's work. Wakarupa was worried that he would die without being able to pass on all the yukar he remembered. Knowing how rare it was to meet an Ainu who could still transmit oral stories for hours on end, Kindaichi appealed to his supervisor and was given enough money to fund a trip to Hokkaido the following year.[18] Kopuanu and Wakarupa visited Kindaichi the following year, and Wakarupa stayed with Kindaichi, where he transmitted fourteen volumes of yukar. Thus the exposition as a place for learning and exchange brought long-lasting results, which can be seen in Kindaichi's major works on Ainu culture.[19]

THEATRICS OF EMPIRE

Despite Tsuboi's hope for humanist cultural exchange, fairgoers at times seemed intent only on the theatrics of the exhibition. In many reports, what stand out the most are the crowds of people who pushed and shoved, trying to get a glimpse of the people on display:

16. KNNS, November 3, 1912.
17. Kindaichi, Watakushi no aruite, 109–11; Kindaichi, Yūkara no hitobito, 59–60; KNNS, November 1, 1912.
18. Kindaichi, Watakushi no aruite, 112–13.
19. Satō, "Zakkan tenjisareta Ainu"; the yukar were compiled in Itadorimaru no kyoku (1944).

The Taiwanese Aborigines and Ainu were surprised by the crowds and of course tended to be extremely retiring inside their houses. Their supervisor exerted great effort to draw them out. Even so, on the part of the Taiwanese Aborigines, they became used to the crowds and went to the next-door house of the Ainu to visit, and with hand gestures they talked to each other. When they did this there was a ton of applause.[20]

At another time when the Atayal had withdrawn into their dwellings, their manager "made a point to get them to sell the commemorative postcards, and outside of the entrance of their dwelling they brought out tatami mats where they could be easily seen, as well as the wife who was weaving on a loom."[21]

Although most of the time participants performed their roles as representatives of their ethnoracial group in the course of everyday activities, Tsuboi occasionally engaged in his own theatrics, sponsoring events such as the much-publicized "Six-Race Handshake Meeting" (roku jinshu no akushukai), a formal public gathering of individuals from all of the groups at the exposition. Tsuboi opened the ceremony with an anthropological lecture and then introduced the guests.[22] He proclaimed that the participants had been brought together with the intention of amity. When translators relayed Tsuboi's speech to the participants in their own languages, they smiled. The presence of translators was important, as they underscored Tsuboi's insistence that the colonial subjects should not be treated as objects to be stared at but would be seen as humans who needed to interact with others. One of the Karafuto Ainu, most likely an elder named Tsubosawa Rokusuke, stood up and relayed his happiness in getting to know his fellow compatriots (dōhō).

PEDAGOGICS OF EMPIRE

Contrary to past research stressing the one-way communication of human displays, with the colonizer gaining a superficial understanding of colonial subjects by viewing them in "native" settings, Tsuboi's displays were

20. *Yomiuri*, October 7, 1912.
21. *Yomiuri*, October 21, 1912.
22. *TNNS*, October 15, 1912; *KNNS*, October 8 and 10, 1912.

designed to foster a two-way pedagogic exchange. The Japanese were meant to learn about their empire from the colonial subjects on display, and the subjects from the different races were expected to learn about their mother country (*bokoku*). Participants in the human displays were shown a film about the various territories of the empire, for example. Shot by photographers who had been dispatched six months earlier to the different colonies, filming the conditions in each region was said to have been one of the most labor-intensive projects undertaken for the exposition: "In Taiwan of course the customs of the suitable regions were filmed. . . . There were also scenes with great energy and full of life filmed in Hokkaido, Korea, Manchuria, and Karafuto." Scenes of Karafuto showed reindeer herds and emphasized its development through shipping and rail transport; scenes from Taiwan focused on battles fought against the Taiwanese Aborigines and the construction of the "guardline" (*aiyūsen*) that demarcated savage territory, where Aborigines had not submitted to Japanese rule, from regions where they had.[23] When the Karafuto participants saw the Taiwanese Aborigines on the screen, they remarked that their numbers were as much as snow, and they were happy when they recognized their houses and scenes from their hometowns.[24] Japanese audiences were shown the same film about the different colonies. The film was meant to be free for the public to view in the exposition's Tourist Pavilion, but because of overcrowding, the fair organizers soon charged three sen for the majority of the seats.[25]

The duality of the pedagogics of empire took dramatic form when a group of Atayal visited the exposition on a tour to the metropolis (*naichi kankō*) and unexpectedly ran into friends who were on display. Reporters and photographers followed the tour group's every movement, and crowds of bystanders would stop in their tracks, trying to catch a glimpse of the tour group as it passed.[26] Such tour groups were anything but inconspicuous at the exposition, and they were typically accompanied by many police officers. Given the scale and spectacle of the Atayal group,

23. *KNNS*, October 9, 1912; *TNNSB*, October 3, 1912.
24. *KNNS*, October 13, 1912.
25. *Yomiuri*, October 21, 1912.
26. Part II of this book focuses on *naichi kankō*. Besides Taiwanese Aborigines, the program took Koreans, Manchurians, and Micronesians to Japan.

it is not surprising that the story of their unexpected encounter with their friends in the exposition made headlines all over the empire.

When the tour group ran into the Atayal family in the exposition, both groups were reported to have tears of happiness in their eyes.[27] The Atayal family in the display was from the village of Wulai (Urai) in the Kusshaku settlement, near where most of those on the tour were from.[28] The family—Patto Chuwasu, his wife, Pisui Yago, and their three children—earned their livelihood weaving baskets.[29] When one of the members of the Atayal sightseeing group saw Chuwasu, he said to him, "We heard you went to Japan, and we worried, thinking about where you went; this is where you were taken to? Your health hasn't changed?" He told Chuwasu that the group was surprised to see that the family had brought their house and rebuilt it right in the middle of Tokyo and that their children had come along. They asked him, with sad faces, whether he was planning on returning to Taiwan. Chuwasu told the tour group that they could not return yet. "Only after the moon changes and the next moon comes out will my business be finished," he replied. He also requested that they relay a message to his father and brother saying that he was perfectly fine in Tokyo.

A reporter for the newspaper *Karafuto nichi nichi shinbun* remarked that the meeting was truly a sight to see, obviously finding it surprising for "people who looked like ogres to express such beautiful emotion, which flowed from their iron-like bodies."[30] *Otaru shinbun* reported that the "ogres had human feelings" and that, on witnessing the reunion, "even the police leader [of the tour group] could not contain tears of sympathy."[31] The reporters' shock at seeing such emotion expressed by "barbarians" makes it clear that despite Tsuboi's best intentions, the colonial status and different appearance of the Taiwanese Aborigines still reinforced doubts among the Japanese that they were fully human.

The Atayal tour group left Chuwasu and toured the rest of the exposition. They were presented with memorial photo albums and given Japanese sake, hand-rolled tobacco, and salted Japanese crackers (*senbei*). They met

27. *OS*, October 14, 1912.
28. *TA*, October 13, 1912.
29. *TNNSB*, October 4, 1912; see KZW for a postcard of the family.
30. *KNNS*, October 20, 1912.
31. *OS*, October 14, 1912.

the Ainu in their display and remarked that they did not look Japanese. Roku, the Ainu elder from Karafuto, reportedly looked at the Taiwanese Aborigines and remarked that the Japanese government had its work cut out for it.[32] When they watched the film about the colonies and the Atayal saw the Uilta people using guns, they asked if the guns had been given to them. The issue of guns was a bone of contention for groups like the Atayal and Bunun, who used them for hunting, because the colonial government was confiscating their weapons, including hunting rifles, in an effort to quell resistance.[33]

Before leaving the exposition, they returned to say goodbye to Chuwasu and his family. Chuwasu told the departing group, "Do you remember asking about our health, well, the truth is Bai Bai Patto [Chuwasu's little daughter] has a fever, but it is no big deal, so please tell everyone we are fine so they do not worry." He had one more message for his father and brother: "Definitely tell them that it's the time to harvest the rice, so please tell them not to steal. If my father and brother harvest the rice, when I return I will give them an appropriate reward."[34]

The reporters' descriptions of this reunion forced readers to confront the fact the Atayal were human beings. The fact that their emotional reactions were under such scrutiny betrays the prejudice directed toward them. The emphasis on their humanity (implying it was not a given) was part of a larger discourse since the colonization of Taiwan in 1895 that fluctuated between seeing the indigenous people as eternally savage or as having the potential to act like civilized humans. As the Atayal encounter at the exposition dramatically demonstrated, both the tourists and those on display were meant to observe and learn about the empire while simultaneously serving as objects of study and fascination.

The idea that colonial subjects were intended to learn about the empire while at the exposition was further demonstrated when Ainu, Nivkh, and Utila participants were taken on a sightseeing tour of Tokyo by car, something they had been eager to do. They drove past the imperial palace, and because they did not have a word for "emperor" in their own languages, the Japanese tried to explain how the emperor was the

32.   *OS*, October 14, 1912.
33.   *TA*, October 13, 1912.
34.   *KNNS*, October 20, 1912.

number one lord in Japan. They were reportedly surprised by the number of people in Tokyo, for they had thought that the people who came to the exposition each day before were the same ones who came the following day, and the next.[35] They visited the Mitsukoshi department store in Nihonbashi, which boasted escalators and elevators.[36] There they were given refreshments and took a memorial photograph. At Mitsukoshi they had the opportunity to try using a telephone and to buy many souvenirs.[37] For these new subjects of Japan, learning about the empire meant enjoying the thrills of modern city life. Riding the elevator at Mitsukoshi was a new experience that was also attracting huge crowds of excited Japanese. Thus the colonial subjects' wonderment at modern city life was no different than that of tourists from rural Japan. They also went to Tokyo's Imperial Theater, where it was said their presence drew more attention than the performance on the stage. Newspaper reports of the event show that even as they were supposed to be learning about the empire, they were simultaneously on display.[38]

RECONFIGURING COLONIAL SUBJECTS

The colonial subjects on display at the exposition were at times fetishized by the Japanese visitors. Women and younger children, in particular, were both doted on and pitied. Twelve-year-old Teru, daughter of the Ainu elder Roku, was one of the more popular participants at the exposition. It was reported in an article on the Japanese prime minister's visit to the exhibit that Teru could even speak Japanese.[39] She was especially popular among the female visitors. In one account describing her popularity, a group of female junior high school students asked Teru to sign the memorial photo albums they had bought from her. She started by signing the books "Tsubosawa Teruko age 12," but as crowds gathered around her table and more and more people begged her to sign their books, it was

35. *KNNS*, October 13, 1912.
36. "Mitsukoshi Department Store, c. 1903–1323," http://www.oldtokyo.com/mitsukoshi-department-store-c-1903-1923/ (accessed July 25, 2018).
37. "Giriya-ku to Ainu no raiten"; see KZW for a photograph of their visit.
38. *TA*, October 25, 1912; *TNNS*, October 25, 1912; *KNNS*, November 1, 1912. Also at the theater was a *naichi kankō* of Koreans. *HT*, October 25, 1912.
39. *KNNS*, October 12, 1912.

reported that she had to resort to writing only "Teru," and even so, she was able to sign only 200 books. Among female visitors, Teru was often called the exposition's "beloved and most popular daughter."[40] Testifying to her popularity, a postcard discovered in the collection of Akino Shigeki (fig. 4.5) features the Karafuto Ainu on the front and has "Teruko" written on the back, signed by the girl herself (fig. 4.6).[41]

Colonial participants at the exposition also subverted the roles they were expected to play. The Karafuto Ainu elder Tsubosawa Rokusuke, also known as Roku, for example, played a leading role at an event called the "Social Gathering of the Races" (jinshu konshinkai), which was held on November 9. This gathering was one of the earliest events in which Japanese subjects from all over the empire gathered to celebrate the empire. Held at the exposition's Tourist Pavilion, it brought together people from all walks of life, from Home Minister Hara Takashi and Foreign Minister Uchida Kōsai to actors and famous entertainers, such as kabuki entertainer Ennosuke, novelist Emi Suiin, comedic storytellers, and geisha from Shinbashi and Shitaya.[42] Yomiuri's over-the-top description proclaimed it the "best social gathering in the world, in which all the assembled races danced together."[43] The purpose of the party was to honor the numerous colonial participants who had agreed to display themselves among the reconstructed dwellings and backdrops of their respective colonies. Newspaper accounts' estimates of the number in attendance varied from 300 to 1,000 people.[44]

The event was memorable not just because people from so many races in Japan's empire were together under one roof but also because it was a party in which Japanese—from all social classes—mingled freely with the colonial participants in drunken revelry. It was reported that the Hokkaido Ainu, Uilta, Nivkh, Karafuto Ainu, Taiwanese Aborigines, and Taiwanese of Han ethnicity moved about freely, for status was not taken into account in determining the seating arrangements. Although there were times when colonial participants got up on stage to entertain the audience, Japanese attendees also joined in the dancing and entertainment.[45] *Tokyo*

40. *KNNS*, October 20, 1912.
41. Conversation with Akino Shigeki in Sapporo, December 2010.
42. *KNNS*, November 23, 1912.
43. *Yomiuri*, November, 10, 1912.
44. *Yomiuri*, November, 10, 1912; *KNNS*, November 23, 1912.
45. *Takushoku hakurankai kinen shashinchō*; see KZW.

FIG. 4.5. From left: Tsubosawa Rokusuke, Tsubosawa Teru, Kimura Chikamaha, and Kageyama Chukaranke. Credit: Author's photograph of Akino Shigeki's postcard.

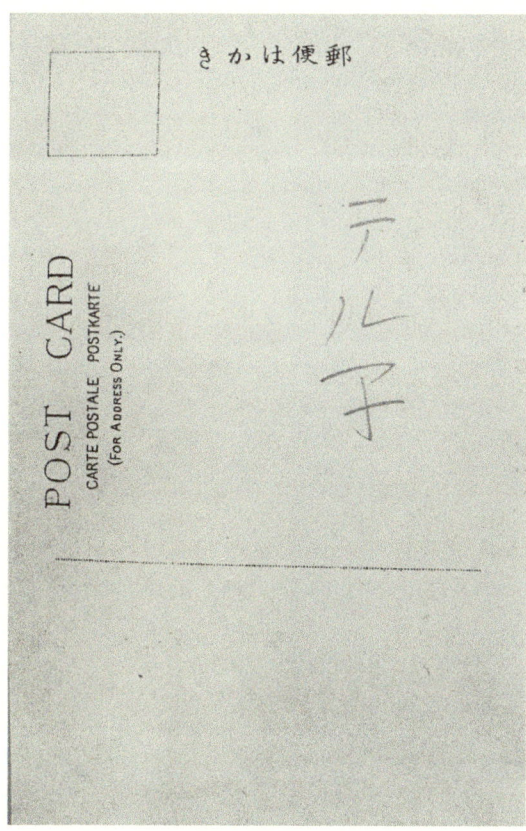

FIG. 4.6. Teru's signature on the back of the card, as "Teruko." Credit: Author's photograph of the back of Akino Shigeki's postcard.

asahi's headline the next day highlighted the unconventional nature of the party: "Unheard of Rare Party: At the Social Gathering of the Races at the Colonial Exposition Barbarians and Tokyoites All Dance."

The speech of the night was given by sixty-year-old Karafuto Ainu Tsubosawa Roku, whose greeting was met with thunderous applause.[46] He wore traditional *attush* (bark-cloth) robes, and as he stroked the beautiful beard covering his chest, he glowered down at the audience. He proclaimed excellently in the language of the metropolis, "We are very happy to have been able to come to the Colonial Exposition and go sightseeing around Tokyo. There is nothing more wonderful than each of the races, from the far south of Japan to the far north, being gathered together and enjoying themselves. On behalf of everyone, I thank you."[47]

Roku, the leader of the Karafuto Ainu in the Otasan region, was the unofficial spokesman for all of the various races at the exposition, both at the party that night and throughout the exposition.[48] Despite his speech in support of the exposition, what he did and said on other occasions during the exposition illustrated that his participation was a bit more complicated, and his view of his place in the empire was far from that of a subdued colonized subject.

In an article titled "It's My Territory" (Ore no ryōbun da), for example, Roku discussed the conflict that the Karafuto Ainu experienced with Japanese officials who had no understanding of the Ainu's territorial claims. He explained,

> In fact, in the past every Ainu had territory stipulated for them. Bafunke [a major Ainu leader from Ai village] lives in Aikawa and his territory is in Tonaicha. My territory is from Otasan until Sakanehama, which has from long ago been fixed and unchanged. The things that come into this territory I deal with as I please. What is so surprising [about the fact] that I do this?[49]

Roku offered a concrete example of how the territorial rights of the Ainu were called into question by Japanese officials in a conflict over a

46. *TA*, November 10, 1912.
47. *KNNS*, November 14 and 23, 1912.
48. *TA*, November 10, 1912; *KNNS*, November 23, 1912.
49. *KNNS*, October 2, 1912.

whale that had beached itself on the eastern coast near his Ainu village. As the person with the rights to the land on which the whale had beached itself, according to the Ainu, Roku was responsible for dealing with the situation. Roku criticized the Japanese for also believing that the Ainu had nothing to do with why whales came ashore, explaining that the reason the whale came to shore was because it "had been given to us by the gods on the basis of prayers."[50] When a fisherman discovered the whale, he went to Roku, who was known as a "wise man for consultation." Roku took care of dividing up the remains of the whale and then misdirected the Japanese officials when they came by inquiring about it, thereby ensuring that the remains of the whale and the resulting profits were divvied up among the Ainu. According to Roku, the young *shamo* (Ainu name for Japanese) officials became a problem for him, so he feigned ignorance and would have nothing more to do with them. He said the officials were mystified and "at sea" when it came to the Ainu territory theory, which in their estimation seemed "to be something out of the history of the age of the gods," a reference to the first chapter of the eighth century book of myths, the *Kojiki*.[51]

The story of the tensions between the Japanese officials and Roku, and how Roku gained the upper hand, illustrates that in some cases the Karafuto Ainu maintained a level of autonomy in the empire. In a photo of prominent Karafuto Ainu leaders taken in the early twentieth century, Roku is among those pictured, along with Chief Bafunke, who he mentioned had significant territorial rights, and Shirakawa Moima, one of the participants of the 1913 exposition.[52] His official portrait was also taken by Bronisław Piłsudski during his research trip to Karafuto (figs. 4.7 and 4.8).

Roku was obviously a man of influence in his region, and it became well known during the exposition that when he was younger he had worked for a Japanese official named Minakami Chūtafu, whom he had accompanied on a trip to Tokyo for five days.[53] During his first visit to the metropolis, Roku had visited the Yoshiwara pleasure quarters and

50.   *KNNS*, October 2, 1912.

51.   History of the age of gods (*shindaishi*) is the first chapter of the *Kojiki* (Records of Ancient Matters). *KNNS*, October 2, 1912.

52.   Kitahara, "Nishihira Ume," 34.

53.   *TA*, October 13, 1912; *KNNS*, November 23, 1912.

FIGS. 4.7 AND 4.8. Roku (left) in photographs taken by Bronisław Piłsudski, in a studio background and dressed in fine clothing. Courtesy of the collections of the Russian Museum of Ethnography, St. Petersburg, Russia.

engaged a prostitute, something of which he was very proud. He kept a paper that had her writing on it as a treasured memento of the experience.[54] His pride in paying for a prostitute represents a claim of power through sexual virility, and the evidence of this encounter puts a different spin on the fetishization of the colonial subject: in this case Roku was not the object of fetishization but the subject exercising the power to fetishize.

Roku was regarded as a master of a form of Ainu debate called *charanke*, which involved debating an opponent to the point of exhaustion; he was called the number-one orator on the eastern seacoast. Being a good orator was an essential skill for Ainu leaders. Roku bragged about how he enjoyed using his skill to toy with the Japanese tourists who asked him about traditional Ainu customs. The presence of orators like Roku, who advanced the cause of his people by talking about the importance of recognizing the Ainu's past claims to land and fishing rights, demonstrated how people in the human displays could appropriate the roles they were supposed to play. Although his primary role at the exposition was to represent his ethnoracial group, by talking about his beliefs concerning territorial rights and his prior experiences in the metropolis, Roku forced many to view him as an individual, not just as a living anthropological exhibit. At the same time that they were being displayed in primitive settings, some colonial subjects were also speaking out about issues involving their political, social, and economic status in the empire.

RECRUITMENT: IT'S WHO YOU KNOW

How participants from the colonies were recruited to take part in the 1912 Tokyo exposition varied; in some cases, members of the indigenous communities helped facilitate recruitment. Tsuboi had dispatched his colleagues to different regions of the empire, each equipped to speak the native language and authorized to offer a salary of one yen a day and the promise of sightseeing in the metropolis. Their success depended on factors beyond the recruiters' control, such as the willingness of local leaders to identify suitable people and word of mouth about others

54. *KNNS*, October 2, 1912.

who had gone to the metropole and returned. An important factor that affected participants' decision to go was other community members' experiences with travel. For example, Patto Chuwasu and his family from Wulai village had spoken to the Atayal who had gone on a tour to the metropolis in April 1912. Members of that group told Chuwasu and his family that Japan had a lot of rice, people, and houses. On arriving in Tokyo, Chuwasu found this to be true—and more. He was surprised by everything, including seeing and riding in a car for the first time. He told reporters that since their arrival a month before the exposition opened, everyone had treated them very well and they were very happy.[55]

At the opposite end of the empire, in Karafuto, a major obstacle to persuading the Ainu participants to travel to the metropolis was their fear that they would never return to their villages. But in a fortuitous turn of events, the return of the Karafuto Ainu Hanamori Shin'yoshi from a much-famed expedition to the South Pole played a big role in successfully recruiting Karafuto Ainu participants to go to Tokyo. In the months leading up to the exposition, the linguists and translators working for Tsuboi in Karafuto and Hokkaido reported that they were having a hard time recruiting Ainu participants. Japanese linguist Nakanome Satoru visited the Karafuto region in August 1912, a few months before the exposition opened, and recorded information about the difficulties Tsuboi's emissaries had in recruiting Karafuto participants, in particular, because they were afraid they would not return home.[56] Among the Ainu, it was said that the original settlers had come to Karafuto by crossing the continent and had encountered many difficulties on the way. Since then, the Karafuto people had heeded their ancestors' advice not to cross the sea, and they believed travel to Hokkaido and Tokyo to be difficult. When exposition participants were about to depart for Tokyo, they suddenly balked and did not want to go.

That was when chance stepped in, in the form of Hanamori Shin'yoshi.[57] Hanamori, along with Yamabe Yasunosuke, a Karafuto Ainu who had fought in the Russo-Japanese War, had gone on an expedition

55. *TNNSB*, October 4, 1912.
56. Nakanome, *Karafuto no hanashi*, 1–2.
57. Chiri Mashiho recorded stories from Hanamori and praised him for his incredible memory. Satō, *Nankyoku ni tatta*, 29.

to the South Pole in 1910.[58] Because Hanamori had not returned for more than two years, the Ainu believed he had died, further demonstrating that traveling abroad was dangerous. But Hanamori finally returned on June 20, 1912, with the other expedition members—all were alive.[59] Fortuitously for the recruiters, Hanamori's return occurred right at the time they were trying to persuade some Ainu to go to Tokyo. Nakanome writes, "It was due to Hanamori's persuasion that at last they were able to depart for Tokyo."[60] The explorer's return—something out of the control of the recruiters—shows how interactions within the empire at times relied on forces that were not under Japanese control.

Elsewhere, recruiters had been working to find willing Nivkh and Uilta participants. They eventually convinced the powerful Nivkh chief Bokon from Bōe village in Shitsuka to come to the exposition with his wife, Chufurendo, and their nineteen-year-old son, Punyon. From the Nivkh point of view, going to the exposition was desirable as it was seen as a way to do foreign travel.[61] Bokon was characterized as a progressive leader whose policies increased the economic viability of his people in the face of their decreasing population.[62] Nakanome considered the Nivkh people more progressive than the Uilta because several Nivkh could read Japanese characters and certain newspapers.[63] Bokon was said to be able to speak Japanese very well and was able to read and write katakana, which he demonstrated by reading kana in a picture book.[64] Bokon's policies—encouraging the use of reindeer to help with agricultural labor, for example, and intermarriage with other races—were seen as crucial to ensuring the longevity of his people. Nakanome described him as a patriotic and powerful chief, whom he viewed as the most intelligent person among not just the Nivkh people but all the races of northern Karafuto.[65]

58. Yamabe founded one of the first schools for Karafuto Ainu in 1909. Satō, *Nankyoku ni tatta*, 7–9.

59. Satō, *Nankyoku ni tatta*, 2; "Nankyoku tanken ni tsuite," http://shirase-kinenkan.jp/tankentai.html (accessed July 25, 2018).

60. Nakanome, *Karafuto no hanashi*, 43.

61. *TA*, October 1, 1912. Tangiku, "Aru Nivufuhito," 141.

62. *KNNS*, October 10, 1912.

63. Nakanome, *Karafuto no hanashi*, 70–71. He specified that these newspapers had *furigana* (smaller kana printed next to the kanji as a reading aid).

64. *KNNS*, October 15, 1912.

65. Nakanome, *Karafuto no hanashi*, 73.

THE IMPERMANENCE OF THE EMPIRE'S BORDERS

Planning the human displays at the colonial exposition and recruiting the participants revealed the instability and impermanence of the empire's boundaries. People from a formally recognized colony of Japan's empire, Korea, were missing from the human displays, and people from an unofficial colony such as Hokkaido, the Ainu, were featured, alongside Taiwanese Aborigines and the various races from Karafuto, which became a prefecture in 1907. In 1912, Hokkaido's inclusion in the exposition alongside other colonies illustrated its ambiguous colonial status and caused some to debate whether it was more like a prefecture or a colony.[66] Yamaji Katsuhiko argues that in 1912, the Japanese people commonly thought of Hokkaido, Taiwan, Korea, and the Kantōshu (Kwangtung) province as colonies.[67] As fig. 4.9 illustrates, although the 1912 exposition was meant to feature the colonies in miniature, the exclusion of Korean participants in the living displays points to another dimension of the exposition and the question of what constituted the empire.

Tsuboi had dispatched an agent to Korea to recruit participants and collect traditional building materials. When the agent, Ōno Nobutaro, a professor from Tokyo Imperial University, failed to get the consent of the Japanese colonial government in Korea, the plans to recruit Koreans and materials for the exhibit were abandoned.[68] The refusal of the Korean government to send people or materials for this display is significant, especially when considered in conjunction with past controversies over the inclusion of Korean participants in the 1903 and 1907 human displays at domestic expositions in Japan. It reveals that human displays in Japan were mediated by certain governments' refusal to participate (in this case, the Japanese colonial government in Korea) and by protests. Interestingly, Okinawans also were not included in the 1912 display; either the perception of their ethnoracial difference had faded away by 1912, or the

---

66. This was evident in an article supporting a discounted train fare for people from Hokkaido going to the exposition, which had been given to people from the other colonies. *KNNS*, September 28, 1912.

67. Yamaji, *Kindai Nihon*, 51.

68. *TA*, October 1, 1912.

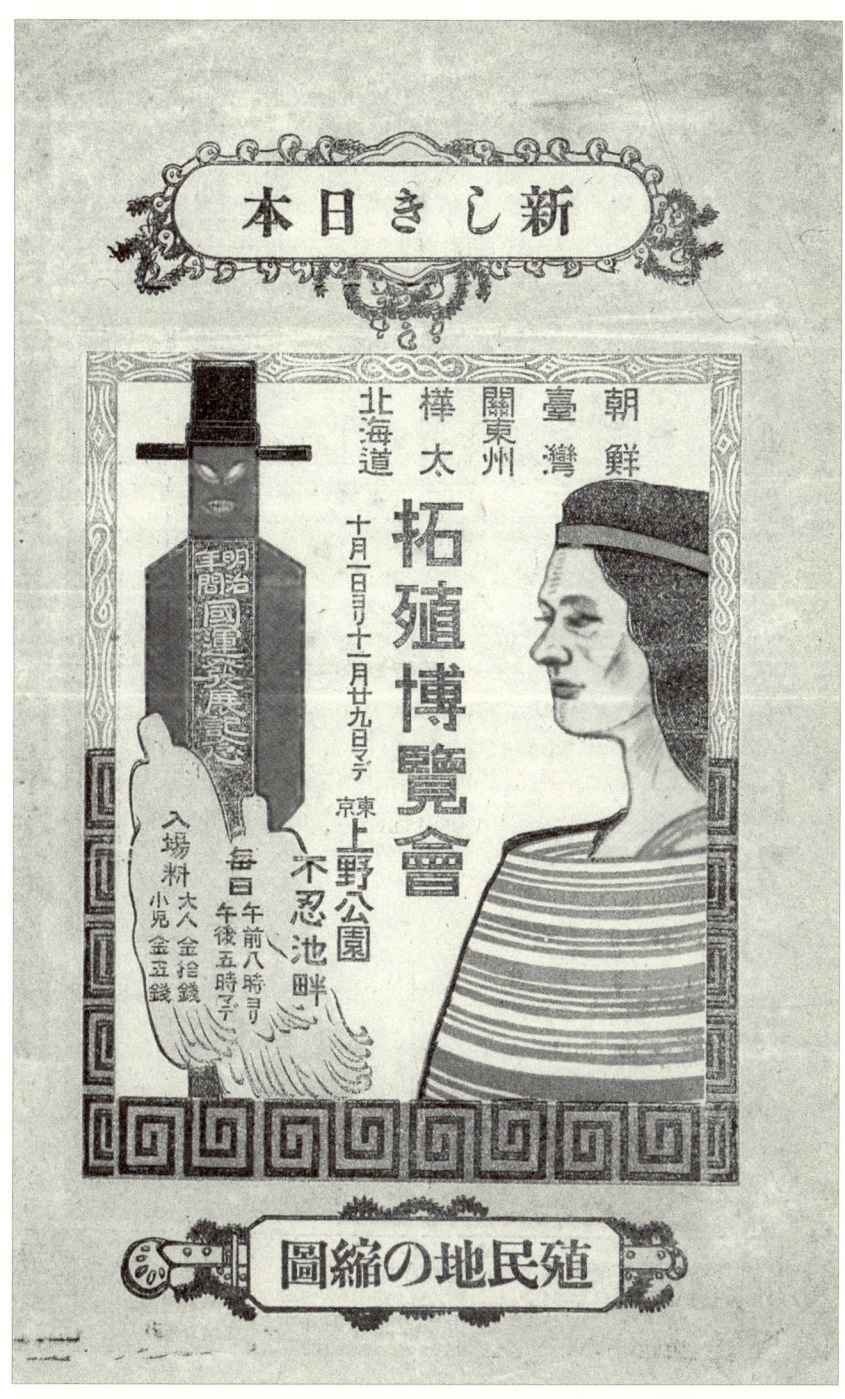

FIG. 4.9. "New Japan" 1912 Tokyo Colonial Exposition pamphlet. "The colonies in miniature: Korea, Taiwan, Kantōshu, Karafuto and Hokkaido." Courtesy of Collection NOMURA Co., Ltd., Japan.

protests in 1903 and 1907 had been enough to dissuade organizers from attempting to include them in future displays.

In addition to the Koreans' absence, the Han Taiwanese were much less visible in the living displays in 1912. Two Taiwanese were displayed in the re-created villages, but they did not feature in news stories about the exposition to the extent that the Atayal, Nivkh, and Uilta displays did, or those of the Hokkaido and Karafuto Ainu. Taiwanese was the only language not included in the book Tsuboi created to help visitors converse with the people on display. There is one photo of a "Taiwanese native," but this image was not widely disseminated.[69] The near invisibility of the Han Taiwanese participants suggests either tensions over their display or a lack of interest in them because they could not be "primitivized" or "exocitized" in the same way the Atayal could be.

When we carefully examine which peoples were exhibited and which were not, we see that in 1912 the exposition reflected imperial realities that are often glossed over today in an effort to reflect an idealized and coherent view of the empire. The facts that Hokkaido was so readily placed alongside the other colonies without much complaint, the Okinawans were not included, the Japanese colonial government in Korea refused to send Korean participants, and the Han Taiwanese were nearly invisible give us an accurate snapshot of the tensions and ambiguities inherent in Japan's imperial project in the early twentieth century.

1913 Osaka Colonial Exposition

The following headline ran in the pages of *Osaka mainichi* near the start of the 1913 Osaka Colonial Exposition:

> BARBARIANS TALK A LOAD OF GARBAGE
> IF THEY AREN'T ALLOWED TO DRINK BEER THEY WILL LEAVE!

In the accompanying article, participants in the fair's human displays aired their disappointments with daily life at the exposition.[70] They

69. *Takushoku hakurankai kinen shashinchō*; see KZW.
70. *OM*, April 26, 1913.

complained partly because of what they had heard from participants in the Tokyo exposition the year before—that they had been taken around the metropolis several times, they had instructors who taught them the language of the metropolis, and they had eaten delicious Japanese and Chinese food. This was not the case for the Osaka participants. The article reported that even though they were paid well—round-trip travel costs were borne by the exposition and the participants received daily wages—the "barbarians" were complaining about the rising cost of living at the exposition.[71] It had been agreed beforehand that the exposition would provide them with meals at a cost of about forty-five sen per person per day. But as the days went by, more and more things were not included in the price, such as cheap kinds of meat, vegetables, and even chopsticks. They wanted beer and *shōchū* (liquor), and they threatened that if they didn't receive them they would return home. According to the report, the exhibit manager was surprised and made no comment. Although the reporter thought the participants' demands were absurd, the article shows that their expectations for their treatment were based on what they had heard from the Tokyo participants.[72] This report further illustrates the importance of word of mouth among the colonial participants and how the travel experiences of some colonial subjects had brought others to the metropolis to participate in the 1913 exposition. Among the participants in Osaka in 1913, there were several interesting connections with the 1912 Tokyo participants that contributed to their agreeing to go to Osaka.

A RETURN PARTICIPANT AND A SICK DAUGHTER

Among the Hokkaido Ainu, Kaizawa Uesanashi was one who had participated in the 1912 Tokyo Colonial Exposition and then returned for the Osaka Exposition, this time bringing his wife, Monunpa, and their thirteen-year-old son, Zentarō. According to reports, Zentarō was in the sixth grade, could read and write, and was said to be a good

71. Wages were determined by sex and age: men one yen a day, women seventy sen, and children fifty sen.

72. *OM*, April 26, 1913.

child.[73] Kaizawa Utorentoku, a renowned wood carver from the same village as Uesanashi and his family, came with them.[74] Both men were artisans from prominent families. In a study of Nibutani village in Biratori in 1953, Kindaichi Kyōsuke identified the seven major families in the village and traced their genealogy. Both men were identified as belonging to the major clans that founded the village.[75] Utorentoku and Uesanashi's relationship had been established when they traveled together to Sapporo in 1893 to sell their hand-carved wooden dishes and plates. The men are credited with starting the wood-carving folk art business in Nibutani, and their woodwork is featured in museums and books as examples of Ainu craftsmanship (figs. 4.10 and 4.11).[76]

From a young age, Utorentoku had enjoyed carving. He carved wooden decorative plates, pipes, sticks, sword handles, and various tools for making tea. In his hometown of Biratori, it is well known that in 1907 the Imperial Household Agency (Kunaicho) bought a variety of handcrafted goods from Utorentoku, a distinction that indicated the skill and value of his work.[77] There was not much written about him during the exposition, except an account of one incident. A group of spectators was crowded outside the window of the Ainu house trying to glimpse them making Japanese wooden shoes. Reportedly, in a sudden explosion of anger, Utorentoku threw a ladleful of water at the heads of the spectators.[78]

Photographs of Utorentoku's work were featured in a 1951 encyclopedia in a section on the Ainu people.[79] His carvings are well known; even today craftsmen make works based on his original designs. In 1999 journalist Satō Yūji interviewed Utorentoku's grandson, who remarked that his grandfather "had been a very beautiful youthful man, he had a good head, was eloquent and was also an educator." He said that Utorentoku had showed him a gold medal he received at the 1913 exposition. The medal was five inches in diameter and several millimeters thick. The

73. OM, April 16, 1913.
74. OS, April 21, 1913; see KZW for a postcard of the Hokkaido Ainu.
75. Kindaichi, "Hokkaido Hidaka," 77–78.
76. Narita et al. (eds.), Kindaika no naka, 303.
77. Satō, "Zakkan tenjisareta Ainu"; Tachibana, Hokkaido-shi, 1:173.
78. OM, April 16, 1913. Utorentoku died a year later. Tachibana, Hokkaido-shi, 1:173.
79. Jidō hyakka jiten.

FIG. 4.10. Plate carved by Uesanashi. Courtesy of Nibutani Ainu Culture Museum.

FIG. 4.11. Plate carved by Utorentoku. Courtesy of Kaizawa Toru.

grandson did not know why his grandfather had received the medal, but the medal is kept in his house as a family heirloom.[80]

Utorentoku and Uesanashi and his family were not the only Ainu at the Osaka Colonial Exposition. More than thirty Ainu had been hired to perform the bear ceremony.[81] They performed the bear dance from ten o'clock in the morning until five in the afternoon.[82] Reports said that during the bear ceremony, even the children who accompanied the performers drank sake.[83] The group was led by sixty-three-year-old Hiramura Ikoratsu from Nibutani, who had come to Osaka with his wife, Shikamura Misuke, and their six-year-old daughter, Shike. Ikoratsu said they had decided to come to Osaka because Shike was sick and suffered from peritonitis. The medical treatment she could receive in Osaka had been the incentive for them to participate in the exposition. After she received medical treatment from a doctor in Osaka, she was said to be progressing nicely, and the family wanted to return to their village when she had recuperated enough to be able to go home. As it did for Fushine Kōzō, who participated in the 1903 exposition to raise money for an Ainu school, the journey to the metropolis could provide colonial participants with opportunity, income, and at times recognition for Ainu causes (better welfare and education), but those benefits came at a price—agreeing to perform traditional Ainu roles for entertainment purposes.

It is significant that the leader of the Ainu hired to perform the bear ceremony came from the Biratori region, and most of the thirty performers probably also came from there. As we have seen, Ainu from Biratori had participated in the 1904 Louisiana Purchase Exposition, the 1910 Japan-British Exhibition, and the 1912 Tokyo Exposition. The fact that Uesanashi returned to take part in a second exposition with his family and Utorentoku suggests that hearing stories of success or seeing the prosperity of former participants who were able to construct new houses after their return encouraged others to participate in subsequent expositions.

Participants at the 1913 Osaka Colonial Exposition also took part largely as a result of their own prior experiences of travel to the metropolis.

80.   Satō, "Zakkan tenjisareta Ainu," 19.
81.   *OA*, April 27, 1913, pictured at Mitsukoshi; see KZW.
82.   *OM*, May 31, 1913.
83.   *OA*, April 24, 1913.

The two Atayal families at the exposition had traveled to the metropolis in 1912 on a government-sponsored tour. They were said to be the families of chiefs. Because they had traveled and gone sightseeing all over the city, it was said they were well versed in metropolitan ways. Although they were not too enthusiastic about Japanese food, they thought the country was beautiful.[84] In addition to having traveled to Japan before, they had heard about the positive experiences of the Atayal family at the 1912 exposition.[85] Watan Paihō and his wife, Chuwashi Watan, came to the exposition from Wulai, the same village as the 1912 participants. The other Atayal family, Bira Omarai, his wife, Bakanrutsukun, and their three-year-old child, Yu-min, came from the village of Rimogan, which is very close to Wulai (see map 2). One exposition visitor wrote on a postcard that featured the family that they sold him the card. Visitors' recordings of their interactions with those in the villages recalls the 1910 postcards and the visitors authenticating their experiences with similar such observations.[86]

A HONEYMOON BEYOND OUR DREAMS

A twenty-eight-year-old Nivkh man named Uerakka and his eighteen-year-old wife, Aruraika, received a lot of press on their arrival at the exposition, owing to their recent marriage. Newspapers reported that the couple had decided to participate in the exposition as a honeymoon trip. Whether this was true or the reporter was taking liberties because of their newlywed status, the domestication of participants in the displays through such human interest stories helped bridge the gap between those on display and those who came to see them. Uerakka was reported to speak broken Japanese, and he asked people to call him Utarō. He was connected to the Japanese anthropologist Torii Ryūzō. The year before, he had been employed as a ship's coxswain on Torii's expedition to Kara-futo and Russia.[87] Although Torii's memoirs do not mention Uerakka by name, in a section devoted to his anthropological surveys in Karafuto and Russia, he does mention his boat journey with several Uilta and

84. *OM*, April 14, 1913.
85. *OM*, April 26, 1913.
86. Author's collection, see KZW for postcard and writing; *OM*, April 14, 1913.
87. *KNNS*, April 3, 1913; *OM*, April 11, 1913.

Nivkh.[88] While Uerakka was employed on Torii's expedition in Russia, he met and fell in love in with his future wife. Although he returned to Karafuto, he did not forget about Aruraika, and he later returned to Russia to marry her. Throughout the exposition she stayed close by her husband's side. It was reported that Aruraika and some others in the human displays envied the kimonos of the metropolitan women.[89]

THE CAPITALIST

A thirty-three-year-old Uilta man named Ushirai and his twelve-year-old daughter, Mariya, also came from Karafuto. The Japanese linguist Nakanome, a proponent of assimilating the various races of the empire, had met Ushirai and described him as "nothing more than a frivolous talented man."[90] Why Nakanome had such a bad impression of Ushirai is a mystery; it could be that he had failed to assist Nakanome in the manner he desired.[91] Although we learn more about Nakanome and his values from his description of Ushirai than we do about Ushirai himself, Nakanome's account is still valuable for its depiction of the kind of Uilta people recruited for the exposition.

Ushirai had a considerable amount of wealth and power among the Uilta, although Nakanome described him as a man "lacking any qualification as a leader of his people and whose virtue of generosity and hospitality was insufficient" and claimed that because Ushirai was seen by the Uilta as a "Japan worshipper," their trust in him was weak. Ushirai was clever in speaking the Japanese language, a rare talent among the Uilta, and this had helped him become a genius at making money. Reindeer were the most valuable commodity in the region, and he raised so many reindeer that no one in his hometown of Shisuka rivaled him in wealth. Ushirai was said to be very good at negotiating the buying and selling of commodities. He was seen as a capitalist among his people, and many were in debt to him financially. Because of his money-lending capability,

---

88.   Torii, *Aru rōgakuto*, 158–63.
89.   *OM*, April 16, 1913; *KNNS*, April 3, 1913; see KZW.
90.   Nakanome, *Karafuto no hanashi*, 86–87; see KZW.
91.   Nakanome had stated he wanted to bring some Karafuto natives back with him to Tokyo, in order to study them. Perhaps Ushirai did not help him with his efforts.

he was seen as a useful person, but with that type of economic power came great control over the welfare of various people. Nakanome, a proponent of preserving the races that he feared were dying out, was alarmed that Ushirai did not have any sense of patriotism and did not take on a leadership role in implementing policies to prevent the extinction of the Uilta or improve their way of life. Ushirai occasionally relayed the thoughts and requests of his people to the Japanese authorities, but in Nakanome's eyes he was nothing more than a translator. Nakanome concluded his condemnation by writing, "he did not have any consistent principles and in his thoughts and actions there were many points of contradiction." Ushirai was a successful man who served as an intermediary and translator for Japanese officials, traders, and researchers. He was most likely recruited for the exposition because of his ability to speak Japanese, and once there, he was relied on to facilitate relations between his people and the Japanese, a role that further raised his status.[92]

ON THE RECOMMENDATION OF THE CHIEF

Sasaki Seiji, who had served as the translator and caretaker of the Karafuto Ainu at the 1912 exposition, returned to Karafuto to recruit participants for the 1913 exposition. At the time, he was employed in the General Affairs section of the Karafuto government. He consulted with Chief Bafunke (Japanese name Kimura Aiyoshi) of Ai village, who along with Roku was a leader in the region. Sasaki did not approach anyone without Bafunke's recommendation. Bafunke's first recommendation was to ask Roku and his family to participate again. Roku's past experience at the exposition and his language abilities made him an ideal candidate. But Roku said his daughter, Teru, was not feeling well and could not travel. After Sasaki failed to secure Roku's participation, Bafunke suggested Shirakawa Shiemon (Ainu name Moima) and his wife, Kuruparumaha, from the town of Horo (see fig. 4.12).[93] It is significant that all of the recommended Karafuto Ainu were leaders and men and women

92. Nakanome, *Karafuto no hanashi*, 86–87.
93. Also called Asowanma in newspapers. Spelling for Kuruparumaha from Uyeda, "Journey of the Tonkori," 109. Japanese reports spelled her name in katakana as Kurubaruma.

FIG. 4.12. From left, Haijō Haibatsutei, Shirakawa Shiemon, Shirakawa Kuruparumaha, and Nishihira Ume. This card is unique as it shows spectators in the shot. Credit: Author's collection.

of influence in their region. Thirty years before, Shiemon had run the Karafuto branch of a Hakodate fishery, and he was now the recognized leader of the East Shiraura village and worked for a freight company on the Horo River. His wife, Kuruparumaha, was a famed *tonkori* (five-string Ainu musical instrument) "virtuoso."[94]

A sculptor who made a wide range of handicrafts, Haijō Haibatsutei was recruited as well, along with Nishihira Ume (Ainu name Ska), who also played the *tonkori* (see fig. 4.12).[95] In newspapers she was reported to be Haibatsutei's thirteen-year-old daughter, Shiyuka [*sic*], and was said to be a second-year student at the Ainu native school (*dojin gakkō*), but current scholarship casts doubt on them being related.[96] She was said to be just as beautiful as Teru, who had been an exposition favorite the year before.[97] Ume took part in the exposition because of her association with *tonkori* players Kuruparumaha and Chikamaha, the latter who had taught

94. Uyeda, "Journey of the Tonkori," 109.
95. Uyeda, "Journey of the Tonkori," 109. Japanese reports reported "Suka."
96. Kitahara, "Nishihira Ume," 26.
97. *OS*, April 10, 1913.

her how to make *tonkori* instruments and had participated in the 1912 exposition.[98]

Ume spoke candidly with a reporter about her experiences. In response to the question about what was the most embarrassing aspect of the exposition, she replied, "showing my face to people of the metropole." When asked what she wished to see, she replied, "Movies," and what she wanted, "A kimono." What she wanted to eat was "candy," the reporter noted, and when "all these things were done, she wanted to return home and see her mother's face."[99] Ume later married, twice, and after 1945 she moved to Hokkaido with the majority of the Karafuto Ainu. She continued to play the *tonkori* with other well-known Ainu musicians. Her legacy lives on today: although she is featured in photographs, the audio recordings preserve her legacy best as one of the most skilled *tonkori* players of her time. Recordings of her singing and playing the *tonkori* are available on CD.[100] In the 1960s she cooperated with the Ainu Folk Museum in Shiraoi to record her performances.[101]

"IN ONE VOICE, THEY CURSE OSAKA"

In June 1913, at the end of the exposition, a reporter interviewed the different groups from the colonies.[102] In a newspaper article with the headline "In One Voice, They Curse Osaka," the participants talked about their Osaka experience. The Nivkh newlyweds said their honeymoon in the metropolis was not all they had hoped it would be. They remarked, "In the beginning we came because we planned on sightseeing. But this promise has not been carried out. The other day because the meat was rotten, we refused to accept it. The director Mr. Ibe said that this was the only meat in Osaka and took no notice of our complaint. In one more day we will go to Tokyo to buy a hunting rifle [their only asset] and then return to Osaka. That will be fun. We don't want to stay in Osaka one more day."[103]

98.   Kitahara, "Nishihira Ume," 26.
99.   *OM*, April 16, 1913.
100.   The CD is included with Ainu Minzoku Hakubutsukan (ed.), *Nishihira Ume*.
101.   Kitahara, "Nishihira Ume," 29. See Uyeda, "Journey of the Tonkori," for Ume's post-exposition life.
102.   See KZW for a postcard of all 1913 participants.
103.   *OM*, June 11, 1913.

Other participants substantiated the claims about rotten food, and it was reported that the Nivkh caretaker Yoshioka had visited them every day to inquire whether the eggs were rotten or the meat was spoiled. When they were bored, Yoshioka had tried to cheer them up by playing cards.[104]

A member of the Atayal group from Rigamon and Wulai who had traveled to the metropolis the year before and had heard about the good experiences of the 1912 participants remarked,

> We came thinking it would be the same treatment as the exposition held in Tokyo. But that was a large mistake. This time of year's temperature is like March in Taipei, and because the climate changed last month I got pneumonia in my windpipe and I checked into the Red Cross hospital. First of all, we cannot put up with the small hut on these grounds. Two or three nights ago the rain fell in from the roof and we could not sleep. We negotiated about this at the office, but they did not give us a helping hand. Before, the people from Tokyo were nice; Osaka people are coldhearted.

The Atayal participant was reported to say this with extreme anger.[105]

The only people who had no complaints were the Karafuto Ainu, who "talked quite composedly of being satisfied," although Ume said she missed her mother. At first they had wanted to return to Karafuto, but soon they came to like Osaka. They talked about their experience visiting Mitsukoshi and being treated to various foods there as one of the highlights of their stay. They said they were friendly with the other participants in the displays and they had all visited each other's houses frequently. They told the reporter with smiling faces, "These days the weather has just been like the weather in Karafuto during August. We rode in a car, and also saw an airplane, a long cherished desire. In one more day we want to return home soon. We are looking forward to buying souvenirs for our relatives and children."[106] On their return to Karafuto, it was said that they and the Nivkh and Uilta participants received about five yen worth of photos, postcards, and clothing from exposition officials.

104. *KNNS*, July 4, 1913.
105. *OM*, June 11, 1913.
106. *OM*, June 11, 1913.

There were reports that they had saved up sixty to seventy yen, since all their sightseeing and travel expenses had been paid by the exposition.[107]

In contrast to the Karafuto Ainu, the Ainu from Hokkaido, whom the reporter described as very sophisticated (*haikara*), had many complaints. Presumably it was Uesanashi who spoke, because he referred to his experience at the 1912 exposition:

> At the Tokyo exposition we learned a lot. Although we are natives [*dojin*], it is troubling to be together with the barbarians [*seiban*, referring to the Atayal]. It was the first time I had heard that the barbarians cut off the heads of their friends, and slurp their blood. Is it really true? We carry a small sword on our back, but in the past we have never decapitated anyone. To be treated the same as them is a disappointment that we can't tolerate. We are putting up with it, but by far the best treatment was in Tokyo. Osaka is completely different. In Tokyo we were nicely taken care of, but in Osaka nobody takes care of us. I also think, with respect to the expositions, in Tokyo it was a better business.[108]

Uesanashi's complaints are interesting when one recalls the Okinawan and Chinese protests against the first Human Pavilion in 1903, when they said that being displayed next to those deemed savage was an insult to their own level of civilization. Ten years later, some of the Ainu were uncomfortable in the human displays for the same reason, when they realized they were to be displayed next to groups they saw as savage. Uesanashi, whose positive experience the year before in Tokyo had induced him to bring his family with him to Osaka, now questioned why the Ainu were presented among those so reportedly barbaric. Based on all the participants' complaints, the reporter remarked, "We should definitely believe the words of the natives," and reported that there was talk they would bring their complaints to the appropriate authorities.

The widespread discontent voiced by the participants in 1913 reinforces the fact that no one believed that the displays merely reflected Japan's superiority over those it had colonized. What was going on at the exposition was a complex, contested process on which the participants themselves

107. *KNNS*, July 4, 1913.
108. *OM*, June 11, 1913.

had strong opinions. Summarizing the critical view of the human displays, an *Osaka asahi* reporter in 1913 questioned the purpose of bringing all the different races from the colonies to the exposition: "Is it to show their lifestyle conditions, by comparatively showing these are the Ainu and these are the Taiwanese Aborigines [*seiban*]? In the middle of the day aren't they just napping? We should not treat humans like goods."[109] The major newspapers in Osaka were willing to air the grievances of the participants indicating that at this stage in Japan's growing empire, the media were also challenging the morality of such displays.

Conclusion

The first Japanese display of colonial subjects in a human pavilion was in 1903 in Osaka Tennoji Park. Fittingly, the last living display of its kind in Japan (in which different races were housed in re-created villages) was presented ten years later on the same exposition grounds. The demise of the anthropological displays occurred in the same year as the death of their originator, Tsuboi Shōgorō. Tsuboi had been involved with running all the human displays held at Japan's domestic expositions. In 1913, though, his presence was barely felt, and there was no sign of the humanist ideals he had promoted in 1912. Certainly, after 1913 colonial subjects continued to travel to the metropolis to perform in various ways that emphasized their racial and cultural distinctiveness from the Japanese. In 1918, for example, thirty Ainu performed at the Kyoto Exposition, showcasing various Ainu customs. The fact that the Ainu looked different from the Japanese certainly made them exotic, but after 1913 their performances were fundamentally different from the human displays enacted solely to represent the ethnoracial groups of the empire. After 1913, displays of colonial subjects continued in various forms but never again in the way Tsuboi had intended them—as interactive exhibits that facilitated an exchange of knowledge regarding Japan's multiracial empire.

Tsuboi left Japan to attend an anthropological meeting in Russia in May 1913; he died unexpectedly in June, a month before his scheduled

109. *OA*, April 24, 1913.

return to Japan.[110] It is no coincidence that his death resulted in the end of his trademark displays. When his successor, Matsumura Akira, who had worked with Tsuboi on the 1903 Human Pavilion, took charge of the South Seas Pavilion at the Taishō Exposition in 1914, he diverged from the precedent Tsuboi had set.[111] He stated, "We have become accustomed to seeing many of the people of the empire like the Ainu, and now I have endeavored to bring people to Japan that the people of the metropolis have never seen before."[112] The South Seas display bordered on the theatrical and advertised cannibals among those featured. Matsumura's keen awareness of the growing connection between consumerism, spectacle, and expositions is clear. His departure from displaying Japan's colonial subjects in favor of more exotic people was perhaps also a response to the lackluster reception the human displays received in 1913. Significantly, the people displayed in the 1914 South Seas Pavilion were not from the Micronesian territories that Japan took control of in 1915. Instead they came from the Philippines, Borneo, Java, and Malaysia. The display reflected a desire to showcase the exotic and was not meant to represent the diversity of the empire.

The change in focus from Tsuboi's displays to Matsumura's reflects the growing expansion and malleability of Japan's empire. For Tsuboi, the Okinawans, Ainu, Taiwanese (of Han ethnicity), and Taiwan's Indigenous Peoples, particularly, were his main areas of study. As the empire expanded with the incorporation of Korea and Karafuto, Tsuboi's interest had also turned in their direction. When Tsuboi died in 1913, Matsumura was one of the first anthropologists to go to Micronesia on several surveys, and the inclusion of the Micronesian islands under the Japanese mandate in 1915 opened up a new frontier of study.[113] Although the influence of Tsuboi's characterization of Japan as a multiracial empire can be seen in articles that Matsumura penned, at his first opportunity to run a human display, Matsumura chose to display people never seen before in Japan, rather than Japan's colonial subjects.

110. *Yomiuri*, April 26, 1913; *Okinawa mainichi*, June 10, 1913.
111. Matsumura, "Osaka Jinruikan."
112. Matsumura, "Taishō hakurankai," 26–29.
113. Matsumura, "Contributions to the Ethnography."

PART II

Journeys between the Metropole and the Colonies

Part II Introduction

The chapters in this part use the context of the Japanese government's tours to the metropolis (*naichi kankō*) program to explore the stories of indigenous subjects from the colonies—from Taiwan in chapter 5 and Micronesia in chapter 6. The tour program, sponsored by the colonial governments in each area, was an attempt to introduce colonial subjects to Japan's advanced civilization, in the hope that they would be inspired to implement modernizing reforms back in the colonies. In Taiwan, the tours started in 1897 and continued until 1941, and were one of the longest-running policies directed toward Taiwan's Indigenous Peoples. In Micronesia, tours began in 1915 and lasted until 1939. In both Taiwan and Micronesia, government officials touted that participants began to partially self-fund the tour costs, starting in 1928 and 1926, respectively.[1] Estimates for the numbers of indigenous people from Taiwan that went to Japan on the tours vary dramatically from Matsuda's estimate of 625 to Yamaji's estimate of 6,543 participants.[2] According to Senju, a total of 660 people from Micronesia went to Japan on the tours.[3]

Previous scholarship has focused on the logistics of the tours to the metropolis and the rationale behind the program, which brought colonial

1. *Riban no tomo*, October 1, 1934, and *Annual Report to the League of Nations* (1926).
2. Matsuda, "Naichi kankō," 88, gives the number of participants from 1897 to 1941, except for 1940. Yamaji's number only includes tours from 1897 to 1933, "Shokuminchi Taiwan," 71.
3. Senju, "Gunseiki Nihon," charts 1 and 2.

subjects from Korea, Manchuria, Taiwan, and Micronesia to mainland Japan.[4] Less has been written about the individuals who actually participated in the tours.[5] These people, through their interactions within their indigenous communities and with the Japanese, were able to shape their own experiences and standing in society. The Japanese relied on them to take on and perform roles that were more multifaceted and nuanced than simply being a colonial subject at the bottom of the racial and imperial hierarchy.

In Taiwan, only the indigenous Taiwanese (not the majority population of Han Taiwanese) were taken on the tours. Intrinsic to the logic behind the tours was Japan's deprecatory view of the intellect of Taiwan's Indigenous Peoples; the government believed that learning through seeing was the most effective way to educate the "savages."[6] Intra-island (*tōnai kankō*) tours also were conducted, the idea being that Japan had progressed so far with its modernizing reforms in Taiwan that the authorities only needed to take participants to see model Aboriginal villages or the capital, Taipei, to show them the glory of Japan's civilizing efforts. Still, tours within Taiwan never replaced the tours to the mainland.

In chapter 5, the focus on individuals connected to the tours shows how the Japanese relied on the very people they maligned to uphold their tenuous position in the highlands of Taiwan—whether as intermediaries or as symbols of colonial submission—to help them rule. For a subject like Yayutz Bleyh, who spoke fluent Japanese and wore a kimono, her value to the Japanese as a leader among the Taiwanese Aborigines was such that she had to be preserved as a model Atayal who was ethnically distinct from the Japanese. On the other hand, the Bunun rebels Dahu Ali and Aliman Siken, who had taken the heads of many Japanese police officers stationed in the mountains, were given immunity from prosecution in exchange for their willingness to engage in public performances of subservience to the Japanese authorities. Why not just execute these men who had defied colonial authority countless times in the past? I argue that the Japanese needed to preserve them as symbols of indigenous

4. Chang, Ueda, and Miyazaki, "Nihon tōchi jidai"; Matsuda, "Naichi kankō"; Zheng, *Rizhi shiqi Taiwan*; Senju, "Gunseiki Nihon" and "Nihon tōchi."

5. Ziomek, "The Possibility of Liminal Subjecthood."

6. Taiwan sōtokufu keimukyoku, *Takasagozoku*, 18.

power tamed. The Japanese worked with willing men and women of influence who agreed to masquerade at times as reified indigenous representatives of their ethnic groups—in exchange for personal or material incentives—to keep the colonial regime running.

Chapter 6 looks at the experiences of colonial subjects who participated in the tour program from the islands of Micronesia—Palau and Saipan, in particular.[7] The tours serve as a common thread binding the chapter's stories, rather than as a defining experience in the individuals' lives. Previous periods of European colonization in the Micronesian islands had resulted in a population of cosmopolitan colonial subjects who had already experienced a hybridity of cultures before they encountered the Japanese. The tours to Japan lacked some novelty and purpose for the Micronesians, who in some ways were already Westernized, thus calling into question Japan's civilizing mission.[8]

In contrast to Taiwan's highlands, where pockets of resistance continued even into the 1940s, there was not any violent opposition to Japanese rule in Micronesia. For one thing, Micronesians were not that impressed by the arrival of the Japanese; they imagined that Japan's rule over the islands would eventually come to an end, just as Spain's and Germany's had. In Palau, traditional leaders who continued to practice the Modekngei religion, a blend of Palauan shamanism and Christian rituals, were seen as participating in subversive and anti-Japanese practices. But in the absence of direct resistance from Micronesian leaders, the Japanese quickly shifted their attention to cultivating the youth to become intermediaries, seeing an opportunity to circumvent the old power structures rooted in traditional customs.

7.   I focus on Palau and Saipan because there were many oral interviews conducted with Palauan and Saipan elders. Palau was the headquarters of the colonial government in Micronesia since 1921 and had a large Japanese community.

8.   The Spanish colonial period was from 1886 to 1899; the German period was from 1899 to 1914.

CHAPTER 5

The Taming of the Barbarian and
Other Savage Love Stories

Japanese rule over Taiwan's Indigenous Peoples required different and contradictory approaches. The Atayal woman Yayutz Bleyh, for example, who was one of the most well known—and highest paid—indigenous women to work for the colonial government, found herself in a liminal position, caught between the metropole and the colony. Her story shows how some colonial subjects were encouraged to assimilate to Japanese ways only to a certain extent, with her ethnic identity as an Atayal never erased but always emphasized. Furthermore, although Yayutz attained a high position within the colonial governing apparatus, the extent of the power she wielded was downplayed. The Japanese dealt with others, such as the notorious Bunun brothers Dahu Ali and Aliman Siken, in a variety of ways. Tactics used to win over or subdue indigenous subjects ranged from gift giving, feasting, and drinking to aerial bombing, torture, and even execution. Other approaches included taking them on intra-island tours and promoting their rehabilitation as former evil savages (*kyōban*) now transformed into ethnic relics of the past.

Yayutz Bleyh: Liminal Colonial Subjecthood

The spark that ignited my research into Yayutz's life was her name. I was researching the tours to the metropolis policy in Taiwan when I came across the mention of an Atayal translator who had been attached to one of the tours: Yayutz Bleyh. The fact that, as a woman and a translator, she was named stood out to me, because articles about the tours typically referred only to one or two leaders by name, if any. Because my goal was to uncover the life histories of various colonial subjects of Japan's empire, Yayutz seemed to be an ideal research subject. Not only had she worked for the colonial government, suggesting the possibility of finding a paper trail, she had also married a Japanese man. At that time, in the late nineteenth and early twentieth centuries, Japanese colonial administrators commonly used interracial unions as a strategy to govern the "savage territories" of Taiwan.[1] But Yayutz's marriage had been different. Her husband was not a colonial official sent to Taiwan to help manage the Aborigines. Rather, theirs was a love story between an everyday Japanese man and an Atayal woman, and that is why their relationship garnered so much attention in the press.

At around the same time I started my research in Japan, an Atayal researcher in Fuxing (長興), Taiwan, Li Hui Hui, stumbled across a noteworthy granite gravestone in the Atayal Toujiao (竹頭角) tribe's cemetery. Li wondered what sort of person was buried there and what he or she had done to merit such a gravestone. Li interviewed the village elders in Fuxing and learned that the stone had been erected for Yayutz Bleyh. To her surprise, Li found she was related to Yayutz. Five years later, in 2013, I met Li in Fuxing and saw Yayutz's gravestone for the first time (fig. 5.1).

The heft of the gravestone, standing over three feet tall, was a tactile remnant of Yayutz's legacy, and its bulk had metaphorical implications, too. The substantial weight of this material object—still intact after eighty years—confirmed the hunch I had five years earlier when I began looking into Yayutz's life: she had been no ordinary woman. But it was not until I met her grandson and the Fuxing village elders that I began to comprehend how significant she had been during the colonial administration. Prior to my 2013 visit to Taiwan I had gathered a significant amount of information about Yayutz, primarily from Japanese documents that celebrated her advancement of education for the Atayal people. What I learned in Taiwan shaped my understanding of that data and in some cases altered it completely.

---

1.   Barclay, "Cultural Brokerage."

FIG. 5.1. Yayutz Bleyh's gravestone in Fuxing, Taiwan. On the side pictured there is an epitaph written in Japanese and dated 1933, one year after her death in 1932. On the other side, in Japanese, is inscribed "the grave of Yayutz Bleyh" (ヤユツベリヤの墓). Credit: Author.

FIG. 5.2. Photo of Nakano Chūzō in Chen Wanfu's photo album. The description reads: "Kyoto born Nakano Chūzō, the husband of my foster mother." Courtesy of Chen Xing Sheng.

YAYUTZ MEETS NAKANO CHŪZŌ

Japanese books, articles, and documents written by various people, including high-profile Japanese contemporaries such as Mori Ushinosuke and Inoue Inosuke, have detailed the fateful first encounter between Yayutz and her future husband. Traditionally the story of their meeting goes more or less like this: in 1899, an eighteen-year-old Japanese pharmacist from Kyoto, Nakano Chūzō, stumbled into one of the most dangerous Aboriginal territories in Taiwan while collecting samples of medicinal plants (fig. 5.2). Chūzō's unwitting entry into the settlement of Dakekan (大科崁, Taikokan), known for its early resistance to the Japanese, quickly resulted in his capture. Brought before the chief, he was told that he would be beheaded the following day. Yayutz, the chief's sixteen-year-old daughter, intervened on Chūzō's behalf, imploring her father to spare his life. The chief hesitated, for he feared losing his dignity if the others heard of his weakness. In the end he gave in to his daughter's wishes and let Chūzō live. But they were forced to flee the mountains under the cover of night and were told they could never return, owing to the shame they would bring on Yayutz's father for being so weak as to spare the life of a foreigner and enemy.[2]

In 1925, Mori Ushinosuke, a Japanese scholar who spent years in Taiwan chronicling various Aboriginal groups, wrote a more violent and less romanticized account of their meeting.

Yayutsu Beriya married Mr. Nakano and left the mountains with him at the time of the Dakekan incident. The settlement that Yayutz had been born in was at war with the Japanese, and while fire was being exchanged, she was unable to abandon Chūzō who she promised to marry but who was still nonetheless the enemy. While it pained her greatly she broke with her familial ties and obligations and followed him to Taipei.[3]

I met Yayutz's grandson in June 2013. In her later years Yayutz had adopted an Atayal child whose Japanese name was Takeno Tsutomu (Atayal name Silan Lesa). After Taiwan's retrocession, he changed his name to Chen Wanfu. His first son, Chen Xing Sheng, told me the Japanese colonial accounts of how his grandparents met were far from accurate. While Chūzō had indeed been in Taiwan to collect camphor plants, the occasion did not involve Yayutz saving his life. Chūzō had been collecting plants by the Daxi (大溪, Daikei) River, near Shixiuping brook, when he spotted Yayutz swimming naked in the river. Yayutz was fourteen at the time, with tattoos on her face; Chūzō was eighteen.[4] Soon after their meeting, Chūzō brought Yayutz to the Daxi police sta-

2. *TNNS*, May 4, 1912; Nojima, "Ogawa Naoyoshi," 51.
3. *TNNS*, June 21, 1925.
4. There is a discrepancy in the ages and dates given by Chen and other accounts of their first encounter.

tion, where her parents agreed that she should go with Chūzō to Taipei. When I asked Yayutz's grandson what had motivated Chūzō to take Yayutz to Taipei with him, he said only the people who were there at the time knew why. He did say that Chūzō had wanted to improve Yayutz's "life and thoughts" and that he thought bringing her to Taipei to study would help do that.[5] The difference between the traditional story of Yayutz and Chūzō's meeting and her grandson's account is remarkable. The former relied on a typical trope of the time, that of the chieftain's daughter saving a young man from her violent, savage people. It allowed those in the colonial regime to celebrate Yayutz's transformation from chieftain's daughter to almost-but-not-quite Japanese girl. In contrast, a chance encounter between a young man collecting plants and a young girl swimming naked in the river focuses more on the romantic attraction between them. Tellingly, the colonial version, which remains the official version of their meeting, highlights Yayutz's willingness to embrace Japanese culture and reject her people to save Chūzō's life. On the surface there appeared to be no room for ambiguity in the colonial regime: it was one way of life or the other. Yet the documents, images, and oral stories about Yayutz show that her position was more in between. If anything, although her outward appearance and speech became more Japanized, other evidence points to her continued attachment and service to the Atayal people.

YAYUTZ AND CHŪZŌ'S EARLY LIFE IN TAIPEI

Nakano Chūzō was said to be the only one of five siblings to make something of himself. Because his father had lost trust in his eldest son, he had transferred all his hopes to his second son, Chūzō, whom he wished to take over the family pharmacy in Kyoto.[6] Chūzō did not follow his father's dream, instead venturing out to Taiwan to collect medicinal plants. After he and Yayutz met, the couple moved to Taipei, where Chūzō began work at the pharmaceutical division of the hospital affiliated with Taipei Imperial University.[7] In April 1904, Yayutz began to study at Taipei

5. Chen interview, Taiwan, June 2013.
6. Nakano, "Taiyaruzoku no obasan," 16, 19.
7. Takezawa, "Yayutsusan wo omou," 7.

Mengjia Girl's School (台北萬華女子學校), now in Wanhua district, Xin-bei City.[8]

In her own writings, which were published in 1933 by the high school she later attended (the No. 3 Girl's High School in Taipei), Yayutz describes her experiences at Mengjia Girl's School where, as a first-year student, she arrived not knowing how to speak Taiwanese, let alone Japanese. She credits her Japanese teacher with translating for her and describes how she learned the Japanese characters one by one. Although she had fond memories of her Japanese teachers, her schoolmates often ridiculed her and made her the target of pranks. She wrote that they often said "horrible things," like "Although that barbarian doesn't under-stand anything, the teacher is always so nice to her." Yayutz credited her Japanese teachers with helping her get through hard times and providing extra help, including private tutoring.[9] It is noteworthy that she says the poor treatment she received at the school came from the Taiwanese students of Han ethnicity; they used the Japanese term seiban ("barbar-ian," sheng fan), which was based on Qing classifications of Aborigine people. Rather than participating in and encouraging Yayutz's marginal-ization as a seiban, her Japanese teachers actually were her allies and, in her account, her saviors in those early times.

According to Japanese records, Yayutz graduated from Mengjia Girl's School in 1910 and was given a job in the Police Bureau's Aborigine Af-fairs Division (Keimukyoku ribanka).[10] There may be visual evidence of Yayutz's early work for the colonial government. In 1912, a photo album titled Taiwan seiban shuzoku shashinchō (Photo album of the barbarian tribes of Taiwan) featured a woman in a kimono speaking to a group of Atayal people. I believe the woman is Yayutz (fig. 5.3).[11] The description accompanying the photograph reads:

During the submission ceremony [帰順式], this photo illustrates the scene of that time's formal ceremony held for the Nan'ao [南澳 , Nanoku]

8.   Chen interview, June 2013. According to Takezawa and Fujin gahō, the school in Japanese was referred to as 台北艋舺公学校 (Taipei Mankō Public School).
9.   Bleyh, "Bango kyōju," 438.
10.   Takezawa, "Yayutsusan wo omou," 7.
11.   Thanks to Paul Barclay for bringing this photograph to my attention.

FIG. 5.3. Yayutz on stage in 1912 during a submission ceremony for the Atayal tribes of the Nan'ao settlement. Credit: Narita Takeshi (ed.), *Taiwan seiban shuzoku shashinchō: fu riban jikkyō* (Taipei: Narita shashin seihanjo, 1912), 155.

settlement.[12] At the top of the photo is the head of the branch office of the Nan'ao jurisdiction, and the woman next to him is a singular woman, revered by the Aborigines as the "Mother of Japan." Presently this woman is also a translator, and she is giving them instructions about the requirements for good behavior in the future.[13]

Furthermore, in the colonial records of the Taiwan police for 1912, Yayutz is listed as one of the employees and is described as a *hontōjin* (person from Taiwan); in 1913 she is listed as being from Taoyuan.[14]

Around the time Yayutz began working for the colonial government in an official capacity, she and Chūzō got married. Soon after her graduation, both Yayutz's and Chūzō's parents had given their blessing for their marriage.[15] Yayutz's grandson stated that Chūzō went back to Kyoto to ask in person for his parents' permission to marry Yayutz. From Kyoto he sent a telegram to Taipei to arrange her registration at a girl's national high school.[16]

12.   This is the Atayal settlement connected to the death of an Atayal girl, Sayun Hayun, who died trying to carry the luggage of her Japanese teacher across a river. This story was made into the film *Sayon no kane* (Sayon's bell) in 1943.

13.   Narita Takeshi (ed.), *Taiwan seiban*, 155–56.

14.   Taiwan sōtokufu minseibu keisatsu honsho (ed.), *Taiwan sōtokufu* (1912), 60, (1913), 16.

15.   Nojima, "Ogawa Naoyoshi," 51.

16.   Chen correspondence, June 11, 2014.

In 1911 she began attending a national (Japanese) school called the No. 3 Girl's High School in Taipei. Yayutz recalled her reaction when she saw the students walking by on their way to the high school: "[I had] the unbearable urge to attend. Furthermore the teachers at the public school told me that the girls' school would be a great place. Also, at the time I visited the Japanese colonial government, and the former head of Barbarian Administration also strongly encouraged me to attend."[17] Yayutz wrote that in her heart, she knew attending the school was the right choice.

1912 TOUR AND EMERGENCE OF YAYUTZ AS MEDIA DARLING

In 1911, the year Yayutz entered high school in Taipei, Chūzō fell gravely ill.[18] Diagnosed with a pulmonary illness, he was advised to return to Japan for his health. Chūzō returned to Kyoto and stayed in a house near the Nanzenji Buddhist temple, where he was bedridden for a while.[19] Yayutz traveled to Japan the next year as the translator for a tour group of Atayal leaders and men of influence, telling metropolitan newspapers at the end of April 1912 that Nakano's illness and the separation it had necessitated were the reasons for her trip. When Yayutz arrived at the port of Moji, reporters—having heard about their love story—were waiting.[20]

Chūzō met Yayutz when she arrived in Kobe, and the couple went to a hotel in Kyoto.[21] Chūzō's relatives later recalled how she caused quite a stir when she arrived in Kyoto by rickshaw, dressed in Japanese clothing. People gathered everywhere she went, and newspapers reported on her arrival and her reasons for coming to Japan.[22] Yayutz became an instant sensation with the press, not only because of her unusual beauty—with her distinctive facial tattoos—but also because she spoke Japanese fluently. The widespread

17.   Bleyh, "Bango kyōju," 438.
18.   *TA*, April 30, 1912.
19.   Nakano, "Taiyaruzoku no obasan," 21.
20.   *TA*, April 30, 1912; *TNNS*, May 4, 1912. Although she had already entered the No. 3 Girl's High School in Taipei, it was misreported that Yayutz was a student at the Taipei Mengjia Girl's School. *TA* has "third-year" student, *Fujin gahō* has "first-year" student.
21.   *TA*, April 30, 1912.
22.   Nakano, "Taiyaruzoku no obasan," 21.

FIG. 5.4. Yayutz pictured in Tokyo. Credit: *Fujin gahō* (no. 70): 41. Tokyo: Fujin gahōsha, June 1, 1912.

reports about how she had met her Japanese husband heightened her allure. Yayutz was cast according to the colonial trope of the chieftain's daughter, and the story about her saving the life of her husband-to-be was well known. But according to her grandson, Yayutz's father was not an important chief. He contends that Yayutz's own prominence in Japan made it necessary to elevate her father's status in the story to fit her persona.[23]

During the Atayal tour group's visit in April and May 1912, the media showered the group and Yayutz with attention, and her activities in the metropolis were reported on regularly. Yayutz was interviewed by *Fujin gahō* (Women's pictorial), one of the leading magazines for women at the time. The caption accompanying her photo identified her as the interpreter for the tour group (fig. 5.4): "Because she can speak Japanese

23.   Chen interview, June 2013.

very well, she has accompanied the group as a translator and is treated as an official." The caption described her clothing carefully, noting a white cotton layer overlaid with striped fabric and her purple-lined kimono, and her white *tabi* (socks), as well as her fashionably styled hair and the tattoo that ran from her cheeks to her ears. The description continued, "This girl is the daughter of the chief of the Dakekan settlement. She saved the life of Kyoto resident Nakano when he had gone deep into the mountains searching for plants and was captured and going to be killed; having received their parents' blessing they exchanged marriage vows; she is the girl of this romance."[24]

There are hints of how Yayutz felt about all the attention directed toward her. *Tokyo asahi* noted her fine clothing and her embarrassment caused by her tattoo. The article noted that she wore a veil over her head that had been lent to her by the women who had initially welcomed her to Tokyo. The reporter remarked that whenever the photographer asked her to turn toward the camera, she quickly hid behind the others.[25] Yayutz's embarrassment over the tattoo was implied in her writing. In a section titled "Happiness and Sadness," she mentioned the things that had made her the happiest and the saddest. Regarding moments of happiness, she referred to leaving the mountains of her Atayal village:

> I had come from the barbarian world of mountains and more mountains, and the first time I entered the plains and I saw their appearance, I had thought to myself were there really places such as this in our world. Repeatedly I gazed as far as I could see and saw luscious green trees and in between the trees, pretty large houses were constructed. From the depths of my heart I was overjoyed.[26]

She also commented on what made her feel sad, and that was how she was often looked at. "Every day, I was embarrassed, not only during the times when I went out, but also when I went into town, everyone looked at my face, I felt embarrassed and sad—even now I will never be able to forget this."[27] According to her grandson, this embarrassment was enough that

24. *Fujin gahō*, June 1, 1912, 41. Same photo in *TA*, April 30, 1912.
25. *TA*, April 20, 1912.
26. Bleyh, "Bango kyōju," 439.
27. Bleyh, "Bango kyōju," 439.

Yayutz eventually had her tattoo removed.[28] For Atayal women, facial tattoos signified they had learned the techniques of weaving and thus were prepared for marriage. The two-stage tattooing process was very painful, and because of the physical ordeal, it was also seen as a test for adulthood. If you were an Atayal woman without a tattoo, you did not have the same status as the women who did have them. It was also believed that after death, only women with tattooed faces could cross the bridge (Hakkau Uttuf) to heaven to meet their ancestors. Removing tattoos was not unheard of at this time, and records show that two Atayal wives of Japanese policemen had their tattoos removed at the hospital affiliated with Taipei Imperial University. Even after the procedure, though, traces of the tattoos could still be seen.[29] If in fact Yayutz had her tattoo removed, as her grandson contends, it is likely that traces would still have been visible, leading her to always be remembered as having a tattooed face. The fact that the procedure to remove the tattoos left these traces mirrors the notion that fully becoming Japanized was not really possible, even on the most superficial and physical level.

Photos taken at this time show Yayutz walking with officials leading the Atayal tour group. One report described the chaotic scene, with many people lined up along the roads to watch the procession. In fig. 5.5, Yayutz is at the center of the group leading the tour. Walking next to her and holding an umbrella is Shige, the proprietress of the inn (*ryokan*) where Yayutz was staying.[30] To the right of Yayutz is Shige's daughter. Yayutz was said to be happy for the female company, as she had found it embarrassing to be the only woman in the group. Her tattoo went from her mouth to her ears, and it was noted that she wore a scarf to cover it. "Yayutz attached herself to the proprietress and walked under the same umbrella."[31] Yayutz and the tour group were also photographed at the Tokyo Artillery Arsenal (fig. 5.6).

Because of Yayutz's employment by the colonial government and her marriage to a Japanese man, she received deferential treatment in the

---

28.   Chen correspondence, April 1, 2014. It is unclear when she had it removed.

29.   Deng, Shimomura, and Uozumi, *Kōnichi Musha jiken*, 142–43.

30.   The inn where Yayutz stayed was the popular inn during the Taishō period, Hanseikan (繁星館). *Fuzoku gahō*, June 5, 1912, 16; *Nihon*, May 6, 1912. http://crd.ndl.go .jp/reference/detail?page=ref_view&id=1000142773 (accessed December 15, 2014).

31.   *Jinruigaku zasshi* (1912), 299.

（入京せる生蕃観光五十二名一行　（タイヤル族四十社の頭目）

FIG. 5.5. Proprietress of Hanseikan, identified as Shige, holding an umbrella (left) and Yayutz (middle) with Shige's daughter on the right, May 5, 1912. The caption of the postcard reads, "The Savage Tour Group which has entered Tokyo has 52 people in its group (Chiefs from 40 Atayal villages)." Credit: Author's collection.

（台灣蕃人観光）　東京砲兵工廠本部前ニ於テ水筒分配ノ實況

FIG. 5.6. Tour group with Yayutz on the right holding an umbrella in Tokyo on May 1, 1912. The caption on the postcard reads: "(Taiwan Savage Tour Group) The actual scene in front of the head branch of the Tokyo Artillery Arsenal when water bottles were being distributed." Credit: Author's collection.

FIG. 5.7. Yayutz in a Ginza café in Tokyo in May 1912. Yayutz is pictured laughing on the left-hand side, with her face slightly turned. Credit: *Niko niko* 17. Tokyo: Niko niko yurakubu, June 1, 1912.

metropolis. According to one report, "Since she came to the capital, the bureaucrat Yayutz of the much-talked-about love affair has been invited along with the landlady of her hotel to the estate of Count Shimazu."[32] Another report remarked: "Among the group there is one star, a beautiful woman with a tattooed face. Yayutsu Beriya wears a patterned kimono and carries a dark crimson parasol. Along with the police officers she oversees numerous things and is always busy; she is seen as the right-hand person in charge."[33]

Yayutz was photographed in a Ginza café during her visit to the metropolis (fig. 5.7). Her kimono-clad body and laughing face distinguish her from the three other Atayal in the group, pictured on the right in their native dress. Yayutz's merriment, shared with her Japanese male companions, and the position of her body, facing away from the other Atayal, illustrate her coeval position with the Japanese. The picture, which was printed in *Niko niko* (Smile) magazine, shows a rare moment when Yayutz is completely off-guard. She is the only one not looking directly at the camera. She remarked in an article accompanying the photo that it would not do if

32. *TNNS*, May 26, 1912.
33. *TNNS*, June 1, 1912.

they were not smiling in the photo because it was being published, after all, in a magazine called *Smile*. When you contrast this photograph with the picture published in *Fujin gahō* (fig. 5.4), it is clear that despite Yayutz's apprehension about being an oddity and being stared at, she did have moments when she was carefree.

In the media coverage of Yayutz's presence in the metropolis, her civilized behavior was continually emphasized, from the repeated references to her fluency in Japanese to admiring comments in newspapers about her signature being proof of her civilized ways.[34] (The association between a signature and civilized behavior was not unusual. Throughout this volume we have seen how various Ainu, Micronesians, and Taiwanese Aborigines impressed the Japanese and Westerners with their ability to write their own names in Japanese.)

After her return to Taiwan, a thank-you note she sent to an internal affairs official was reproduced in Japanese newspapers. The note read: "We arrived back to Taiwan without incident. Thank you for helping me enjoy my stay. In Taipei it is raining; the climate is better in the metropolis."[35] Her simple note, which was more akin to something written to thank one's hosts for their hospitality than a formal letter from an employee of the colonial government, contrasts with efforts—comments on her signature, for instance—to show that this woman, who had a tattoo but could speak fluent Japanese, was in fact truly civilized. No wonder Yayutz hid her tattoo and was ill at ease with the crowds of spectators who wanted to see her face. As much as the media fawned over her and praised her accomplishments, Yayutz's colonial status and indigenous background were inescapable. Beneath every layer of media praise was a subtext that reminded the reader of her true place in the empire.

YAYUTZ'S TIME IN THE METROPOLIS

According to her grandson, at some point after Yayutz and Chūzō married in 1910, Yayutz transferred to a girl's school in Kyoto. Owing to her tattoo, people in Kyoto were curious and surprised when they saw her. In Kyoto she began working for the Japanese colonial government, first as a

34. *Nihon*, April 30, 1912; see KZW for signature.
35. *TA*, June 20, 1912; *TNNS*, June 25, 1912.

sergeant, then an internal affairs officer; later she was involved in integrating Aboriginal affairs.[36] On life in Kyoto, Yayutz remarked,

> At first because I didn't know one thing about the metropolitan lifestyle when I went to buy vegetables, or went shopping at the general store, I didn't understand anything at all and so I was very much in trouble. That wasn't all, I didn't know how to wear a kimono, and didn't know how to tie it, so when I had to wear a kimono I asked how to do it at the dress-maker's. Because I didn't know how to wear a kimono and how to tie an obi it was extremely distressing. As the days went by, I became a little more accustomed to the metropolitan lifestyle. Although I began to enjoy myself a little bit more and more, and although I had thought that I wanted to adapt to the customs and the lifestyle of the metropolis, it was early in this time that my husband had died and that was extremely regrettable.[37]

Yayutz's recollections show a progression from her initial experiences in Taipei. In Taipei she had been embarrassed by her tattoo and singled out by her Taiwanese classmates. In the metropolis, Yayutz had her tattoo removed a year after enrolling in the girl's school.[38] Interestingly, in her own writings she never mentions the removal of her tattoo; instead, her concerns seem more mundane: wearing a kimono and shopping. Evidently, adjusting to metropolitan life encompassed more than just speaking the language (in which Yayutz was now fluent): it was the small everyday things that separated her from the Japanese.

CHŪZŌ'S DEATH

Yayutz's writings seem to suggest that she had to leave Japan before her husband's death. It is unclear, from my conversations with her grandson, whether she had lived in Japan at some point between 1910 and

---

36.   Chen correspondence, April 1, 2014. In her writing, Yayutz refers to her time in Japan as her "time in the metropolis." Chen asserts that she had lived in Kyoto. While I have been unable to find details about how long Yayutz lived in Kyoto, her writing indicates it was for a short time.

37.   Bleyh, "Bango kyōju," 438–39.

38.   Chen correspondence, April 1, 2014.

April–May 1912, when she came from Taiwan with the tour group. It is also possible she lived in Japan for some time between May 1912 and her husband's death in 1913. Complicating matters in determining when she lived where is the fact that the newspapers suggest that she was not at her husband's side when he died. In fact, up until April 1913, while Chūzō was bedridden in Kyoto, he continued to send Yayutz fifteen yen a month for school supplies and other expenses in Taiwan, and they exchanged photos. The climate in Taiwan was not suitable for Chūzō's health, so he had to stay in Japan. It was reported that Yayutz remained in Taiwan because of her elderly father but that after her graduation it would be appropriate for her to go to Japan. Yayutz implored Chūzō many times to let her come visit, and these requests moved him. In April 1913 Chūzō made arrangements with a man identified as Honda, the ship's purser on the *America*, promising to compensate him for Yayutz's safe passage to Japan.[39] According to reports, in April 1913 Chūzō and Yayutz were planning to have a wedding ceremony after she returned to Japan.[40] This suggests that although she was already called Chūzō's wife (*tsuma*), their marriage had not been officially celebrated. Nine days later, the same paper reported that Yayutz's trip to Japan was delayed. The report stated that not only was the Aboriginal Administration office not happy that Yayutz wanted to return to Kyoto, but *seiban* (barbarians) were still not allowed to live in the metropolis. Even though Yayutz worked for the colonial government, the government demanded more paperwork detailing the course of their relationship. This delayed her journey to Japan.[41]

The next mention of Yayutz is from July 1913, when a reporter found her in the third-class section of a ship bound for Japan. Overwhelmed with grief, Yayutz had received a telegram notifying her that her husband was critically ill. The newspaper reporter revealed that the colonial government had approved her request to go and nurse him.[42] No further mention was made of a formal wedding. Chūzō died later that year. His relatives recall that there was public interest in Yayutz not just because

39. *OM*, April 19, 1913, April 28, 1913.
40. *OM*, April 19, 1913.
41. *OM*, April 28, 1913.
42. *TA*, July 13, 1913. Nakano remarked that while she appeared to be an actual wife (*genchi tsuma*), in reality she was not ("Taiyaruzoku no obasan," 20).

she was an Aborigine but also because the people of Kyoto remembered her and could not help but sympathize with her.[43]

A COLONIAL GOVERNMENT OFFICIAL

Yayutz graduated from the national language high school in Taipei in 1914, the year after Chūzō's death. Around this time she reportedly started to assist linguist Ogawa Naoyoshi in his studies of the Atayal language. She continued her association with Ogawa and his family until her death.[44] On September 6, 1915, Yayutz was transferred to Hsinchu province (新竹) and was assigned to work at the branch office in Sugina (樹杞林支庁), now Zhudong (竹東町). She was appointed as a lecturer and official translator at the Neihengping Aboriginal Language Institute (內橫屏蕃語講習所, Neiheipin), where she taught the Atayal language to Japanese officials (fig. 5.8). She also taught Japanese to Aborigines who had been selected to be police officers. The institute functioned as a village office, for it oversaw administrative affairs in the mountainous Taozhumiao region (桃竹苗地區).[45]

Owing to her work at the language institute, it was said that not one official in the savage lands of Hsinchu province had not received instruction from her.[46] Yayutz's white clothing makes her the focal point amid the darkly clothed Japanese police officers and Aborigines (the latter photographed sitting, and thus closer to the ground).

Although documentation of her work at the institute is sparse, in 1917 it was reported that Yayutz had attended the sixth annual inauguration ceremony for the Neihengping Aboriginal Language Institute—along with several high-ranking colonial officials—to commemorate the admittance of seventeen Japanese students. After the ceremony, fifty indigenous men and women of influence who had attended the ceremony from neighboring settlements received official government orders, and they

43.   Nakano, "Taiyaruzoku no obasan," 22.

44.   Nojima, "Ogawa Naoyoshi," 51. When Chen's father studied in Japan, one of his professors was Ogawa. Chen correspondence, April 1, 2014.

45.   Kang, *Taiyazu Msbtunux*, 419. Taozhumiao is an abbreviation that refers to the Taoyuan, Hsinchu, and Miaoli regions of Taiwan.

46.   Takezawa, "Yayutsusan wo omou," 7.

FIG. 5.8. Yayutz pictured when she worked as an instructor at Neihengping Aboriginal Language Institute. This photograph was taken sometime between 1915 (when she was transferred to Hsinchu province) and 1920 (the publication date). Credit: *Taiwan sōtokufu banzoku chōsakai banzoku chōsa hōkokusho* 6, no. 3. Taipei: Taiwan sōtokufu banzoku chōsakai, 1920.

were all given souvenirs to bring back to their villages.[47] In 1918 Yayutz once again traveled to Japan as a translator for another tour group. On this occasion, she visited Chūzō's grave and saw his family. Chūzō's father (his mother had died in 1901) and brothers met her at the port, and it was reported that they had many things they wanted to talk with her about.[48]

The intertwining of Yayutz's personal and public life—seeing Chūzō's family members and visiting his grave while also working as a translator for a tour group—can be seen in the visual record. Postcards of the tour group, featuring Yayutz, were meant for public sale, while the photograph of her in fig. 5.9 was of a personal nature and found in her husband's family album.[49] These dual characteristics—the commercial versus the personal—show that her position in the empire was not just that of a model colonial subject or, in the case of the tours, a translator. She also

47. *TNNS*, December 4, 1917.
48. *TA*, April 25, 1918.
49. I saw this postcard on a Japan Yahoo! auction site.

FIG. 5.9. Formal portrait of Yayutz in Nakano Takashi's family album in Kyoto. Takashi dates the photo as having been taken in 1913, after Chūzō had returned to Kyoto because of his illness. Credit: Nakano Takashi, "Bansha no Yajutsu Beriya." *Mirai* 7 (1981): 38. Courtesy of Miraisha.

had deep ties with the Nakano family, as their possession of her photograph demonstrates. In their eyes she was a daughter-in-law and, in the case of Chūzō's nephew Nakano Takashi, an aunt. As the medium for the images featuring Yayutz changes—from a postcard to a personal portrait—what the images signify changes as well.

Writing about his Atayal aunt, Nakano Takashi recalled meeting her when he was around five years old, at the end of the Taishō period.[50] He and his mother were eating at a restaurant when the waitress told them that a strange, dark-skinned woman with a tattooed forehead—wearing Japanese clothes and speaking Japanese—had to come to see them. His mother rose to greet the woman. Nakano wrote, "I grew brave although I was very young. I still hid behind [my mother's] kimono but peeked through the lower region of her sleeve, and what I saw I clearly remember."

"Are you not Yajutsu?" said my mother, suddenly seeming to understand.

"I am Yajutsu Beriya. It has been a long time. I have come to visit you," she replied in a polite manner, and my mother treated her as any normal guest. I was very surprised but calmed down when I saw that she was deserving of respect.[51]

Years later, relatives confirmed the circumstances of her visit; Yayutz had been working as a translator for a tour group that had come to Japan. When she arrived in Kyoto, she had slipped out of the hotel to visit Nakano's mother, who was the same age as she.[52]

In 1930 one of Chūzō's relatives, Chūjirō, who was in the imperial navy, tried to find Yayutz when their ship stopped in the port of Keelung, Taiwan. The ship's personnel were allowed to hike Mount Jiaoban (角板山, Kappanzan), near Yayutz's birthplace. Chūjirō talked to a waitress at their lodging about Yayutz and mentioned his connection to Chūzō. To his surprise, the waitress knew of her and said that she was teaching in the elementary schools in the area. Unfortunately, sending an express messenger to tell Yayutz that one of her relatives was in the area would have

50. Nakano, "Bansha no Yajutsu," 38.
51. Nakano, "Taiyaruzoku no obasan," 17–18.
52. Nakano, "Bansha no Yajutsu," 38.

taken three days round-trip. Chūjirō had to return to his ship the following day and was disappointed that he would not be able to see her.[53]

Details about Yayutz's work for the colonial government are defined at the start and end of her employment. In the early Taishō period she instructed police officers in the Atayal language, and toward the end of her life she taught Atayal children Japanese in the remote regions of Taiwan where she had been raised.[54] The information about her other positions in the colonial government between 1915 and the 1930s is murkier. Yayutz's grandson says that when she was around thirty years old, she became the assistant manager of Aboriginal affairs in the Taiwan Governor-General's Office (Section 1, Bureau 1) (台灣總督府第一局第一課原住民事務). Ten years later she was promoted to be in charge of that office.[55] I have not yet found government records that corroborate this information, but several key pieces of evidence indicate that she indeed held a high position beyond that of a translator. First, she was one of the highest paid female Aboriginal employees, if not the highest paid. By tracing colonial documents that record her pay, I found that it increased almost without fail each year. Starting in 1912, the first year her salary was recorded, Yayutz was paid three yen a month. In the years that followed, her monthly salary increased from eight yen in 1913 to sixty-two yen in 1926 and 1927 (twice the amount that male Aboriginal patrol officers [*junsa*] earned).[56] Her grandson says that Yayutz's monthly salary was closer to about 100 yen. He recalls that she saved more than 5,000 yen, all of which she gave to her son. To put this into context, her grandson relayed that his father, as a civil engineer, made about eighteen yen a month, meaning it would take him twenty-three years to earn the amount of money that Yayutz had saved.[57] When the Nakano family business fell on hard times, long after Chūzō's death, Yayutz continued to send money to his relatives in Kyoto.[58]

53.   Nakano, "Bansha no Yajutsu," 39–40.

54.   In *Seibanki*, Inoue and Uchimura visited a school where Yayutz was teaching Japanese to Atayal children, 146. Nakano, "Bansha no Yajutsu," 40.

55.   Chen correspondence, April 1, 2014.

56.   Taiwan sōtokufu minseibu keisatsu honsho (ed.), *Taiwan sōtokufu*, 1912, 60; 1913, 53; 1914, 56; 1915, 57; 1916, 218; 1917, 226; 1918, 234; 1919, 262; 1920, 266; 1921, 269; 1922, 279; 1923, 287; 1924, 292; 1925, 279; 1926, 290; 1927, 304.

57.   Chen correspondence, April 1, 2014.

58.   Inoue and Uchimura, *Seibanki*, 146.

義母 ヤユッ ベリヤ

FIG. 5.10. Yayutz is seated in the center of Japanese policemen in Taiwan. The description underneath the photo reads in Chinese "*yimu*" (義母, foster mother) and then in Japanese katakana "Yayutsu Beriya." Courtesy of Chen Xing Sheng.

A photograph in her grandson's album gives another indication of Yayutz's elevated position in the colonial government (fig. 5.10). The photo shows Yayutz in her thirties, in a position of authority: not only is she is seated in the front row in a group of male police officers, she occupies one of the two center seats; according to Japanese photo etiquette, the center seat is usually reserved for the most important person in the group.[59] Her tailor-made colonial uniform, designed for a woman, illustrates that she was a colonial government official, not a mere attaché.[60]

Perhaps most convincingly, the oral stories told about Yayutz even today in her home village attest to her high status. When she died in 1932,

59.   Chen correspondence, June 11, 2014.

60.   In all the photographs I have seen of the Japanese colonial period, this is the first one that shows a Japanese colonial uniform designed for a woman.

a grand and elaborate funeral was held in Taiwan in her honor, and the substantial stone monument was ordered to mark her gravesite.[61] Her influence reportedly was so great in the Taozhumiao region that Japanese and Atayal people had all readily acquiesced to her judgment when she was called on to resolve conflicts between the two groups.[62] In 2007 Atayal Watan Pilaw recounted stories about Yayutz heard from other Atayal elders. The Atayal highly respected Yayutz because of her achievements. She was remembered as a tall, strong lady with tattoos on her face. According to the elders' stories, whenever she went to her home in Qara village, police officers carried her in a sedan chair and assisted her when she got out to walk. Most of the Atayal people could only watch her from afar; they could not approach her. They also had to line up and salute her, welcoming her when her sedan chair passed by.[63]

Yayutz's sudden death in 1932 shocked those who had had seen her in good health only a short time before. According to Boya Maray, Japanese officials sent Yayutz's body back to Fuxing via the push-car railway. All the Atayal people wore white clothes and gloves (for mourning) and lined up on the both sides of the track to pay their respects and condolences as her body passed by.

Yayutz's nephew in Japan, Takashi, recalled finding a photograph of her funeral among his mother's belongings, along with a card announcing her death (fig. 5.11). The photo of her funeral, which was held in a classroom, shows four Aborigine children and three Japanese police officers. White banners in the background read "From all the Aborigine children" and "From all students of the Aborigine language."[64] In the eulogy written by the police department, it was revealed that the several thousand yen she had saved were being given to her adopted son, who was known as Tsutomu, ensuring him "a happy and prosperous future." Tsutomu was a sixth-grade elementary student at that time.[65]

---

61. The Japanese government had banned the traditional Atayal practice of burying bodies underneath houses, thus Yayutz's ashes were interred in a cemetery. The granite gravestone was shipped from Japan to the remote mountains of Fuxing, Taiwan, several years after her death.

62. Chen interview, June 2013.

63. Kang, *Taiyazu Msbtunux*, 420.

64. Nakano, "Bansha no Yajutsu," 41–42.

65. Takezawa, "Yayutsusan wo omou," 7.

FIG. 5.II. Photo of Yayutz's funeral in Taiwan in 1932. From Nakano Takashi's family album. Takashi wrote that he believed her funeral was most likely held in the classroom where she had taught in Taiwan. Credit: Nakano Takashi, "Bansha no Yajutsu Beriya." *Mirai* 7 (1981): 42. Courtesy of Miraisha.

The lengthy inscription on Yayutz's gravestone praises her as honest, pretty, intelligent, and "elegant, with a tattooed face." After listing her efforts in education (primarily her language teaching), Yayutz's chastity is mentioned. She is praised because she never remarried after Chūzō's death but devoted her energy to teaching and writing. Some of her ashes were buried in Japan, next to Chūzō's gravesite in Kyoto, a place her son visited often. In Taiwan, Yayutz's burial site is in the Toujiao tribe's cemetery for Atayal people.

Although no one alive today remembers her directly, her name and the stories associated with her activities in the region are still passed on. One Atayal elder told me that although she had never met Yayutz, her Japanese teacher would take her elementary class to visit Yayutz's gravesite. There the teacher would tell them about a remarkable Atayal woman who had married a Japanese man and had done a lot for the Atayal people.

Yayutz's story is one of competing narratives. In the metropolis, the image that resonated with everyday people was that of a sensational love story. The Shizuma Shōjirō company, which was part of the New School (Shinpa) movement, produced a *sōshi shiba* (a play that dramatizes contemporary material in the news) based on Yayutz and Chūzō's life. The play, which Chūzō's father attended, was performed before large audiences in Kyoto's Minamiza and Meijiza theaters.[66] But in the eyes of the Japanese colonial government, Yayutz was eulogized as the "sole pioneer [*senkusha*] in the northern savage territories." She is remembered for her work in education, though visual images and oral history hint that her position in the colonial government was far greater than that of an instructor.

Rather than opting for one story over the other, it is best to recognize that Yayutz's position was liminal. I borrow Victor Turner's definition in identifying Yayutz as one of the "liminal entities [who] are neither here nor there; they are betwixt and between the positions assigned and arrayed by law, custom, convention, and ceremonial."[67] Although Turner used the term as a mode of analysis for understanding rites of passage in reference to the various African peoples, his discussion of liminality is also useful in this context for understanding the in-between place that colonial subjects found themselves in, trying to assimilate many aspects of their life to the norms of the colonizer while remaining a colonized subject. As Turner writes in a later work, "Liminality represents the midpoint of transition in a status-sequence between two positions."[68] This use of liminal should not be misunderstood as applicable to everyone who during times of colonialism occupied an ambiguous position; I use it to refer to Yayutz who, as a colonial subject, was in the process of still being Atayal and becoming Japanese. This liminal state is one where the colonial subject has neither lost her or his identity as a colonial subject, nor become like the colonizer (something Albert Memmi contends is impossible); thus this type of colonial subject occupies a liminal space. The discussion of whether Yayutz was Atayal or had become Japanese is moot as she was neither, but was somewhere betwixt and between.

66. Nakano, "Taiyaruzoku no obasan," 20; http://www.performingarts.jp/E /overview_art/1005_06/1.html (accessed December 16, 2014). The Shinpa style was established toward the beginning of the Taishō period (1912–26).

67. Turner, "Liminality and Communitas," 95.

68. Turner, "Passages, Margins," 237.

Her own writing illustrates this liminal position, as do the memories about her that are kept alive in both Japan and Taiwan and the burial sites located in both countries. Remarkably, her writing in her high school's commemorative book mentions little about the most sensationalized aspect of her life: her husband. She gives no details about meeting him or their life together. She briefly describes his death and says that she had to leave the metropolis. That is all. Given that her account was written for a memorial book about the No. 3 Girl's High School in Taipei, it is perhaps fitting that Yayutz chose to focus on her experiences in education and teaching (after all, the article is titled "A Teacher of the Savage Language and Various Recollections"). However, the silences stand out. Her failure to mention her husband is notable because in all the written documents and oral accounts about her, meeting him and their romance had been the most publicized aspect of her life. Meeting her husband had triggered her move to Taipei, the start of her studies, and her later employment with the colonial government. When she speaks about leaving the mountains and entering school, she never explains why she was in Taipei in the first place. Her silence might indicate a desire to protect what was closest to her heart, or that she did not—as the colonial authorities often did—define herself in relation to her husband. In her writing, Yayutz's primary struggles were the trials and tribulations involved in her attempts to learn Japanese and fit into a different world.

Her writing highlights the insecurities inherent in her liminal position, especially with regard to living in the metropolis, or her experiences in school, where she was singled out by her Taiwanese classmates. At the same time her use of the term "barbarian" (*seiban*) throughout, when describing where she grew up and what she was called in school, can demonstrate her internalization of the colonizer's rhetoric or conversely the disarmament of its deprecatory intent through her appropriation of it.

Both sides of Yayutz's family have kept alive the duality of her memory. On the Nakano side, her nephew describes the close ties she had to their family. Takashi wrote of his treasured mementos of his Atayal aunt: a photograph of Yayutz dressed formally in a kimono and another photo of her funeral. In Taiwan, her grandson's memories of his father telling him about his grandparents, and the stories told by the Atayal elders in Fuxing village, describe a woman of status who helped the Atayal people and was highly respected. During my visit to Fuxing, I asked the elders and Yayutz's grandson what impression the Atayal people had of her and how she had viewed herself: as Japanese or Atayal. Responding to my first question, the elders all had only good things to say about her, emphasizing that she was sent to mediate problems that arose between Japanese officials and other Atayal. Yayutz always ruled fairly, they said, and never against the Atayal's best interests. Whatever she decided, the Japanese accepted. Her grandson added that she never denied requests from the Atayal people, and she tried her best to foster good relations between them and the Japanese.[69] With respect to how Yayutz had viewed herself, her grandson replied that she always saw herself as an Atayal and never thought of herself as Japanese. He remarked that she always tried to understand her people's way of life and customs and was the bridge that connected the Japanese and the Aborigines.

Perhaps this, then, is the legacy of colonial subjects that is often elided. In the rush to define and categorize, to represent and symbolize, the transitional nature of colonial identity as a process that is ongoing and never complete is obfuscated. Someone of Yayutz's status appeared differently to different people, and she is thus remembered in different ways. The multiplicity of her life and the competing refractions of her image illustrate the destructive and reconstructive forces of colonialism. Trying to piece together one coherent image requires dismissing those aspects that do not fit a specific narrative. Trying to smooth out the wrinkles actually obscures the fact that the discrepancies are what remind us of the colonial context in which people like Yayutz lived. Thus it is the journey and not the destination that matters in attempting to understand whether one can write histories of colonial subjects. Whatever composite image of Yayutz may emerge, it is necessarily incomplete, inevitably a by-product of obfuscations and reconstructions inherent in the colonial archive. Yayutz's grandson told me that his father had recounted many love stories about his grandparents: stories about Yayutz's time in Kyoto and even about their lives together after they married and she was working. He has kept many of these stories private, as is the right of a grandson who holds the stories his father told him close to his heart. It is the role of the historian to use other sources and techniques to try to sharpen the images of colonial subjects.

69.   Chen correspondence, April 1, 2014.

Dahu Ali and Aliman Siken: The Subjugation of (or Peaceful Reconciliation with) "Evil Savages"

In 1933 a grand ceremony was held in Kaohsiung to dramatize what the Japanese called "the subjugation of the last barbarian in Taiwan." The so-called last barbarian was Dahu Ali (拉荷阿雷), a Bunun rebel leader who had holed up in a precipitous mountain area of Taiwan known as Tamaho, in Hualien prefecture, for nearly twenty years. Along with the Atayal, the Bunun were known for holding out the longest in their fierce resistance to Japanese colonial rule.[70] Dahu Ali's so-called submission to Japanese authorities thirty-eight years after Japan first took control of Taiwan marked his people's continuous efforts to stave off the Japanese and the unrelenting drive of colonial officials to establish control over them. However, the Bunun and Dahu Ali's great-grandchildren disagree with the characterization of their ancestor as surrendering or having been "subjugated." They contend that Dahu Ali's ceremony represented him reaching a peaceful reconciliation with the Japanese.[71]

The presentation of Dahu "as the last barbarian to submit" was also a performance, and his persona as the last holdout was bolstered by colonial officials labeling him a *kyōban*, or "evil savage." In actuality, Dahu's subjugation ceremony marked neither the end of indigenous resistance against the Japanese nor the achievement of true control over the indigenous population of Taiwan. Like Yayutz, Dahu was not who he appeared to be. The colonial record shows that Dahu's brother Aliman Siken (阿里曼西肯), who had hidden out with Dahu in Tamaho, was by far the more powerful rebel leader of the two, but because Aliman had submitted to Japanese rule three years before his brother, Dahu was characterized as more notorious, even though he was not the colonial authorities' initial concern.

The road to peaceful reconciliation with Dahu was paved when his son and other members of his tribe were taken on a government-sponsored

70.   Chan, "From Autonomy," 100; see KZW for image of ceremony.
71.   Yan Guoming and Yan Guochang, written correspondence, December 12, 2017, and January 2, 2018.

intra-island tour (*tōnai kankō*) to Taipei (due to an injury, Dahu could not go). Dahu was also taken on a tour of the Pingtung airport, where just years before planes had taken off laden with bombs intended for his hideout. Once again, uncovering the details relating to the people involved in the government's tours shatters the imperial rhetoric that the tours were an effective tool for leading Japan's colonized people toward civilized behavior. Dahu Ali and Aliman Siken's actions and their interactions with colonial authorities reveal that they finally decided to stop resisting Japan's rule not because of the marvels they saw on the tour but because of the material incentives cooperation would bring. In this particular case, the tours functioned more as propaganda than as a colonial policy that brought about real transformation in the thinking of the Bunun brothers.

The Japanese manufactured Dahu's submission narrative to signify a triumphant end to the "savage problem," but in reality the ceremony proved premature. Its central premise, the rehabilitation of evil savages, required the Japanese to magnify the brothers' evil nature (or perhaps even fabricate it). For all the media coverage regarding the ceremony, nothing published at the time explains how, exactly, the Japanese reached a détente with Dahu (although there is some earlier written evidence regarding Aliman's decision to stop resisting the Japanese). Indeed, when looking at the visual evidence of the 1933 ceremony, the Bunun point of view—that what had occurred was actually a peaceful reconciliation— is supported. Considering the enormous amount of manpower, energy, and resources devoted to convincing the brothers to stop fighting and the well-photographed meetings with Japanese colonials after their détente, it is clear that the Japanese chose reconciliation over execution for political purposes. It also points to Japan's trepidation about the influence of these rebel leaders and what their execution could provoke among their supporters. Furthermore, the fact that Aliman had worked closely with the Japanese in the early period of colonial rule is never mentioned in later narratives of his "submission" (*kijun*). Peeling away the layers in the carefully constructed story of the "last barbarian to submit" reveals how colonial identities were rewritten and details were erased to gloss over the complexities of colonial interactions and, consequently, Japan's weakness in enforcing its rule in the indigenous areas.

COUNTERNARRATIVES TO THE STORY OF
PROGRESS IN SAVAGE ADMINISTRATION

Although Japanese officials started with policies of conciliation and appeasement to gain the support of local leaders when they entered the indigenous territories of Taiwan, they eventually shifted to harsher tactics to force the indigenous people into submission.[72] Those harsh policies were ramped up with Governor-General Sakuma Samata's "Five-Year Plan to Subdue the Northern Tribes" (gokanen keikaku riban jigyō), from 1909 to 1914. The Five-Year Plan was viewed largely as a success, in that it "brought most of Atayal country under colonial rule. The Banmu honsho (Bureau of Aboriginal Affairs), the temporary organ established to administer Sakuma's five-year plan, was disbanded in July 1915 and victory was declared in the north."[73] Sakuma's campaign ended with the Truku (Taroko) Battle in 1914, which lasted seventy-four days and involved more than 11,000 Japanese troops (soldiers, police, and laborers) against a Truku population of 10,000.[74] The battle's campaigns involved "burning several Truku villages, taking prisoners, confiscating rifles and killing countless combatants."[75] After declaring victory on August 23, 1914, the Japanese government turned its sights on the Bunun-occupied regions of southern Taiwan.

From 1914, the battle to make the Bunun submit was an ongoing—and long-lasting—concern of the Japanese colonial authorities. In the late 1920s and 1930s, after failing to strong-arm rebels like Dahu and Aliman into submission, authorities turned to earlier policies of conciliation to convince them to stop resisting Japanese rule and thus turn them into symbols of tamed indigenous power. Japan knew that the rebel brothers' value to their communities was such that their outright extermination could have upset the balance of power in the highlands, consequently affecting the stability of Japanese rule. In the early years of colonial rule the Japanese had exerted control through local chiefs and men of influence;

72. Barclay, "Cultural Brokerage," 336–40.

73. Barclay, "Cultural Brokerage," 349–50. See Barclay, *Outcasts of Empire*, 104, for more information about the genesis of this five-year plan, which was not the first of Sakuma's five-year plans.

74. During the Japanese colonial period, the Truku were identified as Atayal, but today they have succeeded in being recognized as a distinct ethnic group.

75. See https://digital.lafayette.edu/collections/eastasia (accessed September 24, 2015).

in later years that policy continued, except that now men of influence had to perform as Bunun leaders and servants of the Japanese state simultaneously—and both roles were facades.

In certain areas of the empire, specifically where there were pockets of indigenous resistance, the Japanese had not been able to advance their policies and the subjugation of the so-called barbarians. The Japanese were at a disadvantage because of the difficulty of the terrain. The Bunun knew the region well and, according to the Japanese, were generally physically stronger people who were used to the climate.[76] Bunun rebels used guerrilla-type tactics. Although at times outmanned and outgunned, they intimidated the Japanese enough that they gave up on forced control and turned to the conciliatory tactics. These included meeting with chiefs and men and women of influence and cajoling them with gifts, feasting, and drinking. Such approaches acknowledged the local power hierarchy, even during wartime. The Japanese did not treat everyone the same—as if all were equally children of the empire—because they realized that some men wielded more influence than others; those who had power were the ones the Japanese wanted to work with.

ALIMAN SIKEN: A MAN OF INFLUENCE

Sometime prior to 1898, Aliman Siken and six other indigenous men of influence were photographed in a makeshift studio in Taiwan (fig. 5.12).

The black-and-white photograph was printed in an undated album titled *Taiwan shashinjō*. Per Japanese etiquette, Aliman's position in the center of the group indicated that he was the most important figure. The caption in the album reads:

> Puli settlement southern savage chiefs: These are the southern savage chiefs who live in the middle of the mountains in the Puli settlement. In comparison to the northern savages, their nature is not as violent and cruel. The power of these chiefs in their jurisdiction is limitless. In important events, like headhunting battles, all these chiefs decide regarding [these practices] and are also the commanders [leading them].[77]

76. Xu and Yang, *Dafen Tamahe*, 83.
77. Jun'eki Taiwan Genjūmin Kenkyūkai (ed.), *Inō Kanori*, 148.

FIG. 5.12. Aliman is center, in the back row. Credit: Jun'eki Taiwan Genjūmin Kenkyūkai (ed.), *Inō Kanori shozō Taiwan genjūmin shashinshū* (Taipei: Jun'eki Taiwan Genjūmin Hakubtsukan, 1999), 148. Courtesy of Sheng Ye Museum of Formosan Aborigines, Taipei.

Aliman and the six others were also photographed with Japanese officials outside an official building, most likely in Taipei (fig. 5.13). This undated photograph also features Atayal, Tsou, and others from various indigenous ethnic groups. Because Aliman and the men he is pictured with in the studio portrait are wearing the same clothing in this second image, it is likely that the photographs were taken at the same time, or at least during the same general time frame. Although it is unclear why these important men from various tribes were gathered, it is likely the Japanese colonial government wished to convince them to help carry out its policies.

Japanese photographer and anthropologist Inō Kanori produced a montage of photographs of individuals from the different Aboriginal groups for the inaugural issue of *Banjō kenkyūkaishi* (Journal of the Society for Research on Aboriginal Conditions) in 1898.[78] The montage is

78.   Barclay, "Playing the Race Card," 49.

FIG. 5.13. Aliman pictured in middle row, third from left. Credit: Record number: F092083, *Taiwan gu xiezhen tie*, "Japanese military officials and Aborigines, unknown date." Courtesy of Taiwan National Library (old Sōtokufu library).

described as being "cobbled together out of black and white studio portraits and field photographs of uneven quality."[79] The photograph of Aliman used in the 1898 montage came from the studio photograph in fig. 5.12. Aliman's image in Inō's montage quickly came to represent the face of the Bunun race, and a watercolor rendering appeared on a poster of the different indigenous people of Taiwan, exhibited at the Paris Universal Exhibition in 1900 (fig. 5.14).[80] The fact that Aliman was photographed several times as early as 1898 indicates that the Japanese recognized him as a man of influence and that he was compliant enough to meet with Japanese officials.

One of the first mentions of Aliman in Japanese documents refers to an encounter that Mori Ushinosuke, an ethnographer and linguist of Aboriginal languages, had with him in 1906.[81] When Mori met him, Aliman was leading a group of twenty-seven men toward Yuli on a headhunting expedition; they were hoping to take a Japanese head. According to Mori's account, the Bunun had a grudge against the Yuli police officers because they were confining and killing the Bunun. Mori describes Aliman as having a commanding face and powerful physique.[82] Aliman asked the chief of the Taranasu settlement, Salidan, for his permission to kill Mori, but Salidan told him that Mori was a friend who should be protected at all costs. Salidan later urged Mori to turn back to avoid Aliman, but Mori refused and insisted on continuing toward Dafen.[83] Although Aliman and his group pursued him, Mori was able to escape unharmed. Aliman is said to have admired Mori's courage in continuing with his journey. A couple of years after their first encounter, Aliman encountered Mori a second time, in the southern part of Dafen village, and this time Aliman helped him with his luggage. They soon became close friends.[84] Yang Nanjun argues that Mori's close relationship with Aliman influenced his ideas about Japanese policies toward the Bunun.

79.   Barclay, "Playing the Race Card," 71; see KZW for 1898 image.
80.   Hu, "Taiwanese Aboriginal Art," 199; Barclay, "Playing the Race Card," 71.
81.   Yang, *Maboroshi no jinruigakusha*, 35.
82.   *TNNS*, part 13, January 21, 1909. Mori wrote a nineteen-part series for *TNNS* in 1909 that documented his journey into Bunun territory in the Central Mountain Range in southern Taiwan. Xu and Yang, *Dafen Tamahe*, 35.
83.   Xu and Yang, *Dafen Tamahe*, 36
84.   Xu and Yang, *Dafen Tamahe*, 36; Yang, *Maboroshi no jinruigakusha*, 83.

FIG. 5.14. Poster sent to 1900 Paris Exposition. Aliman is pictured in the center. Courtesy of Anthropology Museum, National Taiwan University.

Mori disagreed with the harsh punitive tactics of Sakuma Samata's Five-Year Plan, which aimed to bring the Atayal in northern Taiwan to their knees through military force. Mori advocated the idea of creating a land reservation on which the Bunun could live, what he envisioned to be a "savage paradise." He worked to attract both popular and financial support, and he used his own money to set up a fund for the construction of the reservation.[85] Mori's utopian scheme stood in contrast to harsh Japanese policies, but he never gained monetary support or backing from the government. Some said that Mori's death in 1925 by suicide—he jumped into the Pacific Ocean during a journey back to Japan—was due to his despondency over the government's failure to secure this free zone for the Bunun. Others contend that Mori was disillusioned by Japanese interference with the indigenous people, whom he always put on a pedestal.

On March 15, 1908, Aliman was appointed as a chief, or *tōmoku*, by the Japanese.[86] At the time of his appointment, he was described as having a ferocious nature and a very bloodthirsty heart. It was noted that he went headhunting alone and had taken the head of a man from Guangdong. The Japanese were willing to appoint Aliman chief, even though they knew he was dangerous, because of the influence he wielded in the region. In 1911, when the Japanese began constructing police stations in Hualien, it was written that "Aliman's power was felt in all regions."[87] The extent of Aliman's influence was widely demonstrated in 1915, when the Japanese authorities began implementing their policy of confiscating guns from the Bunun in southeastern Taiwan, who relied on guns for hunting.

In June 1914, confident that it would succeed in its battle with the Truku, the colonial government had begun to turn its attention toward southern Taiwan and achieving control over the Bunun there. Compared with military activities in the north, initial relations between the Bunun and Japanese were relatively peaceful, and at first the authorities did not use military force in confiscating Bunun guns. Unlike the Truku Battle, in which thousands of Japanese police officers participated and Japanese

85.   Yang, *Maboroshi no jinruigakusha*, 86–87.
86.   Okuda, *Bununzokushi*. I first saw mention of his appointment in Ishimaru, "Police Officers," 9. Ishimaru cites Okuda but only refers to Aliman's appointment while Okuda also describes Aliman's bloodthirsty nature.
87.   Senō, *Bankai haishi*, 276.

forces finally overwhelmed the Truku with two armies, no army was brought into southern Taiwan.[88] Instead, workers already in place at the police stations implemented the confiscation policy. The police were encouraged not to use force but to calmly persuade the Bunun to hand over their guns. Right before the confiscation of guns began on July 15, 1914, the authorities issued guidelines for the police that included gathering all the local chiefs and men of influence at the police station to inform them of the plan. The Bunun were offered monetary compensation in exchange for handing over their guns.[89]

According to Senō Yasushi, who worked in the Department of Savage Administration in Taipei, Aliman's willingness to cooperate with Japanese officials in the confiscation of guns was a major reason the Bunun gave up their weapons without conflict.[90] Senō described Aliman as not only the chief of Dafen but also the general chief of all the Bunun in neighboring regions. Aliman ceremoniously gave up his own guns first and then visited neighboring villages to encourage the people to give up their guns as well, an approach described as a "huge success." Nevertheless, while the Bunun gave up some of their guns, they did not give up all of them. Rivalries grew among some who felt that their neighbors had managed to stockpile more guns than they had.[91]

Against this backdrop, Lt. Sakamura dramatically departed from the mandated protocol of not using force. He conducted a gun raid in Kashibana village, taking advantage of the absence of the chiefs and men of influence, who had been taken on a tour of an airport in Hualien. While their leaders were gone, Sakamura tied up and hung from beams any men in Kashibana who did not hand over their guns. The men were tortured, and those who could not endure the pain finally agreed to give up their guns, but in the end Sakamura confiscated only five guns. Senō laments that this use of torture, which was largely fruitless, became

88. Senō says 1,700 policemen participated in the Truku Battle, compared to Barclay's number of 3,127 policemen, "as well as 3108 soldiers, 4840 laborers over 11,000 people against a Truku population of roughly 10,000." Victory against the Truku was declared on August 23, 1914. https://digital.lafayette.edu/collections/eastasia (accessed February 9, 2017).

89. Senō, *Bankai haishi*, 257–59.

90. Senō, *Bankai haishi*, 260, 277.

91. Senō, *Bankai haishi*, 260–61.

the root of the deep resentment the Bunun (including Dahu and Aliman) of the Laonong Creek region bore against the Japanese.[92] Other sources corroborate the Japanese deception: "The Japanese police's stratagem [was to trick] the able-bodied men in the Laonung [*sic*] Creek region to tour an airport in Hualien so that the police could search their villages while in [a] weakened state and seize their hunting rifles."[93]

In 1915 there were two attacks on the Dafen police station and one on the Kashibana police station in retaliation for how the Japanese had extorted guns from the Bunun. Dafen was by far one of the largest police stations built along what became known as the Batongguan Trail (八通關), which traced the "alpine spine of Yushan national park" and was part of the Central Mountain Range of southern Taiwan (see map 2). Dafen station was the hub of the region, and next to it were situated a Japanese school, a trading post, a martial arts and ceremonial hall, and an ammunitions depot; a very sizable Japanese population also lived there.[94] A group of Bunun first attacked the Dafen police station on February 23, but when Aliman intervened and pleaded with them to stop, they listened to him and ceased their attack.[95] A few months later, on May 12, the Kashibana station was attacked by a group of Bunun who looted guns and ammunition, burned the station, and killed several policemen.[96] Five days later, on May 17, the Dafen police station was attacked a second time, in what was subsequently known as the Dafen Incident.

The Dafen Incident resulted in the murders of twelve Japanese policemen—some of whom were beheaded—and the burning of the station. The attack was said to have involved fifty-six Bunun men. According to Yang, the incident shook the Japanese police so badly that they waited several months before they returned to Dafen to retrieve the corpses. Even then, they were so afraid of being ambushed that they enlisted the help of nearby Atayal to accompany the police officers to Dafen.[97]

---

92. Senō, *Bankai haishi*, 267.

93. Chan, "From Autonomy," 101.

94. Robert Scott Kelly, "The Batongguan Historic Trail," http://hikingintaiwan .blogspot.com/2008/04/batongguan-menu.html (accessed July 13, 2015).

95. Taiwan sōtokufu keimukyoku, *Riban shikō*, 4:12; Senō, *Bankai haishi*, 268.

96. Taiwan sōtokufu keimukyoku, *Riban shikō*, 4:13–14. Senō dates the Kashibana attack to be on May 13.

97. Conversation with Yang Nanjun, Taipei, June 2015.

The exact circumstances of the Dafen Incident have been the subject of historical debate. The majority of scholars today name Aliman Siken and Dahu Ali as the leaders of the attack, although one scholar, Haisul Palalavi, has challenged this traditional narrative, arguing that no documents written at the time actually name Aliman or his brother as being involved. In fact, *Riban shikō* (Records of Savage Administration) specifically reports that Aliman's family was not involved in the attack.[98] Palalavi points to *Tō Taiwan tenbō* (View of eastern Taiwan), a book published in 1933, the year of Dahu Ali's "subjugation" ceremony, as the first document to link the brothers to the attack.[99] Contrarily, Yang Nanjun argues that the brothers did take part in the attack and cites two indications for why they had to have been involved.[100] First, Aliman, as the chief of Dafen, would have known about everything that was happening in the region and nothing would have been done without his consent. Second, Yang points out that both men left Dafen right away; why would they have fled the area, he asks, if they were not involved?[101]

There is another explanation in Senō's account for why the brothers might have fled the region. According to him, after the May 12 attack on Kashibana, Bunun from various settlements held a meeting to discuss what action to take next. The main leader of the Kashibana attack, Toshiyo's chief Aliman Bukun, argued that they should attack Kashibana again, but Aliman Siken said they should not continue fighting, as the police were mobilizing against them. On May 17 the Dafen police station was attacked a second time, and Senō's account identifies Aliman Bukun and another Bunun rebel from the Hsinwulu region, Lamatasingsing, as the leaders of the attack.

Senō describes how the other Bunun turned against Aliman Siken because he had helped the Japanese confiscate their guns. He was labeled a tool of the Japanese and an enemy. Senō argues that Aliman had the Bunun people's welfare in mind when he acted to dissuade the others from continuing their attacks on the police—he believed that opposition to

98. Taiwan sōtokufu keimukyoku, *Riban shikō*, 4:16–17.

99. Mōri, *Dong Taiwan*, 259.

100. Yang, *Maboroshi no jinruigakusha*, 83. In June 2015 I spoke with Yang about the brothers' involvement.

101. According to Yang, they went to Tamaho in 1916; according to Palalavi, they went after 1922, after the Tusui Incident.

the Japanese would never succeed. The other Bunun failed to recognize his concern for them and cursed and boycotted him. Thus, the implied reason that Aliman and his brother fled to Tamaho on the upper reaches of Laonong Creek was not because they carried out the attack, but because the other Bunun were upset they did not want to fight the Japanese.[102] If Senō's account is accurate, it is ironic that Aliman, a man who tried to dissuade others from attacking the Japanese, has now been labeled one of the main instigators.

Scholars Ishimaru Masakuni and Haisul Palalavi first questioned the fact that documents at the time of the 1915 attack did not name either Aliman or Dahu as the leaders. Palalavi interviewed Dahu's great-grandchildren and other descendants, who claim he did not participate in the attack and contend that Dahu was then still on good terms with the Japanese at the time.[103] An examination of the records makes it clear that it was in the 1930s that Dahu and Aliman began to be linked to the Dafen Incident. The earliest mention I found of Aliman's involvement in the Dafen Incident was in 1929, and Dahu Ali was not mentioned.[104] I found only one account, from 1938, that directly accused Dahu and Aliman of having led the Dafen attack. All other accounts vary in associating one brother or the other with the attack, without specifically stating that they were the leaders.[105]

According to Senō's 1935 account, rumors that Aliman was being accused of having been involved started circulating not long after the Dafen attack, and Aliman himself addressed the rumors. Apparently being labeled a leader of the attack was so vexing to him that when a government official visited Dafen in 1918, Aliman requested a meeting with him. Aliman is recorded to have said, "It appears that I have been called the leader of the Dafen Incident, but that was the work of the men associated with Lamatasingsing and Toshiyo's Aliman Bukun. Please do not get it mistaken. I used to work a little for the officials—the officials all

102.   Senō, *Bankai haishi*, 277.

103.   Palalavi, *Dafen jiken*, 7–13.

104.   *TNNS*, November 1, 1929.

105.   Miyamura, "Hontō saigō," 130; referencing Aliman's involvement: Fujisaki, *Taiwan no banzoku*, 855; Suzuki, *Taiwan no banzoku kenkyū*, 335; *Riban no tomo* 2 (1936), 2; *TNNS*, January 10, 1936 (this says seventeen policemen were killed at Dafen, not twelve). Referencing Dahu's involvement: *TNNS*, February 26, 1933; *Riban no tomo* (1941), 8.

know me."[106] After this, in subsequent interactions Aliman had with the police, they noted that he began to treat them more and more coldly.

Following the introduction of the gun-confiscation policy and then the Dafen Incident, the Japanese began construction on roads like the Batongguan Trail to facilitate access to the mountains where the Bunun lived. Although there was already a trail leading from Dafen to Yuli in Hualien prefecture, built in 1910, construction on the ninety-kilometer Batongguan Trail began in 1919 and was completed in 1921 (map 2). Japan saw such roads as integral to governing the Bunun; the trail was referred to as "the managing natives road."[107] According to Robert Kelly,

> Dafen became the center of the colonial government's attempts to control the Bunun around the Laku Laku River valley. An inflexible policy banning all aboriginal firearm possession was met with such resistance (the Bunun revered guns) that police stations had to be set up every 2–4 km along this part of the [Batongguan Trail]. To this day, commemorative steles marking bloody battles can be spotted every few kilometers.[108]

Authorities also began construction of the Guanshan Road, which was finished in 1932 and provided access to the hideout of Lamatasingsing, one of the Bunun rebels Senō accused of leading the Dafen Incident.

ALIMAN'S TRANSFORMATION INTO "EVIL SAVAGE"

The construction of the Batongguan Trail and the Guanshan Road coincided with Japan's determination to solidify its control over Bunun areas. With Aliman and Dahu residing in Tamaho, they were no longer under constant surveillance (map 2).[109] In 1923 and 1924, during Aliman's time in Tamaho, mentions of him transition from identifying him as a chief to using terms like "evil savage."[110] Senō blames this on Aliman's

106. Senō, *Bankai haishi*, 278.
107. Zeng et al., *Yushan huishou*, 133.
108. Kelly, "The Batongguan Historic Trail."
109. See KZW for a map of Tamaho published in *TNNS* in 1929.
110. Taiwan sōtokufu keimukyoku, *Riban shikō*, 4:465, 671.

hardening demeanor toward the Japanese in reaction to their questionable methods, which included arresting people who had done nothing wrong and a discipline-and-punish system that often caused outrage. Eventually Aliman returned to headhunting, a revered Bunun tradition linked to the passage into manhood and notions of bravery and masculinity.[111] Colonial records mention him going headhunting in 1919 and 1920.[112] During headhunting trips, men proved their bravery by taking the heads of enemy tribesmen. According to Bunun elder Tama Biung Istanda, "If someone says you never *makavas* (headhunt) you will try to join a group so you can go. When you come back, you can be proud. If you don't go ([or] never go) no one will respect you, they won't share meat and wine with you."[113]

In June 1921, the Japanese took their revenge on the purported assailants in the Dafen Incident, identified as Bunun from the Takistalan clan, in Tusui village (杜秀社/ トシヨ). The Japanese police tricked twenty-three Bunun chiefs and men of influence from Tusui village into visiting the Dafen police station, where they were arrested and executed.[114] Among the executed were Lamatasingsing's brother, Dahu (not Dahu Ali), and Aliman Bukun. The killing of his brother fueled Lamatasingsing's continued rebellion against the Japanese until his own execution in 1932. Significantly, there is no mention of trying to round up Aliman Siken or Dahu Ali for their involvement.

The Tusui Incident was not well publicized or known among the Japanese public. In some accounts the mass killing is only alluded to with mentions like: "from this time period more than 20 evil savages have been punished."[115] But it directly influenced many of the Bunun rebels, who resolved to keep resisting the Japanese. Aliman and Dahu ignored requests to submit to the Japanese police because they feared that on doing so, they would be arrested and executed. This fear was not unwarranted, as that proved to be the fate of many rebels. Colonial records state that

111.   Senō, *Bankai haishi*, 278.

112.   *TNNS*, January 10, 1936.

113.   Martin, "Ethnohistorical Perspectives," 132–33.

114.   *TNNS*, December 2, 1922; Republic of China, Ministry of Education website, http://210.240.125.35/citing/citing_content.asp?id=3151&keyword=%A7%F9%A8q%AA%Co%A8%C6%A5%F3 (accessed June 11, 2015). Palalavi cites oral testimony that confirms that those who were killed were targeted due to Dafen connections.

115.   Fujisaki, *Taiwan no banzoku*, 849.

in November 1921, Aliman was asked to submit to police, but he did not because he feared he would be arrested and executed. He also said he saw planes flying over their hideout in Tamaho.[116]

Aliman's continued resistance was so alarming to the Japanese that in 1926 airplanes were dispatched from Pingtung to bomb Tamaho. A description of the bombing campaign included the following statement: "It is said that out of all the hundreds of chiefs, Aliman is a very powerful person, such that his name is well known everywhere, and uttering it can quiet crying babies."[117] Under attack in his precipitous Tamaho hideout, Aliman became labeled a "fighting savage."[118]

DAHU ALI

In contrast to his brother, Dahu Ali was not photographed as frequently prior to his submission ceremony, nor is he mentioned as often in the records. Even so, Dahu is more famous today, primarily because of his moniker as "the last barbarian to submit" and his purported involvement in the Dafen Incident.[119]

One of the first mentions of Dahu relates to his having gone headhunting near the Sakusaku police station in Taidong prefecture in 1926. It was reported that he had gone on the hunt with nine others, including four of his sons, at Aliman's urging.[120] A group of Bunun led by Buruburu village's vice chief, Bionrabiyan, convinced Dahu and his group to stop and return to Tamaho. In return for their help, the Japanese awarded medals to Bionrabiyan and the others who had stopped Dahu and gave them gifts of salt, large iron pots, and cloth. Bionrabiyan credited his people's peaceful life to the Japanese and said it was their natural duty to prevent Dahu and his group from going headhunting.[121] The account shows how the police used a system of material incentives to convince members from the same ethnic group to help them fight the rebels.

---

116. Taiwan sōtokufu keimukyoku, *Riban shikō*, 4:76.

117. Noguchi, *Banchi hikō*, 38; Taiwan sōtokufu keimukyoku, *Riban shikō*, 4:1041–44.

118. Senō, *Bankai haishi*, 278.

119. Chan, "From Autonomy," 101, claimed that Dahu killed seven police officers.

120. Taiwan sōtokufu keimukyoku, *Riban shikō*, 4:1032–34.

121. *TNNS*, December 17, 1926.

Indirectly addressing the lack of photographic or literary documentation on Dahu in comparison with his brother, Senō writes that while Aliman was at the height of his power, Dahu was nothing more "than a nameless savage." Unlike Aliman, who was deemed brilliant and brave, Senō judged Dahu as not as smart as his brother and very obstinate.[122]

THE PURSUIT OF ALIMAN AND DAHU ALI

In 1928–29, when a number of so-called escapee savages from nearby settlements, including Gundaiban (群大蕃), came to Tamaho to join forces with Aliman and Dahu, there was a swift change in the Japanese attitude toward the brothers.[123] They shifted from bombing them to conciliatory measures to induce their surrender. The Japanese relied on the help of police officers, indigenous collaborators, and a Taiwanese intermediary named He Mei, who spoke Chinese, Bunun, and Japanese, to convince Aliman and Dahu to stop resisting Japanese authority.

According to reports in 1928, more than fifty people from Gundaiban fled to Tamaho to join forces with the brothers. As more reports came out, so did claims that their power was increasing.[124] One account said there were twenty-seven clans and 266 people in Tamaho.[125] It was reported that the rebels in Tamaho were crossing the Batongguan Trail to conduct raids and continue their headhunting, striking fear in the hearts of the Japanese.[126] Yang portrays the Japanese decision to try conciliation over heavy-handed tactics as a calculated move, noting that after the 1921 Tusui Incident, many indigenous people had become suspicious of the government and were causing trouble for the Japanese. The Japanese authorities feared if they were too harsh, the indigenous people would come to hate them, making their presence in the region untenable.[127]

---

122.   Senō, *Bankai haishi*, 276.

123.   *TNNS*, June 3, 1928, September 2, 1928, July 2, 1928.

124.   *TNNS*, July 1, 1928, said over fifty people have joined Tamaho; *TNNS*, February 26, 1933, said forty-eight people. *TNNS*, July 6, 1928, said fifty-six escapees joined forces with the brothers.

125.   Chan, "From Autonomy," 101.

126.   *TNNS*, November 1, 1929.

127.   Xu and Yang, *Dafen Tamahe*, 174–75.

Around 1929–30, Japanese police officers finally made some headway with Aliman, cajoling him to move down to a lower elevation on Lilong Mountain in Taidong prefecture, which was still considered part of Tamaho.[128] Aliman acquiesced to the move, according to Yang, because he was tired of the difficulty of living in the higher elevation's cold, harsh climate and was concerned about the welfare of his family and his children's health. Furthermore, he had a tense relationship with Dahu and his brother's children, and living with them in Tamaho was not ideal.[129] Senō's account corroborates that Aliman was poor and suffered from the harsh life in Tamaho as he grew older. He describes Dahu's three grown sons as violent men who defied their uncle, who was still the recognized leader of Tamaho. The antagonism between Dahu's sons and their uncle widened the gulf between Dahu and Aliman.[130]

A Japanese police officer named Kobayashi Masaki was the main contact with the Bunun in this region, specifically with Aliman. Kobayashi worked with He Mei to build friendly relations with Aliman. He Mei offered to let Aliman's youngest daughter, Puni, live with his family so she could be nursed by his wife. The conditions were so harsh in Tamaho that Aliman's wife could not breastfeed her own child. Kobayashi and He Mei also gave Aliman warm clothes and food.[131] The police offered him a brand-new house, which they built for him at the lower elevation, contending that Aliman would enjoy an easier life if he moved to more arable land. According to one account, in December 1929 Aliman had a dream about moving to land outside of the Lilong police line, and he performed a ceremony to interpret his dream.[132]

Aliman eventually chose to move from Tamaho to the house on Lilong Mountain in December 1930. The Japanese claimed that he was now able to have a more enjoyable lifestyle and live peacefully in his old age.[133]

128. *TNNS*, December 10, 1929, describes Aliman's meeting at the Buruburu station and his potential move to lower-level land.

129. Xu and Yang, *Dafen Tamahe*, 173–77. Yang describes his work as reportage (interview, June 18, 2015), which blurs the lines between fact and fiction. While his work takes literary license with imagining conversations between characters, it is based on historical research and fieldwork.

130. Senō, *Bankai haishi*, 279.

131. Xu and Yang, *Dafen Tamahe*, 133–37.

132. *TNNS*, 1929.

133. *TNNS*, December 9, 1930; see KZW for Aliman's house.

Aliman's obituary mentions that the death of his eldest son, Abi, from pneumonia in 1930 had been the turning point for his decision to cooperate with Japanese officials.[134]

After Aliman and his family moved, he was invited to meet with the head of Taidong prefecture, Kodama, in April 1931. Much was made of Aliman's visit to Kodama's house, and their full conversation was published in colonial records and in newspapers. Extracts from their conversation reveal that among other things, Aliman stated his desire to own a camera, and Kodama encouraged Aliman to bring his whole family with him the next time he visited.[135] The conversation did not reference Aliman's previous rebellious actions or the fact that he had been bombed and hunted by authorities.

The dissonance between a formal photograph from their visit, which features Aliman seated in a friendly way, shoulder to shoulder with Kodama, and the published caption, which labeled him an "unsubmitted barbarian," is striking. In the photograph Aliman is seated in close proximity to Kodama's wife and children, so he was hardly perceived as a threat.[136] By 1931 he had reached a mutual understanding with the Japanese. He had ceased his resistance and moved into the house the Japanese had built for him. Figure 5.15, a different, more candid angle on their meeting, shows that sake bottles had been brought out, one of the conciliatory tactics from the early period of colonial rule.

In contrast to Aliman, Dahu Ali held out longer, essentially resisting until the ceremony in 1933. Much of what the Japanese viewed as resistance consisted of continued headhunting and his refusal to move from Tamaho. According to reports in 1930, Dahu Ali claimed he had taken six Japanese heads, whereas a report in 1938 said that Dahu Ali had taken so many heads he did not even know the number.[137]

Officials used Dahu's brother to help them convince him to submit. Although the Japanese depicted Aliman's move to Lilong Mountain as bringing him happiness, Yang's account depicts Aliman being conflicted

134. *TNNS*, January 10, 1936.
135. Suzuki, *Taiwan no banzoku kenkyū*, 538–42; *TNNS*, May 15, 1931.
136. Fujisaki, *Taiwan no banzoku*; see KZW for image.
137. *TNNS*, February 9, 1929; Miyamura, "Hontō saigō," 130. According to *TNNS*, December 15, 1927, Dahu went headhunting in Pingtung and took the head of policeman Tsubouchi.

FIG. 5.15. Aliman with Kodama and other officials, with sake bottles in background. Courtesy of National Taiwan University, Library Database of Taiwanese Old Photos.

about betraying his brother and other clansmen by leaving Tamaho and working with the Japanese. Furthermore, he missed the traditional Bunun ceremonies that Dahu conducted, which previously he had thought his brother took too seriously. Now he wished to conduct the millet ceremony, he said, but only Dahu knew the proper procedures. He decided to return to Tamaho for a visit. When Kobayashi found out about Aliman's trip, he decided to accompany him, seeing it as an opportunity to convince Dahu to submit. Kobayashi's diary entries describing the details of their journey were published in a six-part series in the *Taiwan nichi nichi shinpō* in April 1930.

The Japanese enlisted other Bunun leaders, like Salidan, the Taranasu settlement chief, to try to convince Dahu that if he surrendered he would not be executed. Salidan was the leader who dissuaded Aliman from taking Mori Ushinosuke's head in 1906. In 1929 Salidan had reportedly assured Dahu, "I have done headhunting many times in the past and it has been forgiven." When Dahu hesitated to accept a meeting with the Japanese authorities, citing the infamous Tusui Incident, Salidan told him he would be willing to accompany him to the meeting.[138] In 1932 the Japanese saw Dahu's willingness to let his grandchildren attend the Japanese education center in Masuhowaru, which was seven *ri* (about seventeen miles) from Tamaho, as a sign that he was becoming more amenable to working with them.[139]

Ultimately, Senō attributes Dahu's willingness to submit—or as the Bunun see it, seek reconciliation with—the Japanese to the Bunun rebel Lamatasingsing's arrest.[140] On learning that Lamatasingsing had been arrested, Dahu would have known that he was one of the last Bunun leaders still holding out. Senō described Dahu's decision to stop resisting as an awakening from "this eternal delusion" of continuing resistance.[141] Another Japanese account corroborates the significance of Lamatasingsing's arrest (and later execution) as a "crushing blow," and cites the retaliatory measures taken against the Maebo for the Wushe Rebellion in 1930 as also making an impression on Dahu. Furthermore, the sound of dynamite explosions set off by the road construction crews was signaling that the Japanese were getting closer and closer to Tamaho.[142]

THE CREATION OF THE MYTH OF "LAST BARBARIAN"

One month before Dahu Ali's submission to Japanese authorities, his eldest son, Shida, along with eighteen other Bunun men and one young woman from Tamaho, were taken on an intra-island tour to Taipei. Dahu did not participate because he had a leg injury.[143] The group visited the zoo, the railroad, and factories in Taipei and received numerous gifts from the Department of Savage Administration in Taipei.[144]

138. *TNNS*, February 9, 1929.
139. *Riban no tomo* (1941), 8.
140. Senō, *Bankai haishi*, 279.
141. Senō, *Bankai haishi*, 279.
142. Miyamura, "Hontō saigō," 130–31.
143. Takeuchi, "Banjin no kankō," 8; Saita, "Banjin kankō," 5; *TNNS*, February 26, 1933.
144. *TNNS*, February 26, 1933. The Bunun girl on the tour could speak Japanese and was photographed wearing a white dress and black shoes and carrying an umbrella. She was called a *moga*, or modern girl.

FIG. 5.16. Dahu at the Pingtung Airport. Credit: *Tainichi gurafu*, March 15, 1933.

Even though the tour group did not include Dahu himself, because it featured his eldest son it carried symbolic meaning and was followed in the press. People from one of the last areas to resist Japan's rule were being shown the wonders of Japanese modernity in Taipei.[145] Although he did not go to Taipei, Dahu and twenty other Bunun were taken to watch military exercises at the Pingtung airfield (fig. 5.16). Just seven

145.   See KZW for pictures of the tour group.

FIG. 5.17. Dahu on the far left, with his son Shida next to him. Dahu is wearing the white scarf that Shida bought him while on his sightseeing tour in Taipei. Courtesy of Kaohsiung Museum of History.

years earlier, they had been bombed by planes from the same airfield.[146] After the tours, the press trained its focus on Dahu's submission ceremony in April. Given what we know about the lengthy negotiations that took place prior to the 1933 ceremony, it is clear that his son's tour did not directly influence Dahu's decision to cooperate with authorities.

Pictures of the 1933 ceremony were circulated widely throughout Taiwan and are even found in personal photo albums (fig. 5.17).[146] According to a Chinese source, in return for cooperation with authorities, Dahu Ali negotiated terms to ensure that "his people's livelihoods, assets and security would not be infringed upon and that they could continue hunting at Mt. Yuhui with guns and knives."[147] Japanese sources indicate only that the authorities were willing to give Dahu immunity from his past actions. The current Bunun view that what Dahu did was "seeking peaceful reconcilia-

146.   Mr. Wei at Nan Tien (SMC Publishers) in Taipei showed me an old album that had a photo of the ceremony in it.

147.   See Chen Hui-chu, "The Old Ways: Chung-chih-kuan," http://www.taiwan clayart.org.tw/t_d_01_a.html (accessed April 1, 2011; no longer available).

FIG. 5.18. Dahu presenting antlers of a sambar. Courtesy of Kaohsiung Museum of History.

tion" is supported by Mori Ushinosuke's explanation how the Bunun understood the meaning of the word *submission*: "In their words, there is not a fixed idiom that means obedience [*fukujū*] or submission [*ki-jun*]. What savages say is similar to 'make peace with' [和約] or to 'have good relations' [仲善], for the most part, and the savages saw it as a relationship between equals."[148] The idea that Dahu's "submission" was not a symbol of subjugation but more a performance of the establishment of good relations with the Japanese can be seen in the photographs taken at the same time as the ceremony. Dahu is pictured presenting the antlers of a sambar to the Japanese mayor of Kaohsiung (fig. 5.18). In Taiwan, antlers were highly prized for their medicinal value.[149] The fact that there was also a close-up photograph of the sambar antlers shows that Dahu's gift was seen to be of consequential significance to Japanese authorities in documenting the détente between them and the Bunun.[150]

148. Xu and Yang, *Dafen Tamahe*, 99.
149. Yuasa, *Segawa Kōkichi*, 180.
150. In Kaohsiung Museum of History collection.

CULTURAL RELICS

After Dahu's détente with the Japanese, Tamaho became a destination for adventurers and mountain climbers.[151] From 1933 until his death, tourists and other visitors sought out Dahu, and he gradually became something of a Bunun cultural relic (fig. 5.19).[152] On three occasions, in 1933, 1936, and 1938, ethnographer Segawa Kōkichi visited Tamaho and photographed Dahu and his family, illustrating Bunun culture with their house, clothing, and utensils.

When Segawa and five members of his group visited Dahu on December 31, 1936, they gave him clothing and two cans of rice sake. Dahu welcomed them by throwing a three-day drinking party at his house (fig. 5.20).[153] Photographs of their visit include pictures of the guests passed out after their all-day drinking.

In 1936, Dahu's brother Aliman died after an illness. His obituary, which was written by the police, featured his photo and omits any mention of his cooperation with the Japanese at the beginning of Japan's rule or how he helped convince Dahu to give up fighting. Instead it mentions his headhunting activities that started at the age of twelve, his (supposed) involvement in the Dafen Incident, and his notable transformation into a "good savage" in the later years of his life. As evidence of his transformation, the obituary cites his decision to move down from the top of Lilong Mountain, the fact that he listened to the orders of officials, and the good example he set by farming. On his deathbed, it says, he "apologized to the police officers for the debt he owed them, and he advised his people to follow the orders of the officials."[154] Even in death, Aliman's rehabilitation was upheld as a model to his people.

When Dahu Ali died in 1941, his past was treated very differently. Although still linked to the Dafen Incident, he was described as one of the most powerful chiefs of the region. No other transgressions on his part were mentioned; instead, the focus was on how he began to cooperate with the Japanese by sending his grandchildren to a Japanese school,

---

151. *Riban no tomo* (1941), 8

152. Miyamura, "Hontō saigō."

153. Yuasa, *Segawa Kōkichi*, 211.

154. *Riban no tomo*, February 1, 1936; see KZW for Aliman's photo published with his obituary.

FIG. 5.19. Dahu Ali. Credit: Yuasa Hiroshi, *Segawa Kōkichi Taiwan yuanzhuminzu yingxiang zhi. Bunongzu pian* (Taipei: Nantian, 2009), 61. Courtesy of Moritani Company. Thanks to Yuasa Hiroshi for assistance.

FIG. 5.20. Dahu Ali and his family's party with Segawa. Credit: Yuasa Hiroshi, *Segawa Kōkichi Taiwan yuanzhuminzu yingxiang zhi. Bunongzu pian* (Taipei: Nantian, 2009), 212. Courtesy of Moritani Company. Thanks to Yuasa Hiroshi for assistance.

FIG. 5.21. Dahu (third from right) with several high-level police and Sōtokufu officials. Credit: Published with the permission of Yan Guoming and Yan Guochang.

how he had allowed people from Tamaho to go on an intra-island tour, and his "submission" ceremony. In some of the last photos taken of Dahu before his death, he is pictured with a group of the police officers responsible for reaching their détente (fig. 5.21). The original photo, in the possession of his great-grandchildren, sums up Dahu's transformation from so-called evil savage to ally of the Japanese. Standing shoulder to shoulder with the men who had worked tirelessly to get him to "submit," his Bunun identity seems almost erased as his khaki clothes help him blend in with the other Japanese.

Conclusion

As the lives of those in this chapter illustrate, the Japanese colonial administrative apparatus in Taiwan relied on indigenous interlocutors to maintain rule. What makes the first story (Yayutz's) all the more compelling is how the colonial government presented one view of her to the world, a view that downplayed the amount of power and influence she had in administering the local regions of Taiwan. The large gap between the way she was presented to the public and her actual influence is demonstrated through visual, material, and oral documentation. The colonial government presented her as a "leading pioneer in education," but in reality she had a multifaceted role in the imperial governing apparatus, the extent of which was never revealed to the public. The colonial authorities often consciously elided the complexity of her colonial subjecthood to present her as a model colonial subject. One example of the careful crafting of her image was the subject of the Atayal tattoo on her face. Historical documents and records repeatedly describe her as a beautiful woman who could speak Japanese so well that, if it were not for her tattooed face, one would never guess that she was not Japanese. How shocked I was to learn from her grandson that she had had her tattoo removed after spending a short time living in the metropolis. No colonial record mentions her tattoo removal, only her grandson—who had heard stories from his father and has seen numerous pictures of his grandmother—attests to this as truth. A document written by Yayutz refers to the embarrassment she felt because of her tattooed face, suggesting the motivation behind its removal (though she never mentions removing it). Furthermore, according to her grandson Yayutz had taken a Japanese name. While I found one mention of her as

"Nakano Yaezuko" (中野ヤエズ子), I have been unable to locate any colonial document or any other record that uses this name or any other Japanized name for Yayutz, nor was one used on her gravestone.[155]

For a colonial regime that touted its civilizing effects and celebrated the Japanization of its non-Japanese subjects, the hidden nature of Yayutz's own Japanization may at first be puzzling. I contend that colonial authorities and documents maintained and celebrated the markers of Yayutz's "Atayalness" because that is what made her pioneer spirit all the more noteworthy. Her tattoo—although it was removed—remained indelibly linked to her image as an ethnic other, and the persistence of colonial sources in maintaining this image of her suggests her importance as an ethnic other and a symbol of progress was greater than the importance of representing her actual character. Memmi has written about the colonial relationship as one of interdependence between the colonizer and colonized, neither of whom can exist without the other. This quandary requires the colonized to always be a step behind the colonizer and explains why the removal of Yayutz's tattoo was never discussed and her representation as an ethnic other was so forcibly maintained. Such anomalies and silences are what we need to gravitate toward when writing colonial histories, if we are to learn the greater story. As Stoler and Cooper contend, "We cannot just do colonial history based on our given sources; what constitutes the archive itself, what is excluded from it, what nomenclatures signal at certain times are themselves internal to, and the very substance of, colonialism's cultural politics."[156]

In the 1930s, Japan's efforts to govern Taiwan's Indigenous Peoples expanded to include working to convince the fiercest of rebels to submit to Japanese rule, which involved a lot of the same approaches taken at the beginning of colonial rule in 1895. These included cultivating relationships with men of influence and making conciliatory gestures, such as giving gifts and feasting and drinking together. The return to such policies contradicts the view of the 1930s as a time when Japan's colonial subjects were increasingly subject to imperialization policies that encouraged assimilation to Japanese culture. Although Japan continued to use force and violent punishment to quell rebellions, in some areas of the em-

155.   Chen correspondence, April 1, 2014; "Taiwan seiban no naichi kankō," 299.
156.   Stoler and Cooper (eds.), *Tensions of Empire*, 18.

pire the Japanese were forced to work with indigenous men of influence on their terms. As the Japanese portrayal of Dahu Ali's "submission" ceremony shows, the complexities in how the Japanese worked with local intermediaries to facilitate interactions with influential men were obscured to present a triumphant narrative of success in barbarian administration.

In 1932, the year before Dahu reached a successful détente with the Japanese, the Japanese had executed Lamatasingsing along with members of his family. In addition to being linked to the 1915 Dafen Incident, Lamatasingsing was most notorious for murdering two policemen in 1932, in what was known as the Daguanshan Incident. He took their heads in retaliation for the execution of his brother by the Japanese during the Tusui Incident in 1921. Nine years after Dahu the so-called last barbarian submitted, in October 1942 the Bunun rebel Takis Vilainan Haisul and many of his family members were executed, owing to his involvement in a coordinated attack on three police stations in Laipunuk. Haisul had been angered by Japanese policies of forced migrations into the lowlands, where the Bunun people were supposed to become farmers. This policy threatened the traditional Bunun way of life and was dangerous, as many Bunun were susceptible to diseases in the low regions that were not found in the highlands, such as malaria. The executions of Lamatasingsing and Haisul ten years apart, bookending the peaceful reconciliation reached with Dahu and Aliman, indicate that even at a time when Japan was at war and the mobilization of imperial subjects was a priority, in some areas of the empire Japanese authorities were still trying to establish and maintain control.

The authorities were willing to forgive important men like Dahu and Aliman, who had retaliated against them with actions that they executed others for (even the murder of Japanese police officers) if they participated in public performances of subservience to the empire. The value of a man of influence who pledged cooperation with colonial officials was such that they were willing to overlook past offenses to rewrite the narrative of colonial submission. Looking at the complicated relationships between the Japanese and the indigenous people of Taiwan, it is clear that the Japanese position was at times tenuous and at others showed how individual actors were crucial to the success or failure of the imperial project.

CHAPTER 6

Two Coconuts and a Bonito Stick

For Micronesians living under Japanese imperial rule, there was unending tension between Japan's "civilizing" rhetoric (you can become like us) and its racial rhetoric (you will never be like us). The constant push and pull between these vectors was a reality for most of Japan's subjects in Micronesia's multilayered, racially stratified society, as we will see in the accounts in this chapter. Colonialism was fueled by both premises. If you took one away—the notion that "you can become like us"—there would be no appealing reason for Micronesians to follow Japan's colonial policies. On the other hand, if you took away the racial rhetoric of difference and proclaimed everyone the same, there would be no justification for Japan's rule over Micronesia. The two vectors operated simultaneously and kept colonial subjects pinging back and forth between the promise of becoming Japanese and the realization that it would never be possible. Some dealt with this contradiction by veering to one side and proclaiming they were Japanese, even though they did not receive the same rights and freedoms. Others voiced bitter resentment and contempt for colonial officials owing to the discriminatory treatment they experienced. Some faced execution for their defiance of the Japanese.

This chapter draws from interviews conducted by Higuchi Wakako in the 1980s and Maki Mita in 2008 with various Micronesians and Japanese people who lived in Micronesia during the colonial period, as well as interviews done by Dirk Ballendorf, William Peck, and G. Geiyer Anderson in 1986. Comparing Micronesian and Japanese perspectives on the colonial period underscores the distortions inherent in the colonial record. For example, interviews with Micronesians reveal that Japan's use of local men of influence to counter the power of traditional chiefs caused tensions in Micronesian society, but those tensions were often smoothed away in representations of the South Seas in Japanese popular culture, in which the islands were described as a primitive and exotic paradise. Japanese colonial records, on the other hand, at times reveal some of those tensions, corroborating the oral testimony of the Micronesians.

When writing historical narratives about the Pacific Islands, oral history is key; the indigenous peoples of Micronesia for the most part did not keep written accounts of their experiences of colonialism under the Spanish, the Germans, or the Japanese. In addition, one must consider such issues as who has the right to record indigenous history (Linda Tuhiwai Smith casts doubt on the motives of nonindigenous writers); the use of oral tradition as a means of mediating how sources from the colonial archive are understood, as Greg Dvorak points out; and the actual maintenance of archives and records in the Pacific Islands (see the work of Evelyn Wareham).[1] Melissa Taitano contends that archives in the Pacific "reinforced the legitimacy of colonial authority through the proliferation and preservation of records that perpetuated the indigenous colonized as subhuman, by excluding indigenous oral, kinetic, and non-written traditions from the archive."[2] Yet I believe the Japanese colonial archives do not completely eradicate our ability to understand Micronesians' experiences of colonialism. The Japanese were diligent record keepers, and a number of ethnographers and anthropologists saw it as their mission to record the customs and lifestyles of indigenous people. Although these documents certainly have a Japanese perspective, we can glean from them information that can help reconstruct the colonial period. Disavowing the colonial archive completely reinforces the perception that everything the colonizers wrote was false and everything the indigenous people said was a complete representation of colonial life. Using information from both sides, from the colonial archive and beyond—documents, material objects, imagery, and oral history—produces a fuller picture of colonial lives.

1. Smith, *Decolonizing Methodologies*; Dvorak, "Seeds from Afar"; Wareham, "From Explorers."
2. Taitano, "Archives, Collective Memory," 33.

"We Will Be Splendid Japanese!"

In interviews Maki Mita conducted in 2008, Palauan elders recalled that during the Japanese colonial period they were taught in school to recite *Warera ga rippa ni Nihonjin ni narimasu!* (We will be splendid Japanese!), along with the phrases "We are the children of the emperor" and "We will be devoted to Japan," and to bow toward Tokyo in the north during the morning assembly.[3] As one of those elders remarked, "Even though we declared, 'We will be splendid Japanese!' there was discrimination."[4]

The rhetoric promoting the Japanization of Micronesians was often divorced from the reality of life in the colonies. Institutionalized ethnoracial segregation existed on the islands in many ways, although the boundaries were often tested. Micronesian students went to the public school (*kogakkō*), while Japanese and some half-Japanese, half-Micronesian students attended the national school (*shōgakkō*).[5] Japanese women were trained for colonial life at "bride schools" in the metropolis and then shipped to the islands to be married according to their kind—Okinawans paired with Okinawans and Japanese with Japanese.[6] According to colonial law, indigenous Micronesians were forbidden to drink alcohol except on rare occasions, whereas the Japanese could drink freely.[7] On Palau, if a Palauan beat a Japanese man he was jailed, but a Japanese man would not be jailed for beating a Palauan.[8] Brothels were segregated, with separate facilities for Japanese and non-Japanese patrons, and while Japanese men could frequent whichever brothel they wanted, Micronesians and Okinawans were restricted from visiting Japanese prostitutes.[9] Palauan elders remember that ethnoracial hierar-

3. Mita, "Palauan Children," 22, 59, 153.

4. Mita, "Palauan Children," 71.

5. Mita, "Palauan Children," 104. The Japanese governor of Saipan sent his two children to the school for indigenous children, but they were kept apart from the local Micronesians. Hiery, *Neglected War*, 143, 312.

6. Conversation with Yamaguchi Yoji, 2009.

7. *Annual Report to the League of Nations* (1925), 89. Nevertheless, Micronesian elders have recounted that the rules were often flouted. Micronesians were often cited for drinking alcohol, for example.

8. Mita, "Palauan Children," 123.

9. Mita, "Palauan Children," 241. Some Micronesians flouted the rules and still visited the Japanese brothels. Hiery, *Neglected War*, 138.

chies were evident in the physical layout of the streets of Koror, the heart of Palau, because that was where the South Seas Bureau, the seat of the colonial government, was located.[10] The Japanese lived in houses on the main street, while Koreans and Okinawans lived in the back alleys, next to the brothels and geisha houses.[11] Japanese anthropologist Umesao Tadao visited the side streets of the city where the Okinawans lived. He saw, "where the Okinawans lived, one had the impression of walking into the confusion and poverty of a Chinatown. There the shops were small and dirty, naked children played in the street, and one encountered half-dressed Okinawans, their skins blackened from exposure to the sun."[12] While there was no evidence of this segregation in the Japanese government's annual reports to the League of Nations on the mandate it was given over the islands in 1915, social norms and practices enforced what was in effect an ethnoracial hierarchy. It was often said that in the islands, first-class subjects were Japanese, second-class subjects were Okinawans and Koreans, and third-class subjects were the Micronesians.[13]

In the oral interviews conducted by numerous scholars with Okinawans, Japanese, and Micronesians during the Japanese colonial period, members of all three groups acknowledged the existence of a stratified racial hierarchy in the islands.[14] On the one hand, ethnoracial distinctions between subjects from Japan—for example, between the Okinawans and Japanese—were magnified by the disparate occupations each group dominated. Almost all South Seas Bureau officials were Japanese, whereas Okinawans mostly dominated labor-intensive industries. Businesses that advertised labor jobs in Micronesia, like the Nan'yō Kōhatsu (South Seas Development Company), would restrict applicants to "Okinawans only." Because of poverty and the bad economy in Okinawa at the time, many Okinawans left to take the low-wage jobs offered in

10.   From 1914 to 1918, government headquarters were set up in Dulon (Natsujima Island) in the Truk Islands. In 1921 the Civil Affairs Bureau moved to Koror in Palau.

11.   Mita, "Palauan Children," 161. In Mita's interviews, she includes the honorifics "Mechas" and "Rubak" with the names of female elders and male elders, respectively. For consistency I have decided not to do so here. No disrespect is intended.

12.   Peattie, *Nan'yō*, 221.

13.   Mita, "Palauan Children," 50, 143; Peattie, *Nan'yō*, 220.

14.   Abe, "Ethnohistory of Palau," 151 and 175; Higuchi, *Micronesia under the Japanese*.

Micronesia.[15] According to Okinawan histories of the immigration to Micronesia, the fact that most Okinawans did not occupy administrative or managerial positions was "not necessarily because there was discrimination, but mostly because they were uneducated farmers who had no experience other than manual labor. Once their children became well-educated and qualified for clerical and administrative office, they began to occupy those positions, something unthinkable to the previous generation."[16] This later success among Okinawans alarmed the Japanese administration, and in 1941 "it passed the word to the home islands that further immigration of Okinawans into Micronesia was not desired, and further, began a campaign to deport from the colony all immigrants—mostly Okinawans, presumably—found to have more than one means of support."[17]

Although overt discrimination may not have kept Okinawans from holding the same types of jobs as the Japanese, the fact that they were not initially qualified for those jobs seemed to link their low socioeconomic status with the ethnoracial distinctions that distinguished them from the Japanese. Tellingly, both Japanese and Micronesians referred to Okinawans as metropolitan Kanaka (*naichijin no Kanaka*) or Japanese Kanaka (*Nihonjin no Kanaka*). By calling them Kanaka (indigenous islanders), Micronesians were referring to how the Japanese, like the Europeans before them, distinguished between two ethnoracial groups in the Micronesian islands: the Chamorros, people of mixed heritage (usually European and islander), who were viewed as more civilized, and the Kanaka. In Japanese photo albums, Chamorros can be seen in European dress, in contrast to images of half-naked Kanaka.[18]

"Among Micronesians, the Japanese regarded the Chamorro as more developed because of their longer history of colonization; the Carolinians and Marshallese followed in this ranking[,] with the Yapese being

15. An "Okinawan only" ad was reprinted in Okinawaken Bunka Shinkōkai (ed.), *Kyū Nan'yō guntō*, 7. Okinawans also worked in the fishing industry and bonito production.

16. Okinawaken Bunka Shinkōkai (ed.), *Kyū Nan'yō guntō*, 79.

17. Peattie, *Nan'yō*, 222.

18. Nan'yō Guntō Kyōkai, *Nan'yō guntō*, 296–97; *Annual Report to the League of Nations* (1925), 20; see KZW.

considered the most primitive."[19] Ethnoracial hierarchies were also linked to skin color, with Chamorros generally being lighter skinned in comparison with the Kanakas. The term "Japanese Kanaka" thus indicated Okinawans' position of inferiority relative to the Japanese in a scheme that mimicked the unique Micronesian hierarchy. Tomiyama Ichirō argues that to combat racial discrimination, Okinawans in Micronesia strove to "become Japanese" and rid themselves of Okinawan customs and manners that distinguished them from the Japanese by taking part in what was called the lifestyle reform movement.[20]

Despite such efforts to assimilate, there is evidence that workers' ethnoracial status also affected the wages different people were paid for the same job. Although Koreans and Okinawans were subsumed under the category of "Japanese" in the annual reports submitted to the League of Nations, interviews with Japanese and Micronesians reveal that not all Japanese wages were equal. For example, in 1933 the wages in the government's Angaur phosphate mining operation were as follows: for Japanese workers, three yen and forty-five sen; for Okinawans, two yen and fifty-three sen; Chinese, two yen and fifteen sen; Chamorro, one yen and forty sen; Kanaka, just seventy-six sen.[21] Singeo Techong recalled, "At that time, the pay system was hierarchical according by race. The pay for Okinawans was less than 40 yen a month, and the pay for Palauans was less than 20 or 25 a month, I remember. But if those people were skilled in a specific field, their pay increased to the Japanese level."[22]

As many interviews with elder Palauans make clear, racial divisions between Okinawans and Japanese were acutely felt. For example, Tengranger Oiterong recalled a time when she and her son Benjamin were invited to an Okinawan family's house. Her Okinawan friend was Mrs. Miyashiro, and she had a son, Yukio. Tengranger recalled,

When we let our boys play together, Yukio called Benjamin "*tomin!*" (islander). Even though I did not know that "*tomin*" meant "islander," I felt

19.   Hanlon, *Making Micronesia*, 46.
20.   Tomiyama, "The 'Japanese' of Micronesia," 65–68. Also see an ad for a meeting in Saipan for Okinawans regarding cultural improvement in "Okinawakenmin no bunka kōjō undō," 74.
21.   Tomiyama, "The 'Japanese' of Micronesia," 61.
22.   Mita, "Palauan Children," 36.

offended to hear this. Feeling that we had been insulted, I told my son to reply, "Ryūkyūjin!" [Ryūkyū was the old name for Okinawa when it was a kingdom; "Ryūkyūjin" means Okinawan.] Then, the boys said to each other, "*Tomin!*" "*Ryūkyūjin!*" "*Tomin!*" "*Ryūkyūjin!*"

Then Mrs. Miyashiro said, "He called your boy *tomin*, because you are actually *tomin*. Why do you get mad about that?" I replied, "Why do you get angry when we call you Ryūkyūjin? You are actually Ryūkyūjin, aren't you?" She responded with something in Okinawan dialect. I did not understand what she said, but they were swear words, I suppose.[23]

There were other restrictions that showed how ethnoracial status determined the treatment Micronesians received in comparison to those subsumed under the category of Japanese, like Koreans or Okinawans. Some Palauans were shocked by how poor the Okinawans' or Koreans' pronunciation of Japanese was, yet they could receive the *shōgakkō* education (for Japanese only) that was denied to Micronesians.[24] With technological innovations in aircraft and passenger flights, Japanese could fly to and from the islands, but Micronesians were forbidden to fly. During the 1940s, Micronesians who dared travel to Japan had to do so by ship, which was dangerous during the war. As a safety precaution, in case they were bombed and their ship sank, all passengers were given two coconuts to use as an improvised flotation device and a bonito stick to eat in the event they were set adrift. Ichiro Dingilius Matsutaro recalled how a rich Japanese man he met in the islands invited him to study in Japan. He readily agreed. Ichiro recalled, "I was so happy. This man departed for Japan by airplane. I thought that I could go with him, but *tomin* (islanders) were prohibited to ride in an airplane. So I would have to go to Japan by myself, by ship. The Japanese man said, 'See you in Yokohama!'" Ichiro planned to make the journey by ship, but when he saw a group of Palauans who had just returned, having been rescued at sea after their ship was bombed by the US forces, their sunburned faces changed his mind.[25]

Within Micronesian life and its racial hierarchies, there were loopholes. Half-Japanese, half-Micronesian children often had the option of being classified as Japanese, contingent on whether their Japanese father accepted

23. Mita, "Palauan Children," 174. The use of *tōmin* by Japanese was seen as derogatory.

24. Peattie, *Nan'yō*, 220; Mita, "Palauan Children," 153.

25. Mita, "Palauan Children," 142.

paternity and their Micronesian family consented, which they often did not, for various reasons. During the war, for example, many Micronesians were adamant about not classifying their children as Japanese because it would mean they could be drafted. Mathias Toshio Akitaya recalled, "Because my mother refused to make me a Japanese, I survived [the war]."[26]

Although such anecdotes illustrate the real social divisions that defined many aspects of life in the Micronesian colonies, they do not convey how the process of Japanization was not confined to the islands. Japanization was both accelerated and in some ways abruptly halted by travel between the colony and metropolis.

Tours to the Metropolis: Micronesia versus Taiwan

In Micronesia, while the rhetoric behind the tours to the metropolis program still emphasized showing the modern wonders of Japan's civilization to the islanders (*tōmin*), or natives (*dojin*)—both terms holding pejorative undertones–, there were differences in how the tours were implemented in comparison with Taiwan. The first tour group was formed in Micronesia in 1915, less than one year after the islands came under Japanese military jurisdiction. It was a cosmopolitan group composed mostly of traditional chiefs and men and women of influence. The group included, for example, Achy Moses, chief of Uman; Truk, who had traveled before to San Francisco and Hong Kong and could speak English; King John Singrah of Kosrae, noted for his facility with both English and German; Mac Farland, a board member at the church of Kosrae who had traveled to San Francisco, Hong Kong, and Honolulu and spoke English; Omang, a candidate for Ibedul (high chief) in Koror who understood English and German; and Akosha, a Palauan chief who had spent two years in German prisons.[27]

What to do with so-called primitives who were already cosmopolitan and sophisticated in their European-style suits and Panama hats, even before they stepped off the ship in Japan? The tour program in Micronesia diverged in several ways from the program in Taiwan. First, almost from the start it was focused on the goal of imperialization (*kōminka*)—achieving

---

26. Mita, "Palauan Children," 153–54, 32.
27. Higuchi, "Kankodan," 5; Higuchi, *Micronesia under the Japanese*, 1:20.

full assimilation—for the Micronesians, which precedes the timeline historians have usually claimed imperialization began, in the mid- to late 1930s.[28] Another difference with respect to Taiwan's program was the early encouragement of Micronesian students to participate in the tour program. The tours in Taiwan began in 1897, but it was not until the late 1920s that schoolchildren participated.[29] In contrast, Micronesian children (who had had Japanese schooling) began going on the tours in 1917. The importance of the tours was specifically amplified and reinforced for schoolchildren on the islands. The textbooks used to teach Japanese to Micronesian children included vignettes about tours to the metropolis, reinforcing the desirability of one day traveling to Japan.[30]

When Japan took up the colonizer's mantle from Germany in 1914, the transition for the Micronesians was relatively smooth because certain methods of indirect rule were already in place. Japan's strategy was to use the chiefs and men of influence who had cooperated with the Germans and slowly replace them with people who could speak Japanese. In Palau, a proxy system of governance was set up. The traditional leadership roles of Ibedul and Reklai were maintained, but the Japanese appointed proxies (usually young Japanese-speaking Micronesians) for the traditional chiefs and attempted to rule through them.[31] Japanese officials simultaneously cultivated young Micronesians to work as intermediaries. The youths could speak Japanese and often had traveled and lived in Japan.

From Student Studying Abroad to Prisoner Facing Execution

Pedro Ada was ten years old when he witnessed the changeover from German to Japanese rule in the Micronesian islands. One early morning in October, a naval ship called the *Katuri* pulled up to the Garapan dock in

28.   Ching writes, "*Kōminka* or the 'imperialization of subject peoples' is usually understood as the final stage of Japanese assimilation, or *dōka*, the policy implemented from 1937 until Japan's defeat"; *Becoming "Japanese,"* 4.

29.   The first group of students came to the metropolis in 1928.

30.   *Annual Report to the League of Nations* (1937), 74–79; "Naichi kankōdan," 713–19.

31.   Vidich, *Political Impact*, 195–96.

Saipan. Japanese officials disembarked and walked around the town. In the evening they gave out biscuits, which, Pedro recalled, everyone enjoyed, and this made them like the Japanese. There was no fighting, and the few Germans who were on the island surrendered right away.[32]

Now Pedro was a Japanese subject, and his experience under Japanese colonial rule ran the gamut from being lavished with praise as a Japanized young man to being accused of spying and facing execution during the Asia-Pacific War. Pedro was born in Guam in 1903, and his family had worked as telegraph operators on the Micronesian island of Yap during the German period and then moved to Saipan and became merchants.[33] Pedro's family was one of the wealthiest families on Saipan under the Germans, and they were permitted to keep working during the Japanese period.[34] Some sources say that his family sold goods to the Japanese navy.

Pedro had received a German education until the third grade, and he first went to Japan on a tour in 1917, when he was fourteen.[35] In Japanese eyes, Pedro was classified as a Chamorro. He was one of ten children among the sixty-nine people on the tour, who came from the Micronesian islands of Ponape, Truk, Yap, Palau, Saipan, and Jaluit. The government paid the expenses of forty-five people, and it was reported that the other twenty-four participants paid for themselves.[36] At the time, Pedro was a first-year student in the advanced course (*hoshuka*), the next level of education for the few who excelled in the three years of public school.[37]

Pedro was part of the third tour group to travel to the Japanese metropolis from the Micronesian islands.[38] His diary of the trip, begun when he departed from Saipan in 1917, shows his quick grasp of Japanese after just two years of Japanese education. Writing primarily in

32. Ballendorf, Peck, and Andersen, *Oral History*, 25.

33. *I manåfyi*, 21.

34. Hiery, *Neglected War*, 312.

35. Leo Babauta, "Pedro Martinez Ada," Guampedia, http://guampedia.com /pedro-martinez-ada/ (accessed April 16, 2011).

36. Senju, "Gunseiki Nihon"; *TA*, July 5, 1917. It is unclear whether self-funded participants were completely self-funded or if they received money from others. In Palau there is a tradition of money-raising and lending.

37. Abe, "Ethnohistory of Palau," 147.

38. There are discrepancies between Pedro's account and the colonial record. Pedro says he went on the tour group in 1916 with twenty people. Ballendorf, Peck, and Andersen, *Oral History*, 25.

katakana but interspersed with kanji, Pedro described stopping at the other Micronesian islands to pick up tour group members. They did some sightseeing on the Ogasawara Islands and then continued their journey to Japan, and he wrote of his delight at seeing so many whales on the journey. At last he saw Hachijōjima, which marked their arrival in Japan.[39]

Once there, their itinerary included the Mitsukoshi department store, where they rode the elevator and escalator to the roof and were taken to the soda fountain. They took photographs, climbed the 130-foot tower at the top of the department store, and looked at the view and at Mount Fuji through telescopes. They ate a meal in the store's dining room and bought such items as umbrellas, perfume, Western clothes, bags, eyeglasses, and various "fashionable" (*haikara*) goods that caught their fancy. When the group went to a performance at the Imperial Theater, they were driven in a caravan of fourteen cars.

Although newspaper stories about the visitors identify a fourteen-year-old Palauan named Arugorubai as the translator in the group, Pedro recalled that he also worked as a translator because he was a very good student and was considered one of the best Japanese speakers. He remarked, "I went along as an interpreter and helper for the older Micronesians."[40] He saw his role as helping the older ones feel at ease in new settings. In a photograph of the group, Arugorubai, who was given the Japanese name Kentarō, stands out as the only one dressed in Japanese clothes, wearing *hakama* pants and a *yukata* top. The rest of the tour members are dressed in white, resembling the dress of the military officers who accompanied them. In *Mitsukoshi* magazine and the newspapers, images of the children's handwriting, giving their name, age, and the name of their home island, were published as proof of their good schooling.[41] In one article, a photograph identified three Palauan boys with their new Japanese names, Kentarō (the translator Arugorubai), Momotarō, and Saburō. Arugorubai talked to the reporter in short Japanese sentences about their elementary school in Palau. According to the reporter, in the short span

39. *Yomiuri* (*Yomiuri fujin furoku*), July 5, 1917.

40. Ballendorf, Peck, and Andersen, *Oral History*, 25; see KZW for pictures of some tour members.

41. "Nan'yō no chinkyaku," 10–11; *OM*, July 21, 1917; see KZW for Palauan children's handwriting.

of two years the "children of the occupied islands had quickly become imperialized."[42]

Pedro recalled many years later that the tour was "very enjoyable." He remembered visiting many shrines and historical places, going to the theater, and being entertained at different people's homes. His experience was similar to that of Yayutz, who was invited to parties in the Japanese metropolis, and Zensuke and Gorō, who had been invited into British and American homes when they were living in London and St. Louis. Pedro recalled that they had dances and parties and that he ate Japanese food and liked it very much. He also remembered that a lot of the other Micronesians on the tour liked to walk without their shoes on because they were not used to wearing them. He was amused when they sometimes took them off.[43]

On his return to Saipan, Pedro continued his education, and he eventually became an assistant teacher of Japanese. The Japanese instructors saw how fluent he was and suggested that he return to Japan to further his studies.[44] His grandchildren, Pedro P. Ada and Carla P. Ada, related to me that his decision to study in Japan had to do with family finances. All of his older siblings had studied abroad in Germany. But because Pedro was the youngest, by the time it was his time to study abroad, they did not have enough funds to send him to Europe.[45]

Two years later, in 1919, Pedro Ada became the first student from the Micronesian islands to study in Japan.[46] He stayed in Japan for four years. He first studied at the Oyama shihan gakkō (Oyama teacher training school). While he attended school, he lived with the family of a Japanese judge. Each summer he returned to Saipan, but he ultimately completed the course.[47] At the time of his graduation in 1922, Pedro was described as much beloved by his teacher, and the newspaper reported that he was never regarded with contempt because he was a person from the South Seas. On graduating, he remarked, "I am very happy to graduate but the

42. *OM*, July 21, 1917.
43. Ballendorf, Peck, and Andersen, *Oral History*, 26.
44. Ballendorf, Peck, and Andersen, *Oral History*, 26.
45. Written correspondence with Pedro P. Ada and Carla P. Ada, November 23, 2017.
46. Senju, "Gunseiki Nihon," 179; *TA*, February 17, 1922.
47. Ballendorf, Peck, and Andersen, *Oral History*, 26.

Japanese language is very difficult. In my former school in Saipan we learned kanji, but no one could remember it so now they teach katakana. The most difficult thing for me was Japanese history because it was difficult to remember all the names of the people from the past, so I don't really know it that well."[48] Proof of Pedro's abilities was shown by his signature and a poem he had written, which were published next to the story about his graduation.[49]

After graduation Pedro enrolled at the Jesuit-run Sophia University in Tokyo, where he studied German and English (fig. 6.1).[50] He remained at the university for a year and a half. His family recounts that he mastered written and spoken Japanese during this time.[51] In 1923, after the Great Kantō Earthquake destroyed much of Tokyo and Yokohama, Pedro returned to Saipan. In 1924 he decided to move to Guam, which was under US jurisdiction. He had some family living there, and his sister was going to get married there. This was a controversial decision because the Japanese were opposed to the idea, but despite their disapproval, Pedro left Saipan. He later remarked that "the Japanese . . . scolded me for coming to Guam after they had invested so much in my education."[52]

On Guam Pedro initially drove a morning bus route because although his Japanese and Chamorro were very good, his English was poor. His wife, Maria, worked as a teacher, and eventually they opened two stores.[53] The Japanese occupation of Guam from 1941 to 1944 halted the construction of their third store. From the onset of the occupation, Pedro was jailed along with the Americans on the island. He was seen as a spy because he had worked as an interpreter for the Americans, who had governed Guam since 1898.[54] When Japanese ships came to Guam, he had gone aboard with US authorities to translate the Japanese papers. The Japanese

48.   *TA*, February 17, 1922.

49.   His published signature is reminiscent of the signatures of other colonial subjects that were displayed in Japanese newspapers to demonstrate their education (see, for example, fig. 5.8); see KZW.

50.   *I manåfyi*, 22.

51.   Written correspondence with Pedro P. Ada and Carla P. Ada, November 23, 2017.

52.   Ballendorf, Peck, and Andersen, *Oral History*, 26.

53.   Written correspondence with Pedro P. Ada and Carla P. Ada, November 23, 2017.

54.   Guam was occupied from December 8, 1941, to July 21, 1944. Taitano, "Archives, Collective Memory," 10.

FIG. 6.1. Pedro Ada (middle row left), with friends in Tokyo. Courtesy of Pedro Perez Ada.

occupiers eventually sent some of the Americans to Japan for imprisonment, while Pedro, along with other Chamorros who had worked for the US military, were sent to a naval compound on Guam.

His granddaughter, Carla Ada, recollects the following about her "Pop" Pedro's imprisonment: "Grandma used to cook food for him, and Dad would take it to Pop where he was imprisoned. The Japanese soldiers would eat it all, especially the rice, but Grandma would still cook for Pop and send Dad to deliver it with the hope that maybe one serving may get to Pop." Carla remembers that one of Pedro's Chamorro friends, who could speak Japanese, was executed, and family lore has it that if the Americans had not come, Pedro might have been next.[55]

"I was slated for execution," Pedro recalled after the war. "Some friendly Japanese on Guam, whom I knew, and who knew me, and who had lived on Guam for years, intervened on my behalf with the military and I was released. However, I was very scared then."[56] There are numerous wartime accounts of Micronesians who were accused of spying and then executed.[57] A few years later, when the US forces landed on Guam in 1944, according to Carla, her grandma, Pedro's wife, Maria, kissed the first US GI she saw, knowing that they were being liberated from the Japanese.[58]

It is interesting to see the double-edged sword of Japanization in Pedro's case. His language skills, learned in Japanese schools, earned him praise when he cooperated with the Japanese colonizers, but they got him thrown into prison when he used those skills to work for the Americans. He was saved from his would-be executioners, the Japanese military, by friendly Japanese who lived on Guam and knew him. Thus the Japanese were executioners and also his saviors.[59]

Pedro Ada's experience as a participant in one of the early tours from Micronesia, and later as the first student from Micronesia to study in Japan, illustrates how educating Micronesian youths to serve as intermediaries was a priority from the start of the Japanese administration. The

55.   Written correspondence with Pedro P. Ada and Carla P. Ada, November 23, 2017.

56.   Ballendorf, Peck, and Andersen, *Oral History*, 27.

57.   Ishigami, *Nihonjin yo wasurunakare*, 166–67.

58.   Written correspondence with Pedro P. Ada and Carla P. Ada, November 23, 2017.

59.   Babauta, "Pedro Martinez Ada." After the war, Pedro and his wife ran successful businesses and are known as the first Chamorro millionaires.

students received Japanese schooling, many visited Japan, and then they took up jobs working for the colonial government.[60] Pedro, though, decided to leave Saipan and live in Guam, under US rule. Japan's policy of cultivating a class of young Micronesians who would rise in the world based on merit and language ability helped break down the traditional power structure in Micronesia. In Pedro's case, his education worked against the Japanese in a way they had not anticipated.

The "Fish from the South Seas" and Viscount Mishima

In 1917, the same year young Pedro Ada journeyed to the metropolis, Oikang Sebastian Kōichi was born in Palau. Unlike Pedro, Oikang did not go on one of the tours himself, but he later served as a translator for the tours when he lived in Tokyo. When Oikang graduated from a Japanese-run public school for Micronesian students, his teacher gave him the name Kōichi because he was the smartest student in his class and had the best marks. He then entered the advanced course in Koror. The Micronesian students in the advanced course also worked in the homes of Japanese residents, doing domestic chores after school.[61] Some children were paid, but others were not. School officials encouraged students to put their earnings in a savings account at the post office, just like people did in Japan, but Oikang had fond memories of spending his earnings on movies and donuts.[62] In 1930, while he was working at his teacher's house one day, his teacher asked him if he would like to study in Japan. His relatives encouraged him to go, saying that this was his chance, although his father was hesitant and wanted someone else to be sent instead. Oikang remembered how he was proud that he was the only one from his school chosen to go to Japan.[63]

60. Vidich, *Political Impact*, 193–94.
61. *Renshūsei* (trainees) only worked in houses of Japanese of high status. Mita, "Palauan Children," 122.
62. Yamamoto, "Nana ni nen," 344.
63. Yamamoto, "Nana ni nen," 346.

Viscount Mishima Michiharu visited Micronesia that year on an inspection tour. He was an advocate of furthering education for youth and a cofounder of the Boy Scouts of Japan. When Viscount Mishima returned to Japan in March 1930, he had two Palauan boys in tow: fourteen-year-old Oikang and a seventeen-year-old named Franz (also known as Branz) Polloi.[64] Franz was reported to be the son of a chief, while Oikang was said to be the child of a poor family.[65] Oikang stayed in Japan for three years.

When Oikang and Franz first arrived in Japan, a group of Boy Scouts was waiting at the port to greet them. Because they did not have any proper clothes when they arrived, Viscount Mishima telegraphed an order for clothes and shoes to be brought to them in Yokohama. Oikang recalled the concern the Mishimas had for him when he went to school for the first time: they sent the family maid to accompany him to the train station so he would not get lost. He and Franz were enrolled in the Boy Scouts, and they also went to the same school as most of the scouts. He recalled that because Viscount Mishima was famous, when he brought back with him two boys from the Pacific Islands, the story made the newspapers and various people came to meet him.[66]

Oikang passed the entrance exam for the former Tokyo Agricultural School in Shibuya, where students learned to grow various kinds of vegetables and went to a farm at least once a week. Because he could speak Japanese well, he made friends quickly. There were also students at the school from Korea and China. Despite having friends, Oikang struggled at school; the hardest subject for him was classical Chinese. Viscount Mishima hired a tutor, Marumoto Masao, a university student who was staying at his house, to help him study.[67] Oikang recalled many years later, "Even in the end, I was in trouble and I got a failing grade in it!" He also struggled in history because it was Japanese history and he did not know it. His best subject was math and he could also do English; in sports, he was ranked number two or three in swimming.[68]

---

64. Yamamoto, "Nana ni nen," 173.
65. *Yomiuri*, March 17, 1930.
66. Yamamoto, "Nana ni nen," 348; see KZW for photograph.
67. Mita, "Palauan Children," 30.
68. Yamamoto, "Nana ni nen," 349.

His fondest memories were of playing with his Boy Scout friends and doing various activities with the scouts, like swimming, running relay races, and camping. He recalled that others had called him "the fish from the South Seas" because of his swimming skills. At meals with the Mishimas, Oikang learned to use chopsticks. He recalled later that "they let me sit how I liked. Sometimes, I ate meals with the Mishima family, but usually I ate with the other students staying in the Viscount's house."[69] The most difficult thing for Oikang in Japan, he said, was adjusting to the cold: "It was hard to wake up in the winter, and I did not want to go to school. One day, I pulled my blanket over my head, and held a hibachi [charcoal brazier]. This surprised Mrs. Mishima, who made me stop. I burned my face a little. After this incident, Mrs. Mishima made me a padded room-coat." He remembered that the Mishimas were always very generous to him and once gave him fifty yen as spending money for a school trip to Osaka, Kyoto, and Nagoya.[70]

Oikang recalled how when a group of Micronesians came on a tour to the metropolis in 1933, he guided them around Tokyo. Remembering this responsibility, he remarked, "I was a little proud of myself."[71] Ichiro Rechebei from Palau recalled that his father was on the tour that Oikang helped guide. Rechebei remarked, "My father and other members of the *kankodang* visited them, and my father gave 30 yen to Brans [Franz] because they were both from Airai. In the same way, Temengiil from Ngarchelong gave money to Oikang."[72] Oikang graduated from the middle school in 1933, and when he was about to depart for his return journey to Palau, the papers published an article about him in which he commented on his time in Japan. "My teachers and friends tell me I must come back to Tokyo, I also want to come back, but once I return to Palau, there are things I want to do."[73]

When he returned to Palau at age seventeen, Oikang worked as a translator at the South Seas Bureau. He translated for the traditional

69. Mita, "Palauan Children," 30.

70. Mita, "Palauan Children," 31.

71. Mita, "Palauan Children," 31.

72. The Japanese term *kankōdan* (tour group) has become part of the Palauan vernacular as *kankodang*. Mita email correspondence, July 1, 2009; Mita, "Palauan Children," 181.

73. Yamamoto, "Nana ni nen," 342, 349; *TA*, June 3, 1933; see KZW for picture.

Palauan chiefs during their meetings with the Japanese officials, at which the officials expressed the government's intentions and outlined policies they wanted the chiefs to implement. Oikang worked as a translator in other situations as well, including land disputes between the Japanese and Palauans, since the buying and selling of land often resulted in disagreements. He remarked that such disputes were particularly contentious in Koror, and often the matters were taken to court. Oikang frankly admitted that there were many times at work when he felt embarrassed and confused. Living in Japan had improved his language skills, but in other ways he was ill prepared for his new job. Because he was only seventeen and had spent several years away, he did not know enough about Palauan traditions and the manner in which land was bought and sold. During land disputes and surveys, he did not know how to translate between the two parties. He eventually received help from other Palauans, who taught him about native customs.[74] Oikang quit his translating job after six years and then worked as a teacher.[75]

Years later, in a letter to Viscount Mishima, Oikang wrote, "What Viscount Mishima did. Rather than making money, he made people. *Sensei* really made me." Oikang maintained relations with the Mishima family through letters, and when he returned to Japan in 1985 for his first visit in fifty-five years, he was reunited with Viscount Mishima's wife.[76] Of that trip he remarked, "It was a totally different world!" He met Mishima's daughter in 2002.[77]

The Chieftain's Son Searches for a Japanese Bride

In 1933, the year Oikang returned to Palau, a Japanese newspaper article announced that another Palauan, Ngiraked Atem, the adopted son of Ibedul Tem (also known as Atem), had once again returned to Japan, this time to find a Japanese bride. Ngiraked (written as Eraketsu in Japa-

---

74.   He received help from Oikawasang (Joseph Tellei), the police constable at that time.

75.   Yamamoto, "Nana ni nen," 351.

76.   Yamamoto, "Nana ni nen," 341, 365.

77.   Mita, "Palauan Children," 31. Yamamoto, "Nana ni nen," 360.

nese) had first traveled to Japan in 1924 as part of a twenty-eight-member tour to the metropolis. His status was that of a *joyaku*, a term used for a chief who controlled one village in Koror; because of this, he was named in the news reports covering the tour.[78]

During the colonial period, the Japanese relied on two traditional leaders to help them rule Palau: the head chief called the Reklai, from Babelthuap island in the Melekeok region, and the head chief called the Ibedul, from Koror. Other traditional chiefs of lesser status also worked with the government, but the Ibedul and Reklai were the most prominent. When the Japanese arrived in Palau, they worked with these traditional leaders. Over time they changed the traditional Palauan leadership by appointing proxies for the head chiefs. These proxies would attend leadership meetings, called *sonchō kaigi*, for the first chiefs of every group of hamlets.[79] At these meetings the Japanese would communicate the policies they wanted to implement. Given the proxies' participation, many Palauans considered the meetings a sham and called them *ua isei*, or "yes-yes meetings."[80]

Although touted as the "chieftain's son," Ngiraked was not supposed to be the next successor to the Ibedul, for succession was based on matrilineal lineage. Ngiraked's biological father was Eranbu from Kaishayaru village. When Ngiraked's mother married Ibedul Tem, Ngiraked had been brought to live with Tem and was raised as his son.[81] Tem was the maternal nephew of the previous Ibedul Louch, under the German administration.[82] Despite being "nothing more than a youth from Gashoru village," because of Ngiraked's education in the metropolis he soon became part of an elite class of young Palauans who could speak Japanese and on whom the colonial authorities relied to help them rule the South Seas islands. They were often referred to as the "intelligentsia."[83]

Although Ngiraked was a low-ranking member of the Idid clan, the Japanese eventually named him Ibedul to circumvent his stepfather, who at times defied their authority. Tem was known as someone who would

78. *TA*, July 28 and 30, 1924; Abe, "Ethnohistory of Palau," 122; *Yomiuri*, July 28, 1924.
79. Mita, "Palauan Children," 71.
80. Hezel, *Strangers in Their Own Land*, 196; Vidich, *Political Impact*, 198.
81. Kitamura, *Eraketsukun no omoide*, preface.
82. Office of Court Counsel, *Quest for Harmony*, 13.
83. Kitamura, *Eraketsukun no omoide*, preface.

not be bullied by anyone, Palauan or Japanese.[84] Although Ibedul Tem had gone on a tour to the metropolis in 1918, the purportedly civilizing effect of seeing modern Japan firsthand had not changed him, and he had continued to defy the Japanese.[85] Colonial officials' unequivocal assertion that Ngiraked was Ibedul Tem's son was meant to naturalize his eventual ascension as the next Ibedul.[86] But the local people were not happy with this unnatural succession, for even if he had been Tem's son, according to the rules of succession Ngiraked would not have been next in line to succeed his stepfather.[87]

After his first tour to the metropolis in 1924, Ngiraked returned to Japan at the age of eighteen to study at the Tenri Elementary School in Nara and then at the junior high school. During this time, from 1929 to 1933, he became interested in a branch of Shintō called Tenrikyō, and after finishing junior high school, he entered and later graduated from the Tenrikyō school.[88] The first Tenrikyō representative to visit Palau, Reverend Shimizu Yoshio, had traveled there for missionary work and research in April 1929, the same year Ngiraked went back to Japan to attend school.[89] Ngiraked's placement in Nara, the location of the first Tenrikyō church, just five months after Reverend Shimizu's visit, suggests that Shimizu may have influenced Ngiraked's decision to go there. Ngiraked later lived in the Tenrikyō school dorm, where he received the honorary title of church missionary.[90]

In Nara, Ngiraked, then nineteen, participated in what was known as "Miyatake's salon," a meeting of scholars of foreign languages, culture, and folklore (fig. 6.2). It was organized by Miyatake Seidō, a Japanese scholar who studied the Malaysian language and ran the Nara branch of a group dedicated to communicating in the constructed language

84.   Hezel, *Strangers in Their Own Land*, 162.

85.   Hezel, *Strangers in Their Own Land*, 161–62. When Ibedul Louch died in 1917, his maternal nephew Tem succeeded him. Senju, "Gunseiki Nihon," chart 14, list of 1918 tour participants.

86.   *OA*, October 24, 1933; Noguchi, *Paraoto yawa*, 179.

87.   Kitamura, *Eraketsukun no omoide*, preface, 15.

88.   Kitamura, *Nara ima wa mukashi*, 71.

89.   The inscription on a commemorative structure constructed in 1979 details the introduction of the Tenrikyō religion to Palau and Reverend Shimizu's role. Shuster, "State Shinto," 21, 39; *Short History*, 162.

90.   Kitamura, *Nara ima wa mukashi*, 68.

Esperanto, which was invented in 1887 to promote cross-national communication and pacifism. Ngiraked was treated with kindness in Nara, and the salon members took an interest in him.[91] Miyatake and another of the members, Kitamura Nobuaki, who was then twenty-five, formed a friendship and scholarly collaboration with Ngiraked (fig. 6.3). Miyatake and Kitamura published numerous Palauan myths and stories that Ngiraked told them, penning more than thirty articles and books with his help.[92] Kitamura and Ngiraked, in particular, developed a deep friendship, becoming like brothers.[93]

Kitamura kept more than ninety-two letters from his correspondence with Ngiraked from 1933 to 1941.[94] There is a visual record of Kitamura's friendship with Ngiraked, as well. Kitamura's grandfather had opened a photography studio during the Meiji period. Kitamura was the third generation to run the studio and was a photographer himself. He took many portraits of Ngiraked and other Palauans who visited Japan, photographing them with each other and with Japanese friends (including himself) in his studio (fig. 6.4). Although in other ways Kitamura was quite modern, his photographic style was unique because he continued to work with the old-fashioned glass plates and Meiji-period equipment that by 1925 had fallen out of use.[95]

Ngiraked excelled in learning Japanese; because of his rich vocabulary, Kitamura called him the best Japanese speaker in the Micronesian islands. But there were other outside influences on Ngiraked, including German. Kitamura remembered visiting Ngiraked's room in Nara, for example, and seeing a photograph of Adolf Hitler on his wall, which Kitamura characterized as evidence of his nostalgia for German rule.[96] The extent of Ngiraked's affinity for Hitler is unclear, but Kitamura's recollection points to the lasting influence of the Germans on the Micronesians, as we saw earlier with Pedro's ability to speak German and his decision to

91. Kitamura, *Nara ima wa mukashi*, 68–69.
92. Kitamura, "Paraotō no minkan"; Miyatake, "Waga Nan'yō"; Kitamura, *Nara ima wa mukashi*, 68.
93. Fujimoto, "Kitamura Nobuaki," 12.
94. Permission to read the private correspondence of Kitamura Nobuaki was granted by Kitamura Miyako.
95. Horiuchi, "Kitamura Nobuaki no satsuei sutairu," 9.
96. Kitamura, *Nara ima wa mukashi*, 68–69; Kitamura, *Eraketsukun no omoide*, 14.

FIG. 6.2. Ngiraked, seated center front. Back row from right, Miyatake Seidō, Kitamura Nobuaki, and Yoshia Ryūtarō, 1931, Nara. Courtesy of Nara University Museum, Kitamura Nobuaki Collection.

FIG. 6.3 Ngiraked (left) and Kitamura Nobuaki, 1931, in Nara. Ngiraked's black jacket, next to Kitamura's white coat, seems to mirror the language used at the time, in which Ngiraked was described as "black" in Japanese papers. Courtesy of Nara University Museum, Kitamura Nobuaki Collection.

continue studying German while in Tokyo. Ngiraked's cosmopolitanism is also seen in the signature accompanying his photograph featured in a 1933 publication.[97] His use of English cursive to sign his picture recalls a similar practice among the Paiwan in London, whose signatures on souvenir postcards reveal their intercultural interactions (see fig. 3.6).

In the fall of 1933, Ngiraked appeared on the NHK radio program in Osaka and Tokyo called *Children's Hour*, on which he talked about Palau and its legends and myths, and sang some Palauan songs.[98] Tsukumo Toyokatsu, the founder of the Oriental Folk Museum (Tōyō Minzoku Hakubutsukan) in Nara and a member of Miyatake's salon,

97.   Kitamura, *Eraketsukun sōbetsu.*
98.   *Yomiuri*, October 17, 1933; *OA*, October 17 and 24, 1933.

FIG. 6.4. Josef and Ngiraked (right), 1935. Courtesy of Nara University Library, Kitamura Nobuaki Collection.

advised him on the broadcast.[99] At this same time, Ngiraked also collaborated with Miyatake on writing *The Myths and Folk Songs of the South Seas Island of Palau*, which was published by the Oriental Folk Museum.[100]

After the radio broadcast, a reporter interviewed Ngiraked, who was accompanied by Tsukumo. According to Kitamura, it is unclear whether Tsukumo said it or Ngiraked let it slip, but at some point Ngiraked's desire to one day marry a Japanese girl was expressed.[101] On October 24, one week after his radio broadcast, the *Osaka asahi* announced Ngiraked's desire to find a Japanese wife.[102] The article sparked readers' interest in his search for a bride by referring to him as "the chieftain's son" (*shūchō no musuko*), an allusion to a popular song, "Shūchō no musume" (The Chieftain's Daughter), which was released in 1930 and later became the story line for a film.[103] The song was about a dancing girl from the Marshall Islands who "intends to marry a Japanese singer if he can perform a dance at a tribal headhunting feast."[104] The lyrics include the following verse: "My lover is the chieftain's daughter. / She's dark but in the South Seas she's a beauty. / Just below the equator in the Marshall Islands, / in the shade of the palm trees she dances lazily."[105]

As scholar Naoto Sudo points out, the South Seas (Nan'yō) has traditionally been a "gendered space connected to the 'brown maiden'" that also "connotes a conflict between colonialist desire and fear." The South Seas islands "represent both sexual promise (marriage) and sexual danger (indigenization)," presenting an exotic natural world that is both "seductive" and "destructive."[106] Ngiraked's search for a Japanese wife

---

99.   Kitamura, *Nara ima wa mukashi*, 71. Tsukumo was a friend of anthropologist Frederick Starr, who had accompanied the Ainu group to the 1904 Louisiana Purchase Exposition (Stevens, "Visit to Japan," 36).

100.   Miyatake, *Nan'yō Parao.*

101.   Kitamura, *Eraketsukun no omoide*, 12.

102.   Kitamura, *Nara ima wa mukashi*, 71.

103.   Baskett, *Attractive Empire*, 55. Although the song was popular in the 1930s, references to the chieftain's daughter appeared as early as 1915 with reference to Susan, the daughter of King John Singrah, a participant on the first tour. *TA*, August 5, 1915.

104.   Sudo, *Nanyo Orientalism*, 9.

105.   Dvorak, "Seeds from Afar," 111. Dvorak points out that the Marshalls are not below the equator.

106.   Sudo, *Nanyo Orientalism*, 34.

inverted the traditional objects of lust and desire (brown maiden) and fear (indigenization). Now a Japanese woman was the object of desire for a brown man, which made the Japanese fearful of her loss of civilization and Ngiraked's full Japanization. His search for a bride turned on its head the typical colonial narrative of the brown maiden as the object of the male colonialist's desire and fear.

The article about Ngiraked discussed the song "The Chieftain's Daughter," offering a different perspective on it compared with how the song is usually interpreted today.[107] It explained why the Japanese man had fallen in love with the chieftain's daughter in the first place. He had first fallen in love with a Japanese café girl, and out of despair, presumably because she could not or did not love him back, had jumped into the sea.[108] The chieftain's daughter had rescued him, and they fell in love (apparently he forgot all about the Japanese girl), which led to him dancing for her hand in marriage.[109] This explanation of the song—the trope of the colonized saving the life of the colonizer—recalls the reimagined narrative of how Yayutz Bleyh first met Nakano Chuzō (see chapter 5).

In the article in the *Osaka asahi*, Ngiraked is described as follows: "His color is black, but he is fluent in Japanese and he has become a Japanese young man [*japani–zu yanguman*]." His colonial status, like that of Yayutz, was written on his face: he was racialized as black. The "black but beautiful" trope that applied to Yayutz and other South Seas brown maidens did not extend to Ngiraked.[110] Instead of beauty, his fluency in Japanese mediated the undesirability and inferiority of his blackness. The photo accompanying the newspaper article shows Ngiraked sitting in the shade of a palm tree (fig. 6.5); the same image was included in a book that Kitamura published in 1933.[111]

While the imagery of palm trees evoked a tropical paradise, without the half-naked bodies of colonial brown maidens, the photographs

---

107. Sudo, *Nanyo Orientalism*; Dvorak, "Seeds from Afar"; Baskett, *Attractive Empire*; Kleeman, *In Transit*.

108. Café girls were associated with prostitution, but not all were involved with it.

109. *OA*, October 24, 1933.

110. Dvorak, "Seeds from Afar," 112–13, discusses the "black but beautiful" notion in the context of the Marshall Islands and "Shūchō no musume." *Yomiuri*, July 6, 1930, also refers to Micronesians as black.

111. Kitamura, *Nan'yō Parao shotō*; see KZW.

FIG. 6.5. "Chief's son is searching for a Japanese wife." Credit: *OA*, October 24, 1933.

of Ngiraked were devoid of the sexual innuendo usually present in images of the South Seas. In fact, the picture was a well-constructed facade. As Kitamura later recalled, he took the photo of Ngiraked in the city of Tamba, in the plaza in front of the inner shrine on the Tenrikyō grounds.[112] Because it conjured the feeling of the South Seas, it was used to accompany the newspaper article.

Although the newspaper labeled Ngiraked a "Japanese young man," it did so not in Japanese (Nihonjin) but in katakana, the script reserved for foreign languages. The manner in which the label *japani–zu yanguman* was applied to him, as a term conveyed in a foreign language (English), undermined the very thing the newspaper was suggesting—his successful transformation into a Japanese young man.[113]

112.   Kitamura, *Eraketsukun no omoide*, 12.
113.   *OA*, October 24, 1933.

Ngiraked told the *Osaka asahi* reporter about his hopes for the future: "My father is still young, so after I return to Palau I do not know if I will become chief or not. Regardless of that, as a teacher of the Tenrikyō religion, naturally I want to establish a church and pursue missionary work." Because he considered himself Japanized, he explained, he thought it would be fitting to marry a Japanese woman:

> I hope to continue my current way of life [Japanese lifestyle] for a long time. With regard to this, the people in Palau do not know the customs and temperament. As someone who has become Japanized [*Nihonka shita*] in language and lifestyle, the way I see it, my wife must be Japanese. The Japanese household is warm and gentle; this gentleness is the point that I love the most. The daughters of Japan are very kind. When I first saw kimonos, I did not like them, but recently, just like watching the cherry blossoms, I cannot describe the warmth of seeing a woman wrapped in long sleeves. For me, a good wife would be gentle, have deep compassion, and be in good health.[114]

Ngiraked saw marrying a Japanese woman as a way he could continue living a Japanese lifestyle in Palau. He explained how it would also enable him to obtain a Japanese last name. Often when Japanese people heard the pronunciation of his name in katakana, "Eraketsu," they erroneously believed it was a strange pronunciation of the word *erabutsu* or *ketsubutsu*.[115] He therefore also went by the common Japanese name Satō Eikichi. Ngiraked's friend Tsukumo, who was with him for the interview, added, "It would be good if there were to appear soon a girl who could give him the name of Satō," referring to the fact that if Ngiraked married a Japanese woman he would legally receive a Japanese name.[116]

On October 29 the newspaper followed up with a report on Ngiraked's progress in his search for a Japanese bride. The earlier announcement of twenty-two-year-old Ngiraked's search for a "daughter of Japan" had resulted in ten hopeful applicants. Among them, one woman from Osaka stood out. A photograph of twenty-year-old Shigeki Futōko and her mother, and an interview with Futōko, were published in the Osaka paper (fig. 6.6).

114. *OA*, October 24, 1933.
115. Both words mean a great man.
116. *OA*, October 24, 1933; Kitamura, *Eraketsukun no omoide*, 12.

FIG. 6.6. Futōko and her mother. Credit: *OA*, October 29, 1933.

The reporter pressed Futōko about whether she could really marry "such a 'youth of Japan'" (*Nihon no seinen*). This euphemism and her response reveal that she understood exactly what the reporter was insinuating. She replied, "I don't have such racial [*jinshutekina*] prejudices." Asked if she could handle a lonely life in the "sun-drenched isolated islands of the South Seas," she replied that she was interested in the South Seas and did not hold any romantic notions about what lay ahead.[117] Despite Futōko's professed willingness to marry Ngiraked, the enterprise fell apart.

After a former South Seas Bureau official explained to the mother and daughter the true reality of life in Micronesia, Futōko withdrew her interest in becoming Ngiraked's wife. While interracial relationships were encouraged in some parts of the empire as helping further colonial rule, fulfilling a colonial subject's desire to become Japanese by marrying a Japanese woman was not seen as a legitimate reason for crossing ethnoracial boundaries.[118] Ngiraked was shaken by Futōko's refusal and was heartbroken for a long time.

117.   *OA*, October 29, 1933.
118.   Barclay, "Cultural Brokerage."

Ngiraked's search for a Japanese bride was reminiscent of a search that an Ethiopian prince named Araya Abeba had conducted earlier that year. Ngiraked's friend Kitamura believed that the big sensation caused by the prince's search was one reason the newspaper reported on Ngiraked's similar search for a bride.[119] Abeba also wished to marry a Japanese girl, but he hoped to form such a marriage, newspapers said, because it would create a "yellow-black alliance" against the white powers.[120] Abeba's search for a Japanese wife had turned up numerous Japanese women who expressed an interest in the potential match. After reviewing more than twenty applications, he selected Kuroda Masako, the second daughter of Viscount Kuroda Hiroyuki.[121] Like Futōko, who declared she did not have racial prejudice, Masako explained that "her intention to marry a 'Negro' is simply stimulated by patriotism. In her opinion, every Nipponese girl should go abroad to do something for her country."[122] Masako's bold decision was a hot topic in many women's magazines, and on the day that a half-page story ran on the Ethiopian–Japanese love match, an accompanying article discussed "the leaping modernism of the current day's women," proclaiming that Japanese women had defeated prejudice.[123] Kitamura had described Futōko, like Masako, as a modern girl (*modan gāru*).[124] Modern girls were certainly seen as more sexually liberated, but the *modan gāru* appellation applied to Futōko and Masako expanded that liberation to include an open-mindedness about race and marriage, complicating the usual depiction of modern girls rebelling against traditional norms.[125] Despite the representations of both women as wanting to move beyond racial prejudice, Abeba's potential marriage, like Ngiraked's, fell through under pressure from the governments involved.

119.   Kitamura, *Eraketsukun no omoide*, 12.
120.   Chen, "Growing Rivalry," 68.
121.   Kitamura, *Nara ima wa mukashi*, 71; Clarke, "Marriage Alliance," 3. The *Ethiopia Observer* reported over sixty applicants.
122.   Chen, "Growing Rivalry," 68.
123.   Clarke, "Marriage Alliance," 3–4; *Yomiuri*, January 20, 1934.
124.   Kitamura, *Eraketsukun no omoide*, 12.
125.   The anti-imperialist attitude of modern girls is something worth exploring further.

Both searches occurred in 1933, and although Ngiraked's search for a bride did not cause the same international headlines as that of the Ethiopian prince, it illustrates the same anxiety over interracial marriage when a brown man is the object of a Japanese woman's desire. In the Micronesian islands, these lines were drawn even more clearly. Japanese government employees, for example, were "strictly forbidden to marry a Palauan woman. [If they did] their children were not admitted as Japanese, and were sent to *kogakkō* [schools for Palauan children]. On the other hand, ordinary Japanese were free to marry Palauan women. Often, if the Japanese father acknowledged paternity, the child was treated as Japanese, and went to *shōgakkō*."[126] Marriages between Japanese women and Micronesian men were rare and were seen as completely taboo.

The roles for Japanese women in the Micronesian islands were highly regulated. Some came to the islands via "bride schools" in the metropolis—where women were taught how to adjust to the colonial lifestyle on the islands—and were matched with potential suitors through letters and pictures. Haruji Matsue, the "Sugar King" of Nan'yō Kōhatsu, provided brides for his Japanese workers in this fashion.[127] In later years, women came with their Japanese husbands, who were moving to the islands for work. There were also, of course, Japanese women who worked for the South Seas Bureau, as well as those employed in Micronesia as waitresses, geisha, and prostitutes. One account written in the mid-1930s estimated that there were eighty Japanese brothels in the colony, employing up to six hundred women.[128] Thus Japanese women could go to Micronesia in several roles—just not as the wife of a Micronesian man. Ngiraked's failed search for a Japanese bride reveals the limits of his Japanization and the limits of colonial desire. It also illustrates the constraints on Japanese female participation in the imperial project.

In the span of time that Ngiraked lived in Japan, from 1929 to 1936, he traveled twice to Palau before his final return in 1936. His first trip back to Palau was in November 1933, a few months after his failed bride search.[129]

126.   Mita, "Palauan Children," 51, 99.

127.   Conversation with Yamaguchi Yoji, 2010.

128.   Peattie, *Nan'yō*, 338. Kikuchi Masao's account written in 1937 reprinted in Peattie.

129.   The results of Ngiraked's search for a bride were not published in the papers but were found in Kitamura's memoirs. Kitamura, *Eraketsukun no omoide*, 11–12; Kita-

His Japanese friends threw him a goodbye party and published a book in tribute: *Anthology Commemorating Ngiraked-kun's Departure* (Ngiraked-kun sōbetsu kinen bunshū). After the fanfare of his farewell party, Ngiraked returned just three months later to Tamba with his biological father, Eranbu. Then one to two years later he returned to Palau and lived for a short time in Yap as a Tenrikyō missionary.[130] His stepfather and brothers opposed his propagation of the religion, and he soon returned to Japan in February 1935 and lived in Kobe until 1936.[131] A letter Ngiraked wrote to Kitamura in June 1935 revealed the discord between him and his adoptive father and relatives because of his continued teaching of Tenrikyō. Because of their dissatisfaction with his activities, they had stopped sending money to him and urged him to become a businessman.[132]

During his stay in Kobe, a tour group from Micronesia came to Japan, and he asked Kitamura to meet with him and the group.[133] During this time Ngiraked turned to a new passion—the law. He said he wanted to help those Palauans whose land, inherited from their ancestors, was coopted by the government for the construction of things like shrines.[134] He stayed for one year in Kobe, living at the Tenrikyō Nadabun church. Kitamura visited him several times a month and recalled that Ngiraked was treated very kindly there.[135]

In August 1936, when Ngiraked returned for the last time to Palau, Kitamura accompanied him. Together they traveled throughout Saipan, Tinian, Yap, and Palau. As soon as they landed in Palau, a white-helmeted South Seas colonial official greeted their group, which consisted of Kitamura, Ngiraked, and another Palauan, and took Ngiraked away to the police station. The official behaved in an arrogant and overbearing manner.[136] He accused Ngiraked of saying something disrespectful about the emperor. When Ngiraked denied this and told him to ask Kitamura whether he had said anything, the official scoffed at them. Kitamura at-

mura, *Nara ima wa mukashi*, 71.

130. Ngiraked letters to Kitamura no. 2-12 (April 6, 1934), no. 2-13 (May 9, 1934).
131. *Yamato nippō*, May 1, 1936.
132. Ngiraked to Kitamura no. 2-26 (June 2, 1935); *OA*, April 29, 1936.
133. Ngiraked to Kitamura no. 2-64 (July 15, 1936).
134. Kitamura, *Eraketsukun no omoide*, 14.
135. Kitamura, *Nara ima wa mukashi*, 70.
136. Fujimoto, "Kitamura Nobuaki," 12.

tributed this behavior to what was typical of colonial officials, who often lorded their authority over everyday people, even over other Japanese, like Kitamura.[137] When they went to Ngiraked's village, Kitamura was taken to the police station by an officer. He was deemed a "suspicious person" and was shown documents by the officer. They included a report from the Nara mayor in response to a request for an investigation from the South Seas colonial government. In the report, Ngiraked and "the bride incident" were discussed; the conclusion was that Ngiraked was a "bad youth."[138] According to Kitamura's assessment of the situation, the South Seas government had concluded that when islanders went to the metropolis, incidents often occurred during their time in Japan that made them "cheeky."[139] He referred to the suicide of a young Palauan named Moriesu in 1935 as a case in which a Palauan had seemingly forgotten his place. Moriesu had lived in Tokyo for several years and had fallen in love with a Japanese madam who ran a nightclub where he worked as a cook. When Moriesu learned he had to return to Palau, he killed himself because he could not bear the thought of leaving his love. His death made a big splash in the metropolis and in Palau. At the time, Ngiraked was also living in Japan, and he corresponded with Kitamura about it two days after the death was reported in the papers. In one letter he expressed his shock over the young man's death. He doubted that Moriesu would kill himself over his relationship with the woman, Hatsu-san, and speculated that there must have been a larger reason beyond her that led to his decision.[140]

Kitamura traveled with Ngiraked for thirty days, and he researched Palauan animals, plants, and various other topics.[141] This visit was the last time the friends saw each other. Soon after Kitamura left the islands, Ngiraked wrote to him in October 1936 saying that the South Seas colonial officials were forbidding him from returning to the metropolis. He entreated Kitamura to intercede on his behalf with some Japanese ac-

137. Kitamura, *Eraketsukun no omoide*, 19–20.
138. Kitamura, *Eraketsukun no omoide*, 21.
139. Kitamura, *Eraketsukun no omoide*, 21.
140. Ngiraked to Kitamura no. 2-42 (October 26, 1935).
141. Kitamura, *Nara ima wa mukashi*, 73–75.

quaintances living on Palau.[142] A few days later, he wrote that he was told he could only return to Japan if he was engaged in commerce.[143] In 1937, Ngiraked wrote to Kitamura, saying he was still living a single lifestyle and he had grown to deeply hate living in Palau. He thought about going to Manado in Indonesia, and when he had tried to return to Japan, the government office had stopped it.[144] Also in 1937 a few newspapers published articles in which Ngiraked expressed his support for enlistment into the Japanese imperial military of those from the South Seas who were "children of the emperor." Since the China Incident in 1937, he said, many eager youths in the islands hoped to enlist and were swept up in war fever.[145]

From 1936 on, Ngiraked worked as a Tenrikyō missionary and as a teacher at a public school in Palau. According to some accounts, he was also recognized as the chief of a village of 300 to 400 people.[146] Around this time, conflicting reports about Ngiraked being named Ibedul began to appear. The dates in documents that mention Tem's and Ngiraked's tenures as Ibedul often do not coincide.[147] According to one scholar, in 1934 Ngiraked was Ibedul and Brel was Reklai. It was reported that both men approved a Japanese plan to reform Palau's currency and exchange customs. Although the Japanese were behind the reform, Ngiraked and Brel reportedly convinced the Japanese "that their honor would be preserved, if they, themselves, could anticipate the Japanese sponsored change by proposing the identical plan as their own."[148] This anecdote indicates that the Japanese did not always rule with absolute authority and that local leaders cared about how colonial policies were rolled out and how they affected perceptions of their own power. According to scholar Mita

---

142. Ngiraked to Kitamura no. 2-70 (October 8, 1936).

143. Ngiraked to Kitamura no. 2-71 (October 20, 1936).

144. Ngiraked to Kitamura no. 2-71 (April 26, 1937).

145. *Nara shinbun*, November 1937 (day unclear); *Yamato nippō*, November 2, 1937. The China Incident refers to the Marco Polo Bridge Incident, which ignited the Second Sino-Japanese War.

146. Kawamura, *"Dai Tōa minzokugaku,"* 182.

147. Ngiraked is listed as Ibedul from 1939(?) with the next Ibedul, Mariur, listed from 1950. http://www.worldstatesmen.org/Palau.htm (accessed September 25, 2015); Tem's term was said to be from 1917 to 1943. Office of Court Counsel, *Quest for Harmony*, 13.

148. Vidich, *Political Impact*, 258.

Maki, although Ngiraked was given the title of Ibedul, he was merely a proxy for Ibedul Tem; all the Palauans knew this, and the only people who called Ngiraked Ibedul were the Japanese.[149]

In addition to putting Ngiraked in a position of power, whether as a proxy for Ibedul Tem or as the actual Ibedul, the Japanese appointed others as proxies for leaders who disobeyed their authority.[150] The deposed traditional chiefs maintained their authority in name only, in that they retained their hereditary title and influence in the eyes of their local community, but with the proxies, the Japanese ensured they had people in positions of power who were working for their side—usually individuals who could speak Japanese and had traveled to Japan.[151] The Japanese attempts to circumvent Palau's traditional chiefs were tied to their effort to eradicate local culture and tradition in favor of Japanese culture. By appointing Japanese-speaking allies as chiefs, they hoped to discipline and control the traditional leaders who defied their orders. For example, the Ibedul whom Ngiraked was meant to replace, his stepfather, Tem, had continued to hold the *mur*, a customary Palauan feast, after it was banned by the Japanese. But his defiance led the Japanese and some Idid clan members to try to remove him from his position.[152] Ibedul Tem fled to Ngaraard for a time, although he later returned to Koror.[153]

There is evidence that Ngiraked's appointment as Ibedul caused widespread discontent in Palau because it circumvented traditional rules of

149.   Maki written correspondence, April 21, 2011; Maki, "Palauan Children," 71.

150.   Joseph Tellei was the proxy for Reklai Rruull. Mita, "Palauan Children," 71; Office of Court Counsel, *Quest for Harmony*, 15.

151.   Both Maki Mita and Francis Hezel support the contention that the traditional leaders were still adhered to (*Strangers in Their Own Land*, 162–63). Vidich, *Political Factionalism*, describes the Micronesians who worked for the government as young, speaking Japanese, and having traveled to Japan.

152.   Hezel, *Strangers in Their Own Land*, 162.

153.   Office of Court Counsel, *Quest for Harmony*, 15. Hezel contends that Tem was persuaded to return to head a shadow government (*Strangers in Their Own Land*, 162). Some sources say both Ngiraked and Omengkar succeeded Tem, others just Ngiraked, and others just Omengkar. For the latter see Hezel, *Strangers in Their Own Land*, 162.

succession.[154] Although the locals were certainly unhappy with Ngiraked's appointment because the Japanese had used him to get around the traditional leaders, according to Kitamura it was Ngiraked's ability to speak Japanese that led to feelings of ill will among some Micronesians, especially lower-level officials, who criticized him strongly. Although Japanese people considered Ngiraked to be relatively refined, some Micronesians saw him as "an islander who did not appear to be an islander." Ngiraked, who had been much loved in the metropolis, encountered cold treatment several times in Palau.[155]

A document describing Ibedul Tem's death in 1938 mentions Ngiraked not as the Ibedul but as occupying the position right below him. The document's author, Japanese artist and ethnographer Hijikata Hisakatsu, lived for several years in Palau and Satawal and wrote about the gathering that took place for Tem's funeral. Hijikata describes Ngiraked as being shoved aside and sitting on the ground in the woods behind the house, not taking part in the funeral.[156]

Another account written in 1941 verifies the resentment that local people felt regarding Ngiraked's appointment as Ibedul, and it suggests that Ngiraked had not wanted the job. Noguchi Masaaki, a Japanese editor in Koror who was known for his critical essays about the South Seas Bureau, wrote that although such an appointment was thought to be desirable, Ngiraked was not grateful for it and did not see it as an honor. He thought it was a burden, and he understood that from then on he would have a hard time in his job.[157] Noguchi said Ngiraked tried to decline the position in favor of other Palauans who were of higher rank, but the government insisted on his appointment. Two factions, those for and those against Ngiraked's appointment, fueled the controversy in Ko-

---

154. One source stated that the appointment of Ngiraked as Ibedul had bypassed an important chief, Tem, who was next in line for Ibedul position, failing to acknowledge Tem had been in power as Ibedul since 1917. Ngiraked was chosen over Tem, because Tem was old and did not speak Japanese. Ngiraked was young and spoke Japanese. After his appointment, there was opposition among the islanders that lasted for some time. Taiheiyō Kyōkai (ed.), *Nanpō*, 106–8.

155. Kitamura, *Eraketsukun no omoide*, preface; Kitamura, *Nara ima wa mukashi*, 69.

156. Hijikata, *Society and Life*, 261, 265.

157. Noguchi, *Paraotō yawa*, 155.

ror. Noguchi wrote of Ngiraked's predicament as pitiful and unfortunate, as he had to take on a responsibility that he did not want and that most of his community opposed.[158] Noguchi described him as someone who came from the highest ranks of the Micronesian intelligentsia. Although he wrote that Ngiraked was not a bad person, he said he had no familial connections to the previous Ibedul and his appointment by the Japanese clearly flouted Palauan protocol.[159]

Furthermore, comments about Ngiraked's "bad" reputation persisted long after his unceremonious welcome in 1936 when he returned to Palau. In 1939 Kitamura was corresponding with a young Japanese woman, Kitamura Yaeko (no relation), who had just moved to Palau and met Ngiraked. She and three other women had answered an ad in the paper for jobs as typists for the colonial government. Kitamura had informed Ngiraked of their upcoming arrival in Koror, so he met them when they landed and drove them around the town. According to Kitamura, although Ngiraked seemed "innocent and cheerful," the women's work colleagues warned them that they should not get too close to him.[160]

Yaeko wrote to Kitamura about how she had spent time with Ngiraked a few times, including attending his stepfather's funeral. But, she said, she kept hearing about Ngiraked's bad reputation. Once or twice she could dismiss it, but on hearing it four times, she gave it some credence. Because her friendship with Ngiraked was drawing attention at work, she cut off ties with him. She concluded her letter by saying she hoped that one day he would again be the interesting and cheerful youth they had both known.[161] It is unclear from their correspondence and Kitamura's accounts what exactly had happened, but it is clear that Ngiraked drew continued scrutiny over any relationships he had with Japanese women on the island. After Ngiraked and Yaeko ceased interacting, Kitamura writes, the young women returned to Japan relatively quickly, their stays having lasted only six months to a year. In 1942 Kitamura got a letter from another acquaintance

158. Noguchi, *Paraotō yawa*, 162, 172–73.

159. Noguchi, *Paraotō yawa*, 175, 179. According to tradition, the women of the clan of the current Ibedul selected the next Ibedul from among the most influential village chiefs. Mita written correspondence, April 21, 2011; Leibowitz, *Embattled Island*, 103.

160. Kitamura, *Eraketsukun no omoide*, 24.

161. Kitamura Yaeko to Kitamura no. 12-1 (August 22, 1939). I first learned of these letters in Mitsuishi, "Eraketsu Atem," 29.

in Palau who told him that there was a rumor that Ngiraked had been put in Karubosu (a combined detention center and jail).[162] It is unclear what the circumstances were, and in another account Kitamura merely writes, "Something bad had happened." Kitamura asked several acquaintances in Palau about Ngiraked and because almost all the replies were unfavorable, he wrote he could not help but feel concerned.[163] Kitamura lamented that Ngiraked's pitiful existence back in the islands was extremely regrettable, considering how well loved he was in the metropolis.[164]

There is one last reference to Ngiraked that suggests his isolation increased as conditions deteriorated during the Asia-Pacific War and Palauans began to lose faith in Japanese rule. Prior to the bombing of Palau in March 1944, the popularity of the Modekngei religion had reached its height. The leader of the Modekngei at the time, Rnguul, estimated that he had an active following of 3,000 members, "half of the total [population] and perhaps most of the adult population."[165] Modekngei leaders offered promises of protection against the bombing and help for the wounded. Unbeknown to the Japanese, Rnguul called a secret meeting of all the traditional chiefs.

> When the casualties were getting higher, Rnguul called a meeting of all the chiefs. He was no longer in hiding and many people were going to see him in Airrai [sic]. At this meeting the chiefs were asked to pray for a quick ending of the war. The only person who did not recognize Rnguul and did not attend the meeting was Aibidul [Ibedul]. All the other chiefs went and this in spite of the fact that the meeting was secret and against the wishes of the Japanese.[166]

The Ibedul who did not attend the meeting was mostly like Ngiraked.[167] Near the war's end, all the proxy chiefs gravitated back to Rnguul and the Modekngei religion. If Ngiraked was indeed the only holdout, we can

---

162.   Kitamura and Suigimoto Minori no. 13-1 (October 10, 1942).
163.   Kitamura, *Eraketsukun no omoide*, 24.
164.   Kitamura, *Eraketsukun no omoide*, preface.
165.   Vidich, *Political Impact*, 245.
166.   Vidich, *Political Impact*, 245, quoting interview with Bismark of Airai.
167.   Ibedul Tem died in 1938, and Ngiraked died in 1944. The next Ibedul, Mariur, did not come into power until after the war.

imagine he was truly isolated during the war years; he would have met with disapproval from both the government and his family.

Interviews with numerous Palauan elders after the end of the Asia-Pacific War reveal that from 1944 to 1945, the Modekngei sect attracted many followers through its healing, money lending, and prophesying. Modekngei talismans of red cloth were believed to have saved Palauan lives during the war. As belief in Japan's ability to win the war faltered, more and more Palauans sought comfort in Modekngei beliefs, and some Japanese soldiers sought the protection of the talismans as well, as their faith in Japan faltered.[168] The persistence of the Modekngei religion and its popularity in the late war years shows that Japan's efforts to enact cultural reforms (as it had in Hokkaido, Okinawa, and Taiwan) by forbidding certain practices, discouraging the use of local dialects, and portraying local customs as backward never completely eradicated local traditions and culture in Palau.

After the war broke out in the Pacific, Kitamura tried to send letters to Ngiraked but to no avail. In 1944 Ngiraked was rumored to have died, partly owing to overwork and the stress of his new position as Ibedul.[169] After the war, Kitamura was desperate to know if Ngiraked was alive or dead. In 1952 he enlisted the help of their friend Tsukumo's son, an English teacher, to write a message in English on a postcard that Kitamura sent to Ngiraked's last known residence. Kitamura implored the recipient to forward the message to Ngiraked if he or she knew where he was, and described him as a friend of more than ten years. After being mistakenly routed through Hawaii, several months later the postcard was returned to Kitamura with "deceased" stamped on it. Kitamura later learned that in 1944, at the chaotic time of the first air strike on Palau, Japanese and Palauans had fled from Koror to the main island of Palau. Ngiraked and several others were transferring luggage from Koror to the main island in a small sailboat when their anchor got stuck on a reef. Ngiraked dove into the water to try to free the anchor, but he went too deep. He drowned twelve feet below the surface.[170]

In 1954 Kitamura published a pamphlet titled *Memories of Ngiraked* (Eraketsukun no omoide) that included numerous photos and his

168.   Aoyagi, *Modekngei*, 145.
169.   Taiheiyō Kyōkai (ed.), *Nanpō*, 105, 107.
170.   Kitamura, *Nara ima wa mukashi*, 75.

detailed recollection of Ngiraked and their friendship, including a description of their travels in the South Seas. The pamphlet testifies to Ngiraked's experiences in the metropolis, which stood in contrast to his experiences in Palau after his return. It describes how, in the later years of his life, he endured scrutiny and suspicion from the colonial government and his own family, illustrating the other side to assimilation that was rarely talked about during the Japanese period. It is important to note, of course, that it is mostly Japanese documents that depict Ngiraked as experiencing resentment from some in the Palauan community. We have little oral testimony from Palauans about Ngiraked; if he had in fact been named Ibedul, the silence surrounding him speaks volumes about their ambivalence over his position in the community. One scholar, Mitsuishi Ayumi, went to Palau in 2016 and conducted oral interviews with Palauan elders. Although some did talk about Ngiraked, they did not reveal much information.[171] Because Ngiraked died at the age of thirty-four, without children, he had no direct descendants. Kitamura's writings, photos, and correspondence provide the fullest insight into Ngiraked's life.

Ngiraked's quest to become Japanese was stymied by his failure to secure a Japanese bride. Interethnic relationships between Japanese women and Micronesian men were extremely rare; the two most talked-about cases ended in tragedy. In one, a Japanese nurse from Yamagata prefecture who worked in a hospital in Saipan and fell in love with a Palauan man named Esang (Ceiman). Some say they married, although the legal status of their union is unknown.[172] Others recall that Esang died and his wife returned to Japan, where she gave birth to their child. After the child was born, according to the story, a police officer came and told her the baby had to be returned to Palau. She went back to Palau and gave up the baby to be raised by Esang's parents.[173] The second case was the relationship between Moriesu, the Palauan who had lived and worked for several years in Tokyo, and the Japanese woman with whom he had secretly fallen in love, the madam who ran Café Palau in Tokyo. On learning he had to return to Palau, Moriesu, in anguish, stabbed himself in the neck. His "black

171.   Mitsuishi, "Eraketsu Atem," 30.
172.   Higuchi, *Micronesia under the Japanese*, 20.
173.   Mita, "Palauan Children," 133, 240.

corpse" in a blood-soaked *yukata* was discovered outside the café, and the details of his suicide were later published as a true cautionary tale of the dangers of unrequited "black love."[174] These stories, and Ngiraked's failed search for a Japanese bride, illustrate the perceived dangers and real difficulties of such unions. Ngiraked, who considered himself Japanese, learned that he was not. Futōko's open-minded answers about marrying him at first indicated the possibility of moving past barriers of race and colonial status, but as quickly as the possibility opened, the authorities made sure the barriers stood firm. The prospect of a dark-skinned colonial subject marrying a Japanese girl was simply too threatening.

Augusta Ramarui and the Takarazuka Revue

Descriptions of the first tours to the metropolis from Micronesia claim that the Palauan participants underwent a dramatic physical transformation: "They had left Palau wearing their finest loin cloths, without shoes, and wearing long hair held in place with the traditional comb; and they returned home clothed in Japanese attire with their hair shorn."[175] Stories are still told today about how the chiefs who went on these first tours returned from Japan and encouraged other Micronesians to cut their hair, wear modern clothing, and move their settlements from the highlands to the coast and construct roads. Reklai Uong Ngirateuid of Ngiwal went on the first tour to the metropolis in 1915. After returning, he moved the village of Ngiwal from inland to the shore and created straight roads. Uong's granddaughter Augusta Ramarui recalled that her grandfather "convinced the land-owners of our clan to divide the land into pieces and give it to other clan people who had no land. There was no democracy at this time. The high clan people did not like this. He also had the men cut their hair short."[176] Uong is said to have constructed a Ginza-dōri (a street in Tokyo seen as an exemplar of modernization), putting in a straight paved street with lanterns on both sides, mimicking what

174. *Yomiuri*, October 24, 1935; Nakata, "Jijitsu shosetsu," 92–95, 81.

175. Vidich, *Political Impact*, 190.

176. Augusta Ramarui interview in Micronesian Area Research Center (MARC), *Oral Historiography*, 179.

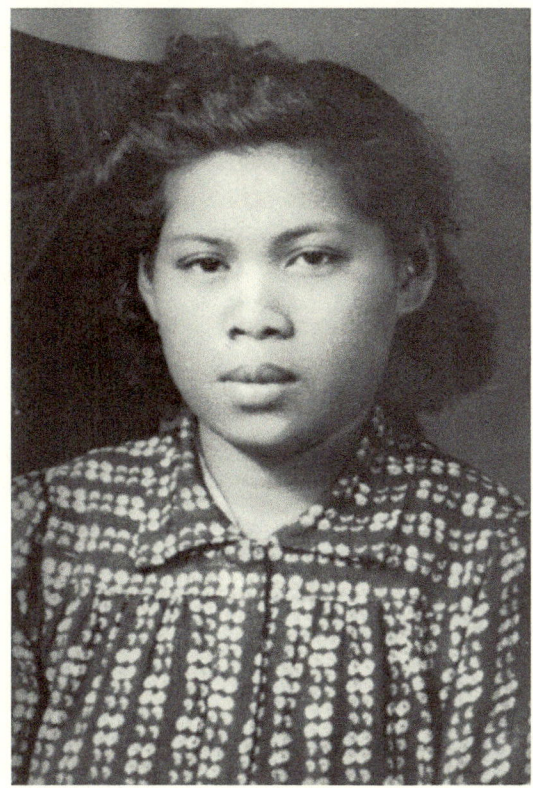

FIG. 6.7. Augusta. Courtesy of Nara University Museum, Kitamura Nobuaki Collection.

he had seen while on tour.[177] Japan lauded the immediate effect of the tours on people from the colonies, writing in its report to the League of Nations, "To judge from their written expressions of the impressions they obtained in Japan Proper, many of them come home, inspired with a fresh zeal to work for the improvement of their villages."[178]

Sartorial changes and government propaganda aside, some Micronesians doubt whether the tours brought equally transformative changes to the participants. One of those who expressed doubt about the civiliz-

177. Iitaka, "Nihon tōchi," and "Conflicting Discourses," concluded that oral stories about Ginza-dōri were a way for Palauans to take control of their own participation in colonial life rather than evidence of the success of the tour program.

178. *Annual Report to the League of Nations* (1935), 92.

ing effects of the tour program was Augusta Ramarui (fig. 6.7), whose grandfather Uong moved their village to the coast and built Palau's Ginza dōri. She recalled that in the beginning, only well-to-do people from the high clans went on the tours. She remarked that "the purpose of the *kankōdan* [tours to the metropolis] was to learn sophisticated culture. The Japanese wanted to change our culture to theirs, to change our primitive life. When [participants] got back, they tried to act like Japanese, wearing *geta* [Japanese-style wooden shoes], shirts, and using *hashi* [chopsticks], but they failed."[179] Although Augusta acknowledged that the participants could speak Japanese, in her eyes becoming Japanese involved more than speaking the language, and their attempts to adopt Japanese ways of life seemed false and resulted in failure.

Augusta's comments are interesting because she herself had lived in Japan from 1939 to 1940. She assessed those who had visited Japan as having only the superficial trappings of being Japanese. Her frank observations about those who returned from the tours and tried to act Japanese are even more interesting when one considers her critical feelings about Japanese rule. She described her stay in Japan: "When I was in the fourth year of *kogakkō*, I went with my teacher and his family to Japan. We went to Osaka, Kobe, and Yokohama, traveling to Japan by ship. Sadao Fukoka, my *sensei*, went on home leave. I worked for them. They lived in Yongo-ken near Osaka. I stayed in Japan for about six months and that's how I learned to speak Japanese well."[180] Kitamura met Augusta, the only girl among the group of Palauans living in the metropolis, and they became friends. He remembered when, as a tall fifteen-year-old, she often came to Nara to visit him.[181] In 1940, when Augusta was seventeen, she took part in a Co-Prosperity Sphere forum, along with children from China and India. During wartime, the articulation of the Greater East Asia Co-Prosperity Sphere was Japanese propaganda that posited Japan leading the countries of East Asia in achieving peace and economic prosperity. Kitamura suggested to Augusta and her Japanese host parents that she should participate in the forum. At the conference she said that she wanted her brother Bapuchiso

179. MARC, *Oral Historiography*, 179–80.
180. MARC, *Oral Historiography*, 182.
181. Kitamura, *Nara ima wa mukashi*, 76.

and sister Panechina to come to study in Japan with her.[182] Kitamura remembered that shortly afterward Augusta visited him and told him about having performed with the Takarazuka Revue, an all-girl group. She told him she had not been embarrassed and had sung and danced on stage, and showed him a picture of the show. The revue's listings show that the program, titled *Saipan Palau: Our South Seas*, ran from the end of July to the end of September 1940.[183]

Augusta seemed like an ideal wartime colonial subject, performing with the Takarazuka Revue and participating in the Co-Prosperity Sphere forum. But her time in Japan did little to change her critical view of life for Palauans under Japanese rule. It is possible that it was seeing the disparity between how the Japanese lived and how the Micronesians were treated that led her to remark, "At that time I hated the Japanese, but we had no choice. What I disliked the most was the limitation of our education and the discrimination. We had only five years of schooling but the Japanese children had ten. These are my major reasons for hating them. Also the Japanese government officials did what they wanted, giving an air of superiority, and acting as if we were animals."[184] In her criticism of the Japanese, Augusta did distinguish between government officials and nonofficials: "I liked the Japanese farmers. We were friends and they mingled with the Palauan villagers. The Japanese government officials were autocrats. We were called *tōmin*, meaning islander. We didn't like this term because it was often used in a negative way."[185]

In her assessment of the tours, her stay in Japan, and Japanese rule in Palau, Augusta rendered the following final verdict: "As far as changing us into Japanese[,] they failed. We couldn't progress because we had no say. The Japanese wanted to make these islands their own. I'm not surprised they left us with only five years of schooling . . . . I hated the Japanese government officials."[186] Augusta's testimony counters colonial records and, in her own case, reports that depicted her as a model subject.

182. Kitamura, *Nara ima wa mukashi*, 77.
183. *TA*, August 25, 1940; Robertson, *Takarazuka*, 119. http://www.hankyu-bunka .or.jp/archive/?app=shiryo&mode=detail&list_id=16898&data_id= 108316 (accessed July 29, 2018).
184. MARC, *Oral Historiography*, 182.
185. MARC, *Oral Historiography*, 182.
186. MARC, *Oral Historiography*, 182–83.

While her grandfather Uong had been upheld as an exemplar of how the tours to the metropolis transformed Japan's colonial subjects, Augusta's ability to speak out later about her time in Japan and in Palau raises the question of how Uong himself would have portrayed his own experience.

Competing Legacies of the Tours

From 1954 until 1967, when Typhoon Sally destroyed the Keptotal Bai, Palau's community center, the legacy of the tours was featured on the center's walls in a sequence of four painted panels. The work is described as depicting

> Ibedul, the paramount chief of Palau's southern confederation [who] was moved to accept western dress, short hair, and use of umbrellas and lanterns as a result of a culture tour [on the panels]. He desired to pass on these accouterments of high civilization on Reklai, paramount chief of the northern confederation, but there was considerable resistance to the short hair the Japanese long shears produced.[187]

The description of the Ibedul seems to describe Uong; interestingly, the panels conveyed a negative reaction to his attempt to implement changes among the Palauan people.

A Japanese who used to live on the islands, Mitsuyasu Kunio, admitted that along with its merits, there were also disadvantages to the tour program. But he said he could not elaborate on the darker side in his account, which was included in a book of recollections by the members of the Nanyō Guntō Kyōkai (South Seas Association), all of whom had lived in Micronesia.[188] One former bureaucrat recalled in these memoirs that when he led several tours to Japan, colonial officials' worst fear was that someone might

187.   An *abai* or *bai* is a traditional Palauan meetinghouse. The Keptotal Bai's artwork was never restored. However, photographs exist and have been reproduced on a map of Japanese Koror. MARC, *Oral Historiography*, 56.

188.   Nan'yō Guntō Kyōkai (ed.), *Omoide no Nanyō guntō*, 97.

die—and in fact several Palauans died (attributed to the change in climate) while on the tours and were buried at a graveyard in Aoyama.[189]

Corroborating the darker side of the tours and the negative reaction some had to changes brought about by the tours, one former participant, Rubach Fritz, recalls the shame he and others were made to feel about their humble background. He was twenty-one years old when, in 1932, he served as a translator for a tour group of eighteen Palauans. Of his experience he recalled,

> We had many surprises on our Japan tour. We traveled by car to Kobe. In Tokyo we saw the Emperor's palace, and met the mayor [of] Tokyo city, visited Yasukuni jinja, Meiji jinja and Akasaka riku. We visited some factories and companies . . . and Yoyomi[,] where we saw a military training center. When we talked amongst ourselves about all the fantastic things we had seen, we had shameful feelings. We were surprised at everything we saw. We thought such things couldn't be created by people but only by gods.[190]

Some, like Fritz, felt a mixture of shame and surprise when they saw life in Japan. Others, like Ibedul Tem, proudly stuck to their Palauan traditions in spite of what they had seen—although Tem's stubbornness led to his replacement by Ngiraked, who fully embraced his time in Japan.[191]

The destroyed Keptotal Bai and the various participants' accounts of their reactions to Japan reveal the competing legacies of the tours. There is one more story that illustrates how some Palauans were able to use the tours for their own purposes. Ongesi, a founder of the Modekngei religion, had long been eager to get a Christian cross, and he asked one of his followers to get one for him on his tour to Japan. Scholar Aoyagi Machiko describes the episode:

> This person visited a Catholic church while he was in Japan. From inside the church, a priest waved to invite him to come in. But he told the priest that he was not a Catholic but a Modekngei, and he was concerned

189. Nan'yō Guntō Kyōkai (ed.), *Omoide no Nanyō guntō*, 59.
190. MARC, *Oral Historiography*, 55.
191. Vidich, *Political Impact*, 191.

that he was not allowed to enter the church. Then the Japanese priest further encouraged him to enter[,] though he was a Modekngei. He said to him, "If you are a Modekngei, that is about the god. So I will give you this." And he handed him a cross with the figure of Christ on it. The man received it respectfully and raised it with both hands over his head more than three times. He returned home [to] Ngebuked, and on the next morning visited Ongesi in Chol. Since then, the cross has become the symbol of the Kodeb title, and it is passed to each new Kodeb when he succeeds to the title.[192]

The story about Ongesi asking one of his followers to bring back a cross from Japan contrasts with other reactions to the tours. Rather than resisting changes that the Japanese wanted to implement or being impressed by Japan's level of civilization, this leader saw the tours as a way to get what he wanted: a cross, which would be used by those who practiced a religion synonymous with challenging Japanese authority.

Conclusion

Among this collection of stories from Micronesia, the individual who appears to have been the most amenable to Japanization was Ngiraked. His search for a Japanese bride, his repeated stays in Japan, and his Japanese friends all reflect his assimilation. His close relationship with Japan began with his involvement in the tour program, and he later worked for the colonial government. His few interviews in various newspapers and letters to Kitamura are the only accounts that feature his opinions. This is unusual for someone of his language ability and status. There are hints as to how he dealt with the failure of his search for a Japanese bride and how he experienced wartime in Palau, but the later years of his life are still murky without any oral testimony. For the other people mentioned in this chapter, I was able use their own testimony to characterize their experiences.

192. Aoyagi, *Modekngei*, 130.

If Ngiraked had lived, how would he have described the Japanization he underwent? Would it be similar to Augusta's? Her testimony contrasts with her presentation in Japanese sources as a model colonial subject. Ngiraked's perspective might resemble that of Oikang, whose own recollections are in sync with the colonial archive. Or perhaps his account would resemble Pedro's, whose Japanization altered his life in the most unexpected way, nearly leading to his execution. The experiences of those who participated in the tours from Micronesia reveal that the Japanese used imperialization rhetoric early in their rule of the islands, in conjunction with supplanting the traditional chiefs who had worked with the Germans. The individual experiences related here show us that for some colonial subjects, who they were in the colony was shaped by their experiences beyond the colony's boundaries.

PART III

Performing and Living Racial-alities

Part III Introduction

Part III shifts the focus back to Japan, this time all the way up north to the island of Hokkaido, and also south to Okinawa. Often referred to as part of the *gaichi*, or "outerlands," Hokkaido, and its Ainu villages in particular, were seen as set apart from the colonial modernity of the metropole (*naichi*). The fluctuation of Hokkaido and the Ainu in and out of conceptions of *naichi* offers a good counterpoint to the people in the metropolis, colonies, and international contexts discussed in parts I and II. In contrast to some of colonial subjects in part II, such as the Palauan Ngiraked, who stated he had "become Japanese," part III showcases the Ainu's understanding of their separateness in the empire and the issue of having Japanese nationality *and* a separate ethnoracial and cultural identity.

With part III, the narrative of Japan's empire and its colonial subjects comes full circle when I examine the experience of colonial subjects who lived through the empire's collapse. Unlike works on Taiwan and Korea that focus on the repatriation of former Japanese colonial subjects, these chapters show that for the Ainu, some colonial continuities persisted beyond the collapse of the empire and well into the postcolonial era in Japan.

Ainu tourist villages, like the human displays described in part I, are often seen as sites of oppression and exploitation by the Japanese. Current scholarship posits that the Ainu have only recently been able to take part in deciding how they are represented in Hokkaido's museums and tourist villages.[1] In contrast, chapter 7 demonstrates that Ainu leaders were the ones to first develop the tourist industry in Shiraoi in the early twentieth century. In response to an influx of tourists, Ainu leaders designated certain *chise* (houses) as proto-museums to regulate the flow of visitors and profit from their presence. At first glance, postcards of the early Ainu tourist villages may seem to show random representatives of the Ainu ethnotype, but in fact many of the people featured on the postcards were the Ainu leaders and families who were involved in the operation of the tourist industry.

Chapter 8 focuses on the postwar period at Lake Akan, where visitors to the area's national park inspired several entrepreneurial Ainu to create a new tourist village. The leaders involved in tourism there had fought for Japan during the Asia-Pacific War, and like many Ainu who had fought in the Pacific, they were affected by the discrimination they faced in the Japanese military and after the war were emboldened to identify more strongly as Ainu. Upending the notion that the Japanese created and used the tourist industry to showcase primitive Ainu culture—and thus Japanese superiority—part III shows how, in response to Japanese discrimination and the government's oppressive policies, some Ainu individuals used tourism to promote their culture as distinct from Japanese culture. After the war, they sought to improve life in the Ainu community and promote Ainu culture within the context of tourism and cultural preservation.

The tourist villages give a glimpse of the transitional period, from the early twentieth century through the Asia-Pacific War when many young Ainu were leaving Ainu (*datsu Ainu*)—frustrated by their elders who spoke the Ainu language, they spoke only Japanese and for all intents and purposes identified as Japanese. In the postwar period there was a spilt: Ainu who had fought in the war as Japanese troops saw that as the final proof of their citizenship; other former Ainu soldiers, having grown up with discrimination and segregated schooling, found their war experience alienating and were further emboldened to break from identifying as Japanese. The end of the war brought hope for a change in the Ainu's situation; in the 1970s, as the human rights era crystallized around the world, Ainu activists became even more vocal. Some denounced tourism

1.   Hiwasaki, "Ethnic Tourism," 400, 407; Morris-Suzuki, "Tourists, Anthropologists"; Higashimura, "'Kankō Ainu,'" 65–85; Sjoberg, *Return of the Ainu*.

in Hokkaido's Ainu villages, whereas other activists denounced the state but saw preserving and performing Ainu culture through tourism as a way to maintain their Ainu identity. The amplified visibility of the Ainu in the 1970s polarized leaders and generations, but significantly, it illustrated that the predictions in the 1930s that the Ainu race would soon die out were wrong. Although the physical ethnoracial characteristics of Ainu a century ago have become more Japanized through intermarriage, and some cultural practices, such as tattooing among Ainu women, have long since ceased, the Ainu people today—those who choose to identify as such—are a vibrant part of the Japanese nation.

CHAPTER 7

Dividing Space, Creating Barriers

Emperor Meiji went to Hokkaido in 1881 with a retinue of 350 people. It was one of the "Six Great Imperial Tours" (roku daijunkō) he conducted in the early Meiji period. He stopped in the Shiraoi Ainu village, where he met, drank, and ate with the Ainu and watched them perform dances, prayers, and an altered version of the bear ceremony (*iyomante*).[1] According to scholars, Emperor Meiji's visit to Shiraoi was the pivotal moment the Ainu village started to become a tourist destination.[2]

Among the Ainu who performed traditional dances (*rimuse*) for the emperor was a fifteen-year-old-boy named Ekashiteba.[3] Although Ekashiteba recalled years later that "it was the greatest honor of his life," it was just one performance of many that he gave in representing Ainu culture to Japanese audiences.[4] Ekashiteba and his family eventually emerged as leaders in the tourism business that developed in response to the influx of tourists during the prewar period. The story of the family's

---

1. Ogawa, "Ainu gakkō," 52–53; Fujitani, *Splendid Monarchy*, 47. No bears were killed. There was only the display of two bear heads. Mitsuoka, *Ainu no sokuseki*, 252–54. As early as the Tokugawa period, Ainu (and Okinawans) had presented themselves—as distinct ethnoracial others—at political meetings with *daimyo* of the Matsumae and during the procession to Edo, for the Ryūkyūans, respectively. Howell, "Ainu Ethnicity"; Toby, *State and Diplomacy*.

2. Saitō, "Hoppō minzoku," 151.

3. Shiraoi Chōshi Hensan Iinkai (ed.), *Shin Shiraoi chōshi*, 18–20. For a picture of Ekashiteba, see Majewicz (ed.), *The Collected Works*, 649.

4. Mitsuoka, *Ainu no sokuseki*, 240

involvement in managing the tourist activities in Shiraoi illustrates how Ainu leaders strove to protect their traditional roles amid changing times.

As the tourist industry in Shiraoi grew in the early twentieth century, Ainu leaders had to adapt to increasing Japanese contact. A few Ainu who had clout in the village designated and oversaw certain traditional Ainu houses (*chise*) that were used as display rooms for Ainu goods and places for lectures about the Ainu. The prewar Ainu tourist villages were still primarily residential spaces, and typically only three or four *chise* were designated for tourists. The villages were not pure artifice (as they were in the postwar period) but were real places where Ainu residents struggled to maintain divisions between tourism and their everyday lives.

The leaders who managed the flow of visitors in the early twentieth century spoke the Ainu language, performed Ainu ceremonies, and were very knowledgeable regarding traditional Ainu life, from hunting and performing the bear ceremony to reciting the deeds of past generations and the epic tales known as *yukar*. Although Japanese audiences accepted them as true arbiters of Ainu culture because of their appearance—they looked Ainu, with their distinct, Caucasian-seeming countenances—their family lineage and knowledge of customs were what solidified their status as leaders in the Ainu community.

The designated tourist spaces were often contested among the Ainu leaders, as the economic success of tourism prompted rivalries over their control. The prewar tourist schemes the Ainu devised worked so well that they attracted Japanese who came in the hope of cashing in on Ainu success. Some set up souvenir shops, and others created "Ainu" goods. Later, in the postwar period, some Japanese even "became Ainu," as they worked in their businesses in the tourist villages.

Leaders Emerge

Ekashiteba was able to trace his lineage back ten generations, to the recognized forefather of the first generation of Shiraoi Ainu, Ipenikkuru. Ipenikkuru was from the Hidaka region of Appetsu and moved to Shiraoi after his village lost a battle with another village. Ipenikkuru chose Shiraoi as a strategic location for his retreat, and with his men he awaited the pursuing army. A battle ensued, and Ipenikkuru and his men prevailed. The defeated Ainu retreated to Volcano Bay (Funkawan), except for one of the daughters, whom Ipenikkuru took as a wife. He negotiated with the few Ainu households already in Shiraoi and gave them treasures; in return, he received all of the land of Shiraoi.

In the sixth generation, the Matsumae domain, which handled Ainu relations for the Tokugawa shogunate, first established a government office and trading post (*kaisho*) in Shiraoi. The Ainu worked in the fisheries as seasonal workers (*basho ukeoijin*) and lived in small villages scattered throughout the area. The Matsumae ordered them to move as a group to the coast. The settlement near the coast became the foundation for the Shiraoi Ainu village known in the nineteenth and twentieth centuries as a prime destination for travelers.[5]

Ekashiteba was the first of his lineage to have a Japanese last name and the first of his family to be entered into the Japanese national registry (*koseki*). He took the name Kumasaka. As the recognized leader of Shiraoi village, Ekashiteba was able to recite the names of all his great forefathers and their characteristics and accomplishments.[6] Mitsuoka Shin'ichi, the son of one of the Japanese state-sanctioned "farming soldiers" (*tondenhei*), who were tasked with developing Hokkaido, settled in the area and became good friends with the Shiraoi Ainu. Mitsuoka worked as the head of the post office but also devoted much of his time to recording the traditions and daily life of the Ainu. He knew Ekashiteba well, and their friendship enabled him to describe prewar Shiraoi based on what Ekashiteba recounted. He wrote that Ekashiteba was skilled in reciting *yukar* and often recited them when he had had a little sake.[7]

After Ekashiteba died at the age of seventy or so, his only son, Shitappire, was recognized as chief.[8] In the national registry, Shitappire was listed as Kumasaka Unnosuke, although he was most commonly referred to by

---

5. Mitsuoka, *Ainu no sokuseki*, 236–38.

6. Because the Ainu did not have a writing system, they relied on oral tradition to preserve family histories and stories and legends. Hilger, *Together with the Ainu*, 191.

7. Mitsuoka, *Ainu no sokuseki*, 236–40, 256.

8. There is doubt if Shitappire is eleventh generation or thirteenth generation. The account that says he is thirteenth generation does not cite where the information came from, thus it cannot be verified. Ekashi to Fuchi Henshū Iinkai (ed.), *Ekashi to fuchi*, 2:29.

his Ainu name.[9] Before Ekashiteba's death, he and Shitappire were involved in tourist activities in the late nineteenth and early twentieth centuries. Shitappire had attended Shiraoi's first elementary school and was
known as its first student because he was the oldest one in the first class
of seven or eight Ainu students. He was able to write his name in kana,
but he told Mitsuoka he had forgotten everything else he learned about
writing.

Even before the emperor's visit in 1881, tourists and Japanese and
foreign researchers had journeyed to Shiraoi, but after the imperial
visit the number of tourists increased, helped by the construction of a
new train station in 1892.[10] Several of the Hokkaido travel guides printed
in the late Meiji period informed travelers as to which train stations were
near Ainu villages. The 1908 edition of *Hokkaido ryokō annai* (Hokkaido
travel guide), for example, described six Ainu villages and mentioned the
unique character and attributes of the people in each. For example, the
Ainu of Yakumo made a living in the fishing industry and were "foolish
and slow and had not yet evolved," whereas the Ainu in the village near
Oshamambe station were described as largely progressing and no different from ordinary Japanese who were able to support themselves; they
were also noted for going to school and earning good grades.[11] The travel
guide advertised the Shiraoi Ainu village as a famous location.[12] In addition to villages, old Ainu battlegrounds and castle ruins were described
as interesting sites for tourists to visit in Hokkaido.[13] Based on the 1908
guidebook's descriptions of the six Ainu villages, it is clear that the transformation of certain villages into tourist destinations had been under way
for some time.

Not all Ainu villages became tourist destinations. The transformation
of Shiraoi into a tourist village came about for several reasons. The first
was the fame it received after the visits by the emperor and other dignitaries. Second was its proximity to the railroad, which made access convenient. Third, the village's Ainu leaders created places where people could
look at Ainu objects and watch Ainu performances; their willingness to

9.   Ekashi to Fuchi Henshū Iinkai (ed.), *Ekashi to fuchi*, vol 2:29.
10. Bird, *Unbeaten Tracks*; Sasaki et al. (eds.), *Ainu no michi*, 76.
11. Sawa (ed.), *Hokkaido ryokō*, 52, 58.
12. Sawa (ed.), *Hokkaido ryokō*, 132–33.
13. Sawa (ed.), *Hokkaido ryokō*, 183–84, 49–50.

interact with tourists marked Shiraoi as tourist friendly.[14] Other attractive Ainu villages, such as Fushiko, had no infrastructure to receive tourists, and the villagers were often hostile to visitors, running away rather than allowing themselves to be seen, or posting signs forbidding visitors to enter certain buildings, such as the native schools.[15] Distinguishing tourist-friendly Ainu villages from those that were not encouraged more tourists to frequent the ones with established reputations and simultaneously deflected some of the unwanted attention from other villages in the region.

In 1914 the Shiraoi Ainu village had a population of 329 Ainu. Tours usually included a stop at the native school where the local children studied, and the children were often pulled out of school to participate in the bear ceremony when a dignitary passed through the village.[16] Three Ainu *chise* had been built and designated as places where tourists could hear an Ainu *ekashi* (elder) talk about customs and watch Ainu women perform dances.[17]

The idea of the Ainu creating *chise* for tourists interested in their culture was not unusual at this time. In fact, in 1916 in Chikabumi village in Asahikawa, Kawamura Itakishiroma opened the first Ainu museum in Hokkaido.[18] Kawamura built a *chise* separate from the one he lived in and filled it with Ainu goods and instruments. There, he would explain to the numerous visitors the purpose of the various goods on display and tell them about Ainu culture. If visitors desired it, he would gather Ainu women to perform traditional dances. Kawamura's main competition in the village's tourist business was another leader in Asahikawa, Kawakami Konusa, who, a guidebook noted, had "long been accustomed to receiv[ing] sightseeing visitors[,] for whose inspection he has built some old-fashioned huts." By 1941, Kawamura's son Kawamura Kaneto had built an Ainu museum "at his own expense for sightseeing tourists." The guidebook advised visitors that Mr. and Mrs. Kaneto Kawamura lived in a modern house of their own

14.   Kindaichi, *Ainu Life*, 78.

15.   Maeda, "Fushiko Ainu," 133. Signs forbidding visitors to the native schools were often ignored.

16.   Higashimura, "'Kankō Ainu,'" 67; *TA*, September 29, 1914; Howell, "Making 'Useful Citizens,'" 17.

17.   *Shiraoi kotan*, 1–2, 92.

18.   See http://ainu-museum.sakura.ne.jp/index.php/ (accessed November 9, 2018).

and would accept lodgers on request.[19] By 1951 Kawamura Kaneto's museum was officially named the Kawamura Kaneto Ainu Memorial Hall.[20]

In Shiraoi, Ainu tour guides would wait at the train station to meet tourists and bring them to the village by foot. In 1917 a series of illustrated vignettes describing a visit to the Shiraoi Ainu village was published in the *Yomiuri* newspaper. According to the reports, when visitors alighted at the train station, a sign reading "Former Aborigine Information Center" directed them to the tour guide who would take them to the village.[21] On arriving in the village, the guide led the sightseers into an Ainu house, where they met one of the leaders of the village, Mori Hisakichi, who was described as resembling Tolstoy.[22] They visited a house where they saw numerous treasures that had been obtained through trade with the Japanese.[23]

As some of the sightseers observed, the Ainu tourist businesses had started to include Japanese participants. When the group's tour guide promised to show the participants Ainu crafts, they were taken inside an Ainu *chise* where a Japanese man had rented space; the numerous handicrafts he had lined up for sale looked like imitations. When they left the *chise*, the sightseeing party questioned their tour guide, asking, "Wasn't that a Japanese?" He responded, "The goods are influenced from the Ainu, so the created products are no different." They visited one more *chise* that had two signs posted: "Native Language Instruction Center" and "Former Native Workshop, Ishii Kiyoshi." A Japanese "group that had become Ainu" was crowded into the *chise*, and when the sightseers entered, the instructor emerged from the back; he was the artist, a white-bearded Ainu man who went by the Japanese name Ishii Kiyoshi.[24] He was teaching the Japanese how to make Ainu handicrafts and how to speak the Ainu language. At this time during the Taishō period, it is evident the Ainu still had

19.   Kindaichi, *Ainu Life*, 80.

20.   Ayabe, *Ushinawareru bunka*, 300. Kawamura Kaneto had fought in the Asia-Pacific War.

21.   *Yomiuri*, August 25, 1917; see KZW.

22.   *Yomiuri*, August 28, 1917. Mori was educated from a young age and grew to be a leader in Shiraoi. In 1946 he became the first director of the Hokkaido Ainu Association.

23.   Tourist postcards circulating at this time showed the interiors of *chise* full of Ainu goods, indicating they were more display houses than residences.

24.   *Yomiuri*, September 3, 1917; see KZW.

the upper hand in running the tourist activities in Shiraoi, as exemplified by Ishii Kiyoshi.

Moritake Takeichi, who is remembered today as a famous Ainu poet and activist for Ainu rights, worked at the Shiraoi train station during the Taishō period. His experience hints at how the tourist business was developed with the arrival of the railroad. Moritake was born in Shiraoi and graduated from the native school for Ainu children. He began to work as a cleaner at the Shiraoi train station in 1919, when he was seventeen. He was responsible for directing tourists to the Shiraoi Ainu village, which was located two kilometers from the train station. As there was no transportation to the village, Moritake led the tourists on foot, carrying a flag bearing the name of a tour company.[25] Later, after passing the railroad employee placement exam, Moritake oversaw the finances of each station within the Iburi district of Hidaka, and in 1930 he was elected to the Committee on Current Employees of District 1 for the National Railroad. He resigned from his position in 1935, saying he could no longer remain silent regarding the railroad companies' advertisements to attract tourists to the land where the Ainu lived.[26]

While Moritake's story informs us how tourists got to Shiraoi, another account provides insight into the village's inner workings. In 1921, a *National Geographic* photographer visited Shiraoi and wrote about the strict controls on taking photographs during an Ainu ceremony:

> I was the guest of a Japanese official and the right to take the official photograph of this auspicious occasion had been given to a commercial photographer. I had no desire to buy a formal picture of this group, in which the Japanese clothed in fine western dress mixed with the fine-looking old Ainu chiefs and their wolfish looking sons. I hinted as broadly as possible that I would like to secure some poses of my own, but all in vain.[27]

After the ceremony was over, the photographer was at liberty to take all the photographs he desired. Monetary valuations were even assigned

---

25.   In the prewar period I could not find evidence of any Japanese tour groups or agencies directly involved in running Ainu tourist villages, so any tour company was most likely associated with one of the Ainu leaders.

26.   Arai, *Ainu jinbutsuden*, 90.

27.   "Using a Camera," 109.

according to how Ainu were photographed, although it is unclear who was behind the regulation of photographs.

KUMASAKA SHITAPPIRE

During the Taishō period, one of the *chise* open to tourists in Shiraoi was a house belonging to Shitappire, the son of Ekashiteba, who had danced for Emperor Meiji. In 2006, an Ainu elder named Nomoto Riyo recalled that the house she was born in was near Shitappire's *chise*, which she said exhibited traditional Ainu culture.[28] A photograph of this *chise* was published in 1929 in an article documenting the visit of a Hokkaido newspaper's women's association to Shiraoi.[29]

The fact that these houses were built specifically for tourists shows that the Ainu were creating tourist spaces separate from the houses they actually lived in. One account from 1926 confirms that these new houses were built specifically for the tourism business. Mitsuoka Shin'ichi, who worked as the head of the post office and was a good friend of Shitappire, guided one visitor around the Shiraoi village. When the visitor asked him, "Is this the house of the chief?," he responded, "No, in Shiraoi this is the oldest house. The chief died last year and afterward it was decided that if researchers came they should be guided around this house.[30] The owners have decided not to work in the fields and have stayed here." On seeing the house, the visitor challenged Mitsuoka, asking him, "Is the house fairly new?" Slightly changing his answer, he replied, "This house became the research material for the researchers; it is specifically constructed as a model." The visitor looked into the kitchen area and was disappointed to see modern objects, such as a pot and an aluminum ruler. When he looked into the sleeping area he saw a trilby hat. He concluded disappointedly, "Their everyday lifestyle was already Japanized [*naichika*]."[31]

Mitsuoka's presence as an intermediary is noted in many accounts. In 1930, he led Maeda Yūgure, a famous poet, around the Ainu village and

---

28. "Shiraoi-chō dentō bunka keishōsha Nomoto Riyo," originally published in Shiraoi-chō hōkokushi, *Genki*, September 2007, http://www.town.shiraoi.hokkaido.jp /ka/jinya/singikai/H18/keisyousya.htm (accessed May 20, 2011; no longer available).
29. *HT*, October 11, 1929.
30. I believe this is Ekashiteba who died.
31. Saitō, "Hokkaido kankō," 3.

was with him when Maeda held a freestyle *tanka* (poem) recitation and various lectures at night.[32] When government dignitaries visited Shiraoi, they often stopped at Shitappire's house to learn about the Ainu. In 1931, when a newspaper reporter visited the village in February to see the bear ceremony, Mitsuoka guided him around the village. The *iyomante* was traditionally held in the winter; despite the freezing temperatures, it was a big draw for tourists. The reporter wrote that a bear cub was to be sacrificed outside Shitappire's house. The *iyomante* was often performed outside of Shitappire's garden, which was known for having an elaborate *nusa*, or shrine, made up of a row of *inaw* (prayer sticks), often with bear skulls and other fetishes attached. *Nusa* varied according to the importance of local gods, traditions, customs, and the tastes of the different elders. In Shitappire's *nusa* there were *inaw* that dated back to a god that the seasonal workers prayed to during the Matsumae period, as well as gods that protected their ancestral lands.[33]

One month after the reporter's visit to Shiraoi, under the direction of Shitappire, ten Ainu men and women performed what was advertised as a bear ceremony and women's traditional dances, for about 300 spectators at the hot springs (*onsen*) at Noboribetsu. Because this bear ceremony was held so soon after the ceremony in Shiraoi, what was presented was likely an abbreviated version, carried out primarily for entertainment.[34] The annual bear ceremony continued to be held in Shiraoi, although abbreviated versions were simultaneously performed elsewhere and marketed to tourists. Noboribetsu, which is close to Shiraoi, began featuring Ainu performances in the 1930s as attractions for tourists, a practice that continued over the years. Sunazawa Kura recalls working at the "gods' village" (*kamui kotan*) at Noboribetsu *onsen* after being recruited, with her family, by Mori Hisakichi. While she demonstrated weaving, her husband recited *yukar* and their son carved wooden bears in a large *chise*. Mori explained her weaving or her son's carving to sightseers. Sunazawa wrote, "In this way, because it was nothing other than showing true Ainu culture and tradition, the *chise* was always full of visitors." They

32. *HT*, July 29, 1930; *OS*, July 29, 1930.
33. Mitsuoka, *Ainu no sokuseki*, 92; *HT*, February 11, 1931; see KZW for postcards of Shitappire.
34. *HT*, March 31, 1931.

could hardly keep up with all the orders for their handicrafts. The reputation of their son's carvings grew, increasing demand, and they received
a lot of money.[35] In the postwar period, Ainu from all over Hokkaido traveled to Noboribetsu to work there during the tourist season.[36]

Postcards of Shiraoi document Ainu leaders involved in tourism in
the early twentieth century. On some of the early cards featuring his
image, Shitappire is named in the caption, and on another card his name
is handwritten.[37] Ainu women pictured on the prewar postcards are rarely
identified, but it was not uncommon for the male leaders to be identified
by name. As tourism advanced into the postwar period, names disappear
from most of the cards that feature Ainu leaders, transforming them
into anonymous examples of Ainu culture. This change indicates significantly that in the prewar period, postcard makers were not using
random Ainu individuals but were photographing the village leaders. It
mattered which Ainu leader was being depicted, and their importance is
bolstered by evidence pointing to their centrality in creating and promoting the tourist industry.

In the early twentieth century, filmmakers started to come to Shiraoi
to film Ainu daily life. In 1925 Okada Kazuo made a silent film titled *Ainu
Life in Shiraoi Village* (Shiraoi Ainu kotan no Ainu seikatsu). In 1930 the
Railroad Ministry filmed scenes throughout Hokkaido, including an
Ainu village, to use for publicity to "entice tourists."[38] By the 1930s, Ainu
tourism was so well established that official signs directed visitors to the
Shiraoi Ainu village. When people entered a *chise* designated for tourists,
they had to pay the Ainu person in charge, and they also had to pay if
they wanted to take photographs of the Ainu in the village or of themselves posing with the Ainu.[39]

Because Shitappire's Japanese was not good, he asked a young Ainu
named Kaizawa Tōzō to work for him as a tour guide. In 1931 Tōzō published a book titled *The Cry of the Ainu* (Ainu no sakebi) in which he described his role as a tour guide:

35. Sunazawa, *Watakushi no ichidai*, 214–15.
36. Kayano Shigeru worked at Noboribetsu each summer of 1961–1967. Kayano,
Our Land, 118–19.
37.   See KZW for postcards.
38. *HT*, June 6, 1930.
39. Higashimura, "'Kankō Ainu,'" 68–69.

Comparatively speaking[,] transportation to Shiraoi village is convenient. From the station, the road to the village is about seven blocks. In a short time you can observe about seventy to eighty small grass huts that make up the village [*kotan*]. It is because of these [huts] that still today, in the Shōwa period, [the village evokes] a primitive lifestyle. I was requested by the elder Kumasaka [Shitappire] to greet the modern visitors who visit in great numbers the village's former houses and explain to them our community [*utari*] and the conditions of life.[40]

The fact that Shitappire himself approached Tōzō to act as a tour guide suggests that he and other Ainu leaders were the ones managing tourist activities in Shiraoi in the prewar period. Certainly reports from Japanese visitors, advertisements by the Railroad Ministry, and various guidebooks were the main ways tourism was encouraged throughout the country, but initially it was Ainu leaders who were in charge of the village's daily tourist operations.

KAIZAWA TŌZŌ

A self-described "bearded samurai" who wore glasses attached to the lapel of his coat, Tōzō was a modern Ainu whom some may have been quick to label as Japanized. Tōzō could speak Japanese and he did not wear traditional Ainu clothing, but he was not Japanized to the extent that he rejected his Ainu heritage. Quite the contrary, he was fiercely proud of being Ainu and never sought to eradicate Ainu practices in favor of living a Japanese lifestyle. At the same time, he believed the economic and social status of the Ainu was pitiable and should be rectified.

Tōzō's recollections of his involvement in the tourist villages as a guide indicate his struggle to promote an understanding of Ainu culture among ignorant Japanese tourists while simultaneously conveying that many Ainu could speak Japanese and in fact lived lives similar to the Japanese. Tōzō believed in the heterogeneous nature of the Ainu people and did not endorse an idealized or monolithic notion of who the Ainu were or should be. He resisted being characterized as one of the older generation, not because he was ashamed of the *ekashi* but simply because

40.   Kaizawa, *Ainu no sakebi*, 381–92.

it was not true. Tōzō, like Fushine Kōzō of the first Human Pavilion, envisioned a space for Ainu in the empire where they could participate as Japanese subjects and speak Japanese but also continue to take pride in being Ainu.

Tōzō wrote that his unstoppable passion for his people compelled him to write *The Cry of the Ainu*: "As the Ainu continue to gasp for breath as we bitterly struggle for existence, I want to get rid of the mistaken beliefs about the Ainu." He described the experience of meeting tourists who were confused by seeing an Ainu dressed in modern clothes. He spoke about the general ignorance of visitors who asked him basic questions about the Ainu and their lifestyle, such as whether they could speak Japanese. When schoolteachers responsible for educating children asked him these questions, he said he wanted to cry. The lack of education about the Ainu in Japanese schools was the cause of this ignorance. Furthermore, Tōzō believed that newspapers were to blame for perpetuating the misconception that the Ainu lived in the past. When high-profile guests visited Hokkaido, the newspapers printed pictures of Ainu elders in *attush* (bark cloth) robes and women with tattoos around their mouths. No pictures of the younger generation were printed, so the people of the metropolis thought all Ainu looked like those images of the elders.[41]

While Tōzō was passionate about uplifting his people, whom he saw as economically downtrodden and living in poor conditions, he did not think the solution lay in eradicating Ainu culture. Although he acknowledged, for example, that many Japanese criticized the *iyomante* as barbaric, he defended its practice as a sacred and meaningful ceremony that had been practiced for generations. Some young Ainu did think that the bear ceremony should be abolished (as did some elders, including Fushine Kōzō), but Tōzō defended it as a noncriminal act and as the Ainu's most important ceremony in honor of the gods. Despite its traditional importance, because the bear population was decreasing and some Ainu were opposed to it, the *iyomante* was being celebrated less and less. Tōzō described the sorrow of the *ekashi*, who saw the younger generation not celebrating the *iyomante* or praying to the gods, and also the sorrow of the *fuchi* (female elders) on seeing young Ainu women without tattoos on

41. This was a common critique by Japanese sympathizers as well, like Yoshida Iwao and Kindaichi Kyōsuke. Howell, "Making 'Useful Citizens,'" 17.

their mouths and arms. He was ambivalent about traditions being slowly lost. He wondered rhetorically whether the fact that the Ainu's countenances were becoming modernized "was tragic, or something to be happy about."[42]

Tōzō's respect for Ainu customs and traditions and his own lived experience made him struggle with the duality of his role as a guide to tourists from the metropolis. On one hand, he was there to teach the tourists about the rich Ainu history and culture, which he thought had value and about which most tourists knew nothing. On the other hand, he wanted the Japanese to be aware of the diversity of the Ainu, something especially evident across the different generations. According to Tōzō, Ainu under the age of thirty spoke only Japanese and were in many other ways similar to the Japanese.[43]

Tōzō had great respect for Ainu culture and history, but he thought that their living conditions should be improved, education should be encouraged, and, most important, they should be urged to give up drinking. In August 1931, Tōzō attended the Convention of Ainu Youth (Ainu seinen taikai), a conference organized by the English missionary John Batchelor. Tōzō recalled the presence at the conference of Fushine Kōzō, who was then more than eighty years old and whose white beard hung down to his chest. Fushine demanded that the young Ainu forsake alcohol because he saw it as the cause of the Ainu's population decline. Tōzō recalled Fushine yelling, "Young Ainu! Outlaw alcohol!! Etch firmly and distinctly into your brains the two characters of temperance [kinshu]!" Tōzō concluded, "Due to the alarm bells that have been rung by our people's hands, our community members [utari], whose dreams have been destroyed, have risen up in rage!"[44]

Through the diversity of Ainu people involved in tourist activities in Shiraoi, the experiences of different Ainu clearly varied a great deal at this time. Tōzō's own life was very much divorced from the life that Shitappire represented, as one of the last great ekashi of his lineage whose primary language was Ainu. Tōzō later filled Shitappire's shoes, as he

42.   Tanigawa (ed.), Kindai minshū, 382.

43.   Tanigawa (ed.), Kindai minshū, 387. A writer in 1936 wrote that all Ainu under age forty spoke Japanese. Saitō, "Hokkaido kankō," 3.

44.   Tanigawa (ed.), Kindai minshū, 393.

FIG. 7.1. Kaizawa Tōzō (right) and his wife, Koyo. Credit: Author's collection.

eventually emerged as one of the most influential leaders of tourism in Shiraoi (fig. 7.1).[45]

Along with Shitappire, Nomura Ekashitoku, and Kaizawa Tōzō, one other leader, Miyamato (Inosuke) Ekashimatoku, played a central role in explaining Ainu customs to the tourists and researchers who visited Shiraoi.[46] Tōzō and Miyamoto continued to play a big part in the tourist industry during the postwar period in Shiraoi.

The most famous description of Kaizawa Tōzō and his involvement in the tourism industry was written during wartime, when an American woman, Neill James, visited Shiraoi in 1940.[47] Certainly James's account, like many travelogues, contains some errors. In her account of her visit to Shiraoi she identifies Kaizawa Tōzō as Kozo Kaisawa, but an examination of the pictures included in the book, which feature James and

45. The prophecy of Fushine Kōzō regarding alcohol as the cause of the Ainu's decline was fulfilled when Shitappire, who was a big drinker according to Mitsuoka, in 1942 one day on the way home from the pub fell down and died.

46. Throughout my research, I came to a conclusion about which four Ainu leaders operated in Shiraoi; later on I found this supposition verified in Sasaki et al. (eds.), *Ainu no michi*, 77.

47. *Shin sekai asahi shinbun*, September 30, 1940.

Tōzō and his wife, Koyo, does not leave any doubt that she was in fact referring to Tōzō.

James's privileged position is quite clear, and there are several pictures of her with Tōzō and Koyo, wearing Ainu clothing and jewelry (figs. 7.2 and 7.3). Recalling photographs of Pete Gorō standing next to Mathilda Krieckhaus at the 1904 Louisiana Purchase Exposition, the images show that for some Westerners, the experience of visiting the Ainu included "trying on" their culture by trying on Ainu garments (fig. 7.3). James's account, which should be taken with a grain of salt, offers some insight into Tōzō's involvement with tourism. She describes coming to Shiraoi and wanting to stay in a grass hut. She explained that Tōzō had "recently advanced a step in the economic scale and built for himself just such a cold-proof house with double wooden walls, shingled roof, and glass windows. He agreed to let me have his former chiefly abode, the largest grass house in the village."[48] One postcard of Tōzō shows him standing in front of his modern house. It is a rare image of him in Western clothing, as he was most frequently photographed in traditional Ainu dress.[49] In the 1930s, postcards of "modern Ainu" became popular, featuring Ainu in Western-style clothing. Often they were pictured next to traditionally dressed Ainu; the novelty of modern Ainu was enhanced when juxtaposed with the latter.[50] Tōzō's lifestyle—outside of tourist work—was also captured and acknowledged. In Ainu Sunazawa Kura's autobiography, she included a picture of her and her family with Tōzō and Koyo, at Noboribetsu *onsen* (fig. 7.4). The picture taken in 1935, found in the collection of a dear friend, shows Tōzō in a suit and on vacation. Although Tōzō worked in the tourist industry in Shiraoi, he also traveled and this photograph shows the multidimensionality of Tōzō's life, which also recalls Gorō's candid photographs of his time in St. Louis, which contrast with the official exposition photos.

From the description of the *chise* that James stayed in during her visit, it is clear that it was the same *chise* that tourists were brought to when they visited. "It was an exotic Ainu house, completely furnished Ainu style. It had nothing in it, nothing but a row of Ainu treasures along the

48. James, *Petticoat Vagabond*, 92.
49. See KZW for Tōzō outside his home and other cards showing "modern" Ainu.
50. See KZW.

The Author with Chief and Chiefess of Siraoi
standing before grass house in which she
lived.

(Frontis)

FIG. 7.2. From left: Koyo, Neill James, and Tōzō. Courtesy of Lake Chapala Society.

FIG. 7.3. Neill James dressed as an Ainu. Courtesy of Lake Chapala Society.

FIG. 7.4. Visiting the Noboribetsu hot springs in 1935 on vacation, Kaizawa Tōzō second from right, his wife, Koyo, second from left, seated. Sunazawa Kura is center standing and her husband Yutarō is seated in front. Credit: Sunazawa Kura, *Watakushi no ichidai no hanashi: Ku sukuppu orushipe* (Tokyo: Fukutake Shoten, 1990), 286. Courtesy of Sunazawa Yoeko.

wall[,] a god shelf in one corner, some old Ainu swords and native costumes hanging from pegs on a wall beam, a few woven mats spread about on the bare plank floor," wrote James.[51] Tōzō explained that the treasures in his house were given "by Japanese in the days of feudal lords in exchange for hides of bear, deer, and other fur bearing animals, and also in exchange for fish. We old Ainu of today know that our grandfathers and fathers were cheated by such transactions! . . . [The items] were already in our family before my father's time."[52]

James describes being awakened the next morning when about twenty people filed into the room.

> The men picked flat square cushions from a pile near the wall and squatted on them while the Chief crossed the room to the north wall. In astonishment I watched the strange proceedings. He unhooked the ceremonial

51. James, *Petticoat Vagabond*, 93–94.
52. Hilger, *Together with the Ainu*, 147.

robe from a peg, slipped it on, placed his willow crown upon his brow, [swung] his sword gear across his shoulders. Now fully clad in the robe of the Ainu Chieftain he was, he faced his audience and began a lecture on the Ainu. I had rented and was living in the local museum.[53]

During her stay in Shiraoi, James, in an ironic twist, became a part of the tourist show. She remarked,

> Daily visitors came and went through my house and I had no more privacy than if I lived in the lobby of a post office. They examined my zippered eiderdown sleeping bag, my portable typewriter with as much interest as they did the "treasures[,]" the old swords, shaved fetishes, ancient *attush*, bearskin, bow and arrow. The hairy Chief, clad in garments in style a thousand years ago, a pagan man of mystery and glamor, was a wonderful sight; but he attracted not one whit more attention from visiting settlers, and travellers than the Petticoat Vagabond.[54]

James explained that news of her presence in Shiraoi caused tourist traffic to increase, and soon Tōzō was incorporating explanations and observations about her in his talks. She wrote, "I became such a distraction to the Chief's lectures that I soon learned to vacate my house when I spied him plodding down the road from the station with a group of information hungry males."[55] Tōzō deftly incorporated James into his lectures, capitalizing on her rarity for tourists.

MIYAMOTO EKASHIMATOKU

At this time Tōzō's main rival in Shiraoi's tourist industry was Miyamoto Ekashimatoku. Born in 1876, like Fushine Kōzō, Ekashimatoku represented the multidimensionality of Ainu imperial subjecthood. He had fought in the Russo-Japanese War in the Japanese cavalry and was proud of being Ainu.[56] His association with the Ainu village in Shiraoi and with

---

53.   James, *Petticoat Vagabond*, 95.
54.   James, *Petticoat Vagabond*, 95–96.
55.   James, *Petticoat Vagabond*, 98–99.
56.   Miyamoto, *A Nisei*, 124.

FIG. 7.5. Prewar postcard of Ekashimatoku and his wife Saki. The caption reads: "Finely dressed Ainu, Miyamoto Ekashimatoku and his wife, Shiraoi." Credit: Author's collection.

tourism generally was perhaps the longest of all Ainu leaders, lasting from before the war into the postwar period. His long tenure in Shiraoi can be seen in a prewar souvenir postcard (fig. 7.5) and later postwar photographs, which show him and his wife, Saki, their countenances the same but aged over the many decades (see fig. 7.8 later in this chapter).[57] He lived next door to Japanese photographer, Kinoshita Seizō, who was responsible for many of the Ainu postcards produced at this time, and their close friendship and collaboration united their families for several decades. Ekashimatoku was able to control the dissemination of numerous images of him and his family through his close collaboration with Kinoshita.[58] His knowledge of Ainu customs and the fact that he could explain them in Japanese made him popular with tourists. Many tourists flocked to Ekashimatoku's reconstructed *chise*, where he provided lectures on the lifestyle of the Ainu.

When Prince Satonari came to Shiraoi in April 1934, he looked inside Ekashimatoku's *chise*, watched Ainu dances, and visited the elementary

57. For additional postwar photographs and postcards, see KZW.
58. Turull, "Eudald Serra," 206.

school, guided by Mitsuoka Shin'ichi.[59] In 1938, a second-generation Japanese American named Kazuo Miyamoto visited Shiraoi village with his family. At the station, an Ainu man on a bicycle greeted them and asked if they were bound for the village. Kazuo recorded that he discovered the Ainu man on the bicycle was the son of the "mightiest contemporary bear-hunter, Miyamoto Ikashimatoku [sic]. The son himself is a photographer and a corporal in the reserve. To see the house and listen to his father lecture, we were charged thirty *sen* apiece and to get them to pose in pictures twenty *sen*." Kazuo remarked, "They do a thriving business."[60] Kazuo reprinted the whole of Ekashimatoku's speech in his travel account, and it is clear that by 1938, Ekashimatoku, who was sixty-three years old at the time, had mastered his delivery of his lecture on Ainu culture, in which he talked about the Ainu's relationship to the Japanese, his profession as a bear hunter, his hunting trips, and the methods he used to catch bears. He introduced himself in the following way, according to Kazuo: "Many people come to see me. Every year there are princes of the blood, ministers, generals and scholars that come to this humble dwelling as you have today, for I am the mightiest bear hunter living today in all Hokkaido."

Among the Ainu goods he showed to Kazuo and his family were "numerous lacquer wares bearing the coat-of-arms of Tokugawa, Toyotomi and the lesser daimyos." Ekashimatoku explained, "You see the fifty or more swords. Swords used at the time of Jimmu tennō, Shotoku Taishi and the different periods. Most of them belong to the Kamakura Era."[61] That these goods were really authentic "national treasures" dating as far back as the legendary first emperor is unlikely. It was not uncommon for the Ainu to dupe naive Western and Japanese scholars with fake artifacts.[62] But it is possible that some of the objects in his collection did in fact date back several centuries. There are also suggestions that some Ainu sold their goods to other Ainu. Kayano Shigeru recalled that his father had sold most of his Ainu objects to residents of Shiraoi in the winter of 1933; presumably they wished to build up the collection of objects on display in the village *chise*.[63]

59.   *HT*, April 13, 1934.
60.   Miyamoto, *A Nisei*, 120–21.
61.   Miyamoto, *A Nisei*, 122.
62.   Ainu chief Penri tried to sell Yoshitsune's sword to Polish scholars.
63.   Kayano, *Our Land*, 100.

Ekashimatoku talked about his bear-hunting trips and explained how they captured cubs to be sacrificed for the annual bear festival. He demonstrated his knowledge of Ainu culture and emphasized his and his wife's rarity: "Out of 500 now in this village only about thirty have tattoo marks around the mouth. This wife of mine will perhaps be about the last to wear this mark of her ancestors." He predicted very few pure Ainu would remain, owing to intermarriage. At the same time Ekashimatoku, like Tōzō, made it clear to visitors that he was like other Japanese subjects in other ways. He stated, "I am sixty-three and have lived in Shiraoi for fifty-three years. I was in the cavalry and fought in the Russo-Japanese War. My three sons are also soldiers waiting for their summons."[64]

Upon researching the tourist business in Shiraoi in the late 1930s, I came across a photograph of Miyamoto Ekashimatoku with a Japanese tourist. I managed to contact the owner of the photograph, Uehara Masami, who told me that the picture was of her grandfather, who visited Shiraoi in 1938. Uehara points out that her grandfather is wearing what her family believes is a rented costume, a *tanzen* (worn at a *ryokan* or *onsen*) for the photograph. This *tanzen* helps juxtapose the representation of a traditional Japanese with a traditional Ainu (fig. 7.6).

By the 1940s the Ainu leaders in Shiraoi had developed a well-coordinated system of managing tourists. A Japanese linguist who studied the Ainu language, Kindaichi Kyōsuke (who worked with the Ainu at the 1912 Tokyo exposition; see chp. 4), explained that Ainu boys would wait for tourists at the train station and then guide them to the house of an Ainu *ekashi*. For this service, Kindaichi recommended sightseers pay the Ainu boys one yen. He also detailed the systematic way visitors would be guided to an *ekashi*'s house.

There are three chieftains' houses at Shiraoi. It is prearranged that sightseers who alight at the station at such and such a time should go to such and such a chieftain's house. Accordingly, if you engage a guide you must follow this pre-arrangement—that is to say, the house where you take rest is previously arranged for you. After that it is optional whether you call at the other chieftains' houses or not.[65]

64. Miyamoto, *A Nisei*, 124.
65. Kindaichi, *Ainu Life*, 78–79.

FIG. 7.6. Ekashimatoku with Uehara Masami's grandfather in 1938 and another Ainu woman. Courtesy of Uehara Masami.

Kindaichi's description corroborates Kazuo's account of visiting the village in 1938, when Ekashimatoku's son met him and ensured he was taken directly to his father's *chise*.

The realities of war touched the Ainu villages in Hokkaido, many of which sent Ainu soldiers to the front lines. Ekashimatoku's second son, Mitsuo, died in north China in August 1940.[66] In 1941 it was reported that Ekashimatoku went to Tokyo with his wife, his daughter, and eldest son, Yoshio (Tomoramu), who was dressed in a first-class officer's uniform, to collect Mitsuo's remains. Within his regiment, Mitsuo's bravery was well known. Although he was a corporal when he died fighting in

66.   GHQ SCAP, "Biographical Sketch," October 24, 1947.

China, such was his bravery that after his death he was promoted to sergeant. At the time, Ekashimatoku proclaimed, "There have been a lot of
Ainu who as soldiers have gone to war and many have died. Mitsuo's
brother, Noboru, is now in the battlefield in China, for his country."[67]
While Ekashimatoku's presence in the metropolis brought some attention to the fact that many Ainu were fighting and losing their lives in the
war, it was not until the postwar period that former Ainu soldiers began
talking about how their experiences of the war affected how they viewed
their Ainu identity vis-à-vis the state.

The Postwar Boom and Growing Problems

For the Ainu in Hokkaido, the immediate postwar period was a time of
transition and potential change, as US occupation officials took control
of Japan from 1945 to 1952. Some former Ainu soldiers believed that having fought in the war meant they were no different than other Japanese
nationals and deserved equal treatment. Other Ainu former soldiers
viewed their experiences in the war as further confirmation of their distance from the Japanese.

After the end of the Asia-Pacific War, a *Life* magazine photographer
in Japan in June 1946 photographed Ekashimatoku as he officiated over
the bear ceremony in Shiraoi.[68] In one photo, former Ainu soldiers returned
from the war are wearing the uniforms of the imperial army as they help
skin a bear (fig. 7.7). Many Ainu from Hokkaido, including Ekashimatoku's sons from Shiraoi, had served in the army. The picture of the
uniformed soldiers participating in the bear festival serves as a striking reminder that the Ainu were not "strange relics of primitive man," as the *Life*
headline stated, but were imperial subjects who had fought in the war
alongside other Japanese soldiers. After their return, the Ainu soldiers
had to reconcile their place in a changing society. Some felt that the expressions of Ainu culture and tradition exhibited for tourists were in-
authentic representations of their current life. Others saw the tourist

67. *Shin sekai asahi shinbun*, January 13, 1941.
68. "The Hairy Ainus."

FIG. 7.7. Returned Ainu soldiers skin a bear. Ekashimatoku is in the background, right-hand side. Credit: Photographer Alfred Eisenstaedt, The LIFE Picture Collection, Getty Images.

villages as some of the few sites where Ainu culture could be proudly shown and experienced.

In the period right after the war, Ekashimatoku was one of the main leaders running Shiraoi tourist operations. US occupation officials represented a large portion of the tourists who visited Shiraoi at this time, and the bear ceremony was frequently performed especially for them.[69] These

69.   John Bennett, "Doing Photography and Social Research in the Allied Occupation of Japan, 1948–1951: A Personal and Professional Memoir," Ohio State Univer-

performances continued until concern over the savagery of the ceremony prompted occupation officials to ban them.[70] Perhaps owing to his visibility in Shiraoi, Ekashimatoku was selected to visit the General Headquarters (GHQ) of the Supreme Commander for the Allied Powers (SCAP), which was under the command of General Douglas MacArthur. His visit to GHQ in Tokyo on October 23, 1947, was widely reported in US newspapers.[71] In the MacArthur archives, there are documents and photographs of Ekashimatoku taken during his visit. The accompanying text describes him as "the chief of the Ainu tribe from Northern Hokkaido" and says he was in Tokyo to visit his friend Colonel Tilton and to give MacArthur some Ainu lacquerware as a gift.[72] During his visit, he asked the Americans for help in improving the economic status of the Ainu. According to SCAP documents, he was described as a bear hunter who opposed the restrictions on hunting in Hokkaido. Furthermore, "His only request is that the Ainus be given some land for cultivation because the hunting and fishing are now so poor that the Ainus are being driven to agriculture for the first time in the history of the race. This turning to agriculture is not by choice but of necessity for their existence."[73] Unfortunately, his request was not taken seriously.[74]

The centrality of Ekashimatoku's role during the occupation can be seen in an incident that occurred two months after his visit to GHQ, when he encountered a group of US officials in Hokkaido. The encounter also sharply conveyed the growing dissension between younger Ainu and the *ekashi* over issues of tourism. Occupation official Herbert Passin met Ekashimatoku during his visit to Hokkaido, where he also visited with John Batchelor's adopted Ainu daughter, Yaeko, who was then in her sixties and living in the village of Usu. Passin later recalled the Ainu of Usu as being very sensitive about their heritage, writing that they "refused in an

---

sity Libraries, 2003, http://wayback.archive-it.org/8650/20171002212036/https://library.osu.edu/projects/bennett-in-japan/2_9_photos.html (accessed August 1, 2018).

70. *Saturday Evening Post*, November 10, 1951.

71. *Los Angeles Times*, November 6, 1947.

72. MacArthur Archives Ph 3489, October 23, 1947.

73. GHQ SCAP, "Biographical Sketch"; see KZW for photo of visit.

74. Also in the MacArthur archives are nine color photographs of Ekashimatoku and his wife, Saki. These photographs have not been in wide circulation and have not been reproduced elsewhere.

exemplary fashion to turn themselves into tourist curiosities as did some Ainu groups in other towns." In contrast to those in the tourist villages, who "lived on the Japanese tourists' thirst for the exotic," the Usu Ainu "bent over so far backward that they would not wear Ainu clothing or draw attention to themselves as Ainu in any way."[75] In Passin's estimation, "They refused to be tourist Ainu not only because they were too proud to do so but because they were ashamed of being Ainu at all." In response to Passin's desire to see traditional music and dance, two of the older Ainu said they would gladly show him the traditional dances. They met him the next day, bringing with them five other elders, two women and three men, among them Ekashimatoku. Apologizing for their age, one of the elder Ainu remarked, "Young people don't know the old dances."

Passin talked with Ekashimatoku at length. Although Passin did not identify him by his name or village, that it was Ekashimatoku is evident through the details of a story he told about being the only Ainu who had been to the United States, specifically Alaska and San Francisco. Of course Ekashimatoku was not the only Ainu to have gone to the United States, but other written and oral evidence corroborates the fact that he had been to San Francisco, something that he was immensely proud of.[76] Ekashimatoku's granddaughter Tsuda Nobuko recalled her grandfather talking about America:

My earliest memory of my grandfather Matoku-ekashi is of sitting on his lap, running my fingers through his long beard while listening to him tell a story. He was making the image of a big wave as he told a story about how difficult it was to shoot a gun on the sea, because the waves rocked the boat. He told me that they had been to northwestern America to catch sea otters and he specially mentioned the coffee he drank there—it must have been very fine coffee because he never forgot that memory.[77]

Passin's recollection of their encounter includes Ekashimatoku's account of his visit to the United States:

75. Passin, *Encounter with Japan*, 165.
76. Clark, *All the Best*, 208.
77. Tsuda, "A Personal Rebirth," 309.

"You won't believe it," one of the old men said, "but I am probably the only Ainu who has ever been to the United States. I spent a year in San Francisco once."

In 1897 or so, when he was seventeen years old, he had been hired on board a Japanese sealing ship as rifleman. "We Ainu had the best shooting eye around here, and all the Japanese sealers wanted us to work for them." One day they were boarded by an American Coast Guard vessel for some suspected violation. "All those *shamo* (the Ainu word for "dirty Japs") pointed to us and said it was our fault. Of course we didn't know what it was all about. We were taken off the sealer and put aboard the American ship, and then taken to Alaska." Since it was deep winter, they spent the season there living in a small post where there were many Eskimo.

"What did you think of the Eskimo," I asked, delighted at this choice anthropological tidbit, the encounter of Ainu and Eskimo.

"Well," he thought back, "you know, their music is like ours. But they look just like the damn Japs."[78]

After spring came, Ekashimatoku and the other Ainu were taken to San Francisco for trial. The city impressed them, as it was the first modern city they had ever seen. Passin noted Ekashimatoku's description: "'San Francisco,' he recalled, 'was all mountains and light. I had never seen anything so bright. I had never seen such tall buildings. At first we were frightened.'" After a year, Ekashimatoku said, they were sent back to Yokohama and visited Tokyo for the first time, which they thought was bigger than San Francisco. (Interestingly, in retelling Ekashimatoku's tale of his arrest, Passin focuses on the trickery of the *shamo*—the Ainu name for the Japanese, which Passin translates as a purely derogatory term; often *shamo* is used simply to distinguish the Japanese from the Ainu.)

After several drinks, Ekashimatoku and the others began to loosen up and started to sing and perform dances. Just when a woman was going to teach Passin an Ainu song, the party was interrupted by a young Ainu man in steel-rimmed glasses whom Passin described having an expression that was between "proper respectfulness and controlled anger." There were two other young men with him, and they told Passin they were there to "protest your making a spectacle of these old people." After Passin told them he didn't understand, he said they continued: "You are deliberately

78. Passin, *Encounter with Japan*, 161.

getting them drunk to make them do those barbaric songs and dances. We would like you stop immediately. It's an insult to us. You are making a spectacle of us, treating us as barbarians." Passin relayed that one of the youths explained:

> I am as good a Japanese as anyone else here. I served in the army and several of my friends, from this very village, died in the war. The only difference is that my ancestors spoke a different language. But that doesn't make me different from other Japanese. In the past, every part of this country had its own dialect. Today we all speak standard Japanese. But every Japanese, not just us, has ancestors who spoke a different dialect. Our dialect happens to have been called Ainu. But like everybody else, we have progressed, and now we want the old dialect to disappear so that we can stand up as equals.[79]

The young man's appeal to Passin has several noteworthy points. First, the basis of his protest was the fact that he was Japanese, as proved by his service in the army. Second, he reduced all differences between the Ainu and Japanese to the single issue of language. From the viewpoint of the older generation, who willingly performed for Passin, it was sad that the younger generation did not want to know how to perform traditional Ainu dances and songs. Passin seemed to connect the reluctance to showcase Ainu culture with a sense of embarrassment about being Ainu. His account provides a snapshot of the debates that the tourist villages crystallized during the occupation period. On one hand, the younger Ainu wanted to connect the older generation's desire to perform Ainu songs and dances with being duped or exploited—in this case, they were given drinks and taken advantage of. They did not seem to recognize the pride or value their elders may have put in showing their culture to the Americans.

Passin declined to call off the party because the Ainu had come in good faith, and instead he invited the young men to join them. They refused and again condemned him. When Passin returned to the room, the spirit of the party was gone. He remarked that he later had several meetings with the same young Ainu who had interrupted the party, and

---

79. Passin, *Encounter with Japan*, 163.

they eventually forgave him for not knowing any better. He also described another conversation he had with them:

> "In two generations," one argued, "this whole problem will become part of history. We will all be Japanese. The Ainu memory will fade, unless it is deliberately kept alive. That's why we were so angry at you the other night. You were doing just what those *shamo*, who despise us, always do. They would rather have us continue as a quaint, primitive enclave, to be stared at and to be felt superior to, rather than become equals."[80]

The young man's words show that they viewed being Ainu as something the Japanese or foreigners forced them to be, rather than the true articulation of a heritage they actually identified with. The younger generation saw the older as continuing a lifestyle that was inauthentic to their own. At the same time, the older Ainu, who had lived through the transition from a time when everyone spoke the Ainu language to the present, when most Ainu youth were unable to speak it, believed they were upholding the last vestiges of a culture that was rapidly fading. A striking contrast in the young man's words was the hopeful sentiment—not a lament—that in time the "Ainu memory will fade."

John Bennett, an anthropologist and occupation official who traveled to Shiraoi in 1948, also noted the generational divide between the Ainu. He wrote, "The professional 'chief' of the village, who has an enormous old thatched house full of Ainu relics, and who insists on going through the various empty old rituals—exactly like Indians in the Western reservations. The similarities are very detailed, even to the resentment shown this sort of thing by the younger people."[81] After his trip, on which he met several wealthy Ainu who had succeeded in lumber and mining businesses, Bennett described the Ainu problem as stemming from their status as a minority group that faced discrimination—a subject he felt was neglected in Japan. He remarked,

> It is high time someone wrote about the Ainu as [a] minority group, instead of some sort of fossil aboriginal element. Not only that, but as a

---

80. Passin, *Encounter with Japan,* 164.
81. Bennett, "Doing Photography."

minority they present many striking differences to the American minority situation. Imagine a member of a minority (Japanese), wealthiest man in his village, accorded all due prestige, but who hesitates to sit next to the guest of honor at an ordinary dinner, preferring to sit in the corner! The Ainu are "held back" as much by their own self-effacement as by discrimination. But this is changing, and the younger generation on the whole doesn't show humility.[82]

Besides the generational divide and whether being identified as Ainu enabled discrimination and inequality to continue, the postwar Ainu tourist villages were also contentious owing to competition between leaders. US anthropologist Ted Bank's account of his visit to Hokkaido in 1956 revealed this competition among leaders in Shiraoi. Unlike Bennett, who had been accompanied by Japanese officials who had no connection to the Ainu, Bank visited Nibutani·with a Japanese professor, Kodama Sakuzaemon, who had formed close relationships with the Ainu through his research. Kodama accompanied Bank on a trip to the Hidaka region that resulted in the following representation of the Ainu: "Whenever we arrived at some Ainu village, everyone was lined up waiting in his finest clothes. Swiftly they posed for photographs, then they were dismissed, and we would be off."[83] The Ainu paid deference to Kodama and bowed deeply to him. His connections to the community at the time meant that Bank was also treated well. (Years later, Kodama's medical inquiries and scientific cataloging of the Ainu, as well as his excavations of Ainu graves, brought him notoriety and criticism.)

In Nibutani, it was clear that the Ainu were doing Kodama a favor by dressing up in their clothes and agreeing to be photographed. There was no mention of money changing hands. After staying in Nibutani for a night, Bank and his wife decided to go on their own to Shiraoi with Honjo, their Japanese research assistant. During the planning of their trip, the full nature of the tourist business there became evident, as well as the tensions between the Ainu leaders who managed the tourists. Honjo was sent in advance, Bank explained, "to get the cooperation from the two Ainu elders, Miyamoto [Ekashimatoku] and Kaizawa [Tōzō], each of whom claims to

82. Bennett, "Doing Photography."
83. Bank, "The Ainu," 49.

be the headman." But Bank said Honjo failed to obtain their cooperation because they maintained that "previous Americans had 'cheated' by expecting them to pose for nothing. When Honjo promised them I would pay, they agreed to help, but said I would have to choose between them; they would not work together." Honjo picked Ekashimatoku because he was older, and consequently "Kaizawa stalked away in anger."[84]

Besides the apparent competition over visitors, Bank's account reveals that a disagreement ensued over the price that Ekashimatoku should charge Bank. Everyone in the village got involved in the disagreement, including Moritake Takeichi. As mentioned previously, Moritake had led tourists to the Ainu village from Shiraoi station when he was a teenager, and he eventually quit working for the railroad company because he disliked the commodification of the Ainu. Moritake entered this debate even though, according to Bank, he "apparently was not involved in the tourist business."

When Bank and his small party arrived, Ekashimatoku immediately started "to speak excitedly" to Honjo, and soon several Japanese managers of the nearby tourist stalls joined in, until "there was quite a racket." When Bank inquired about the source of contention, his assistant told him that they were complaining that the agreed-on price was not high enough. Honjo conveyed their demands:

"They say you must pay 5,000 yen ($14.00) before they pose for pictures. It's too much!" Honjo looked as if he were going to cry; his reputation with me as an arranger was at stake. "And they say you must buy them two *shyuo* [sic] of sake for the wine ceremony; and the old woman says you must pay 5,000 yen more for using the old-time Ainu things in your pictures."[85]

The "old woman" to whom his assistant Honjo referred was Ekashimatoku's wife, Saki, whom Bank unkindly said was "scowling their way" like one "of the witches of Macbeth." Nevertheless, Bank's reference to Saki illustrates her active role in negotiating rates. At this point Moritake stepped in and took Bank's side, which caused Saki to turn on him "with a fury of violence." Bank said he had "no trouble following her string of

84. Bank, "The Ainu," 50.
85. Bank, "The Ainu," 50.

epithets." This account of their haggling over prices indicates that the Ainu leaders priced every interaction carefully. For those interested in a scientific study of the Ainu and not a straightforward tourist visit, or perhaps because they were foreigners, prices were set even higher.

Bank agreed to the prices because he understood that US reputations were already low in the village and he would rather be thought "a sucker than a cheat." In the end, though, he thought he did not get what he paid for. One interesting aspect of his account hints at direct Japanese involvement in running the tourist village in the postwar period. Bank said, "the Miyamotos and their Japanese manager rounded up a few additional Ainu."[86] It is not clear if they had a Japanese manager in the official sense of the word, or if the manager to whom Bank referred was a Japanese associate, like photographer Kinoshita Seizō. According to all other accounts, the Miyamotos were in firm control of their business, especially during the prewar period, and it is possible that with the influx of tourists after the war, collaborations with Japanese were forged to execute more effective business arrangements.

Bank was rattled by his treatment, so he quickly took some photographs and tried to "beat a retreat." His status as viewer was reversed when Saki demanded a photo with him.

> The old lady ran after us however, demanding that I pose with them for one last picture, using our camera, and our film, of course. She wanted the picture for publicity purposes[,] to induce other Americans to visit Shiraoi. Obviously, we had convinced her, much to my regret, that Americans are a lucrative source of revenue, if nothing else.[87]

Bank's account reveals the flip side of the tourism business, where the Ainu working in the villages had grown wary of researchers and tourists who did not adhere to the rules regarding payments. Although Bank felt he should be allowed to photograph the Ainu for the lower price, in this situation the Ainu maintained control over their own commoditization. In her last salvo, Saki recognized the value Bank represented in publicity for their business and was able to commodify his visit to their village, just like Tōzō did with Neill James.

86. Bank, "The Ainu," 50–51.
87. Bank, "The Ainu," 51.

Ekashimatoku's major competitor in Shiraoi tourism in the postwar period was Kaizawa Tōzō, the man who had hosted James and continued to work in the tourism industry in Shiraoi well into the 1960s. In 1961 a European traveler, Vlasta Hilska, visited Shiraoi and wrote about her interactions with Tōzō. In the following account she described entering a large ceremonial hut where there was a table covered with handicrafts.

> The chief put on an Ainu frock[,] which had turned red with old age, over his European trousers. He seated himself in the carved armed chair, as if on a throne[,] and started his narration in rapid Japanese just as a guide in an old castle. The howling of the wind and the rattling of the skulls mingled with his words and formed a strangely sad monologue. He spoke of the mild and kindhearted temper of the Ainus, of the way they respect their women[,] who have a higher position than Japanese women, about the Iomante [*sic*].

Hilska said she asked him to say something in Ainu, but he politely refused. He sold her a few sets of postcards that were on the table and signed his name in Japanese kanji, then wrote his Ainu name in the Japanese kana alphabet. Then Ainu women and girls danced for her, putting on Ainu garments that had been hanging on the walls over their European dresses.[88]

One of the women who danced for Hilska was the mother of Yamazaki Shimako. In 2011, at age seventy, Yamazaki recalled Tōzō's involvement in the Shiraoi tourist industry in the postwar period. Yamazaki had lived next door to Tōzō's *chise*, where "tourists watched Ainu dances."[89] She remembered that starting around 1948, her mother had danced at Tōzō's *chise* as part-time work, for which she received 300 yen a day. Yamazaki recalled that at that time, 300 yen a day was a tremendous amount of money. For comparison, in 1941 Kindaichi recommended tipping the Ainu boys leading tourists to the villages one yen.[90] When her mother returned from dancing, Yamazaki remembered, she would spend her time weaving Ainu *ruumpe* (robes), but she never talked about it to Yamazaki. Although her mother spoke the Ainu language with the other

88. Hilska, "In an Ainu Village," 13.
89. Ryō Michiko, "Ainu kōgei sakuhinten 2011/2/5-8 Gyararī matsumori," February 9, 2011, https://ryomichico.net/bbs/review0012.html#review20110209173959 (accessed August 10, 2018).
90. Kindaichi, *Ainu Life*, 78–79.

old women, she didn't teach Yamazaki the Ainu language or how to weave. Yamazaki recalled, "I was raised by my parents that I must not use the Ainu language." After she married a Japanese man at age twenty-five, her husband worked carving Ainu wooden dolls called *nipopo*, but she herself had nothing to do with Ainu culture. Later in her life, she became involved in learning Ainu cultural practices, including weaving.[91] Her recollections are important not only because they establish how Ainu performers were paid but also because they illustrate the rise of another leader in the local tourism business who competed directly with Ekashimatoku, a competition that eventually led to hostility.

By 1960 the number of *chise* in Shiraoi that were used to host tourists rose from three to four.[92] A Japanese visitor in 1961 had a completely different experience from Bank's at Shiraoi and reported that there "they did not get as fleeced as much as in the Asahikawa Chikabumi Ainu village." At Shiraoi, he said, they enjoyed the talk given by the chief, which was filled with jokes and made the audience laugh and smile. He reported that if they wanted to see dancers perform they had to pay money, and then four or five women came out and danced.[93]

As the tourist operations in Shiraoi grew, so did the antipathy toward the Ainu involved in tourism, who were often called *kankō* Ainu (tourist Ainu) or *misemono* Ainu (spectacle Ainu). Although in the 1930s a few Ainu individuals, such as Moritake Takeichi and Yoshida Kikutarō, had spoken up against turning their people into spectacles, by the 1960s the opposition against Ainu tourist villages had become a full-blown movement.[94]

Hokkaido's Tourist Boom and the Corporatization of Shiraoi

The number of tourists visiting Shiraoi continued to climb, reaching unprecedented heights. From 1956 to 1960, one million visitors traveled to Hokkaido, including Japanese tourists, many children on school trips,

91.   Ryō, "Ainu kōgei."
92.   Saitō, "Hokkaido kankō," 6.
93.   Tominaga, *Hokkaido ryokō*, 104.
94.   Morris-Suzuki, "Tourists, Anthropologists," 55–57.

FIG. 7.8. School trip to Shiraoi village in 1953. Saki and Ekashimatoku in the middle of the photo. *Nusa* pictured in the back. Courtesy of Uehara Masami.

and American tourists (fig 7.8).[95] In 1964, 56,000 people visited Shiraoi.[96] Shiraoi was constantly adapting to deal with the flood of visitors.

The increase in visitors to Shiraoi during the 1960s eventually had two major consequences. The first was a decision to move the tourist village a kilometer away, to the shore of Lake Poroto. The second was the formation of a vocal opposition movement led by young Ainu activists who were against this move. The Ainu leaders' influence on tourist operations was waning at this time, with the increasing role of the Shiraoi town board and other tourism operators who wanted to maximize revenue. Only after the 1970s and the height of antidiscrimination campaigns in Japan that protested unequal treatment of the Ainu and Burakumin, did the Shiraoi Ainu tourist village begin to be reshaped by Ainu leaders who spearheaded tourist activities to foster cultural preservation.

With the influx of tourists, the sustainability of Shiraoi village and the effect of tourism on its residents reached the point that town officials

95. Higashimura, "'Kankō Ainu,'" 70.
96. Shiraoi Chōshi Hensan Iinkai (ed.), *Shin Shiraoi chōshi*, 4.

decided "to move the village to an uninhabited tract of land in order to divert tourists away from the residential neighborhoods."[97] The phrase "moving the Ainu village" was disingenuous, because only the souvenir shops and reconstructed *chise* where Ainu goods were displayed were to be moved to the new location.

In 1935, Japanese scholar Takakura Shin'ichiro had been concerned about tourism's effect on Ainu villagers and had urged "that the government establish an Ainu museum for the benefit of officials and tourists," arguing that "it should be located in Sapporo or some other place away from any Ainu community," but the Japanese government had not acted on his suggestion. In the 1960s, the driving force behind moving the Shiraoi Ainu village to Lake Poroto was the Shiraoi Tourism Consultant Corporation (Shiraoi kankō konsarutanto kabushiki kaisha), which was established in 1965.[98] It worked closely with the Shiraoi city office regarding the plan to move the Ainu village. Its goal was to relieve the congestion and address residents' hygiene concerns, since there were no restrooms or other facilities for the crowds of tourists now arriving by bus, car, and on the train. The Shiraoi city office also cited its concern with preserving Ainu culture and establishing a place where visitors could see Ainu materials.

According to an employee of the consultant corporation, the company was not concerned with profits but with preserving Ainu culture. The head of the company made this position clear to the public in Shiraoi and was backed by several high-profile community members, including Ekashimatoku's son Tomoramu, Tōzō, and Nomura Giichi.[99] For the move, the town contributed 2.3 million yen, and several important residents contributed 700,000 yen.[100] One of the men who contributed was the aforementioned Nomura Giichi, who had served as the leader of the Hokkaido Ainu Association (Hokkaido Utari Kyōkai) and the tourist Ainu abolition movement (kankō Ainu kaishō undō) in 1962.[101] Nomura was related to Nomura Ekashitoku, one of the four Ainu leaders in the prewar period who domi-

97.   Howell, "Making 'Useful Citizens,'" 17.

98.   Shiraoi kankō konsarutanto kabushiki kaisha is also referred to as the Poroto kohan kankō kaihatsu kaisha.

99.   Hashine, *Ware Ainu*, 214–15.

100.   Hashine, *Ware Ainu*, 213–14.

101.   *AS*, July 8, 1962.

nated the Shiraoi tourism business.[102] Nomura's attempts to stop Ainu from working in tourist villages had failed a few years before, and in 1965 he saw the value in the proposal to move the village to Lake Poroto.

There is some discrepancy over whether Ekashimatoku worked in the new village. According to an Ainu informant, when Ekashimatoku worked in the new village, he walked from the part of Shiraoi town where his large modern home was located and crossed the street to where he stood in front of a re-created Ainu *chise*.[103] Discrepancies over the year that Ekashimatoku died coupled with the fact that due to his popularity, even after his death, signs advertising his *chise* remained up has led to confusion in the historical record regarding his involvement in the new venture.[104]

By the 1960s, Ekashimatoku's son Tomoramu had became a frequent fixture next to his father, and he had a specially named *chise* set up where he posed for photographs with visitors (fig. 7.9). In the 1960s Tomoramu began to be referred to as a chief of Shiraoi, reflecting his increasing visibility. In one notable incident, he had not been taking photographs with tourists because it was a rainy day, but when a group of former soldiers stopped in Shiraoi, he agreed to a photograph with them for the newspaper. Although the paper did not report it, Tomoramu's service in the army—and that of his brothers—probably influenced his decision to take a photograph with them.[105]

Moving the village to Lake Poroto would help manage visitor traffic because the village would be even closer to the train station (about 600 or 700 meters away). However, the new, separate village would also create the illusion that the Ainu were frozen in time. No one would really be living in the *chise* in the village near the lake. If the tourists could see where the majority of Ainu actually lived in Shiraoi, they would see an increasing mix of newer homes.[106]

102.   Nomura Giichi's grandmother's brother was Ekashitoku, who some sources claimed was the last traditional chief of Shiraoi. Honda, *Hinkonnaru*, 194.

103.   Ainu informant, December 2010.

104.   *News from the Pacific* (1968–69), 34, states that Ekashimatoku visited the Anthropology Society of Hawaii in 1968 "where he produced a fieldwork sensation" and translated a *yukar* in the library's collection. *Montreal Gazette*, October 5, 1974, mentions Ekashimatoku. Ōsuga, *Shiraoi Ainu*, and Ekashi to Fuchi Henshū Iinkai (ed.), *Ekashi to fuchi*, 2:57 state that he died in 1957.

105.   *Yomiuri*, June 15, 1962; *AS*, July 10, 1962.

106.   Shiraoi Chōshi Hensan Iinkai (ed.), *Shin Shiraoi chōshi*, 5.

FIG. 7.9. Sign reads: "Chief Miyamoto Tomoramu," Shiraoi 1963. Courtesy of Phil Peters.

Not everyone saw the benefits of constructing a new village. Some of the Ainu youth, in particular, were unhappy about the plan and started an opposition movement against the village's transfer—an effort that ultimately failed. They employed tactics like removing the sign that directed people to the tourist village from the train station. Each time the sign was replaced, they took it down again. They also criticized the fact that the *iyomante* was being held only to satisfy tourists and that it was being put on by Japanese.[107]

One of the move's critics put it this way, "Ainu hate from the bottom of their hearts the selling of Ainu. For Ainu the fundamental cause of discrimination and prejudice is the tourist villages."[108] Journalist Sugawara Kōsuke visited various Ainu tourist villages in the mid-1960s, including Shiraoi. His account offers a counterpoint to the consultant company's employee's version, which emphasized that the company had the support of Ainu leaders like Tomoramu, Tōzō, and Nomura.

107.   Sugawara, *Gendai no Ainu*, 82.
108.   *AS*, July 8, 1962.

According to Sugawara, tour operators said "it was fine if the local Ainu did not cooperate. There were many impoverished Ainu in the Hidaka backlands and they would hire those people and make a splendid tourist village."[109] Sugawara also talked to Nomura and questioned him regarding his support for the new Poroto Ainu village. According to Sugawara, Nomura spoke with regret but said that even if the new Shiraoi Ainu tourist village had not been built, tourist operators would have built another one and poor Ainu from other areas would have worked there. Nomura explained,

> The tourists from Honshu have a deep impression of Hokkaido, that it is a place where you can get close to the Ainu. Today's tourist village is modern and you cannot see the natural figure of the Ainu. The present tourist village is separated from the town by one kilometer, and moved to Lake Poroto, where the traditional Ainu lifestyle and ceremonies are made up. Because there is an increase in interest, there are also performances. By doing this, we are able to increase profits, and improve the lifestyle of the Ainu and develop the tourist town of Shiraoi.[110]

Sugawara's account includes his meeting in Shiraoi with an *ekashi* (elder) who worked in the tourist village who was called the "bear hunter" and who had lost two sons in the war. Although Sugawara does not name him, he is probably not referring to Ekashimatoku, who only lost one son in the war. By Sugawara's visit, it is likely that other Ainu *ekashi* were using appellations, like bear hunter, that had previously only applied to Ekashimatoku.

In response to a question from Sugawara about whether he had made a lot of money that year, the elder responded that although the Japanese liked to make Ainu into spectacles, they did not like to pay money. He said that photographers kept taking pictures, but they did not pay. He talked about the prime minister and other officials who had visited him: "Important *shamo* (Japanese) have said, we must protect the Ainu. . . . They have even said to me 'take care of yourself.' However their true intention is just to come and see us Ainu as rare spectacles. I know all about

---

109. Sugawara, *Gendai no Ainu*, 84.
110. Sugawara, *Gendai no Ainu*, 83.

it! Therefore young Ainu from the bottom of their hearts hate *misemono* Ainu (spectacle Ainu) and criticize them."[111]

He said that there were those who thought this embarrassing business was going to end soon, because the young Ainu hated it and there would be no one left to be tourist Ainu. They believed the tourist villages would naturally disappear. But he disagreed: "Even if I don't show up to the tourist village, fake Ainu [*nisemono* Ainu], that is to say, Japanese pretending to be Ainu, would come to make money." According to the elder, Ainu were being hired only to stand next to a sign or to sit and carve bears for show in front of a shop. He said that in reality the people who carved the bears sold to tourists were all Japanese, and they made the bears in the back of the store with machines that allowed them to mass-produce them.[112] He said the girls who walked around the village selling flowers were also Japanese, pretending to be Ainu. Real Ainu hated the tourist villages and fled from them, and Japanese "became" Ainu because they were engaged in the greedy moneymaking scheme of tourism.

This elder's response to the villages seemed to correspond with Nomura's thinking—that the villages were inevitable and there was enough demand for employment that you could find sufficient numbers of Ainu to work in them. One of his major concerns seemed to be with the number of Japanese who had infiltrated the villages to make money, a phenomenon that had become quite noticeable. In 1962 a newspaper article exposed the "fake Ainu" working at the tourist villages.[113] Not only were Ainu goods with Ainu labels being made by Japanese workers, but some goods were also coming from Taiwan and Korea.[114] By 1965 the majority of the fifty souvenir shops at Lake Poroto Ainu village were run by Japanese workers, many of whom the tourists thought were Ainu.[115] According to one report, some Ainu began to think, "If Japanese are making money by performing as the Ainu, who are diminishing in numbers, we ourselves should play the real thing."[116]

111.   Sugawara, *Gendai no Ainu*, 81.

112.   Sugawara, *Gendai no Ainu*, 82.

113.   *AS*, July 8, 1962.

114.   Higashimura, "'Kankō Ainu,'" 71.

115.   Higashimura, "'Kankō Ainu,'" 72; Gōnai and Wakabayashi, *Ashita ni mukatte*, 173.

116.   Saitō, "Hokkaido kankō," 9.

The Greatest Revenge Is to Succeed as Ainu: Moritake Takeichi

Moritake Takeichi, who had worked as tour guide in the Shiraoi village when he was a young man, had witnessed the evolution of the Ainu tourist village industry and was a vocal critic of the form it eventually took, especially in the postwar period. Significantly, it was Moritake who had interceded on anthropologist Ted Bank's behalf when Ekashimatoku and others were demanding higher prices, and his presence in that encounter symbolizes his centrality in the growing debate over Ainu tourism in the Shiraoi region. Moritake's willingness to argue with Ekashimatoku on behalf of Bank illustrates how the Ainu held diverse opinions regarding the tourist industry.

After resigning from the National Railroad Company in 1935, Moritake had started a small restaurant in Shiraoi and worked in the fishing industry. But he devoted most of his energy to encouraging the preservation of Ainu culture, which he saw as being changed and destroyed by the tourist industry. In 1961 he became the museum director of the Ainu Memorial Hall in Tōyako, where he worked for about three years. He helped establish the Shiraoi Ainu Folk Museum in 1967, which was located next to the Shiraoi Ainu village, and served for three years as its first director. As director, he was an acknowledged expert in Ainu culture and was primarily focused on promoting cultural preservation. A photo series titled "Tourist Ainu," featured in *Chūō kōron* in 1968, included his photo (fig. 7.10), along with an image of tourists watching Miyamoto Tomoramu and other Ainu dancing (fig. 7.11).

It is ironic that the 1968 photo essay was accompanied by a photograph of Moritake on the cover next to the words "tourist Ainu," a label he detested. He had fought for years against the discriminatory practices that arose out of tourism, and in his role as museum director he was far from being a tourist Ainu. The photo essay was problematic in that it did not detail how the issue of tourism divided the Ainu community in Shiraoi. It implied that all the photos of Ainu people were "tourist Ainu" when in fact Moritake was a critic of Ainu engaged in tourism.[117] In a

117. "Kankō Ainu," 229–36.

1971 piece titled "The Tourist Industry That Uses Ainu as Spectacles," Moritake laid out his position against the Ainu tourist business. He wrote the article at a time when *jinken mondai* (human rights issues) were important in Japan, with respect to the Burakumin, Zainichi Koreans, and Okinawans (following Okinawa's reversion in 1971 after US occupation ended), as well as around the world. Moritake wrote, "Today when people are clamoring for human rights, it is especially problematic that the tourist industry is nonchalantly displaying Ainu as spectacles."[118] The international context was readily apparent in his treatise when he referred to the treatment of African Americans in the United States, which he compared to the treatment of the Ainu. Moritake argued that the Japanese used sophistry in attempting to justify the display of the Ainu, claiming it was done out of a call to "preserve the important traditions of *furusato* [the hometown]" and to "praise our place of origin and the beautiful customs of our ancestors."[119]

Moritake pointed out that if the greatness of the Ainu ethnic culture were truly being recognized, then their display would elevate the whole Ainu race. However, what occurred in Ainu villages was exactly the opposite—the performing Ainu, though finely dressed, were seen as mere stage props; the tourists did not recognize the greatness of Ainu culture. Moritake wrote that the three- or four-minute performances by the Ainu in the tourist villages were not traditional performances but a way to increase profits, as tickets to the village and the tickets to performances were sold separately. Unlike the Living National Treasures (Ningen Kokuhō), such as Kabuki or Noh, in which Japanese performances of the past were accepted as ancient art forms, Ainu performances, as promoted by the tourist industry, were to be examples of a still living past.

Moritake believed that rather than helping celebrate Ainu culture, the villages only misled tourists into thinking that they represented places where the Ainu currently lived. Moritake wrote that eight or nine years before (in 1962–63), Shiraoi had become a village flooded with tourists. At the heart of the village was a block of modern houses where Ainu lived that had such modern amenities as running water, indoor bathrooms, electric washing machines and vacuum cleaners, color televisions,

---

118. Moritake, *Rera korachi*, 79.
119. Moritake, *Rera korachi*, 79.

観光アイヌ
開道百年のなかの虚像

白老民俗資料館館長 森竹竹市氏

FIG. 7.10. Moritake Takeichi, identified in caption as the Shiraoi Ainu Folk Museum director. Credit: *Chūō kōron* 83, no. 973 (October 1968): 229. Photograph by Yamada Kenji, *Chūō kōron* photography division.

FIG. 7.11. Miyamoto Tomoramu dancing with other Ainu. Credit: *Chūō kōron* 83, no. 973 (October 1968): 232. Photograph by Yamada Kenji, *Chūō kōron* photography division.

refrigerators, and telephones; some Ainu even owned cars. According to Moritake, these Ainu followed the much-desired lifestyle pursued nation-wide during the 1960s, what was known as "a cultured lifestyle" (*bunka seikatsu*). However, when tourists were told the Ainu lived in the same way the Japanese did, many believed this to be a lie. Moritake wrote that the tourist companies deliberately left the Japanese in the dark about the Ai-nu's present living conditions. If the Japanese knew how Ainu really lived, the companies feared, interest in them would fade and the number of tourists would decrease.[120]

Moritake criticized how Ainu tourist villages operated, with their in-authentic dances and Ainu crafts that were made by machines but sold as genuine handicrafts. Furthermore, he thought it was wrong that cer-tain Ainu pretended to be village chiefs (*shūchō*).[121] But he said he sup-ported tourism if the Ainu benefited directly from the business and if they were in control of how they were represented. He concluded his treatise by arguing that the Ainu people themselves should have the sole right to the Ainu name and should use it to become economically independent. Significantly, he referenced two Ainu communities, Lake Akan and Nibutani, that were starting to create tourist industries under their own local, independent control. Moritake wrote that the best revenge for the long period of contempt and ridicule the Ainu had endured would be for Ainu men and women to succeed economically by using the Ainu name. The Ainu should never be content with being an exploited people, he said.[122]

Conclusion

Moritake blamed tourist companies for the commodification of the Ainu. In Shiraoi, we have seen that although in the postwar period the pres-ence of Japanese tour companies increased, that came about only after several Ainu leaders had established the precedent of welcoming tourists

120.   Moritake, *Rera korachi*, 81.
121.   Moritake, *Rera korachi*, 82.
122.   Moritake, *Rera korachi*, 82.

to their village. The arrangements that tour companies in the postwar period had with Ainu working at Shiraoi are harder to find in the records, but Moritake's anger was focused on the areas of the tourism industry that had tipped into Japanese hands.

Anger at the tourist operations in Shiraoi culminated in two incidents in 1974. The first was the stabbing of the mayor of Shiraoi by a Japanese man who was upset about the commodification of the Ainu. A few months later, the headquarters of a tourist company was bombed by non-Ainu activists.[123] While tensions were high in Shiraoi, at the same time, some Ainu, like Moritake, pushed the Ainu to appropriate their own culture and present it in a way that was beneficial for them, not just for the amusement of tourists. Moritake's sentiments became part of a growing push toward the regeneration of Ainu culture through tourism, a movement that was intertwined with the legacies of the Asia-Pacific War, as the following chapter details.

123. Siddle, *Race, Resistance*, 165; Hashine, *Ware Ainu*, 181–90.

CHAPTER 8

A Mountain of Bones

In 1965 Teshi Toyoji peered into a cave in Maehira, Okinawa, a place where he had experienced the horrors of war during the Battle of Okinawa. Twenty years after the end of the war, what Teshi saw inside the cave was a mountain of human bones, amounting to nearly 4,500 pieces (fig. 8.1).[1]

The bones had been collected by nearby residents, who had found them in the forest, the mountains, and nearby fields and deposited them in the cave. The bones were those of soldiers and Okinawan civilians, including Okinawan students who had been mobilized to help the Japanese military, all of whom had died during the war. They were a tangible reminder that more civilian lives were lost in the Battle of Okinawa than in any other battle in the Pacific theater during the Asia-Pacific War.[2] In the town of Maehira alone, about two-thirds of its population—551 of its 900 residents—perished during the battle.[3]

When Teshi, an Ainu and a former soldier, traveled to Okinawa in 1965, he did so as a member of an Ainu cultural group that had been in-

---

1. Hashimoto, *Nanboku no tō*, 120.
2. Hashimoto (ed.), *Haha to ko*, 133. Out of 122,228 Okinawans killed in the Battle of Okinawa, 94,000 were civilians and 28,228 were soldiers. Numbers from a display in the Okinawa Prefectural Peace Prayer Museum. (The total represents more than half of the estimated 200,000 deaths in the battle and means more Okinawan civilians died than Japanese soldiers.) Ōta, *Battle of Okinawa*, xi.
3. Hashimoto, *Nanboku no tō*, 103.

FIG. 8.1. The cave in Maehira, Okinawa, where the bones of the war dead from the Battle of Okinawa were gathered before the construction of the *Nanboku no tō* memorial. Courtesy of Itoman city office.

vited by the local Yaeyama school board to perform traditional dances and songs for Okinawan schoolchildren. During this three-month trip to Okinawa, ostensibly to showcase Ainu culture, Teshi renewed his connections to Okinawa, the scene of so many nightmares during his time in the war.[4] He returned again to Okinawa in 1966. Along with the residents of Maehira, he helped construct the North-South Memorial (Nanboku no tō), which commemorates the soldiers from Hokkaido, including thirty-nine Ainu soldiers, and local residents of Maehira who died during the Battle of Okinawa (fig. 8.2).[5]

The Ainu writing on one side of the stone reads, "Kimun utari" (Mountain compatriots), referring to the bond between those from extremes of the empire—Hokkaido and Okinawa—whose fates were intertwined at their final resting place. The memorial is also the location of the charnel house that holds the bones stored in the cave. Prior to the

4.   Hashimoto, *Nanboku no tō*, 120.
5.   *AS*, January 14, 1989.

FIG. 8.2. "Nanboku no tō" memorial. Courtesy of Itoman City Tourist office.

memorial's construction, government officials had wanted to transport the bones to a memorial in Naha. Teshi joined with Okinawans in protesting the move and arguing for burying the bones in the area where they had been found. The dedication ceremony for the memorial was held in February 1966, and more than sixty local residents attended.[6]

The same year that Teshi was peering into the mouth of the cave and wondering what to do with the bones, he was pictured in an article in *National Geographic* magazine about the Ainu, written by M. Inez Hilger. The caption with the photograph, which showed him working in an open-air booth, identified him as a wood carver in charge of tourist operations in Lake Akan, where many Ainu owned tourist shops.[7] In 1971 Hilger, writing about her study of the Ainu in the book *Together with the Ainu: A Vanishing People*, described Teshi as the "go-between for tourist-trade companies and Ainu performers" at Lake Akan. She notes that he gave lectures on Ainu customs for tourists and arranged dance performances.[8]

6.   Hashimoto, *Nanboku no tō*, 121.
7.   Hilger, "Japan's 'Sky People,'" 280.
8.   Hilger, *Together with the Ainu*, 71–72.

Hilger was an anthropologist mostly known for her fieldwork on Native American and Latin American indigenous peoples. But from 1965 to 1966, she traveled throughout Hokkaido to record the customs of the Ainu, taking advantage of what was purportedly one of the last opportunities to record the traditions of a "dying race." The dying-race appellation, which had been applied to the Ainu people since the nineteenth century, was often used to justify anthropological and ethnographic studies. Hilger's account, ostensibly about recording the traditions and customs of the Ainu before they disappeared, unwittingly captured a snapshot of the Ainu tourist industry in the mid-1960s. Many of Hilger's interviewees who knew the most about Ainu oral history and culture were also leaders in the tourism business. While tensions regarding the "tourist Ainu" controversy can be gleaned in some of the interviews, Hilger was primarily concerned with the traditional aspects of Ainu culture. Thus the multidimensionality of Teshi's life and his experience as a former soldier who had fought in the Asia-Pacific War were not discussed.

These two seemingly disparate depictions of Teshi—as a war veteran and an artisan and tourism promoter—have never been reconciled in one account.[9] By looking at Teshi's involvement in the tourist industry in light of his wartime experiences, one can understand how Ainu involvement in tourism during the postwar period moved beyond issues of cultural representation and shifted toward criticism of the state and its treatment of the Ainu. In the early twentieth century, representing oneself as Ainu and promoting one's Ainu culture were seen not as subversive acts but to some onlookers as a sad display of what the Ainu were resigned to because of the lack of other economic opportunities. By contrast, in the postwar period in Lake Akan, Teshi and another Ainu former soldier, Yamamoto Tasuke, used the platform that tourism provided to promote Ainu cultural preservation as a direct critique of the Japanese state. By promoting Ainu tourism, at the height of the backlash against it, they also challenged the assumption that all Ainu felt the same way about the tourist-Ainu issue. Both men were linked to the Ainu liberation movement in the early 1950s, and both were former soldiers who

9. While Hashimoto, *Nanboku no tō Ainu*, and Hashimoto (ed.), *Haha to ko de miru*, discuss both aspects of Teshi's life, it is not done within a larger discussion of the Ainu experience in the postwar period (including *kankō* Ainu).

had been shaped by their travel to other parts of the empire. Teshi's experiences with the Okinawan people encouraged him to promote the idea that they shared a common bond as indigenous peoples that set them apart from the Japanese.

Teshi and Yamamoto witnessed Japan's empire, its collapse, and the emergence of the postcolonial era. What happens to former colonized subjects when an empire collapses but the subjects remain? Instead of viewing the tourist villages as evidence of Japan's oppression of the Ainu—as places where the Ainu were forced to perform their "Ainuness"—we can see, through the lives of Teshi and Yamamoto, that in spite of (or perhaps because of) Japanese oppression, they became places that promoted Ainu culture and its value.

I do not mean to promote Ainu agency at the expense of diminishing the oppressive nature of the Japanese state against the Ainu. Tourism was, rather, the nexus point for Ainu people like Yamamoto and Teshi, who were subjected to economic and ethnoracial marginalization and responded by promoting Ainu culture as separate from Japanese culture. It also exposed the falseness of imperial rhetoric that implied fighting for the emperor could make one Japanese. Ainu soldiers who were conscripted and fought for Japan found that their social and economic marginalization continued after the war. This led them to turn to tourism as one of the few occupations in the postwar period that offered not only economic advancement but a way to advance Ainu issues and rights.

The First Ainu President? Yamamoto Tasuke and Lake Akan

After the Asia-Pacific War, Yamamoto Tasuke was one of the voices calling for the creation of an independent republic for the Ainu apart from Japan.[10] In 1946 he wrote a piece in the newly created and short-lived *Ainu shinbun*, a newspaper he founded with Takahashi Makoto. He proclaimed that it was time to take action:

10.   Shin'ya, *Ainu minzoku*, 236–38. Chiri Mashiho, the first Ainu to earn a Ph.D., also supported this movement.

The twin villains of exploitation and invasion, thought to be the business of the emperor, have finally driven us to the point of being one step away from the destruction of our fatherland [*sokoku*]; however, now they are dying as war criminals. You reap what you sow. The Ainu must stop wishing for peace in Japan and democratization. At this time, at this moment, all of our community [*utari*] must really wake up and rise to action! If we don't wake up, we also will be destroyed. It is necessary that we secure land for the Ainu, improve housing, expand education, and have our land returned that was taken by corrupt bureaucrats, to be communal land. We elders [*ekashi*] have performed distinguished services in the development of Hokkaido; Hokkaido is the country of the Ainu. To protect our pride, Ainu now must rise up!![11]

Yamamoto's call to action was all the more shocking coming from someone who went to war. He saw Japan's defeat in the war as a kind of karmic retribution for Japanese actions taken during the war and presumably against the Ainu people.

Yamamoto's ally, Takahashi, who was also a big proponent of creating an independent Ainu republic, sent General Douglas MacArthur a deerskin and antlers "as a token of our grateful appreciation for what he has done to secure land for our people and to give to Japan a democratic society, based on law and order."[12] Similar to Ekashimatoku, who used his visit to General Headquarters during the US occupation as an opportunity to ask for land for the Ainu, Takahashi hoped the Americans could secure them land and an increased standard of living, which the Japanese government had failed to provide. In fact, as Takamae Eiji has pointed out, land reform implemented by occupation officials in 1946 actually ending up hurting Ainu farmers instead of compensating them for colonization policies that had taken away their land and fishing rights. Part of the land reform initiated after the war mandated that the land of absentee landlords—including some Ainu who tilled only part of their land—qualified for redistribution to Japanese farmers.[13]

11. *Ainu shinbun* no. 3 (1946) reprinted in Tanigawa (ed.), *Kindai minshū*, 257–58.
12. Yūki, "Teshi Toyoji," 38; Takamae, *Inside GHQ*, 349. Takahashi's letter was signed on behalf of all Ainu of Hokkaido and called MacArthur the greatest hero of the present world. Sodei, *Dear General MacArthur*, 141.
13. Takemae, *Inside GHQ*, 439–40.

There was one defining moment in the spring of 1947 that had ramifications for the success of the Ainu independence movement. Four Ainu
representatives were called to the Hokkaido occupation headquarters at the
Sapporo Grand Hotel, where they were asked if they wanted independence
from Japan. They all answered in the negative. U.S. General Joseph Swing
gave each of the Ainu 100,000 yen and dismissed them.[14] More than forty
years later, that lost opportunity was one that Yamamoto still recalled with
passion and a twinge of regret. As he explained in an interview in 1989
when he was eighty-four, "At that time I called for us to take drastic action.
It was now or never if we wanted to have an Ainu republic. Even if it was
impossible, we should have seized the initiative to abolish the bad law
known as the Protection Act for Former Natives." Laughing, he said wryly,
"If we had created an Ainu country, there is no doubt that I would have
been the first president."[15] The interviewer noted how Yamamoto's spirits
were lifted by referring to those times: "This one moment of history, even
today, has taken hold of his thoughts, and he cannot let it go."[16]

The Ainu liberation movement never gained much steam, even
though the few passionate people who wanted to create a republic pursued every viable path, including approaching the Chinese for help. In
July 1948 an Ainu representative addressed a petition for emancipation
from Japan to the Chinese delegate to the Allied Council for Japan. The
document requested the help of President Chiang Kai-shek in securing
independence for the Ainu, "who had long been subjected to Japanese
oppression. The request was based on the right of self determination of
minorities and the hope was expressed that Japan would provide a tribal
reservation for the Ainus [sic] so that they can preserve their independence
and identity."[17] The petition was forwarded to the US State Department,
where it was filed without comment.[18]

Although his varied efforts for Ainu independence were not successful,
Yamamoto made his mark for the Ainu through his work in cultural preservation and tourism. We can see, through his varied life experiences, how

14.   Koshiro, *Trans-Pacific Racisms*, 110.
15.   Yoshihisa, "Maboroshi no Ainu," 90.
16.   Yoshihisa, "Maboroshi no Ainu," 90.
17.   MacArthur Memorial archives, "Incoming Airgram dated July 20, 1948 from
American Consulate General, Shanghai China to Department of State."
18.   Takemae, *Inside GHQ*, 439–40.

he came to endorse the revitalization of Ainu culture through tourism, specifically at Lake Akan. Born in Kushiro in 1905, six years after the passage of the aforementioned Hokkaido Former Natives Protection Act and two years after the Human Pavilion in Osaka, Yamamoto said he had to shoulder the burden of discrimination throughout his life. He attended a Japanese-run "native school" (*dōjin gakkō*) for Ainu children led by Nagakubo Shūjirō, whose former students included Yūki Shōtarō, who had gone to the 1907 Tokyo exposition to work in the Ainu Building. Yamamoto recalled how his life was divided between school, which was *shamo*, and the village, which was Ainu. He remembered one time he went to town with his mother to go shopping and *shamo* children jeered at them on their way home, calling "Ainu, Ainu," and throwing rocks at them. He said he was naughty and tried to break away from his mother to fight the boys, but she did not let him and told him to be patient. Yamamoto recalled that he was not able to contain himself and said that later that night he escaped from his house and ran into town. He found some *shamo* children and beat them up, even though he could not see who they were because it was dark. To Yamamoto it did not matter if he was retaliating against his bullies or not; all Japanese were his persecutors. He believed that because the Japanese had won the Sino-Japanese and Japanese-Russo Wars, they had grown arrogant and felt entitled to belittle the Ainu. Yamamoto looked back with pride at his childhood. When other Ainu children ran off when they were bullied, he said he stood his ground. He recalled that it was no good if he faced a gang of *shamo* boys, but fighting one on one was no problem; he actually enjoyed it. After he graduated, at the age of sixteen he went to work in a coal mine, helping with transportation by lining up the horses and walking with them and their heavy cargo.[19]

Yamamoto began to work in the Ainu tourist industry by chance in the 1930s. He had gone on a week-long trip to the Kawayu *onsen* near Kussharo village at Lake Akan to recover from an illness. This was right around the time the area was designated a national park in 1934. Yamamoto said that when he saw the crowds of tourists who came to the area, he realized the "potential of tourism."[20] The next year he went

19. Yamamoto, "Ainuzoku wo hokoru," 10–11.
20. According to Cheung, "Rethinking Ainu Heritage," 202, tourism started in the 1920s.

to the shore of Lake Kussharo and began a business selling carved bears he made himself. When he was kid, he had received carving tools from a shipwright and would carve small pieces of wood when he had free time; ultimately he grew to like wood carving. No one else in Lake Akan National Park did similar work, and his business became very popular. He remarked, "At this time Ainu were rare [in the tourist business], so I directed my attention toward this pursuit," realizing the worth of Ainu commodities. He bought a large house on the side of the road that he used for his business, and when tour buses stopped, the store would fill up with customers. Despite not having a special arrangement with the buses, their passengers continued to fill his store. He did not sell things at a high price, he said, but because he had such a high volume of sales, he made two to four times his costs in profit each day.[21] He retained a *shamo* partner, and the business went well. Business was good until the worsening of the situation with China in the late 1930s; when tourists stopped coming, he turned to farming and raising cows. In the early years of Yamamoto's involvement in the tourist industry in Lake Akan, he benefited financially, admitting that he was successful because Ainu artisans and businesses were rare in that region.

In 1941 Yamamoto was deployed to the Micronesian island of Truk as a civilian member of the Japanese navy. He remarked, "Even if there had not been a war, we had already been invaded and suffered due to the *shamo*. However, if Japan lost, I knew that our defeated countrymen would be wretched, and so I had the feeling to go." He went off, thinking, "Win, and I will return."

Yamamoto remembered that the Korean soldiers fighting for Japan were treated poorly, and because of this they held anti-Japanese feelings. He recalled violent clashes between Korean and Japanese soldiers. Because he could speak Japanese, he said, the soldiers and islanders did not know he was an Ainu. During the war they suffered air strikes every day. In one attack a piece of shrapnel pierced his left eyebrow, and he eventually lost sight in his left eye. His hand was burned, and his left arm was injured so that afterward he could only partly raise it. They had no food rations and ate whatever they could find. Yamamoto recalled

---

21. Yamamoto, "Ainuzoku wo hokoru," 14–15.

soldiers dying because they had eaten poisonous plants, and he described how five or six men worked together to catch lizards, and because they were so hungry, they even ate the bones and skin. According to him, the most pitiful victims of the war were the comfort women. He remembered a time they came ashore on a small island in Micronesia, the island girls greeted them loudly, but one girl dropped to her knees without saying anything and quietly smiled. Yamamoto thought she must be sick, but he later found out she was a comfort woman who provided sexual services to the Japanese army. She ended up throwing herself into the traffic in the middle of a crowded street. He also recalled another comfort woman who wanted to stay and live out her life in the islands. She married an islander but eventually ended up killing herself.[22]

Yamamoto said he had seen many men die during the war, and that he had never heard anyone say when he was dying, "Long live the emperor!" Instead, he remarked, they called out the names of beloved women, and the word he heard most often cried out was "mother."[23] After Japan was defeated in the war in 1945, he and his fellow soldiers received the order to repatriate, but many starved while waiting to go home. In Yamamoto's eyes, all he saw in the war was dying and destruction.

When Yamamoto returned from Truk, he was bedridden from December 1945 until the following spring because of extreme malnutrition. Knowing that so many young men had died from malnutrition or injury on the battlefield, he wondered for what purpose he was still alive. After regaining his health, in May 1946 he helped form the Kushiro branch of the Hokkaido Ainu Association and was elected its president. Explaining his involvement in the association he remarked,

As a people we were in reality still living, and so we needed to unite in order to encourage lifestyle improvement and cultural transmission. At this time the Ainu had been gradually driven into *shamo* society. There were many who denied their Ainu identity. Those who succeeded economically fled to Honshu, where they hid their Ainu identity and, secretly in pain, carried out lifestyles like *shamo*.[24]

22. Yamamoto, "Ainuzoku wo hokoru," 16–18.
23. Yamamoto, "Ainuzoku wo hokoru," 18.
24. Yamamoto, "Ainuzoku wo hokoru," 19.

Despite the work of Yamamoto and others, the Ainu independence movement did not gain traction. When three Ainu candidates ran for election to the National Diet in the spring of 1946, they failed to garner enough votes.[25] US papers reported on one of the three candidates, Okakura Tokuemon, and although he did not win, it is clear that the Ainu had caught American interest.[26] US occupation officials, in particular, saw the Ainu as a minority group, just as they distinguished Okinawans as "non-Japanese" during their control of Okinawa from 1945 to 1972.[27]

The Start of Tourism at Lake Akan

By the 1950s a small Ainu community had settled in the Lake Akan region and became involved in running businesses centered on Ainu tourism. Unlike in Shiraoi, there was no long-established Ainu community at Lake Akan. The first Ainu who moved to Lake Akan in the 1920s and 1930s opened up a couple of shops in the area, with mostly seasonal Ainu workers who came from Kushiro, Urakawa, Shiranuka, Bihoro, and Asahikawa.[28] When the Maeda family, who owned the land in what is now known as Lake Akan National Park, gave some Ainu workers land on which they did not need to pay rent, the Ainu were able to truly establish and sustain a tourism industry centered on their culture.[29]

There are different accounts of how the Ainu came to establish the Ainu *kotan* (village) in Lake Akan. According to fieldwork conducted by Ann-Elise Lewallen, Maeda Mitsuko had given the land to the Ainu in an act of benevolence.[30] According to a relative of the Maeda family, Maeda

25. Koshiro, *Trans-Pacific Racisms*, 110.

26. *Newsweek* vol. 27 (1946) and *St. Louis Dispatch*, February 5, 1946; *Official Gazette*, April 7, 1947, 5.

27. Aniya, "Okinawasen wo kataritsugu," 40.

28. Shitaku, *Ainu oman*, 38; Irimoto says there were about eleven households in the early 1950s. Irimoto, "Creation of the Marimo Festival," 22.

29. The Maeda family worked in the forestry business for three generations and owned a paper production company.

30. Maeda Mitsuko was the wife of Maeda Shoji, the son of Meiji bureaucrat Maeda Masana, who was well known for his agricultural endeavors. Maeda was granted the land in Lake Akan as a reward for his services to the government. See Crawcour,

had "urged local Ainu to 'abandon the bottle in favor of the blade,' apportioning rent-free land for houses so that local Ainu might reside year-round, producing and marketing woodcarvings and other folk-art objects to tourists."[31] This recollection emphasizes the Maedas' charity and paternalism by focusing on their role in guiding the Ainu to forsake alcohol to focus on employment. In contrast, according to Shitaku Toyojirō, who worked in the Lake Akan Ainu village (and incidentally accompanied Teshi to Okinawa in 1965), the Ainu approached Maeda in 1953 because they were frustrated with their working conditions under Japanese business owners.

The request for land that they presented to Maeda had the signatures of thirty Ainu workers who were employed as carvers or accessory makers, all of whom were seasonal workers. Shitaku explained that the thinking behind their petition was that if they had houses in the Ainu village, they could focus on wood carving. Furthermore, they could portion off sections of their houses to be used as shops in which they could sell the things they made without a middleman. If they did this, the petitioners said they could live happy and long lives. As it was, under Japanese management the Ainu workers' behavior was regulated by owners who wanted the tourists to be able to see the Ainu at work. According to Shitaku, Maeda Mitsuko gave a portion of the family's land to the Ainu for free, for them to use as they wished, saying, "In the past you used to live on this land." That land became the foundation of the Lake Akan Ainu village.[32] Shitaku's account emphasizes the role Ainu workers played in helping themselves. The agreement between Maeda and the workers, allowing Ainu people to live and work in the *kotan* area without paying rent, was finalized in 1959.[33]

During this time, Teshi set up a tourist shop that also became a lodging house. Teshi would let university students and other travelers who had little or no money stay with him.[34] He led an initiative to set working

---

"Kōgyō iken," and http://kam-kankouken.jp/tourism/en/akanko/special/71/html (accessed July 31, 2018).

31. Lewallen, "'Hands that Never Rest.'" Ainu *kotan* residents and shopkeepers, who are required to be Ainu-identified persons or employed by Ainu families, live rent-free and are only billed for their cold water (73–74).

32. Shitaku, *Ainu oman*, 38–42.

33. Cheung, "Rethinking Ainu Heritage," 202.

34. Hashimoto, *Nanboku no tō*, 120.

standards for Ainu wood carvers, wages for winter work, and standard-ized expectations for customer service, as well as to encourage savings.[35] He created an association for wood carvers and other workers. In the mid-1950s, members of the community built a *chise* where they put on dancing performances and held the *iyomante*. In 1962 the Ainu workers at Lake Akan formed a craftsmen's cooperative. Among other things, the cooperative purchased raw materials in bulk, such as trees for carv-ing, thus lowering the cost.[36] They also opened a branch of the Hok-kaido Ainu Association in Lake Akan, signaling their involvement with prefecture-wide policies regarding the Ainu.

The Creation of the Marimo Festival

While Teshi was working to secure fair treatment for workers, Yamamoto shifted from his earlier efforts to establish an independent Ainu republic to promoting the teaching and performance of traditional Ainu dances and songs as a way to regenerate the culture. He established and became the chair of the Kushiro Classical Ainu Dancing Preservation Society in 1948. Along with several others, both Japanese and Ainu, he created the Marimo Festival, which was first held in 1950. This annual festival at Lake Akan has become one of the ways Ainu cultural traditions are still transmitted and revitalized today. The Marimo Festival was not a traditional Ainu ceremony; it was invented to recognize and praise nature and return the *marimo* (spherical algae plants) that had been removed from the lake and sold all over Japan back to the waters of the lake. The festival included the performance of Ainu dances and some traditional ceremonies. Yamamoto began holding the bear festival in the town of Teshikaga, with Yamanaka Torizō presiding over the ceremony and Yamamoto assisting.[37]

Some foreign observers mistakenly thought that the Marimo Festi-val was a traditional event. Hilger, who visited in the late 1960s, proclaimed, "Since ancestral days the Ainu have celebrated an autumn festival to

35. Shitaku, *Ainu oman*, 43.

36. Shitaku, *Ainu oman*, 46–47.

37. He validated Yamanaka's expertise by citing his history of having killed more than eighty bears and having officiated the bear ceremony for more than twenty years.

honor the *marimo*."[38] Because the festival was not part of Ainu tradition, some Ainu leaders were critical of it, saying that "Ainu culture was being abused for the sake of tourism."[39]

Yamamoto responded to this criticism by commenting, "The Marimo Festival, the *iyomante*, all of it is for the future of the Ainu. As a people if we are excited, we are able to regain our pride. Eighty-year-old grand-mothers, although they are in pain, still extend their arms and dance."[40] He acknowledged the concern about "tourist Ainu" and pointed out that although the same questions had been raised about the bear festival, which had been performed for tourists for years, it retained its spiritual value.

> At this time, there was the criticism regarding tourist Ainu [*kankō* Ainu] who sold their "Ainuness." We clearly expected that when we performed the *iyomante*, it would attract a lot of people. As a people who have respect for the gods, our strict belief in the bear has not faltered. It is an idea that has endured from the past. If there are a hundred people, or a thousand, it does not matter because we are taken over by the Ainu spirit.[41]

The first Marimo Festival drew about 600 people and twenty Ainu elders. Yamamoto recalled the struggle to establish the event: "In the beginning there was no money or understanding, which was the biggest obstacle. Five years after the war [1950], everyday life was very difficult and it was only natural that the Ainu had the lowest level of lifestyle." The organizers worked hard to ensure they could provide round-trip transportation to ease the worry of the Ainu grandmothers who would perform the dances, because, as Yamamoto said, "If there were no Ainu, there would be no festival." They negotiated a deal with a bus company, and for the first several years the people who came to dance from Tokachi and Kushiro received free transportation. The Ainu's in-volvement in the Marimo Festival differed from events at other Ainu tourist villages, because the Marimo Festival relied on inviting Ainu people from all over Hokkaido to participate—to proudly wear their

38.   Hilger, *Together with the Ainu*, 76.
39.   Irimoto, "Creation of the Marimo Festival," 13.
40.   Yamamoto, "Ainuzoku wo hokoru," 28.
41.   Yamamoto, "Ainuzoku wo hokoru," 28.

Ainu clothing and perform their dances and traditional ceremonies. While the presence of so many Ainu people was undeniably a tourist draw, the Ainu who participated did so of their own volition and were not paid to attend or perform.[42]

Yamamoto saw the Marimo Festival as an important way to practice Ainu traditions and language that had fallen out of use over the previous decades. In regions, such as Lake Akan, that did not have extensive tourism programs in which the bear festivals and traditional dances were regularly performed, there was no reason to practice Ainu cultural traditions. He remarked,

> As soon as the war started there was no cultural interaction among the Ainu. Therefore when the Ainu came to gather for the festival, I saw a forgotten people [*wasuretta minzoku*] become excited. It was planned as a cultural exchange. As a result, in each region the practice of Ainu dances began again. Each year the Ainu came together and the level of the arts continued to improve, and their spirit changed. Elders came who heard about the festival from other elders, and it gradually became a marvelous thing.[43]

Although the Ainu participating in the Marimo Festival might have been labeled tourist Ainu, they participated voluntarily as a way to practice Ainu traditions that were no longer part of their everyday lives. For those who did earn money as tourist Ainu, Yamamoto retorted, "You can say that tourist Ainu are bad; however, if we did not have the tourist business, there is no [other] policy for the people who cannot eat. The carrying out of the festivals is correct and there isn't anything [in them] that is not from Ainu traditions."[44] Despite Yamamoto's fierce defense of the Marimo Festival, it was still criticized as an "invented tradition" that promoted discrimination through its perpetuation of so-called tourist Ainu.[45] Yamamoto was featured in round-table discussions about "the Ainu problem" in the 1970s, and although he spoke up about discrimination and condemned

---

42. Zaidan Hōjin Ainu Bunka Shinkō (ed.), "Yamamoto Tasuke," 374; Yamamoto, "Ainuzoku wo hokoru," 27.

43. Yamamoto, "Ainuzoku wo hokoru," 27.

44. Yamamoto, "Ainuzoku wo hokoru," 28.

45. Hirasawa, "Kojin kara mita Ainukan," 101.

how the Japanese took Ainu land and oppressed the Ainu, he did not participate in discussions about the tourist Ainu controversy.[46]

Yamamoto's promotion of cultural revival activities was occurring at a time when the Japanese government still denied the Ainu people's status as an indigenous group in Japan. In 1974 Yamamoto was part of an Ainu group that visited China. The group was impressed by Chinese government policies that recognized the culture of minority ethnic groups, such as the Mongols. Everywhere the Ainu group went in China, they were greeted enthusiastically, which Yamamoto said contrasted greatly with their treatment in Japan.[47] This visit brings to mind the Ainu's earlier appeal to China through the Chinese delegate to the Allied Council for Japan and illustrates how travel outside of Japan caused people like Yamamoto to compare the treatment of the Ainu with that of other indigenous groups in other countries. Yamamoto also traveled abroad to perform the Ainu *yukar* in 1976 in Paris, for a meeting of the United Nations Educational, Scientific and Cultural Organization. Yamamoto's devotion and commitment to the preservation of Ainu cultural traditions was recognized in 1974, when the Ainu dances of Akan and Kushiro were designated as Japanese "intangible cultural assets." In 1984 the number of Ainu classical dances designated as intangible cultural assets grew to eight.[48]

War Memories That Never Fade

In the 1960s, during the height of criticism directed at Ainu who worked in tourist villages, an article featuring Teshi Toyoji, titled "Living as a Tourist Ainu, Independence Rhetoric Reverberates," appeared in the papers. Teshi was the leader of the Lake Akan Ainu Association at the time, and he defended Ainu who worked in tourism, saying it was the only way that they could achieve a "cultured life style" (*bunka seikatsu*)—the term in vogue at the time for economic prosperity—in the Lake Akan region, where natural resources for fishing were scarce. He proclaimed

46. Gōnai and Wakabayashi, *Ashita ni mukatte*, 201–2, 206–14.
47. Yamamoto, "Ainuzoku wo hokoru," 21.
48. Yamamoto, "Ainuzoku wo hokoru," 31–32.

that the Ainu took pride in being modern Japanese people, and his views were characterized as advocating ethnic nationalism and challenging Japanese (*wajin*) humanism, which criticized Ainu tourism.[49]

Around this same time, Teshi returned to the site of the horrific Battle of Okinawa and then worked to establish the North-South Memorial in Okinawa in 1966. The memorial did not garner much interest, however, until a nationwide educational conference was held in Okinawa in 1978, where it was brought up and discussed.[50] In 1981, the Hokkaido Ainu Association sponsored a performance of the *icarpa* (an Ainu mourning ceremony) at the war memorial to appease the spirits of the dead.[51] Among those who attended were Teshi and Kaizawa Tadashi, as well as some relatives of soldiers who had died in the battle.[52] Kaizawa was a prominent Ainu leader who had gone to Manchuria as part of the youth volunteer corps. He is the grandson of Kaizawa Uesanashi, who had participated in the human displays in Tokyo in 1912 and Osaka in 1913. Since this first *icarpa*, different Ainu groups have returned to Okinawa to perform the *icarpa*, typically every five years.[53]

During the 1980s Teshi was interviewed by several writers and recorded his experiences during the war, particularly about the Battle of Okinawa. Teshi said he had been drafted, and he joined the Asahigawa Seventh Division, Twenty-Fourth Infantry Division, Eighty-Ninth Regiment, also known as Mountain Division 3476, in February 1944. Before he left home, he told the mother of his childhood friend Fumi that if he returned from the war, he wanted to marry her.[54] Teshi was first sent to Manchuria, and then his regiment was transferred to Okinawa in August 1944.[55] Two of the lengthiest accounts recorded by the writer Hashimoto Susumu reveal that at age twenty-two, Teshi's experiences in the

49. *Yomiuri*, May 17, 1962.

50. Nakano, "Nanboku no tō," 270. One participant at the conference, Ainu Washitani Sato, had a nephew who died in the Battle of Okinawa. She met Okinawan teacher Aniya Masaaki, who recalled that an Ainu memorial had been built and took her to see it.

51. Hashimoto (ed.), *Haha to ko*, 132; Kaizawa, *Ainu waga jinsei*, 140–46.

52. For Kaizawa Uesanashi, see chapter 4.

53. Ceremonies have been held in 1981, 1986, 1991, 2006, and 2011. *Senkusha no tsudoi*, January 1, 1982, vol. 29, 471; *RS*, May 18, 2006; *Okinawa taimuzu*, May 17, 2011.

54. Shitaku, *Ainu oman*, 63.

55. Hashimoto, *Nanboku no tō*, 87.

war were defined by two struggles: one with the top-down nature of the imperial military command, and the other with trying to help the Okinawan civilians caught in the midst of battle.[56] Although military orders forbade soldiers from fraternizing with civilians, Teshi defied those rules.[57] He made friends with one Okinawan family in particular when he went to purchase eggs from a farmer. An Okinawan woman who saw him immediately started to weep. She said he looked exactly like her son, who had died in the war. Teshi grew close to her and her other son, a young boy of thirteen, Nakayoshi Kikō. He would visit their house for tea, and the mother, Mrs. Kamado, cut his hair. Nakayoshi would wait for Teshi's return when he went out on missions. Teshi gave Nakayoshi's family some of his military rations, and he brought them to watch the army newsreels and movies.

Teshi's memories of the Battle of Okinawa, recorded when the accounts of war survivors and wartime oral history projects were gaining traction in Okinawa, are remarkable in that they emphasize the suffering the Okinawans endured in the war.[58] At that time, in the 1980s, there was no well-known body of writing on the Ainu soldiers' experiences during the Asia-Pacific War, only undocumented claims, much of it oral, that no Ainu villages had been left untouched by the war.[59] During the Battle of Okinawa, Teshi recalled, he found a ten-year-old boy lying in a foxhole in the arms of his dead mother. The boy had a chest wound that was full of maggots. Teshi and another soldier rescued him and brought him to an army doctor. This Japanese doctor did not make any distinctions between saving the lives of civilians and soldiers. Teshi said they gave the boy soldiers' clothes, and he became very attached to him. Teshi worked as a messenger, running messages between commanders by hand because radio communications on the island were almost nonexistent. When he would go out to deliver a message, the boy would often wait for him at the mouth of one of the caves, where soldiers took refuge from the battle, until he returned. One day there was a bombardment near the mouth of the cave, Teshi said, and the boy was killed. Teshi recalled an

56. Hashimoto, *Nanboku no tō*, 84–89.
57. Hashimoto, "Nanboku no tō: Okinawasen," 195.
58. Ikeda, *Okinawan War Memory*, 9.
59. Peng and Geiser (eds.), *The Ainu*, 284.

encounter with seven nurses and a seven-year-old boy outside of Garabi Cave. They were about to commit group suicide. Teshi said he told them not to kill themselves. He gave them a white flag and told them to surrender to the Americans. After the war, when he entered the Ishikawa POW camp, he met the same nurses. Teshi recalled how they greeted him with tears streaming down their faces.[60] Although at times Teshi spoke of Japanese generals who were indifferent to the welfare of everyday soldiers, he recalled Japanese doctors who risked their lives to save the lives of Okinawan civilians and soldiers.

Even after Teshi was captured at the end of the war and sent to the POW detention camp, he made sure to identify himself as an Ainu. At the camp, Teshi's *inaw*, or Ainu prayer stick, which his uncle Shōtaro had given to him when he entered the army and which Teshi had kept with him at all times, was taken away from him. Teshi said he asked to speak with the head of the camp's military police. He told him, "I am an Ainu. An *inaw* is the same as a cross. If your cross was taken would you be silent?" The head of the military police had lived in Yokohama and could understand some Japanese, Teshi recalled, and he also had some knowledge of the Ainu. They returned his *inaw*.[61]

Today the young Okinawan boy whose family Teshi befriended during the war, Nakayoshi Kikō, is the living "memory keeper" of Teshi's war experiences.[62] In 2005 Nakayoshi, at age seventy-one, would recall that his relationship with Teshi was like one with a longtime *Uchinānchu* (Okinawan) friend.[63] In one instance, he says, Teshi helped his family when Japanese soldiers commandeered the caves where local residents were taking shelter. Teshi chased the Japanese soldiers away by putting on his dead commander's uniform and commanding them to leave.[64] Nakayoshi told of how Teshi had escaped from the Ishikawa POW camp when he heard that they were sending Japanese prisoners to Hawaii. He stayed with Nakayoshi's family for a while before going to Yanbaru and working with the reconstruction army. With the pay he earned in that work, he was able to purchase an Okinawan soldier's demobilization card

60.   Hashimoto, *Nanboku no tō*, 98–99.
61.   Hashimoto, *Nanboku no tō*, 118.
62.   *Nihon keizai shinbun*, June 21, 2005.
63.   *Nihon keizai shinbun*, June 21, 2005.
64.   Hashimoto, *Nanboku no tō*, 97.

for 300 yen. Nakayoshi's account stresses how his uncle helped find Teshi an Okinawan soldier's uniform so he could return to Japan as a demobilized soldier and not an escaped POW.[65] Nakayoshi recalled that Teshi "became Okinawan"—and that by doing so he was able to finally return to Hokkaido in February 1947.[66]

When recalling his wartime experiences, Teshi expressed the kinship he felt, as an Ainu, with Okinawans, and in several interviews he stressed the similarities between Okinawans and Ainu not only in their appearance but also in their greetings. He discussed how their similarities ranged from gestures of greeting and dances to what they ate and even certain boats they constructed.[67] He thought Okinawan women's hand tattoos were similar to the tattoos of Ainu women, his grandmother's in particular.[68] Teshi's affinity for Okinawans was something that other Ainu who had fought in Okinawa also expressed.[69] In the same way, Nakayoshi and his mother had such a warm reaction to Teshi partly because he was not like a *Yamatochū* (the Okinawan term for a Japanese person) but seemed more like an Okinawan.[70]

By 1985 Teshi's views about being Ainu had dramatically changed. Gone was the pride he expressed in 1962 in being both an Ainu and a modern Japanese citizen. In 1982, he opened the Kussharo Ainu Kotan Folk Museum in Teshikaga and served as its director. Although many tourists visited the museum, the tour guides often gave visitors incorrect information. For example, one guide said that Ainu still were not in the national registry. A reporter described how Teshi could not stand this and said he glared remonstratively at the guide. His views about the status of the Ainu had also darkened. "The Ainu have ceased to exist," he stated in an interview for a US magazine. "We have lost our language, our culture. We are Ainu only because we feel that we are, deep down."[71] The writer who interviewed him attributed the dire state of the Ainu to the fact that they were restricted to making a living by farming or by "carving wooden bears, or

65. Nakayoshi, "Nanboku no tō," 26.
66. Nakayoshi, "Nanboku no tō," 25.
67. Yūki, "Teshi Toyoji," 33–34.
68. *AS*, January 14, 1989; Yūki, "Teshi Toyoji," 33–37.
69. Tomimura, *Kōgun to Ainuhei*, 134.
70. Nakayoshi, "Nanboku no tō," 25.
71. Di Salvatore, "Hokkaido," 45–46.

posing in authentic costumes for tourists' cameras." Teshi said he had been researching cultural ties with other indigenous peoples—Saudi Arabians, Malaysians, Swedes: "'I met with a group of American Indians last summer,' he explained. 'I thought they had been hurt badly. Now I realize that it is [we] who have gotten nothing. Nothing.'"[72] The US journalist noted of Teshi's Ainu appearance, "There was no mistaking him for a Japanese. His eyes are round and his skin the color of an American Indian." According to the reporter, Teshi's non-Japanese features had enabled him to masquerade as a Mexican American during the war.[73] Again, through interactions with other indigenous groups, Teshi and others saw how far behind Japan was in relation to other governments in the treatment of indigenous people. This realization inspired the Ainu to demand better treatment and acknowledgment from the government as an indigenous people.

With the death of Emperor Hirohito on January 8, 1989, the Shōwa period (1929–1989) ended, and the beginning of the new period—the Heisei—began. Teshi thought this new period should be the time when Japanese culture and politics were reinterpreted from the perspectives of the north (Ainu) and south (Okinawa).[74] He saw the death of the emperor and the beginning of a new era as an opportunity to rectify how the Japanese had long written about their history and culture, without mentioning the Ainu and Okinawans.

Yamamoto, on the other hand, reacted differently to the emperor's death as it approached (fig. 8.3). In 1988 people were debating whether the thirty-ninth Marimo Festival should still be held that year, in the face of Emperor Hirohito's illness, which was growing more severe. In the end the prefestival activities and the dancing procession were canceled but the ceremony itself went on as planned. Yamamoto explained,

Although the Ainu made a big deal out of the emperor's life and death, and hesitated [about] celebrating the festival, I swore to myself that I would make them carry it out and perform the Marimo Festival conscientiously. . . . [I]f he die[d], we would only pray that his soul may rest in peace, and if he [were] alive, we would pray for his recovery, and hold the festival.

72.   Di Salvatore, "Hokkaido," 47.
73.   Di Salvatore, "Hokkaido," 46.
74.   *AS*, January 14, 1989. This reassessment has occurred in both Japanese and English scholarship.

FIG. 8.3. Yamamoto Tasuke (1905–1993). Credit: Featured in Bryan Di Salvatore, "Hokkaido: The Narrow Road to the Deep North," *Islands* (May–June 1985): 43. Photograph by Harley Hettick and published with his permission.

[Ainu] formalities have been practiced even before the emperor system was established, so there is no reason to refrain from continuing to do so.[75]

From this statement it is clear Yamamoto did not believe that Ainu culture and practices should be superseded by the Japanese tradition of the emperor system.

Both the emperor-based system of rule and the Marimo Festival were invented traditions, designed to create a new sense of belonging and affiliation. But the emperor system fell short, as Yamamoto and Teshi observed

75. Akan Kankō Kyōkai, *Marimo matsuri*, 16; Irimoto, "Creation of the Marimo Festival," 17.

during the war, when they saw how dying soldiers never said the emperor's name but instead called out for their mothers or loved ones.[76] For Yamamoto, his unwillingness to cancel the Ainu Marimo Festival in deference to the looming death of Hirohito speaks to the defiant attitude he maintained until his death. It also illustrates his belief that the intrinsic value of Ainu culture did not derive from the Japanese state but from the Ainu people's own actions.

In 1993, when a very frail Teshi was in hospice the year before he died, he was interviewed for a television program that aired on the Hokkaido Broadcasting Channel.[77] For the first time, he revealed that on the orders of their superiors, he and other soldiers had been forced to shoot Okinawan civilians during the war. In a barely audible voice, he uttered his wish to go back to Okinawa once more to offer prayers to the dead.[78] In this interview, who was victim and who was victimizer finally became blurred by the horrors of war. Prior to this, Teshi's wartime stories framed him as a fearless fighter aligned with the Okinawan civilians, who were victims of the war. His admission that they had been ordered to shoot civilians reveals not only the painful process of coming to terms with the war but also that his connection with Okinawa involved atonement and reconciliation.

In a similar fashion, an Okinawan involved with the intercultural exchanges between Ainu and Okinawans at the North-South Memorial, Aniya Masaki, wrote that Okinawans had forgotten that they were not just victims but were victimizers during the war. He referred to the Korean soldiers and comfort women who had suffered during the Battle of Okinawa.[79] Forced laborers from Korea had also died during the battle.[80]

Shitaku Toyojirō, Teshi's friend and ally in cultural preservation and tourism at Lake Akan, took care of Teshi in his later years. In an interview in 2005, Shitaku reiterated the connection between Ainu and Okinawans, saying that they resembled each other in appearance and in the way they

76.   Yamamoto, "Ainuzoku wo hokoru," 18.

77.   *Nihon keizai shinbun*, June 27, 2005.

78.   Hokkaido Broadcasting Channel (HBC), June 23, 1993, also mentioned in Hirano, "Okinawasen," 536. Thank you to Nambu Hajime at HBC, who assisted me in viewing the program featuring Teshi.

79.   Aniya, "Okinawasen wo kataritsugu," 45.

80.   Ryūkyū shinpō (ed.), *Descent into Hell*, 432–33.

thought and their religious beliefs.[81] In the postwar period the Ainu found it advantageous to ally themselves with other indigenous groups, such as the Okinawans. In contrast to the Meiji period, when an association with other ethnoracial groups was seen as potentially detrimental to one's status, now Japan's former colonial subjects sought such connections as a way to strengthen their standing vis-à-vis the Japanese state.

Conclusion

Tellingly, in the postwar period some Ainu saw the advent of the US occupation as an opportunity to lobby for more land and equal rights, an indication that they did not view Japanization as the only way to live their lives as Ainu-Japanese nationals. Although that effort failed, it showed the continued resilience of the Ainu in their struggle to rectify the consequences of Japanese colonization. The fact that it was not until 1996 that they were able to repeal the 1899 Hokkaido Former Natives Protection Act, something that Yamamoto had been pushing for since the end of the war, speaks to the drawn-out nature of the Ainu fight for recognition within the Japanese state. The Japanese government finally recognized the Ainu as an indigenous people in 2008.[82] Yamamoto's and Teshi's efforts to preserve and transmit Ainu culture and traditions, and their constant reiteration of the distinctiveness of Ainu culture, can be directly linked to this outcome.

The Ainu people discussed in these chapters illustrate how colonial subjects can contest colonial boundaries not just breaking them down but by choosing how they want to reinstate them. By reaffirming the ethnoracial and cultural distinctions that set them apart from the Japanese, people like the Ainu have found a way to regenerate their culture and reassert its value.

One of the main arguments of this book is that Japan's approach to empire involved dividing colonial subjects based on ethnoracial differences, in contrast to studies that have characterized Japan's empire as a

81. *Nihon keizai shinbun*, June 21, 2005.
82. Lewallen, "Indigenous at Last!"

case of Asians colonizing Asians, with race a nonfactor.[83] Ethnoracial differences were used and mobilized by both colonized and colonizer, for different and varying reasons, all invariably connected to power. Although some colonial subjects saw assimilation as a potential path to take, the hyperracialization of colonial subjects worked to ensure assimilation was not possible. Not all of the emphasis on ethnoracial difference was negative, and some of Japan's subjects used these differences as the basis from which they could protest against the Japanese. Ironically with regard to the Ainu today, ethnoracial difference—or the lack thereof—has become the latest factor used by some ethnographers and critics to argue that the Ainu have ceased to exist because they lack the visible, clear ethnoracial features their ancestors once had. The muting of these distinctions is the ammunition now being used to delegitimize their position as an indigenous group. But by allying with other recognized indigenous groups around the world and continuing their own cultural traditions, the Ainu have been able to sustain their position despite the challenges that remain.

83. Peattie, "Introduction," 7.

CONCLUSION

Colonial remnants are fragmented, scattered, and disparate. What can be collected is reconstructed, destroyed, and cast anew. Many presume that there is little point in writing histories of colonial subjects because their histories are unknowable or always told from the viewpoint of those who ruled them. Or that their stories do not need to be told because they all tell the same story—a tale of oppression. Admittedly, there are huge challenges to writing colonial histories, and not all stories of the colonized can be told. But a few can.

The colonized individuals in Japan's empire whose history can be told were primarily the subalterns on which the empire was run. In focusing on three sites of colonial experience—ethnographic human displays, the tours to the metropolis program, and Ainu tourist villages—we have seen that such ventures did not involve nameless or randomly chosen people. For example, those who participated in the human displays in Japan and at international expositions in London and St. Louis were often affluent and elite members of their ethnoracial groups. Some who can be traced in the colonial records were men and women of influence and power in their communities. Although those who had such influence were the people Japanese officials gravitated toward, describing them as collaborators does an injustice to the variety of motivations and influences that affected their interactions with the Japanese and their own communities. In some cases, advancing their local community's best interests conflicted with the interests of the empire. At other times, cooperating with Japanese authorities did not necessarily mean the interests of the local community were disadvantaged.

Some of the colonial people included in this book had considerably less power than others. On one end of the spectrum, the glimpses of the Okinawan women in the first Human Pavilion in Japan illustrate the essential invisibility of the pure subaltern. Their brief statements to the press and, after their return to Okinawa, rumors of a house being constructed and a suicide are the only hints to their fates. The very murkiness that envelops them illustrates that even if some subalterns can access a line of social mobility, they can just as easily lose it. The stories of the Palauans Oikang Sebastian Kōichi and Augusta Ramarui show how the Japanese sought to cultivate an elite youth core that would facilitate rule in the islands through their ability to acquire Japanese language skills. Although they did not have the stature of an individual like Fushine Kōzō, who spoke impressively on behalf of the Ainu, they were an important part of the infrastructure of empire and illustrate Japan's reliance on a wide spectrum of colonial subjects. Japanese colonial administrators also worked with indigenous people like the Bunun brothers Aliman Siken and Dahu Ali, for example. While the brothers' past actions taken against the Japanese police in Taiwan would appear to be the perfect reason to punish them as savages, in fact the Japanese colonial government did its utmost to "domesticate" them and get them to publicly submit to Japanese rule—although in doing so, they also exposed the colonial officials' relatively weak position.

The location and movement of colonial subjects affected their relationship to the empire; their position was constantly in flux as they traveled from the colony to metropole. Ngiraked was much beloved in the Japanese metropolis, in contrast to his final years in Palau, when hints of his increasing isolation appear. Teshi Toyoji and Yamamoto Tasuke, who fought for Japan in the Asia-Pacific War (in Okinawa and Truk, respectively), were changed by their experiences of war and further emboldened to identify as people distinct from the Japanese in the context of the Ainu tourist villages.

One of my main goals with this book was to bring into relief the colonial context in which Japan's subjects were living, as well as their motivations, influences, and actions. The variegated terrain of the three colonial sites of this book show, through the lived experiences of individuals in those sites, a world in which things were not clear-cut in terms of how power was wielded. The shape of power was distinct in each locale, and some of the operators of empire were colonial subjects. Other people's stories illustrate how the Japanese were often at the mercy of those they ruled. Despite Japanese attempts to perpetuate notions of a perfectly run empire, neither the operators of the imperial infrastructure nor the people they ruled conform to that rhetoric.

The process of writing colonial histories for this book demonstrated that relying on only one set of documents or materials—those labeled as perpetuating the colonizer's perspective or those from the perspective of indigenous people—can result in a skewed history. For example, take the process of discovery regarding Yayutz Bleyh. I started researching her when I saw her name mentioned several times in a Japanese newspaper. Among the copious material I turned up, however, it was her grandson's photograph of her, seated among the Japanese policemen, that was the greatest indicator of the level of power she had. Yet this photograph was never reproduced in colonial documents or records. It was only by considering this image along with the oral stories told by the Atayal and the colonial records that it became clear that the Japanese had relied on Yayutz to mediate in local communities to a high degree, more than simply by working as a teacher or a translator for tour groups. There is a simple explanation for why the Japanese would not want to reveal how much responsibility Yayutz actually had: by acknowledging the extent of her power, they would be revealing their own limitations.

The relationships between colonized and colonizer are so intertwined, as Albert Memmi wrote, that you cannot understand one without examining the other. The same is true with the writing of colonial history. Jean-Paul Sartre, in his introduction to Memmi's *The Colonizer and Colonized* (1965), described this interdependency as "a relentless reciprocity [that] binds the colonizer to the colonized—his product and his fate."[1] Liam O'Dowd, in the book's revised introduction ten years later, further elaborated on Sartre's idea of "relentless reciprocity," writing that Memmi's "colonizer and colonized are linked together in a reciprocal but mutually destructive relationship within which the identity of each is forged, and once forged, is frozen."[2] The research I conducted for this

1. Sartre, "Introduction," 24.
2. O'Dowd, "New Introduction," 40.

book showed me how Sartre and O'Dowd's characterization of relations between the colonizer and colonized operated as a never-ending process of destruction and reconstruction. Writing colonial histories using only one perspective cannot capture the relentless reciprocity that in reality binds colonizer and colonized together. These connections are inherent in the colonial archive as well as in the visual, oral, and material objects found beyond it.

The process of writing the colonial histories herein involved locating names in the colonial archive and seeking documents and records of that person in official colonial documents and popular culture and mass-media sources.[3] After starting with traces in the colonial archive, I tracked down oral history, images, documents, and material objects from indigenous sources that either corroborated or stood in contrast to the version of events in the colonial archive. Of course, the two realms are not equal. One could argue that the material coming from those who have been colonized is sparser, with evidence that traditional histories leave out. One could also argue that the colonial archive is tainted by a version of events that suits the imperial project. Writing histories of colonial subjects means accounting for the weaknesses on both sides and then forging ahead. There are no perfect histories waiting to be reconstructed on either side, but trying to excavate some of those presumed to be lost to history can bring us closer to understanding how vibrant and dynamic their presence really was during times of imperial rule. The Japanese did not interact with faceless, interchangeable representatives of ethnoracial groups. They relied on, pursued, cajoled, and in some cases hoped to diminish the power of specific people. Those today who have been muted and moved into the background of grand colonial histories, or transformed into monolithic ethnotypes, back then were individuals who mattered greatly, not just to those around them but also to the Japanese, and they helped shape the trajectory of Japan's imperial project.

---

3. See Corbin, *A Life of an Unknown*, for another approach to how to write histories of the unknown.

Bibliography

Newspapers

Asahi shinbun (after 1945) (*AS*)
Daily News (London)
Grey River Argus
Hōchi
Hokkai taimuzu (*HT*)
Illustrated London News (*ILN*)
Karafuto nichi nichi shinbun (*KNNS*)
Kobe shinbun (*KS*)
Los Angeles Times
Mainichi (Yokohama) (*MY*)
Miyako
Nara shinbun
Nihon
Nihon keizai shinbun
Okinawa mainichi
Okinawa taimuzu
Osaka asahi (*OA*)
Osaka chōhō (*OC*)
Osaka mainichi (*OM*)
Otaru shinbun (*OS*)
Otautau Standard and Wallace County Chronicle (*OSWCC*)
Riban no tomo
Ryūkyū shinpō (*RS*)
Shin sekai asahi shinbun
St. Louis Post-Dispatch (*SLPD*)
St. Louis Republic (*SLR*)
Sydney Morning Herald
Tainichi gurafu

Taiwan nichi nichi shinpō (TNNS)
The Times (London)
Tokyo asahi (TA)
Tokyo nichi nichi shinbun (TNNSB)
West London Observer (WLO)
Yamato nippō
Yomiuri

Books and Journals

Abe, Goh. "An Ethnohistory of Palau under the Japanese Colonial Administration." PhD diss., University of Kansas, 1985.

Ainu Bunka Shinkō Kenkyū Suishin Kikō (ed.). *Umi wo watatta Ainu no kōgei: eikokujin ishi Manrō no korekushon kara.* Sapporo: Ainu Bunka Shinkō Kenkyū Suishin Kikō, 2002.

Ainu Minzoku Hakubutsukan (ed.). *Nishihira Ume to tonkori.* Shiraoi: Ainu Minzoku Hakubutsukan, 2005.

"Ainu mura no daihanjō." *Taiyō* (Nichiei daihakurankai rinji zōkan 6) 16, no. 9 (1910).

Ainu no bi–kamui to sōzō suru sekai–. Sapporo: Zaidan Hōjin Ainu Bunka Shinkō Kenkyū Suishin Kikō, 2009.

Akan Kankō Kyōkai. *Marimo matsuri go jū shūnen kinen shashinshū.* Akan: Akan Kankō Kyōkai, 2000.

Anderson, Clare. *Subaltern Lives: Biographies of Colonialism in the Indian Ocean World, 1790–1920.* Cambridge: Cambridge University Press, 2012.

Aniya Masaaki. "Okinawasen wo kataritsugu Ainu minzoku to Maehira buraku jūmin no kōryū." *Tsubute,* no. 51 (2006): 40–47.

Annual Report to the League of Nations on the Administration of the South Sea Islands under Japanese Mandate. Tokyo: Nan'yōchō, 1925.

———. Tokyo: Nan'yōchō, 1926.

———. Tokyo: Nan'yōchō, 1935.

———. Tokyo: Nan'yōchō, 1937.

———. Tokyo: Nan'yōchō, 1938.

Aoyagi Machiko. *Modekngei: A New Religion in Belau, Micronesia.* Tokyo: Shinsensha, 2002.

Arai Genjirō. *Ainu jinbutsuden.* Sapporo: Katō Yoshio, 1992.

Ashcroft, Bill, Gareth Griffiths, and Helen Tiffin (eds.). *Post-Colonial Studies: The Key Concepts.* London: Routledge, 2001.

Atkins, E. Taylor. "Colonial Modernity." In *Routledge Handbook of Modern Korean History,* ed. Michael Seth, 124–40. London: Routledge, 2016.

Ayabe Tsuneo. *Ushinawareru bunka ushinawareru aidentiti.* Tokyo: Akashi Shoten 2007.

Ballendorf, Dirk, William Peck, and G. G. Anderson. *An Oral History of the Japanese Schooling Experience of Chamorros at Saipan and in the Commonwealth of the Northern Mariana Islands.* Guam: Micronesian Area Research Center, 1986.

Bank, Ted, II. "The Ainu: Last Days of a Lost Tribe." *Best Articles and Stories* 5 (1961): 49–53.

Barclay, Paul. "Cultural Brokerage and Interethnic Marriage in Colonial Taiwan: Japanese Subalterns and Their Aborigine Wives, 1895–1930." *Journal of Asian Studies* 64, no. 2 (2005): 323–60.

———. *Outcasts of Empire: Japan's Rule on Taiwan's "Savage Border," 1874–1945*. Berkeley: University of California Press, 2018.

———. "Playing the Race Card in Japanese Governed Taiwan, or: Anthropometric Photographs as 'Shape-Shifting Jokers.'" In *The Affect of Difference: Representations of Race in East Asian Empire*, ed. Christopher Hanscom and Dennis Washburn, 38–80. Honolulu: University of Hawaii Press, 2016.

Barthes, Roland. *Camera Lucida: Reflections on Photography*, trans. Richard Howard. New York: Hill and Wang, 1981.

Baskett, Michael. *The Attractive Empire: Transnational Film Culture in Imperial Japan*. Honolulu: University of Hawaii Press, 2008.

Berg, Shelly C. "Sada Yacco in London and Paris, 1900: La Rêve Réalisé." *Dance Chronicle* 18, no. 3 (1995): 343–405.

Bird, Isabella. *Unbeaten Tracks in Japan: An Account of Travels in the Interior, Including Visits to the Aborigines of Yezo and the Shrines of Nikkō and Ise*. London: John Murray, 1880.

Bleyh, Yayutz. "Bango kyōju to omoide no samazama." In *Taipei Daisan Kōtō Jōgakkō sōritsu man san jū nen kinenshi*, ed. Ono Masao, 437–39. Taipei: Taipei Dai San Kōtō Jōgakkō dōsōkai gakuyūkai, 1933.

Bogdan, Robert. *Freak Show: Presenting Human Oddities for Amusement and Profit*. Chicago: University of Chicago Press, 1988.

Brooks, Barbara. "Peopling the Japanese Empire: The Koreans in Manchuria and the Rhetoric of Inclusion." In *Japan's Competing Modernities: Issues in Culture and Democracy 1900–1930*, ed. Sharon Minichiello, 25–44. Honolulu: University of Hawaii Press, 1998.

Bruner, Frank. *The Hearing of Primitive Peoples: An Experimental Study of the Auditory Acuity and the Upper Limit of Hearing of Whites, Indians, Filipinos, Ainu and African Pigmies*. New York: Science Press, 1908.

Caprio, Mark. *Japanese Assimilation Policies in Colonial Korea 1910–1945*. Seattle: University of Washington Press, 2009.

Carlson, Lew. "Giant Patagonians and Hairy Ainu: Anthropology Days at the 1904 St. Louis Olympics." *Journal of American Culture* 12, no. 13 (1989): 19–26.

Chan Su-chuan. "From Autonomy to Subjugation: Taiwan Aboriginal Struggles during the Japanese Colonial Era." In *Taiwan lishi de jing yu chuang* (The mirror and the window of Taiwan history), ed. Dai Baocun, 98–105. Taibei: Guo jia zhan wang wen jiao ji jin hui, 2002.

Chang Wei-Chi, Ueda Akira, and Miyazaki Kiyoshi. "Nihon tōchi jidai ni okeru Taiwan no genjūmin kankō no keisei." *Sōgō kankō gakkaishi sōgō kankō kenkyu*, no. 2 (November 2003): 47–55.

"A Chat with Dr. Munro about the Ainu." *New East* 3, no. 5 (1918): 454–58.

Chen, Edward I-te. "The Attempt to Integrate the Empire: Legal Perspectives." In *The Japanese Colonial Empire, 1895–1945*, ed. Ramon H. Myers and Mark Peattie, 240–74. Princeton, NJ: Princeton University Press, 1984.

Chen, T. H. "Growing Rivalry of Italy and Japan." *China Weekly Review* 69 (1934): 68.

Cheung, Sidney. "Rethinking Ainu Heritage: A Case Study of an Ainu Settlement in Hokkaido, Japan." *International Journal of Heritage Studies* 11, no. 3 (July 2005): 197–210.

"Chief of Subon Village." *Taiwan shashinchō* 1, no. 7 (1915).

Chikamori Kiyomi. "Ainu bunka to watashi—sofu Pete Gorō no ashiato wo tadotte–." *Sapporo kaijō*, July 28, 2007.

Ching, Leo. *Becoming "Japanese": Colonial Taiwan and the Politics of Identity Formation.* Berkeley: University of California Press, 2001.

Chou, Wan-yao. "The Kominka Movement in Taiwan and Korea: Comparisons and Interpretations." In *The Japanese Wartime Empire, 1931–1945*, ed. Peter Duus, Ramon H. Myers, and Mark R. Peattie, 40–70. Princeton, NJ: Princeton University Press, 1996.

Christy, Alan. "The Making of Imperial Subjects in Okinawa." *positions: east asia cultures critique* 1, no. 3 (1993): 607–39.

Clark, Sydney. *All the Best in Japan and the Orient Including Hong Kong, Macao, Taiwan, Thailand and the Philippines.* New York: Dodd, Mead, 1958.

Clarke, J. Calvitt, III. "Marriage Alliance: The Union of Two Imperiums: Japan and Ethiopia," *Selected Annual Proceedings of the Florida Conference of Historians* 7 (December 1999): 105–16.

Claypool, Lisa. "Sites of Visual Modernity: Perceptions of Japanese Exhibitions in Late Qing China." In *The Role of Japan in Modern Chinese Art*, ed. Josh Fogel, 154–80. Berkeley: University of California Press, 2012.

Corbey, Raymond. "Ethnographic Showcases, 1870–1930." *Cultural Anthropology* 8, no. 3 (1993): 338–69.

Corbin, Alain. *A Life of an Unknown: The Rediscovered World of a Clog Maker in Nineteenth-Century France.* New York: Columbia University Press, 2001.

Cortazzi, Hugh. "Overview: Organization, Aims, and Results of the Exhibition." In *Commerce and Culture at the 1910 Japan-British Exhibition: Centenary Perspectives*, ed. Ayako Hotta-Lister and Ian Nish, 17–25. Leiden: Brill, 2012.

Crawcour, Sydney. "Kōgyō iken: Maeda Masana and His View of Meiji Economic Development." *Journal of Japanese Studies* 23, no. 1 (1997): 69–104.

Daigokai naikoku kangyō hakurankai jōnai annai shōka. Osaka: Nakamura Torakichi, 1903.

Deng Xiangyang, Shimomura Sakujirō, and Uozumi Etsuko. *Kōnichi Musha jiken wo meguru hitobito.* Osaka: Nihon Kikanshi Shuppan Sentā, 2001.

Deriha Kōji. "Furederikku Sutā ga 'eranda?' Ainu shiryō Sento Ruisu bankoku hakurankai sono ato." *Hokkaido Kaitaku Kinenkan kenkyū kiyō*, no. 37 (2009): 95–114.

———. "Sento Ruisu bankoku hakurankai 'tenji' sareta Ainu ifuku ni tsuite." *Hokkaido Kaitaku Kinenkan kenkyū kiyō*, no. 35 (2007): 25–42.

———. "Shashin ni nokosareta Ainu shiryō Sento Ruisu bankoku hakurankai ni sankashita Ainu no hitobito to sono dōgu." *Hokkaido Kaitaku Kinenkan kenkyū kiyō*, no. 34 (2006): 41–56.

Di Salvatore, Bryan. "Hokkaido: The Narrow Road to the Deep North." *Islands* (May–June 1985): 42–59.

Doak, Kevin. "What Is a Nation and Who Belongs? National Narratives and the Ethnic Imagination in Twentieth-Century Japan." *American Histoical Review* 102, no. 2 (April 1997): 283–309.

Driscoll, Mark. *Absolute Erotic, Absolute Grotesque: The Living, Dead, and Undead in Japan's Imperialism, 1895–1945*. Durham, NC: Duke University Press, 2010.

Duara, Prasenjit. "The New Imperialism and the Post-Colonial Developmental State: Manchukuo in Comparative Perspective." *Asia-Pacific Journal* 4, no. 1 (January 4, 2006).

Durbach, Nadia. *Spectacle of Deformity: Freak Shows and Modern British Culture*. Berkeley: University of California Press, 2010.

Dvorak, Greg. "Seeds from Afar, Flowers from the Reef: Re-Membering the Coral and Concrete of Kwajalein Atoll." PhD diss., Australia National University, 2007.

Ehagaki ni miru Okinawa Meiji Taishō Shōwa. Naha: Ryūkyū shinpōsha, 1993.

Ekashi to Fuchi Henshū Iinkai (ed.). *Ekashi to fuchi*, vol. 1, *Kita no shima ni ikita hitobito no kiroku*. Sapporo: Sapporo Terebi Hōsō Kabushiki Kaisha, 1983.

———. *Ekashi to fuchi*, vol. 2, *Shiryōhen bunken jō no ekashi to fuchi*. Sapporo: Sapporo Terebi Hōsō Kabushiki Kaisha, 1983.

Elwes, Henry John. *Memoirs of Travel, Sport, and Natural History*. London: Ernest Benn, 1930.

Endō Hiroya. *Taiwan banzoku shashinchō*. Taipei: Endō Hiroya, 1912.

Engei no tomo 3, no. 7 (Tokyo kangyō hakurankai rinji zōkan) (1907).

Everett, Marshall. "Mysterious Little Japanese Primitives." In *The Book of the Fair: The Greatest Exposition the World Has Ever Seen Photographed and Explained, a Panorama of the St. Louis Exposition*, 385–94. Philadelphia: Ziegler, 1904.

Fernsebner, Susan. "Expo 2010: A Historical Perspective." *Journal of Asian Studies* 69, no. 3 (2010): 669–76.

Fowler, Don, and Nancy Parezo. *Anthropology Goes to the Fair: The 1904 Louisiana Purchase Exposition*. Lincoln: University of Nebraska Press, 2007.

Fraleigh, Matthew. "Transplanting the Flower of Civilization: The 'Peony Girl' and Japan's 1874 Expedition to Taiwan." *International Journal of Asian Studies* 9, no. 2 (2012): 177–209.

Frey, Christopher. "Ainu Schools and Education Policy in Nineteenth-Century Hokkaido." PhD diss., Indiana University, 2007.

Frühstück, Sabine. *Colonizing Sex: Sexology and Social Control in Modern Japan*. Berkeley: University of California Press, 2004.

Fujimoto Yū. "Kitamura Nobuaki to Atem Eraketsu no yūjō." In Kida Takafumi et al., *"Nara ima wa mukashi" ten: Kōki no hito Kitamura Nobuaki no sekai Nara Daigaku Hakubutsukan kikakuten*, 11–12. Nara: Nara Daigaku Hakubutsukan, 2016.

Fujin gahō 70. Tokyo: Fujin gahōsha, June 1, 1912.

Fujisaki Seinosuke. *Taiwan no banzoku*. Tokyo: Kokushi Kankōkai, 1931.

Fujitani, Takashi. *Race for Empire: Koreans as Japanese and Japanese as Americans during World War II*. Berkeley: University of California Press, 2011.

———. *Splendid Monarchy: Power and Pageantry in Modern Japan*. Berkeley: University of California Press, 1996.

Fushine Kōzō. "Ainu seikatsu no hensen." In *Keimeikai daijūhachi kōenshū*, ed. Kasamori Tadashige, 52–72. Tokyo: Keimeikai Jimukyoku, 1926.

Gen Ansei. *Nihon ryūgaku seishinshi: Kindai Chūgoku chishikijin no kiseki*. Tokyo: Iwanami Shoten, 1991.

GHQ SCAP. "Biographical Sketch of the Ainu Chieftain Who Visited GHQ 23 October 1947." MacArthur Archives, October 24, 1947.

Gibbs, Philip. *Crowded Company*. London: Wingate, 1949.

———. *England Speaks*. Garden City, NY: Doubleday, Doran, 1935.

"Giriya-ku to Ainu no raiten." *Mitsukoshi* 2, no. 12 (1912): 17.

Gōnai Mitsuru and Wakabayashi Masaru. *Ashita ni mukatte: Ainu no hitobito wa uttaeru*. Tokyo: Maki Shoten, 1972.

Gotō, Ken'ichi. "Cooperation, Submission, and Resistance of Indigenous elites of Southeast Asia in the Wartime Empire." In *The Japanese Wartime Empire, 1931–1945*, ed. Peter Duus, Ramon H. Myers, and Mark R. Peattie, 274–301. Princeton, NJ: Princeton University Press, 1996.

"The Hairy Ainus: Japan's Aborigines Are Strange Relics of Primitive Man." *Life*, June 10, 1946.

Hamada Hiroshi. "Nibutani no ekashi Meiji 43 nen Rondon he iku." In *Kita no shima ni ikita hitobito no kiroku*, vol. 1, ed. Ekashi to Fuchi Henshū Iinkai, 334–42. Sapporo: Sapporo Terebi Hōsō Kabushiki Kaisha, 1983.

———. "Nibutani no ekashi Meiji 43 nen Rondon he iku." In *Ekashi to fuchi wo tazunete*, ed. Kawakami Yūji, 163–72. Tokyo: Suzusawa Shoten, 1991.

Hämäläinen, Pekka. *The Comanche Empire*. New Haven, CT: Yale University Press, 2008.

Hanlon, David. *Making Micronesia: A Political Biography of Tosiwo Nakayama*. Honolulu: University of Hawaii Press, 2014.

Hanson, John. *The Official History of the Fair, St. Louis*. St. Louis: Monarch, 1904.

Hashimoto Susumu. "Nanboku no tō: Okinawasen de shinda Ainu heishi no kiroku." *Bunka hyōron*, no. 213 (1979): 184–201.

———. *Nanboku no tō Ainu heishi to Okinawa sen no monogatari*. Tokyo: Sōdo Bunka, 1981.

——— (ed). *Haha to ko de miru: Okinawa-sen to Ainu heishi*. Tokyo: Kusanone Shuppankai, 1994.

Hashine Naohiko. *Ware Ainu koko ni tatsu*. Tokyo: Shinsensha, 1974.

Heishi Susumu. "Ainu shibai." *Kabuki* 37 (1903): 52–54.

Henry, Todd. *Assimilating Seoul: Japanese Rule and the Politics of Public Space in Colonial Korea, 1910–1945*. Berkeley: University of California Press, 2014.

———. "Assimilation's Racializing Sensibilities: Colonized Koreans as *Yobos* and the '*Yobo*-ization' of Expatriate Japanese." *positions: east asia cultures critique* 21, no. 1 (2013): 11–49.

————. "Sanitizing Empire: Japanese Articulations of Korean Otherness and the Construction of Early Colonial Seoul, 1905–1919." *Journal of Asian Studies* 64, no. 3 (2005): 639–75.

Hezel, Francis X. *Strangers in Their Own Land: A Century of Colonial Rule in the Caroline and Marshall Islands.* Honolulu: University of Hawaii Press, 1995.

Hiery, Hermann. *The Neglected War: The German South Pacific and the Influence of World War I.* Honolulu: University of Hawaii Press, 1995.

Higashimura Takeshi. "'Kankō Ainu' ni miru wajin no Ainu minzoku sabetsu." *Kaihō shakaigaku kenkyū* 9 (1995): 65–85.

Higuchi Wakako. "Kankodan." *Islander*, May 31, 1987, 4–9.

————. *Micronesia under the Japanese Administration: Interviews with Former South Sea Bureau and Military Officials,* 2 vols. University of Guam, 1987.

Hijikata Hisakatsu. *Society and Life in Palau: Collective Works of Hijikata Hisakatsu,* ed. Endo Hisashi. Tokyo: Sasakawa Peace Foundation, 1983.

Hilger, M. Inez. "Japan's 'Sky People,' The Vanishing Ainu." *National Geographic* 131, no. 2 (February 1967): 268–96.

————. *Together with the Ainu: A Vanishing People.* Norman: University of Oklahoma Press, 1971.

Hilska, Vlasta. "In an Ainu Village on Hokkaido Island." *New Orient* 2, no. 2 (April 1961): 12–13.

Hirano Masami. "Okinawasen to Ainu minzoku Nanboku no tō no gakushū wo megutte." *Toshokan zasshi* 87, no. 8 (1993): 536–38.

Hirasawa Ryūichi. "Kojin kara mita Ainukan Ainu minzoku to shite no watashi kojin." FRPAC lectures, 2005, 99–102.

Hisaki Yukio. "Yamagata Ryōon no Ainu kyōiku katsudō." *Yokohama Kokuritsu Daigaku kyōiku kiyō* 20 (1980): 1–21.

Hiwasaki, Lisa. "Ethnic Tourism in Hokkaido and the Shaping of Ainu Identity." *Pacific Affairs* 73, no. 3 (2000): 393–412.

Hokkaido Kyōiku Kenkyūjo (ed.). *Hokkaido kyōikushi,* vol. 4. Ebetsu: Hokkaido Ritsu Kyōiku Kenkyūjo, 1998.

Hokkaido Shinbunsha Henshū (ed.). *Hokkaido daihyakka jiten.* Shitamaki. Sapporo: Hokkaido Shinbunsha, 1981.

Honda Katsuichi. *Hinkonnaru seishin B shū.* Tokyo: Yahiro Shunsuke, 1989.

Horiuchi Yasuhiko. "Kitamura Nobuaki no satsuei sutairu." In Kida Takafumi et al., *"Nara ima wa mukashi" ten: Kōki no hito Kitamura Nobuaki no sekai Nara Daigaku Hakubutsukan kikakuten,* 9. Nara: Nara Daigaku Hakubutsukan, 2016.

Hotta-Lister, Ayako. *The Japan-British Exhibition of 1910: Gateway to the Island Empire of the East.* Richmond, UK: Japan Library, 1999.

————. "Japan Seeks an Image as an Emerging Colonial Empire: The Japan-British Exhibition of 1910 in London." In *The 38th International Research Symposium Questioning Oriental Aesthetics and Thinking,* ed. Inaga Shigemi, 115–33. Kyoto: International Research Center for Japanese Studies, 2010.

Howell, David. "Ainu Ethnicity and the Boundaries of the Early Modern Japanese State." *Past and Present* 142, no. 1 (1994): 69–93.

———. *Geographies of Identity in Nineteenth-Century Japan.* Berkeley: University of California Press, 2005.

———. "Making 'Useful Citizens' of Ainu Subjects in Early Twentieth Century." *Journal of Asian Studies* 63, no. 1 (2004): 5–29.

Hu, Chia-yu. "Taiwanese Aboriginal Art and Artifacts: Entangled Images of Colonization and Modernization." In *Refracted Modernity: Visual Culture and Identity in Colonial Taiwan,* ed. Yuko Kikuchi, 193–216. Honolulu: University of Hawaii Press, 2007.

Hur, Hyunguju. "Staging Modern Statehood: World Exhibitions and the Rhetoric of Publishing in late Qing China, 1851–1910." PhD diss., University of Illinois at Urbana-Champaign, 2012.

I manåfyi, Who's Who in Chamorro History. Agaña, Guam: Political Status Education Coordinating Commission, 1995.

Iitaka Shingo. "Conflicting Discourses on Colonial Assimilation: A Palauan Cultural Tour to Japan, 1915." *Pacific Asia Inquiry* 2, no. 1 (2011): 85–102.

———. "Nihon tōchi shita Parao, Ogiwaru sonraku ni okeru Ginza dōri kensetsu wo meguru shokuminchi gensetsu oyobi o-raru hisutori- ni kansuru shōsatsu." *Ajia Afurika gengo bunka kenkyū* 77 (2009): 5–34.

Ikeda, Kyle. *Okinawan War Memory: Transgenerational Trauma and the War Fiction of Medoruma Shun.* London: Routledge, 2014.

Inagaki Yochitarō. "Genshi jinshu no kōi kōkan." *Kiristokyō shūhō,* June 8, 1904.

Inoue Inosuke and Uchimura Kanzō. *Seibanki.* Tokyo: Keiseisha Shoten, 1926.

Irimoto Takeshi. "Creation of the Marimo Festival: Ainu Identity and Ethnic Symbiosis." *Senri Ethnological Studies* 66 (2004): 11–40.

Ishida Masaharu. *Okinawajin no genronjin Ōta Chōfu: Sono aikyōshugi to nashonarizumu.* Tokyo: Sairyūsha, 2001.

Ishigami Masao. *Nihonjin yo wasurunakare: Nan'yōno tami to kōkoku kyōiku.* Tokyo: Ōtsuki Shoten, 1983.

Ishimaru Masakuni. "Police Officers in Aboriginal Administration: The Japanese Period of Taiwan." PhD diss., Taiwan Chengchi University [in Chinese], 2008.

James, Neill. *Petticoat Vagabond in Ainu Land and Up and Down Eastern Asia.* New York: Scribner's, 1942.

Japan British Exhibition, 1910 Official Guide. London: Bemrose and Sons, 1910.

Jidō hyakka jiten. Tokyo: Heibonsha, 1951.

Jinruigaku zasshi 29 (January 1913).

Jun'eki Taiwan Genjūmin Kenkyūkai (ed.). *Inō Kanori shozō Taiwan genjūmin shashinshū.* Taipei: Jun'eki Taiwan Genjūmin Hakubutsukan, 1999.

Kaizawa Tadashi. *Ainu waga jinsei.* Tokyo: Iwanami Shoten, 1993.

Kaizawa Tōzō. *Ainu no sakebi* (1931). Reprinted in *Kindai minshū no kiroku Ainu* 5, ed. Tanigawa Kenichi, 381–92. Tokyo: Shinjinbutsu Ōraisha, 1972.

Kang Peide. *Taiyazu Msbtunux de meili yu aichou: toujiao yu kuihui buluo Kbuta shixiqun jiazushi.* Nantoushi: Guoshiguan Taiwan wenxianguan, Xingzhengyuan yuanzhuminzu weiyuanhui, 2009.

"Kankō Ainu: Kaidō hyakunen no naka no kyozō." *Chūō kōron* 83, no. 973 (October 1968): 229–36.

Karlin, Jason. "The Gender of Nationalism: Competing Masculinities in Meiji Japan." *Journal of Japanese Studies* 28, no. 1 (2002): 41–77.

Kawamura Minato. *"Dai Tōa minzokugaku" no kyojitsu.* Tokyo: Kōdansha, 1996.

Kayano Shigeru. *Iyomante no hanaya zoku Ainu no ishibumi.* Tokyo: Asahi Shinbunsha, 2005.

———. *Our Land Was a Forest: An Ainu Memoir.* Boulder, CO: Westview Press, 1994.

Kerr, George. *Okinawa: The History of an Island People.* Boston: Tuttle, 2001.

Kindaichi Kyōsuke. *Ainu Life and Legends.* Tokyo: Board of Tourist Industry, Japanese Government Railways, 1941.

———. "Hokkaido Hidaka koku Nibutani kotan ni okeru kakei to pase onkami." In *Ainu minzoku no shūkyō to girei,* ed. Kubodera Ituhiko, 73–101. Tokyo: Sofukan, 2001.

———. *Watakushi no aruite kita michi.* Tokyo: Nihon Tosho Sentā, 1997.

———. *Yūkara no hitobito.* Tokyo: Heibonsha, 2004.

Kitahara Jirōta. "Nishihira Ume to tonkori." In *Nishihira Ume to tonkori,* ed. Ainu Minzoku Hakubutsukan, 26–38. Shiraoi: Ainu Minzoku Hakubutsukan, 2005.

Kitamura Nobuaki. *Eraketsukun no omoide: Rememoroj de S-Ro Ngiraked.* Nara: Mikuroneshia Minzokukai, 1954.

———. *Eraketsukun sōbetsu kinen bunshū.* Nara: Dōhōsha, 1933.

———. *Nan'yō Parao shotō no minzoku.* Osaka: Tōyō Minzoku Hakubutsukan, 1933.

———. *Nara ima wa mukashi.* Nara: Nara Shinbun Shuppan Sentāa, 1983.

———. "Paraotō minkan no ryōhō." *Tabi to densetsu* 8, no. 12 (1935): 87–88.

Kitaoka Masako. "Daigokai naikoku kangyō hakurankai to shinkoku ryūgakusei." In *Bunka jishō to shite no Chūgoku,* ed. Kansai Daigaku bungakubu Chūgokugo Chūgoku bungakuka, 205–36. Suita: Kansai Daigaku Shuppanbu, 2002.

Kleeman, Faye. *In Transit: The Formation of a Colonial East Asian Cultural Sphere.* Honolulu: University of Hawaii Press, 2014.

Koshiro, Yukiko. *Trans-Pacific Racisms and the U.S. Occupation of Japan.* New York: Columbia University Press, 1999.

Kwon Hyeokhui. "An Analysis of Korean Intellectual Responses to the Exhibition of Koreans at Japanese Expositions: Nationalism and the Discourse on Northeast Asian Solidarity at the Turn of the Century." *Sungkyun Journal of East Asian Studies* 17, no. 1 (April 2017): 19–40.

———. "A Study on 'Korean Displays' in Industrial Exhibitions of Japan: Focus on the Fifth National Industrial Exhibition (1903) and Tokyo Industrial Exhibition (1907)." MA thesis, Seoul National University [in Korean], 2006.

Landry, Donna, and Gerald MacLean. "Subaltern Talk: Interview with the Editors (29 October 1993)." In *The Spivak Reader: Selected Works of Gayatri Chakravorty Spivak,* ed. Donna Landry and Gerald MacLean, 287–308. London: Routledge, 1996.

Leibowitz, Arnold. *Embattled Island: Palau's Struggle for Independence.* Westport, CT: Praeger, 1996.

Lewallen, Ann-Elise. "'Hands that Never Rest': Ainu Women, Cultural Revival, and Indigenous Politics in Japan." PhD diss., University of Michigan, 2006.

———. "Indigenous at Last! Ainu Grassroots Organizing and the Indigenous Peoples Summit in Ainu Mosir." *Asia Pacific Journal: Japan Focus* 6, no. 11 (November 1, 2008).

Lorde, Audre. "The Master's Tools Will Never Dismantle the Master's House." In *Sister Outsider: Essays and Speeches*, 110–14. Berkeley: Crossing Press, 2007.

Maeda Yūgure. "Fushiko Ainu kotan no dojin gakkō wo otonau." In *Kōjitsu kikō*, ed. Yanokura Shoten, 126–33. Tokyo: Yanokura Shoten, 1938.

Majewicz, Alfred (ed.). *The Collected Works of Bronisław Piłsudski*, vol. 3, *Materials for the Study of the Ainu Language and Folklore 2*. Berlin: Mouton de Gruyter, 1998.

Martin, Steven. "Ethnohistorical Perspectives of the Bunun: A Case Study of Laipunuk, Taiwan." MA thesis, National Chengchi University, 2006.

Mason, Michele. "Manly Narratives: Writing Hokkaido into the Political and Cultural Landscape of Imperial Japan." PhD diss., University of California, Irvine, 2005.

Mathur, Saloni. *India by Design: Colonial History and Cultural Display*. Berkeley: University of California Press, 2007.

Matsuda Hiroko. "Becoming Japanese in the Colony: Okinawan Migrants in Colonial Taiwan." *Cultural Studies* 26, no. 5 (2012): 688–709.

———. "Moving Out from the 'Margin': Imperialism and Migrations from Japan, the Ryūkyū Islands and Taiwan." *Asian Studies Review* 32 (December 2008): 511–31.

Matsuda Kyōko. "'Naichi kankō to iu tōchi kihō: 1897 nen no Taiwan genjūmin no 'naichi' kankō wo megutte." *Akademia jinbun shinzen kagakuhen: Nanzan Daigaku kiyō*, no. 5 (2013): 85–103.

———. *Teikoku no shisen: Hakurankai to ibunka hyōshō*. Tokyo: Yoshikawa Kōbunkan, 2003.

Matsumura Akira. "Contributions to the Ethnography of Micronesia." *Journal of the College of Science, Imperial University of Tokyo* 40 (1918): 1–174.

———. "Osaka Jinruikan." *Jinruigaku zasshi* 18, no. 205 (April 1903): 289–92.

———. "Taishō hakurankai ni okeru shojinshu." *Jinruigaku zasshi* (1914): 26–29.

Matsumura, Wendy. *The Limits of Okinawa: Japanese Capitalism, Living Labor, and Theorizations of Community*. Durham, NC: Duke University Press, 2015.

Matsuoka Tadasu. "Gendai Taiwan genjūmin shakairon shotan tōmoku" wo tegakari to shite." *Taiwan genjūmin kenkyū* 8 (2004): 74–93.

McDonald, Kate. *Placing Empire: Travel and the Social Imagination in Imperial Japan*. Berkeley: University of California Press, 2017.

Micronesian Area Research Center (MARC). *An Oral Historiography of the Japanese Administration in Palau*. University of Guam, 1986.

Mita Maki. "Palauan Children under Japanese Rule: Their Oral Histories." *Senri Ethnological Reports* 87 (2009).

Mitsuishi Ayumi. "Eraketsu Atem, Kitamura Nobuaki no Parao." In *Dai 31 kai chirigakuka kaigai kenshū puroguramu "gaikoku kenkyū kaigai kenshū," Parao hōkokusho*, ed. Fujimoto Yū, 27–31. Nara: Nara Daigaku bungakubu chirigakuka, 2017).

Mitsuoka Shin'ichi. *Ainu no sokuseki*, 8th ed. Shiraoi: Ainu Minzoku Hakubutsukan, 1991 [1924].

Miyamoto, Kazuo. *A Nisei Discovers Japan*. Tokyo: Japan Times Press, 1957.

Miyamura Kenya. "Hontō saigō no kijunban Raho Are no honkyo Tamaho wo saguru." *Taiwan sangaku*, no. 11 (August 1940): 129–58.

Miyatake Kimio. "Aija ni okeru hakurankai no kenkyū—1904 nen Sento Ruisu hakurankai ni okeru Ainu tenji to himoji shiryō–." Unpublished paper, University of Hokkaido, 2008.

———. "Hakurankai no kioku: 1904 nen Sento Ruisu hakurankai to Ainu." *Hokkaido Daigaku Bungaku Kenkyūkai kiyō*, no. 118 (2003): 45–93.

———. "Shikago Fui–rudo Hakubutsukan shozō no Ainu kōgeihin: 1904 nen Sento Ruisu hakurankai to futatsu no tekunpe." *Hōpō jinbun kenkyū*, no. 1 (2008): 41–54.

———. *Umi wo watatta Ainu: Senjūmin tenji to futatsu no hakurankai.* Tokyo: Iwan-ami Shoten, 2010.

Miyatake Seidō. *Nan'yō Paraotō no densetsu to minyō.* Nara: Tōyō Minzoku Hakubut-sukan, 1933.

———. "Waga Nan'yō Paraotō no shinwa." *Kyōdo fukei* 1, no. 10 (1932): 14–17.

Mizuno, Norihito. "Meiji Policies towards the Ryūkyūs and the Taiwanese Aboriginal Territories." *Modern Asian Studies* 43, no. 3 (2007): 683–739.

Mōri Yukitoshi. *Dong Taiwan zhanwang* [Higashi Taiwan tenbō], ed. and trans. Chen Azhao. Taipei: Yuanmin wenhua shiye youxian gongsi, 2003 [1933].

Moritake Takeichi. *Rera korachi: kaze no yō ni.* Shiraoi: Ezōya, 1977.

Morris, Rosalind. "Introduction." In *Can the Subaltern Speak?: Reflections on the History of the Idea*, ed. Rosalind Morris, 1–20. New York: Columbia University Press, 2010.

Morris-Suzuki, Tessa. "Heroes, Collaborators and Survivors: Korean Kamikaze Pilots and the Ghosts of War in Japan and Korea." In *East Asia beyond the History Wars: Confronting the Ghosts of Violence*, ed. Tessa Morris-Suzuki, Morris Low, Leonid Petrov, and Timothy Tsu, 164–90. New York: Routledge, 2013.

———. "Migrants, Subjects, Citizens: Comparative Perspectives on Nationality in the Prewar Japanese Empire." *Asia-Pacific Journal* 6, no. 8 (August 1, 2008).

———. "Tourists, Anthropologists and Visions of Indigenous Society in Japan." In *Beyond Ainu Studies: Changing Academic and Public Perspectives*, ed. Mark Hudson, Anne Elise Lewallen, and Mark Watson, 45–66. Honolulu: University of Hawaii Press, 2014.

Munro, Neil Gordon. *Ainu Creed and Cult.* New York: Columbia University Press, 1963.

Murakami Kyūkichi. *Ainu jinbutsuden.* Tokyo: Heibonsha, 1942.

"Naichi kankōdan." In *Kōgakkō hoshūka kokugo tokuhon*, 713–19. Tokyo: Nan'yō chō, 1937.

Nakamura Kazue. *Nagakubo Shūjirō no kenkyū.* Kushiro: Kushiro-shi, 1991.

Nakano Hideo. "Nanboku no tō wo megutte." In Abe Takeshi and Tamura Sadao, *Meijiki Nihon no hikari to kage*, 269–92. Tokyo: Dōseisha, 2008.

Nakano Takashi. "Bansha no Yajutsu Beriya." *Mirai* 7 (1981): 37–42.

———. "Taiyaruzoku no obasan." *Mirai* 6 (1981): 15–23.

Nakanome Satoru. *Karafuto no hanashi.* Tokyo: Sanseidō, 1917.

Nakata Chikao. "Jijitsu shosetsu Moriesu no shi." *Nan'yō guntō* 10, no. 11 (1935): 92–95, 81.

Nakayoshi Kikō. "Nanboku no tō to Teshi Toyojisan." *Tsubute*, no. 51 (2006): 25–26.

"Nanban no kyoseichi ni otsu." *Taiwan keisatsu kyōkai zasshi* 208 (1926).

Nanta, Arnaud. "Colonial Expositions and Ethnic Hierarchies in Modern Japan." In *Human Zoos: Science and Spectacle in the Age of Colonial Empires*, ed. Pascal Blanchard et al., 248–58. Liverpool: Liverpool University Press, 2008.

Nan'yō Guntō Kyōkai. *Nan'yō guntō Parao Nan'yō chōnai.* Tokyo: Nan'yō Kyōkai Nan'yō Guntō Shibu, 1935.

——— (ed). *Omoide no Nan'yō guntō.* Tokyo: Nan'yō Guntō Kyōkai, 1965.

"Nan'yō no chinkyaku." *Mitsukoshi* 8 (1917).

Narita Takeshi (ed.). *Taiwan seiban shuzoku shashinchō: fu riban jikkyō.* Taipei: Narita Shashin Seihanjo, 1912.

Narita Tokuhei et al. (eds.). *Kindaika no naka no Ainu sabetsu no kōzō.* Tokyo: Akashi Shoten, 1998.

"Native Dwellings at the St. Louis Exposition." *Scientific American* 91, no. 13 (1904): 218.

News from the Pacific Anthropological Society of Hawaii 19 (1968–1969): 1–39.

Nihon Koten Bungaku Daijiten Henshū Iinkai (ed.). *Nihon koten bungaku daijiten,* vol. 6. Tokyo: Iwanami Shoten, 1985.

Nish, Ian. "On the Commercial Periphery of the Japan-British Exhibition, 1910." In *Commerce and Culture at the 1910 Japan-British Exhibition: Centenary Perspectives,* ed. Ayako Hotta-Lister and Ian Nish, 51–67. Leiden: Brill, 2012.

Nishihara Renta. *Watashitachi no rekishi to fukuin rikai. Shu gomoto ni tachikaerasete kudasai.* Tokyo, 1995.

Noguchi Masaaki. *Paraotō yawa.* Tokyo: Kensetsusha Shuppanbu, 1941.

Noguchi Takashi. *Banchi hikō.* Tokyo: Shinkōasha, 1942.

Nojima Motoyasu. "Ogawa Naoyoshi no kenkyū." In *Taiwan genjūmin kenkyū gairan: Nihon kara no shiten,* ed. Nihon jūneki Taiwan Genjūmin Kenkyūkai, 49–53. Tokyo: Fūkyōsha, 2001.

Obata, Eri. "The Display of Taiwan's Aborigines in the Japan-British Exhibition of 1910 as a Showcase of Japan's Colonial Power." MA thesis, National Chengchi University, 2012.

O'Connor, Peter. "The Exhibition and the Media in the Springtime of Propaganda." In *Commerce and Culture at the 1910 Japan-British Exhibition: Centenary Perspectives,* ed. Ayako Hotta-Lister and Ian Nish, 89–101. Leiden: Brill, 2012.

O'Dowd, Liam. "New Introduction." In Albert Memmi, *The Colonizer and the Colonized,* trans. Howard Greenfeld, 29–66. London: Earthscan, 1990.

Office of Court Counsel, Supreme Court of the Republic of Palau. *The Quest for Harmony: A Pictorial History of Law and Justice in the Republic of Palau.* Palau: Office of Court Counsel, 1995.

Ogawa Masahito. "Ainu gakkō no secchi to 'Hokkaido kyūdojin hogohō,' 'kyūdojin jidō kyōiku kitei' no seiritsu." *Hokkaido Daigaku kyōiku gakubu kiyō* 55 (1991): 257–325.

———. "Hokkaido kyūdojin hogohō kyūdojin jidō kyōiku kitei shita no Ainu gakkō." *Hokkaido Daigaku kyōiku gakubu kiyō* 58 (1992): 197–266.

Oguma Eiji. *"Nihonjin" no kyōkai Okinawa, Ainu, Taiwan, Chōsen shokuminchi shihai kara fukki undō made.* Tokyo: Shin'yōsha, 1998.

Okinawaken Bunka Shinkōkai (ed.). *Kyū Nan'yō guntō to Okinawajin: Tenian (Okinawa kenshi bijuaru ban 9 kindai 2).* Okinawa: Okinawaken Kyōiku Iinkai, 2002.

"Okinawakenmin no bunka kōjō undō." *Nan'yō guntō* 1, no. 8 (September 1935): 74.

Okuda Iku. *Bununzokushi.* Unknown publisher, 1931.

Okurashō Insatsukyoku. *Shūgiin Gikai giji sokkiroku dai ichi nijūhachi kai.* Tokyo: Insatsukyoku, 1890–1912.

Omskaiā sensatsiiā : seriiā akvareleĭ Bëzana Khirasavy "Zhizn' i obychai aĭnov" iz sobraniiā Omskogo oblastnogo muzeiā izobrazitel'nykh uskusstv imeni M.A. Vrubeliā. Moscow: Izdatel'skaiā programma "Interrosa," 2008.

Ōsuga, Rueko. *Shiraoi Ainu no kenkyū 1. Miyamoto Ekashimatoku—tsuma Saki wo chushin ni.* Shiraoi: Shiraoi Tanoshiku Yasashii Ainugō Kyōshitsu, 2013.

Ōta Masahide. *The Battle of Okinawa: The Typhoon of Steel and Bombs.* Tokyo: Kume, 1984.

———. *Okinawa no minshū ishiki.* Tokyo: Kōbundō Shinsha, 1967.

"Paiwan woman in full dress." *Taiwan shashinchō* 1, no. 5 (1915).

Palalavi, Haisul. *Dafen jiken Bununzoku Daho Ari = (Dahu Ali) shubōsetsu no shinsō.* Unpublished paper, 2008.

Passin, Herbert. *Encounter with Japan.* Tokyo: Kōdansha, 1982.

Peattie, Mark. "Introduction." In *The Japanese Colonial Empire, 1895–1945,* ed. Ramon Myers and Mark R. Peattie, 3–60. Princeton, NJ: Princeton University Press, 1984.

———. *Nan'yō: The Rise and Fall of the Japanese in Micronesia, 1885–1945.* Honolulu: University of Hawaii Press, 1988.

Peng, Fred, and Peter Geiser (eds.). *The Ainu: The Past in the Present.* Hiroshima: Bunka Hyōron, 1977.

Phillips, Steven E. *Between Assimilation and Independence: The Taiwanese Encounter Nationalist China, 1945–1950.* Stanford, CA: Stanford University Press, 2003.

Piłsudski, Bronisław, and Jan Rozwadowski. *Materials for the Study of the Ainu Language and Folklore.* Krakow: Imperial Academy of Sciences, 1912.

Preston, Douglas. *Dinosaurs in the Attic: An Excursion into the American Museum of Natural History.* New York: St. Martin's Press, 1986.

Price, William. *Life of a Botanist.* October 1974. PRI/2/2.

———. Personal diary, 1912. PRI/1/1.

———. *Plant Collecting in Formosa.* Unpublished manuscript, August 16, 1961. PRI/2/1.

———. *Plant Collecting in Formosa.* Taipei: Chinese Forestry Association, 1982.

Proetz, Arthur. *I Remember You, St. Louis.* St. Louis: Zimmerman-Petty, 1963.

"The Racial Exhibit at the St. Louis Fair." *Scientific American* 91, no. 24 (1904): 412, 414.

Refsing, Kirsten. *Early European Writing on Ainu Culture: Travelogues and Descriptions,* vol. 1, 5. Richmond, UK: Curzon, 2000.

Robertson, Jennifer. *Takarazuka: Sexual Politics and Popular Culture in Modern Japan.* Berkeley: University of California Press, 1998.

Rousselot, Jean. "Phonétique d'un groupe d' los Aïnos." *Revue de Phonétique* 9 (1912): 5–49.

Ruoff, Kenneth. *Imperial Japan at its Zenith: The Wartime Celebration of the Empire's 2,600th Anniversary.* Ithaca, NY: Cornell University Press, 2010.

Rydell, Robert. *All the World's a Fair: Visions of Empire at American International Expositions, 1876–1916.* Chicago: University of Chicago Press, 1984.

Ryūkyū shinpō (ed.). *Descent into Hell: Civilian Memories of the Battle of Okinawa,* trans. Mark Ealey and Alastair McLauchlan. Portland, ME: Merwin Asia, 2014.

Saita Satoru. "Banjin kankō no enkaku to sono jisseki." *Riban no tomo* 3, no. 10 (1934): 3–5.

Saitō Reiko. "Hokkaido kankō annai no naka no Ainu bunka shōkai no hensen: Shōwaki no ryokō annai Hokkaido shōkai kiji no kōsatsu wo tōshite." *Shōwa Jōshi Daigaku kokusai bunka kenkyūsho kiyō* 6 (2000): 29–42.

———. "Hoppō minzoku bunka kenkyū ni okeru kankō jinruigakuteki shiten: Edo-Taishōki ni okeru Ainu no baai." *Hokkaido Ritsu Hoppō Minzoku Hakubutsukan kenkyū kiyō* 3 (1994): 139–60.

Sakamoto Hiroko. "Chūgoku minzokushugi no shinwa: shinkaron, jinshukan, hakurankai jiken." *Shisō*, no. 849 (1995): 61–84.

Salwey, Charlotte. "Japanese Monographs no. XIV: The Ainu, Past and Present." *Imperial and Asiatic Quarterly Review* 31 (1911): 315–31.

———. "Japanese Monographs no. XV: Formosa." *Imperial and Asiatic Quarterly Review* 32 (1911): 348–62.

Sand, Jordan. "Imperial Tokyo as a Contact Zone: The Metropolitiation Tours of Taiwanese Aborigines, 1897–1941." *Asia Pacific Journal* 12:10, no. 4 (March 3, 2014).

Sartre, Jean-Paul. "Introduction." In Albert Memmi, *The Colonizer and the Colonized*, trans. Howard Greenfeld, 17–26. London: Routledge, 2013.

Sasaki Toshikazu et al. (eds.). *Ainu no michi*. Tokyo: Yoshikawa Kobunkan, 2005.

Satō Chūetsu. *Nankyoku ni tatta Karafuto Ainu: Shirase Nankyoku tankentai hiwa*. Tokyo: Tōyō Shoten, 2004.

Satō Yūji. "Zakkan tenjisareta Ainu." *Aida* 46 (1999).

Sawa Sekita (ed.). *Hokkaido ryokō annai*. Hakodate: Kōbunsha, 1908.

Scholtz, Amelia. "'Almond-Eyed Artisans'/'Dishonoring the National Polity': The Japanese Village Exhibition in Victorian London." *Japanese Studies* 27, no. 1 (May 2007): 73–85.

Senju Hajime. "Gunseiki Nihon tōchi shita Nan'yō guntō ni okeru naichi kankōdan." PhD diss., Rikkyō Daigaku Daigakuin, 2006.

———. "Nihon tōchi shita Nan'yō guntō ni okeru naichi kankōdan no seiritsu." *Rekishi hyōron* 661 (2005): 52–68.

Senō Yasushi. *Bankai haishi junshoku hiwa*. Taipei: Senō Yasushi, 1935.

Sharpe, Jenny, and Gayatri Chakravorty Spivak. "A Conversation with Gayatri Chakravorty Spivak: Politics and the Imagination." *Signs: Journal of Women in Culture and Society* 28, no. 2 (2002): 609–24.

Shin'ya Gyō. *Ainu minzoku teikōshi: Ainu kyōwakoku he no taidō*. Tokyo: Kadokawa Shoten, 1974.

Shiraoi Chōshi Hensan Iinkai (ed.). *Shin Shiraoi chōshi*. Shita maki. Shiraoi: Shiraoichō Yakuba, 1992.

Shiraoi kotan: Kindai Shiraoi Ainu no ayumi. Kinoshita Seizō isaku shashinshū. Shiraoi: Shiraoi minzoku bunka denshō hozon zaidan and Ainu Minzoku Hakubutsukan, 1994.

"Shiri-zu Japan debū—Daiikkai Ajia no 'ittōku.'" NHK, April 5, 2009.

Shitaku Toyojirō. *Ainu oman = aynu ga yuku bunka shisetsudan Okinawa he* (Part 1). Akan: Shitaku Toyojirō, 2001.

A Short History of the Tenrikyō. Nara: Headquarters of Tenrikyō Church, 1956.

Shuster, Donald. "State Shinto in Micronesia during Japanese Rule 1941–1945." *Pacific Studies* 5, no. 2 (1982): 20–43.

Siddle, Richard. *Race, Resistance and the Ainu of Japan*. London: Routledge, 1996.

Sieroszewski, Waclaw. "Among Hairy People." In *The Collected Works of Bronisław Piłsudski, Materials for the Study of the Ainu Language and Folklore 2*, ed. Alfred Majewicz, 3:661–99. Berlin: Mouton de Gruyter, [1926] 1998.

Simon, Scott. "Formosa's First Nations and the Japanese: From Colonial Rule to Postcolonial Resistance." *Asia-Pacific Journal* 4 (January 4, 2006).

Sjoberg, Katarina. *The Return of the Ainu*. London: Routledge, 1993.

Smith, Linda Tuhiwai. *Decolonizing Methodologies: Research and Indigenous Peoples*. New York: Zed Books, 1999.

Smits, Gregory. "Jahana Noboru: Okinawan Activist and Scholar." In *The Human Tradition in Modern Japan*, ed. Ann Walthall, 99–113. Lanham, MD: SR Books, 2002.

Sodei, Rinjirō. *Dear General MacArthur: Letters from the Japanese during the American Occupation*, ed. John Junkerman, trans. Shizue Matsuda. Lantham, MD: Rowman & Littlefield, 2001.

Spickard, Paul. "Race and Nation, Identity and Power: Thinking Comparatively about Ethnic Systems." In *Race and Nation: Ethnic Systems in the Modern World*, ed. Paul Spickard, 1–32. London: Routledge, 2005.

Spivak, Gayatri. "Can the Subaltern Speak?" In *Marxism and the Interpretation of Culture*, ed. Cary Nelson and Lawrence Grossberg, 271–316. Chicago: University of Illinois Press, 1988.

———. "Can the Subaltern Speak? Revised Edition, from the 'History' chapter of Critique of Postcolonial Reason." In *Can the Subaltern Speak?: Reflections on the History of the Idea*, ed. Rosalind Morris, 21–78. New York: Columbia University Press, 2010.

———. *A Critique of Postcolonial Reason: Toward a History of the Vanishing Present*. Cambridge, MA: Harvard University Press, 1999.

———. "Extempore Response to Susan Abraham, Tat-siong Benny Liew, and Mayra Rivera." In *Planetary Loves: Spivak, Postcolonality, and Theology*, ed. Stephen Moore and Mayra Rivera, 136–46. New York: Fordham University Press, 2010.

———. "In Response: Looking Back, Looking Forward." In *Can the Subaltern Speak? : Reflections on the History of the Idea*, ed. Rosalind Morris, 227–36. New York: Columbia University Press, 2010.

Starr, Frederick. *The Ainu Group at the St. Louis Exposition*. Chicago: Open Court, 1904.

Stevens, Jean. "A Visit to Japan: Professor Starr Returns." *Japan: Overseas Travel* 16, no. 3 (1927): 36–37.

Stoler, Ann, and Frederick Cooper (eds.). *Tensions of Empire: Colonial Cultures in a Bourgeois World*. Berkeley: University of California Press, 1997.

Sudo, Naoto. *Nanyo Orientalism: Japanese Representations of the South Pacific*. New York: Cambria Press, 2010.

Sugano Tadashi. "Osaka hakurankai (1903) Chūgoku." *Narashigaku* 13 (1995): 124–47.

Sugawara Kōsuke. *Gendai no Ainu: Minzoku idō no roman*. Tokyo: Genbunsha, 1966.

Sunazawa Kura. *Watakushi no ichidai no hanashi: Ku sukuppu orushipe*. Tokyo: Fukutake Shoten, 1990.

Suzuki Akira. *Takasagozoku ni sasageru.* Tokyo: Chūō Kōronsha, 1976.

Suzuki Sakutarō. *Taiwan no banzoku kenkyū.* Taipei: Taiwan Shiseki Kankōkai, 1932.

Tachibana Bunshichi. *Hokkaidoshi jinmei jiten*, vol. 1. Sapporo: Hokkaido Bunka Shiryō Hozon Kyōkai, 1953.

Taiheiyō Kyōkai (ed.). *Nanpō he teshinsuru hitobito he: Nettai seikatsu hikkei.* Tokyo: Nihon Hyōronsha, 1944.

Taitano, Melissa. "Archives, Collective Memory: A Case Study of Guam and the Internment of Chamorros in Mañenggon during World War II." PhD diss., Univeristy of California, Los Angeles, 2007.

"Taiwan seiban no naichi kankō." *Jinruigaku zasshi* 28, no. 5 (1912): 299.

Taiwan Sōtokufu Banzoku Chōsakai banzoku chōsa hōkokusho 6, no. 3). Taipei: Taiwan Sōtokufu Banzoku Chōsakai, 1920.

Taiwan Sōtokufu Keimukyoku. *Riban shikō*, vols. 2–3. Taipei: Taiwan Sōtokufu Keimukyoku, [1921] 1989.

———. *Riban shikō*, vol. 4. Taipei: Taiwan Sōtokufu Keimukyoku, 1938.

———. *Takasagozoku no kyōiku.* Taipei: Taiwan Sōtokufu Keimukyoku, 1942.

Taiwan Sōtokufu Minseibu Keisatsu Honsho (ed.), *Taiwan sōtokufu keisatsu shokuinroku.* Taipei: Taiwan Sōtokufu Minseibu Keisatsu Honsho, 1912–1927.

Takakura Shin'ichirō. "Ryokushō ni kataru: Fushiko mura no kyūdojin Hotene-kun danwa kikigaki." *Hokkaido shakai jigyō* 51 (July 1936): 88–93.

Takamae, Eiji. *Inside GHQ: The Allied Occupaiton of Japan and Its Legacy*, trans. Robert Ricketts and Sebastian Swann. New York: Continuum, 2002.

Takeuchi Susumu. "Banjin no kankō ni tsuite." *Riban no tomo* 2, no. 4 (1933): 8–9.

Takezawa Shin'ichirō. "Yayutsusan wo omou." *Riban no tomo* 1, no. 4 (1932): 7.

Takushoku hakurankai kinen shashinchō. Tokyo: Meiji Kinenkai, 1912.

Tamura Suzuko. *Ainugo onsei shiryō senshū inbunhen.* Tokyo: Waseda Daigaku gogaku kyōiku kenkyūjo, 1993.

Tangiku Itsuji. "Aru Nivufuhito no senzen to sengo." *Wako Daigaku* gendai ningen gakubu kiyō 4 (March 2011): 129–143.

Tanigawa Kenichi (ed.). *Kindai minshū no kiroku* 5 Ainu. Tokyo: Shinjinbutsu Ōraisha, 1972.

Taro. "Takushoku hakurankai wo miru." *Yōnen sekai* 14 (December 1912).

Tierney, Robert. *Tropics of Savagery: The Culture of Japanese Empire in Comparative Frame.* Berkeley: University of California Press, 2010.

Toby, Ronald. *State and Diplomacy in Early Modern Japan: Asia in the Development of the Tokugawa Bakufu.* Stanford, CA: Stanford University Press, 1984.

"Tokyo kangyō hakurankai ekai." *Fuzoku gahō* 360 (1907).

Tomimura Jun'ichi. *Kōgun to Ainuhei: Okinawa sen ni kieta Ainuhei no shōgai.* Tokyo: JCA Shuppan, 1981.

Tominaga Jirō. *Hokkaido ryokō.* Tokyo: Akimoto Shobō, 1961.

Tomiyama Ichirō. "The 'Japanese' of Micronesia: Okinawans in the Nan'yō Islands." In *Okinawan Diaspora*, ed. Ronald Nakasone, 57–70. Honolulu: University of Hawaii Press, 2002.

Torii Ryūzō. *Aru rōgakuto no shuki; Kōkogaku to tomo ni rokujūnen.* Tokyo: Asahi Shinbunsha, 1953.

Trouillot, Michel-Rolph. *Silencing the Past: Power and the Production of History*. Boston: Beacon Press, 1995.

Tsuboi Shōgorō. *Jinruigaku kōwa*. Tokyo: Waseda Daigaku Shuppanbu, 1907.

———. "Meiji irai teikoku no hanto ni hairishi jinshu." *Shinkōron* (1908).

———. "Nihon zenjinshu no ōshirimochi to ōwarai." *Shōgakusei* 2, no. 9 (1912): 14–17.

Tsuboi Shōgorō and Kindaichi Kyōsuke. *Nihon kokunai shojinshu no gengo*. Tokyo: Tokyo Jinrui Gakkai, 1912.

Tsuda Nobuko. "A Personal Rebirth through Ainu Traditional Basketry." In *Ainu: Spirit of a Northern People*, ed. William Fitzhugh and Chisato Dubreuil, 309–12. Washington, DC: Arctic Studies Center, National Museum of Natural History, 1999.

Tsurumi, Patricia. *Japanese Colonial Education in Taiwan, 1895–1945*. Cambridge, MA: Harvard University Press, 1977.

Tsuzuki, Chushichi. "Conditions in Japan and Britain at the Time of the Exhibition." In *Commerce and Culture at the 1910 Japan-British Exhibition: Centenary Perspectives*, eds. Ayako Hotta-Lister and Ian Nish, 9–16. Leiden: Brill, 2012.

Turner, Victor. "Liminality and Communitas." In *The Ritual Process: Structure and Anti-Structure*, 94–113. New York: Aldine de Gruyter, 2011.

———. "Passages, Margins and Poverty: Religious Symbols of Communitas." In *Dramas, Fields and Metaphors: Symbolic Action in Human Society*, 231–71. Ithaca, NY: Cornell University Press, 1974.

Turull, Ricard Bru. "Eudald Serra i el poble ainu. L'estada a Hokkaido de 1947." *Locus Amoenus* 14 (2016): 199–214.

Uchida, Jun. *Brokers of Empire: Japanese Settler Colonialism in Korea, 1876–1945*. Cambridge, MA: Harvard University Asia Center, 2011.

Uchigasaki Sakusaburō. *Eikoku yori sokoku he*. Tokyo: Hokubunkan, 1911.

Uechi Miwa. "'Jinruikan' jiken no aramashi." In *Jinruikan: Fūinsareta tobira*, ed. Engeki 'Jinruikan' jōen wo jitsugen sasetai kai, 19–26. Osaka: Atto Wākasu, 2005.

Umeki Takaaki. *Ainu dendōsha no shōgai: Ega Torazō ikō*. Sapporo: Hokkaido Shuppan Kikaku Sentā, 1986.

"Using a Camera in Japan." *National Geographic* 40 (July 1921).

Uyeda, Kumiko. "The Journey of the Tonkori: A Multicultural Transmission." PhD diss., University of California, Santa Cruz, 2015.

Vanstone, James. "The Ainu Group at the Louisiana Purchase Exposition, 1904." *Arctic Anthropology* 30, no. 2 (1993): 77–91.

Vidich, Arthur. *Political Factionalism in Palau: Its Rise and Development*. Washington: Pacific Science Board, 1949.

———. *The Political Impact of Colonial Administration*. New York: Arno Press, 1980.

Wareham, Evelyn. "From Explorers to Evangelists: Archivists, Recordkeeping, and Remembering in the Pacific Islands." *Archival Science* 2 (2002): 187–207.

Weiner, Michael (ed.). *Japan's Minorities: The Illusion of Homogeneity*. London: Routledge, 1997.

Xu Rulin and Yang Nanjun. *Dafen Tamahe: Bunong kangri shuangchengji*. Taipei: Nantian, 2010.

Yamaguchi Mamoru (ed.). *Kōza Taiwan bungaku*. Tokyo: Kokusho Kankōkai, 2003.

Yamaji Katsuhiko. *Kindai Nihon no shokuminchi hakurankai*. Tokyo: Fūkyōsha, 2008.

———. "Nichiei hakurankai to ningen dōbutsuen." *Shakai gakubu kiyō* 108 (2009): 1–27.

———. "Shokuminchi Taiwan to 'kodomo' no rhetoric Musha no yabanjin to jinruigaku." *Shakai jinruigakau nenpō* 20 (1994): 63–87.

Yamamoto Tasuke. "Ainuzoku wo hokoru." In *Watashi no naka no rekishi 7*, ed. Hokkaido Shinbunsha, 8–32. Sapporo: Hokkaido Shinbunsha, 1987.

Yamamoto Yūko. "Nana ni nen mae no kizuna, ima mo nao—Aru koron no shōnen to Mishima shishaku." In Kurata Yōji Inamoto Hiroshi and Sudō Kenichi, *Parao kyōwakoku: kako to genzai soshite 21 seiki he*, 341–60. Nagasaki: Orijin Shobō, 2003.

Yamamuro Shin'ichi. "The Evolving Meiji State: Its Dual Character as a Nation-State and Colonial Empire." *Senri Ethnological Studies* 51 (2000): 9–24.

Yang Nanjun. *Maboroshi no jinruigakusha: Mori Ushinosuke*, trans. and ed. Kasahara Masaharu, Miyaoka Maoko, and Miyazaki Seiko. Tokyo: Fūkyōsha, 2005.

Yoshida Iwao. *Higashi Hokkaido Ainu koji fudoki shiryō dai yon hen (Aikyō soshi)*. Obihiroshi: Obihiro-shi Kyōiku Iinkai, 1958.

Yoshihisa Masuko. "Maboroshi no Ainu dokuritsuron wo ou: chōrō ni 'shikin' wo okutta GHQ no shini." *Asahi jānaru* 31, no. 10 (March 3, 1989): 87–90.

Yoshimi Shun'ya. *Hakurankai no seijigaku: manzashi no kindai*. Tokyo: Chūō Kōronsha, 1992.

Yuasa Hiroshi. *Segawa Kōkichi Taiwan yuanzhuminzu yingxiang zhi. Bunongzu pian*. Taipei: Nantian, 2009.

Yūki Shōji. "Teshi Toyoji ni kiku." *Tsubute*, no. 51 (2006): 27–39.

Yūki Shōji Kenkyūkai (ed.). *Yūki Shōtarō kenkyū hōkokusho*. Sapporo: Yūki Shōji Kenkyūkai, 2005.

Zaidan Hōjin Ainu Bunka Shinkō (ed.). "Yamamoto Tasuke denshō shita Ainu bunka wo chūshin to shita Hokkaido tōbu no Ainu bunka kenkyū." *Ainu kanren sōgō kenkyū tō josei jigyō kenkyū hōkoku* 4 (2007): 357–81.

Zeng Huixiang et al. *Yushan huishou = Reflections on Jade Mountain, 1696–1985*. Nantou sian shuili xiang: Yushan guo jia gong yuan guan li chu yuan gong xiao fei he zou she, 1990.

Zheng Zhengcheng. *Rizhi shiqi Taiwan yuanzhumin de guanguang xinglu*. Taipei: Boyang chuban, 2005.

Ziomek, Kirsten. "The 1903 Human Pavilion: Colonial Realities and Subaltern Subjectivities in Twentieth-Century Japan." *Journal of Asian Studies* 73, no. 2 (May 2014): 493–516.

———. "The Possibility of Liminal Colonial Subjecthood: Yayutz Bleyh and the Search for Subaltern Histories in the Japanese Empire." *Critical Asian Studies* 47, no. 1 (2015): 123–50.

Zwick, Jim. *Inuit Entertainers in the United States: From the Chicago World's Fair through the Birth of Hollywood*. West Conshohocken, PA: Infinity, 2006.

Index

Page numbers for maps are in italics.

Harvard East Asian Monographs
(most recent titles)